Language and Muslim Immigrant Childhoods

Wiley Blackwell Studies in Discourse and Culture

Linguistic anthropology evolved in the 20th century in an environment that tended to reify language and culture. A recognition of the dynamics of discourse as a sociocultural process has since emerged as researchers have used new methods and theories to examine the reproduction and transformation of people, institutions, and communities through linguistic practices. This transformation of linguistic anthropology itself heralds a new era for publishing as well. *Wiley Blackwell Studies in Discourse and Culture* aims to represent and foster this new approach to discourse and culture by producing books that focus on the dynamics that can be obscured by such broad and diffuse terms as "language." This series is committed to the ethnographic approach to language and discourse: ethnographic works deeply informed by theory, as well as more theoretical works that are deeply grounded in ethnography. The books are aimed at scholars in the sociology and anthropology of language, anthropological linguistics, sociolinguistics and socioculturally informed psycholinguistics. It is our hope that all books in the series will be widely adopted for a variety of courses.

Series Editor

James M. Wilce (PhD University of California, Los Angeles) is Professor of Anthropology at Northern Arizona University. He serves on the editorial board of *American Anthropologist* and the *Journal of Linguistic Anthropology*. He has published a number of articles and is the author of *Eloquence in Trouble: The Poetics and Politics of Complaint in Rural Bangladesh* (1998) and *Language and Emotion* (2009) and the editor of *Social and Cultural Lives of Immune Systems* (2003).

Editorial Board:

Richard Bauman – Indiana University
Eve Danziger – University of Virginia
Patrick Eisenlohr – Georg-August-Universität Göttingen
Per-Anders Forstorp – Royal Institute of Technology, Stockholm
Elizabeth Keating – UT Austin
Paul Kroskrity – UCLA
Norma Mendoza-Denton – University of Arizona
Susan Philips – University of Arizona
Bambi Schieffelin – NYU

In the Series:

1. *The Hidden Life of Girls*, by Marjorie Harness Goodwin
2. *We Share Walls: Language, Land, and Gender in Berber Morocco*, by Katherine E. Hoffman
3. *The Everyday Language of White Racism*, by Jane H. Hill
4. *Living Memory: The Social Aesthetics of Language*, by Jillian R. Cavanaugh
5. *Lessons from Fort Apache: Beyond Language Endangerment and Maintenance* by M. Eleanor Nevins
6. *Language and Muslim Immigrant Childhoods: The Politics of Belonging* by Inmaculada Mª García-Sánchez

Language and Muslim Immigrant Childhoods

The Politics of Belonging

Inmaculada Mª García-Sánchez

WILEY Blackwell

For Wafiya, Worda, Sarah, Manal, Karim, Mimon, and Kamal
whose real names I cannot reveal but whom I shall never forget.
And
for my nephews Mateo López Gil and Yasin Fervenza Rabah,
whose young smiles give me hope and faith.

And in memory of
Josefa Sánchez Naranjo (1942–2007)
Juana D. Naranjo Argüello (1914–2012).

Contents

Acknowledgments

This book is the fruit of a long journey; a journey that would not have been possible without the help and support of many people and institutions. I would first like to express my deepest gratitude to the Moroccan children and families who let me into their lives and made this study possible. I could never repay their kindness, generosity, patience and forbearance they exhibited, even towards the most taxing methods of data collection. Apart from their participation in this research, the focal children and their families offered something at least as, if not more, valuable: their warmth, care, and friendship throughout the study, providing me with several "homes from home." In addition to the children and their families, I also want to thank teachers, doctors, trainers, and other individuals in Vallenuevo who participated in this study and who generously opened the doors of their classrooms, offices, school, clinic, and mosque. This study could not have been carried out without their involvement, trust, and enthusiasm. The support and generosity of some of these individuals went well beyond their participation in the study. Among them, I must mention teachers and administrators of the public school, as well as the head coach of the local track-and-field club. I am sorry that, for reasons of confidentiality, I cannot mention their real names here, but I do hope they know that I will always be in their debt. Many other people in Spain helped me at various stages of research. In particular, I am extremely grateful to government officials who were very enthusiastic about my research and instrumental in helping me obtain official permits to conduct my study.

I would like to thank my research assistants Wafiya and Omar for their patience and talent. Their skills, persistence, knowledge of the community, and insights into language varieties were instrumental in allowing me to produce rich, ethnographically-informed transcripts. Omar Rabah, in particular, spent countless hours with me refining transcripts and discussing nuances of language use. He offered me not only his insight and knowledge, but also the hospitality of his household (along with Silvia) and his friendship.

Several institutions have generously funded this study. The Center for Near Eastern and North African Studies at the University of California, Los

Angeles (UCLA) supported the preliminary stages of this research with a Summer FLAS Fellowship. The main periods of data collection were funded by a Wenner-Gren Foundation for Anthropological Research Individual Dissertation Grant (Grant #7296), by a Harry and Yvonne Lenart Foundation Graduate Research Travel Grant, and by a UCLA Center for European and Eurasian Studies Summer Dissertation Research award. Sustained periods of writing and revision at different stages of this project were funded first by a UCLA Graduate Division Dissertation Year Fellowship, and later supported by a Faculty Fellowship of the Center for the Humanities at Temple University (CHAT), as well as by a Temple University Sabbatical and Grant-in-Aid. A Spencer Foundation/National Academy of Education Postdoctoral Fellowship also facilitated final revisions, while also allowing me to start working on new research projects. I am deeply grateful to these organizations for their generous support and assistance. The views articulated in this book are my own and those of the research participants and do not reflect the opinions of the funding sources.

Intellectually, I am very grateful for the support, dedication, and encouragement of my dissertation committee at UCLA: Elinor R. Ochs, Candy Goodwin, Reynaldo F. Macías, Marjorie F. Orellana, and Kris Gutiérrez. Very special thanks to Elinor and Marjorie, my mentors, role-models, and my co-producers, as I affectionately call them. Beyond the vision and intelligence they brought to this project, they have both continued to provide steadfast support and guidance whenever I have needed it. I feel very honored and privileged to have had the opportunity to work and learn with mentors of the caliber of Ellie and Margie. My luck in mentors has only been matched by my luck in my senior colleague in linguistic anthropology at Temple University. Only in my dreams could I have imagined having a colleague as smart, as generous, and as helpful as Paul B. Garrett. Very special thanks to Paul who, in addition to reading several drafts of most of the chapters, has unwaveringly offered support, analytic insights, and friendship. In general, I also want to thank my colleagues in the Department of Anthropology at Temple University who have been very supportive of my research and my writing sabbaticals. In particular, I want to thank Mindie Lazarus-Black who was the chair during my first four years at Temple and who always went above and beyone to protect junior faculty. I also want to thank a group of Temple colleagues and graduate students who helped with final proofreading: Michael Hesson, Melissa Krug, Nicole Nathan, Kristina Nazimova, Dave Paulson, Eryn Snyder, and Ben Wilson.

This study has also benefited from intellectual insights and generous feedback, of many other colleagues at UCLA, Temple, and elsewhere who have helped me along the way, offering moral support, and commenting on earlier drafts or presentations on which this work is based. In particular, I would like to thank Sandro Duranti, Bambi Schieffelin, Ayala Fader, Patricia Baquedano-López, Heather Loyd, Jennifer Reynolds, H. Samy Alim, Amy Kyratzis, and Satomi Kuroshima. I also would like to thank various members of my informal writing group (Kathy Howard, Mary Ebeling, Rachel Reynolds, and Cati Coe) who read and commented on earlier versions of Chapter 5 and parts of the introduction, and who offered helpful suggestions for the organization of the book. I also wish to thank the students and faculty of the UCLA Linguistic Anthropology Discourse Laboratory, the UCLA Center for Language, Interaction, and Culture (CLIC), and the UCLA Center for the Everyday Lives of Families (CELF), who listened several times to my work-in-progress and offered feedback and encouragement during 2007–2009. I am also grateful to the 2011–2012 participants in the Fellows Seminar of the Center for the Humanities at Temple University who read and commented on Chapter 7 and other aspects of this study. In particular, I want to thank Peter Logan and Heather Ann Thompson who ran the Fellows Seminar and provided a space to write and to think. I also would like to thank the four anonymous reviewers for Wiley-Blackwell- for their helpful suggestions and thought-provoking questions. My thanks also go to Jim Wilce, series editor of *Blackwell Studies in Discourse and Culture*, as well as to the editorial and production team of Wiley-Blackwell. I appreciate their patience, encouragement, and commitment to this project.

I am deeply grateful to my friends and family for their constant and never-ending support and excitement about this project. I want to thank my parents for their help throughout the years and I remember especially my mother, Josefa Sánchez Naranjo and my grandmother, Juana Naranjo Argüello, who always encouraged me in all my journeys, projects, and explorations. I wish they could have been here to see this project completed and to hold the printed book in their hands. My profound gratitude goes to my aunt Lola, my uncle Manolo, and my partner, Doug, *mi calvito*. You three deserve a t-shirt with "We survived Inma's Book" printed on it. I thank my *tía Lola* and my *tío Manolo* for their love and unyielding faith in me. As for *mi calvito*, only he knows how much I owe him. Thank you for being there through everything.

Finally, some of the analyses in this book have appeared in earlier forms in three previous publications: "Language Socialization and Exclusion," in A. Duranti, E. Ochs, B. Schieffelin, eds. *The Handbook of Language Socialization*. Wiley-Blackwell: 391–420, Copyright © 2012, Wiley-Blackwell, reprinted with permission; "The Politics of Arabic Language Education: Moroccan Immigrant Children's Socialization into Ethnic and Religious Identities," *Linguistics and Education*, 21(3): 171–196, 2010, Copyright © 2010 Elsevier, reprinted with permission; and "Serious Games: Code-switching and Identity in Moroccan Immigrant Girls' Pretend Play," *Pragmatics* 20(4): 523–555.

1

Introduction

In late October 2005, barely two months after I arrived in Spain with my suitcases and equipment to document the sociocultural and linguistic worlds of the Moroccan immigrant children of Vallenuevo, a small rural community in the central southwest of the country,[1] riots erupted in hundreds of immigrant housing estates in France, and spread temporarily into Germany and Belgium. The rioters were not newcomers, but rather second- and third-generation immigrant youth of North African descent who had been born and raised in Europe. Perhaps because Spain is now witnessing the solid emergence of a second generation of Moroccan immigrant youth, the conflicting sentiments aroused by the 2005 events in France found a strong echo in the Spanish media, as well as in Vallenuevo, where 38% to 40% of the population has a Moroccan immigrant background.

The string of editorials about the riots that filled the Spanish press during those days emphasized the discontent of marginalized Muslim youth in Europe, as well as how these youth often felt more discriminated against and excluded from the European countries where they were born/raised than their parents' generation.[2] In spite of the likely relationship between these events and the structural conditions of the daily existence of these youth, the French riots in fall 2005, along with the July 2005 London bombings and the March 2004 Madrid bombings, were portrayed as the main triggers of what soon became widely discussed in the political arena as a full-blown failure of immigrant integration in Europe, or "una crisis de los modelos de integración." Although the actual promotion of coherent and systematic policies of inclusion prior to these events is highly debatable,[3] the discourse that has indeed come to dominate contemporary political discussion surrounding immigration in Spain, and throughout Europe, is

Language and Muslim Immigrant Childhoods: The Politics of Belonging, First Edition. Inmaculada Mª García-Sánchez.
© 2014 John Wiley & Sons, Inc. Published 2014 by John Wiley & Sons, Inc.

that of a crisis of the politics of inclusion, especially when it comes to immigrants from North African or other Muslim backgrounds.

The feelings that the 2005 riots in France had generated in Spanish political and cultural circles also reverberated among the local, non-immigrant population of Vallenuevo. I remember vividly the first time I actually saw live images of the pandemonium that had erupted in France. It must have been the third or fourth day of the riots, since I did not have television in the apartment I had rented. That morning I had gone to the local *churrería* – a bar serving the traditional Spanish breakfast of fried bread – to have coffee and *churros* with Álvaro, a local farmer and one of my research contacts, who was going to introduce me to some Moroccan families in the town. The television in the *churrería* was showing the early morning news, and when the riot images of the previous night came on the screen almost everybody stopped going about their business and focused on the small monitor hung high in one of the corners of the bar. My own sense of shock at the level of violence and destruction was compounded by the comments of a few vocal patrons, applauding the actions of the French police and agreeing with the opinions of the most conservative French politicians. As I was pondering over the despair evidenced by the actions of the young rioters, and simultaneously wondering about the complex interethnic dynamics of this rural community that I was by then only beginning to discover, one of the owners of the establishment, to whom Álvaro had just introduced me, looked at me directly and said: "Hay que echarlos a todos, porque esto – esto ahora está pasando en Francia, pero esto va a terminar pasando aquí con *los moros*" **(They must all be kicked out, because this – this is happening now in France, but this is going to end up happening here with *los moros*[4]).**

The chilling nature of this statement, suggesting an ominous inevitability of civil unrest, renders almost invisible a question that was neither adequately posed nor satisfactorily answered by the media, politicians, and the public: how do these youth come to develop such an insidious sense of exclusion and alienation from the European countries where they were born and raised? This was a question that I thought about more and more as the weeks went on, especially in the face of political and everyday discourses that seemed to be more concerned with the emergence of headscarves and other *Islamic symbols* among the younger generations than with the quality of these youths' sociocultural lives.

This book is about how Moroccan immigrant children in Vallenuevo negotiate everyday forms of difference and belonging in the contemporary sociopolitical climate of Spain and, to some extent, of Europe. While current

scholarship has increasingly focused on issues of belonging, identity formation, exclusion, and forms of citizenship for those whose lives are characterized by mobility and for those who have to navigate the liminality of
geographical and ideological borders (Agamben 2005; Appadurai 1996; Brubaker 1992, 1998, 2001, 2004a, 2004b, 2010; Clifford 1994; De Genova
2005; Ong 1996, 1999, 2003, 2006; Rosaldo 1994, 1999; Waldinger 2001,
2008, 2010), few studies have examined how these processes emerge and
unfold through everyday discursive practices and social interaction. Even
fewer have focused on how children who experience migration specifically
are affected by and affect these processes through their everyday participation in the multiple communities and institutions that make up their sociocultural milieus. This book attempts to provide a nuanced picture of
Moroccan immigrant children's lifeworlds, by developing a holistic analysis
of the constraints and affordances that this group of immigrant children
routinely encounter and negotiate across the social contexts of their daily
lives, including family, public school, religious institutions, medical clinics,
and neighborhood peer groups.

In my examination of Moroccan children's social interactions in all these
contexts, I have placed special emphasis on the multicultural politics of difference and belonging in a country, like Spain, increasingly characterized by
multilingualism and cultural diversity. In showing how both social difference
and commonality of belonging are products of everyday interaction, I have
adopted an ethnopragmatically-informed approach, which involves the close
study of everyday language use coupled with long periods of ethnographic
research to investigate the ways in which speech is both constituted by and
constitutive of sociocultural forms of interaction and social organization
(Duranti 2007). With this approach, I examine not only the everyday ways
in which Moroccan immigrant children become socially *marked* and discriminated against, but also how they actively and creatively respond to these
practices of racialized exclusion and position themselves with respect to the
multiple communities to which they can claim membership.

Spain, and Vallenuevo in particular, were interesting places to study
Moroccan immigrant children's lives for several reasons. With increasing
numbers of Moroccan immigrants into rural and urban Spanish centers over
the last decades of the twentieth and the first decades of the twenty-first
centuries, Spain has witnessed the emergence of strong North African and
Muslim diasporic communities that are pushing taken-for-granted boundaries of social and institutional notions of membership and identity. The
effects of these migratory trends on the demographic, ethnic, and linguistic
make-up of Spanish society have generated a number of points of social
and political contention.[5] In Vallenuevo, a small rural community that in
the span of a decade saw its population of immigrant origin increase from

zero to 37%, these points of contention have been particularly heart-felt by both Spanish and Moroccan communities. Indeed, Vallenuevo was among the growing number of small farming communities all over the country that were rapidly becoming important centers of settlement for migrants attracted to jobs in the agricultural sector.

Ironically, some of these rural communities, like Vallenuevo, had had a long history of emigration during the 1960s and 1970s. By the 1990s and 2000s, however, they had become a prime destination for immigrants and were absorbing a large percentage of the migration flow into the country. Even so, much of the literature on immigrant communities in Spain has continued to focus on the large industrialized centers, like the areas surrounding Madrid and Barcelona (Erickson 2011; Lucko 2007; Martín Rojo 2011; Mercado 2008, etc.), and other urban spaces (see Rogozen-Soltar 2012a, 2012b in Granada). This under-attention to immigration into rural areas is also characteristic of much of the ethnographic work on North African and other Muslim immigrant communities in Europe as a whole (e.g., Bowen 2007, 2010; Ewing 2008; Mandel 2008; P. A. Silverstein 2004).

Of course, there are many important reasons to pay attention to immigration into the hyper-diverse, cosmopolitan cities of the twenty-first century. But it is also crucial to study such processes in rural areas. There are also good reasons to think that immigrants' participation dynamics will be different in smaller places, where the receiving context is often more homogenous and where the history of immigration is shallow and fast-paced, rather than characterized by longer histories of immigration and by more sociocultural, economic, religious, and linguistic heterogeneity, as in cosmopolitan cities.

Vallenuevo was also a good place to investigate the social and ideological constraints and affordances Moroccan immigrant children experience because, while not immune to the growing problematization surrounding Muslim and North African immigration to Spain, this town's social services and education institutions had been heralded in the Spanish media for their active promotion of multicultural policies and integration programs. This made it possible for me to consider the extent to which these efforts to mitigate exclusion and promote tolerance and integration were actually experienced by the children in their everyday negotiations of difference and belonging.

1.1   About this Introduction

Attempting to integrate different levels of analysis – macro and micro, global and local, public and private, social and individual forces – that shape the experience of growing up in immigration contexts is a daunting task. Certainly it is one that defies the artificial boundaries of traditional disciplines and the parameters of single theoretical paradigms or theoretical models. For this reason, this book project draws from theoretical approaches in anthropology, ethnomethodology, sociology, and philosophy to address the lives of immigrant children growing up in a multilingual, multicultural community undergoing rapid social change. The body of theories framing this book illuminate the situated and processual nature of culture, socialization, belonging, inclusion/exclusion, and identity formation within the migration context of contemporary Spain.

For clarity and ease of exposition, my discussion of these framing theoretical ideas and bodies of literature will unfold in the next four sections. I begin by discussing the ideological and geopolitical backdrop of North African and Muslim immigration in contemporary Europe, emphasizing how a new *Orientalism qua security* is the unacknowledged elephant in the room affecting Moroccan immigrant children's everyday negotiations of difference and belonging. I then discuss the theoretical importance of examining immigrant children's everyday lives holistically in a variety of social settings, particularly immigrant children from heavily scrutinized and racialized communities. This holistic perspective is important so that we can obtain a balanced view of both how immigrant children are affected by these larger geopolitical forces, but also of how they actively negotiate these forces and other structural constraints. In the section that follows, I address some contemporary theories of sociopolitical *markedness* and membership that frame my understandings of how Moroccan immigrant children negotiate the micropolitics of belonging. The introduction closes with a discussion of how ethnomethodologically informed linguistic anthropology provides a particularly helpful set of theoretical and analytical tools to investigate Moroccan immigrant children's daily constraints and affordances in negotiating belonging and participation in their multiple communities.

1.2 Orientalism Revisited: North African and Muslim Immigrant Communities in Europe

Although the figure of the immigrant has often been constructed as a problem of integration into national polities both in lay and academic discourses,[6] the experience of Muslim immigrant groups in contemporary Europe falls into a distinctive racialized category of exclusion regardless of country of origin and settlement and other contextual differences.[7] Indeed, the widespread debate about *la crisis de los modelos de integración*, or failure of integration, in Spain, as well as in the rest of Europe, must be understood against the backdrop of growing levels of problematization regarding immigrants from North Africa and the Muslim world. In the last three decades, European nations have witnessed how Muslim diasporic communities have taken visible and strong roots in their countries due to both an increase of immigration and of policies of family reunification. The concerns expressed about this taking of roots have significantly gone hand-in-hand with a feeling of exclusion experienced by many members of Muslim immigrant communities.

The feelings of anxiety, mistrust, and suspicion that the presence of Muslim immigrant communities generate among local populations of different European nations have been partly explained by a deeply rooted historical attribution of *Otherness* to Islamic culture that stems from Orientalist interpretations of the Muslim world (e.g., Asad 2000; Bowen 2004a; Cesari 2004; Said 1978; Werbner 2002). Asad (2000), in exploring the role of historical narratives in the formation of European identity, traced how Muslims since the early Middle Ages have consistently been positioned in historical accounts and other forms of cultural representation as the primary violent and uncivilized *Other* to Christians; this positioning has been critical to the construction of the modern notion of the cultural and historical unity of Western European civilization.

This historical Orientalist perspective alone, however, cannot explain the current revival of hostilities towards Muslim immigrant communities in Europe. Many scholars have argued that the Orientalist discourse has found renewed prominence in the wake of the September 2001 terrorist attack in the United States, the March 2004 train bombings in Madrid, the July 2005 London bombings, and the ensuing War on Terror.[8] The high profile nature of these international events have intensified the focus on Muslim immigrant communities in Europe, putting entire communities under suspicion and surveillance.

As a result, Muslims are seen not only as a threat to European security, but to European identity itself. This combined problematization has made possible the emergence of a new kind of *Orientalism* that has found its maximum expression in theses closely aligned with Huntington's (1992) controversial analysis of the *clash of civilizations*. A significant amount of attention has indeed been paid to the processes of *othering* of Muslim populations brought about by new anti-terrorism laws and by the hotly contested issue of racial profiling, which singles out this specific ethnic group as being dangerous for the rest of the society. Since 9/11, much has been written about how immigrants from the Muslim world are viewed from a security paradigm and are subjected to special scrutiny by the state, as well as to potentially discriminatory treatment under the law.[9] With regard to Muslims as a threat to European identity, the construction of Muslims as intrinsically incompatible with principles of European democracies has become the flagship of a culturalist brand of racism that highlights cultural differences, such as religion, language, dress and so on, and that has also found resonance in state policies targeting Muslims, such as the *headscarf law* in France (Balibar 1991; and Bowen 2004b, 2006).

In Spain, more specifically, it is also easy to identify the conflation of perceived unbridgeable cultural differences in way of life and religious views with a security paradigm that positions the Moroccan community under suspicion in the eyes of the majority of the population. There are several particularities of the Spanish context, however, that deserve separate attention and that will be addressed at length in Chapter 2. Two that I will mention briefly here are the pervasive cultural representations of Moroccan immigrants as *los inasimilables* (the "unassimilable") (Bravo López 2004) and the many studies suggesting that Moroccan children are the most racialized and most socially marked immigrant group in Spanish public schools (e.g., Mijares 2004a and Martín Rojo 2010). This positioning as the ultimate *Other* that Moroccan immigrant communities are confronted with must not only be understood within the more general European reaction against the increasing immigration of the last 60 years from Africa, Asia, and the Middle East, but also against the background of a Spanish-specific kind of *Orientalism* that has historically constructed Spain as the last fortress protecting Europe from Islamic invasions (Martín Rojo 2000; van Dijk 2005; Flesler 2008). Undoubtedly, this deeply ingrained historical consciousness differentiates to a large extent the prejudice and mistrust faced by Moroccan immigrant communities in Spain from other brands of anti-immigrant sentiment directed at other groups.

Specific immigration policies undertaken by successive Spanish governments in the 1990s are of crucial importance as the most immediate sociopolitical context of contemporary representations of Moroccans as the "unassimilable." During the mid- to late 1990s, the immigration policies in Spain promoted the idea that there were immigrant groups more compatible with the Spanish way of life and, therefore, more easily assimilable to the fabric of Spanish society. Immigration policies during these years blatantly favored the arrival of Latin Americans and Eastern Europeans who were seen as more desirable for cultural and linguistic reasons, as opposed to other immigrant groups, such as Moroccans, whose language, religion, and culture were regarded as more distant and alien (Bravo López 2004).

These ideas, and the ways in which they resonated with international and national political events,[10] have furthered the association of Moroccan and Muslim immigration with insecurity and have amplified the cultural and historical representations of Moroccans in Spain as *the Other*, not only different from *us*, but also dangerous to *us*. This increased problematization resonated particularly forcefully during the period I was conducting my primary fieldwork, from early fall 2005 to the end of summer 2007. Just before the beginning of my fieldwork, two events put the Moroccan immigrant community under a brighter spotlight than ever before in its history of immigration into Spain: (1) the Madrid train bombings of March 11, 2004, many of whose perpetrators were Moroccan nationals, and (2) the 2005 "extraordinary regularization process" (*proceso de regularización extraordinaria*) of thousands of undocumented immigrants approved by the then newly elected government of José Luis Rodríguez Zapatero on December 30, 2004. This was a legal measure that was opposed by the conservative opposition and hotly debated in all spheres of politics, from local town hall and union offices of small rural communities, like Vallenuevo, to the highest seats of European Union policy-making institutions.[11] The convergence of greater surveillance and suspicion, brought about by the March 2004 terrorist attacks, and the higher visibility of the actual size and proportions of the Moroccan immigrant community, engendered by the process of regularization, is a pivotal historical moment. This is true for both its more negative aspects of how this confluence of factors made the environment in Spain less hospitable for the Moroccan immigrant community, but also for its more positive aspects of renewed hopes for fuller membership and a more permanent future in the country.

The historically-constituted ideologies for "understanding the problem" of Muslims in Europe, as well as the sociopolitical landscape through which their *Otherness* has been constituted, have received much scholarly attention. Less attention, however, has been paid to how these policies, surveillance, and general suspicion have affected immigrant groups' ordinary lives and everyday experiences. Yet, examining how the newer generations of North African and Muslim immigrants in Europe, in this case Moroccan immigrant children in Spain, are able to negotiate membership on the ground amidst these complex cultural politics of belonging is particularly important if we want to understand how the immigrant second generation may grow up to develop a sense of commonality of belonging, or conversely, a feeling of not-belonging and alienation, like the young French rioters in 2005.

This book attempts to refocus scholarly attention on the everyday experiences of racialized immigrant groups by focusing on how Moroccan immigrant children in Vallenuevo navigate (and are affected by) both local and national politics of inclusion/exclusion. I emphasize the timing of my study because the dramatic bombings of 2004 (Madrid) and 2005 (London), on the one hand, and the 2005 *proceso de regularización extraordinaria* were the macro sociopolitical backdrop to the daily social encounters of Moroccan immigrant children in Vallenuevo during the period of my study (2005–

2007). In this sense, I want to emphasize, more generally, the importance of studying immigrant children's everyday lives and discursive practices to trace how forces at play in transnational, diasporic settings impact these children's emerging sense of belonging and processes of identification in the most immediate contexts of their daily existence.

1.3 The Everyday Landscapes of Immigrant Childhoods

In the last few years, a growing number of ethnographic studies have considered issues of identity and community identification in the lives of transnational migrant youth (e.g., Baquedano-López 1998, 2000; Hall 2002; Klein 2009; LaBennet 2011; Lee 2005; Maira 2002; Mendoza-Denton 2008), as well as how children's everyday lives are shaped by sociopolitical forces, including the attitudes, stereotypes, and ideologies of the receiving community towards specific immigrant, diasporic groups (e.g., Hall 1995; Orellana 2009; Sarroub 2005; Shankar 2008; Reyes 2007). In spite of these important studies, the dominant tendency is still to consider the different spheres of immigrant children's everyday lives in relative isolation from one another. One of the most important goals of this book is to consider the social contexts of immigrant childhoods integrally in order to construct a holistic understanding of the sociocultural and linguistic matrix of Moroccan immigrant children's everyday lives. Documenting immigrant children's experiences and across contexts, and studying family, educational, institutional, religious, community, and peer practices, highlights both the constraints and affordances that Moroccan immigrant children face in and negotiating membership and belonging in different realms of their social relationships.

Each of the following chapters presents how Moroccan immigrant children negotiate participation in different but concurrent spheres of their lives. Taken together, the chapters allow us to examine integrally the (co-)occurrence of features of both communicative and social practices. Building on a strong tradition of scholarship that has already established that immigrant children, the world over, have the daunting task of coping with the sociocultural expectations of their immigrant and receiving communities,[12] this book aspires to trace the landscapes of Moroccan immigrant children's worlds in a way that allows us to capture and appreciate holistically the social complexity of immigrant childhoods.[13] Understanding the sociocultural and linguistic lifeworlds of immigrant children is ever more important now, with children and youth being the fastest growing sector of the more than 214 million transnational migrants found throughout the world (Suárez-Orozco et al. 2011).

In accounting for how Moroccan immigrant children in Vallenuevo manage the local and global forces that impinge upon their lives and upon their emerging sense of belonging and identification, I have tried to avoid two common traps that characterize the study of immigrant and minority children: either romanticizing the affordances and agency that these children are sometimes able to exercise, or, conversely, highlighting social, political, and economic constraints to the point of abnormalizing their childhoods. Documenting different arenas of the children's social lives has helped me with this difficult task. Being able to examine a wide variety of contexts has allowed me to present the interplay between the constraints and affordances children experience in different settings. Another way in which I have tried to avoid these pitfalls is by capturing as faithfully as possible the perspectives of the children themselves. Listening to children's ongoing reflections on their lives has been the main compass I have used when I felt I was being pulled too far in one of those two directions.

Throughout the writing of this book, I often found myself drawn to a series of interviews and *lifemaps* (see Chapter 3) that I collected from some of the children featured in the study. The drawings always reminded me of the exceptional but also of the more commonplace circumstances of immigrant childhoods. They struck me as powerfully illuminating perhaps because, as forms of self-presentation and narration, they function as *tours* in De Certeau's (1984) sense of the term – Moroccan immigrant children's everyday narrations of movement through their lives as subjectively experienced by them. In these pictorial narrations, children casually traverse national boundaries, lived-in spaces, temporal boundaries, linguistic codes, and cultural and imaginative domains. In the lifemap reproduced in Figure 1.1, Worda, age 9, represents with drawings and text captions significant events in her life, from her birth in Morocco to her current life in Spain, as well as favorite activities and her future dreams. At first glance, this lifemap may not seem very different from one that any Spanish girl of Worda's age could have produced, and, in many ways, it is quite similar: the prominence of school and play in her life, her love for sports and physical activities, such as swimming and running in the track-and-field team, and her aspirations to become a computer science teacher and to have a family when she grows up.

A closer look, however, reveals a more complex picture. As illustrated in the three subsections of Worda's map featured in Figure 1.2 below, we see the intrinsic hybrid nature of her daily life, as well as the situated negotiation of languages and practices that children like her must perform on a daily basis. For example, in Worda's own representation of her favorite play activities, she seamlessly transcends linguistic boundaries and displays her

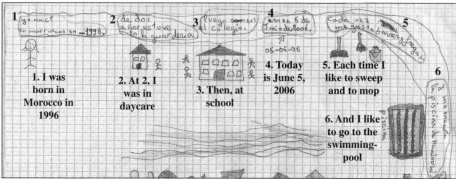

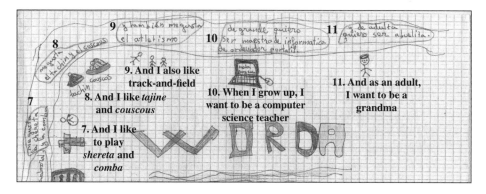

Figure 1.1 Worda's life map.

bicultural repertoire, by describing these children's games as *chereta* (šereta[14] – Moroccan Arabic word for "hopscotch") and *comba* (Spanish word for "jump-rope") in the same sentence.

The enduring importance of the practices of her immigrant diaspora community are represented in culinary traditions, such as Moroccan tažine

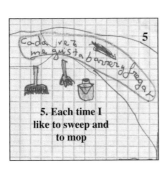
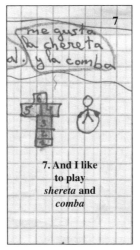
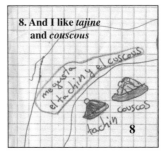

Figure 1.2   From Worda's lifemap.

and couscous. These meals are not only presented as Worda's favorites, but from further conversations I learned that these are dishes that she routinely helps her elder sister prepare when their mother is working (see Chapter 4). In many Vallenuevo Moroccan households, children are expected to under-take significant household responsibilities from an early age as part of an ethos of generational interdependence and appropriate development. Moroc-can immigrant children's contributions to the sustainability of their com-munities, through the responsibilities expected of girls like Worda, are also prominently represented in the depiction of the household chores that Worda enjoys doing, that is, sweeping and mopping. These tasks, which would be rare in lifemaps produced by Spanish children of her same age,[15] are even represented before Worda depicts her favorite games and pastimes.

Thinking seriously about Moroccan immigrant children's critical role and active participation in important sociocultural processes of settlement and transformation, such as when they help in their homes or when they trans-late for families and doctors in institutional contexts, may seem paradoxical, given forms of social exclusion and discrimination that Moroccan immi-grant children in Vallenuevo face and that this book also describes. It is precisely this nuanced complexity in Moroccan immigrant children's lives, however, that this book attempts to capture. Yes, Moroccan immigrant chil-dren's dreams and aspirations for the future, like Worda and Wafiya's illus-trated in Figure 1.3, may be challenged by social exclusion and discrimination, structural economic disparities, community expectations, and differential access to (and distribution of) resources. Yet, Moroccan immigrant children in Vallenuevo are not passive subjects in these processes of inclusion/

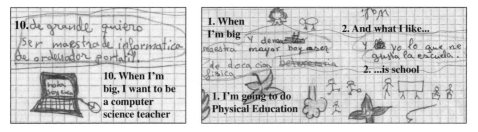

Figure 1.3 "When I'm big . . ." from Worda's and Wafiya's lifemaps.

exclusion through which belonging (or lack thereof) is negotiated. One of the most important things that this book shows is how this group of children actively try to negotiate their positions in their social worlds from a very early age, even in the midst of social relations that are clearly asymmetrical, and involving large power differentials. Yes, Moroccan immigrant children act contextually against a number of adverse constraints due to their subordinate positions as *children* and as *immigrants* from a particularly undesirable group (*los moros*). Yet, social actors are never wholly drained of agency, even those who occupy subaltern positions or are on the margins of power (Ortner 2006). As the new second immigrant generation in the making, Moroccan immigrant children in Vallenuevo often find themselves at the forefront of the negotiation of some of these sociocultural processes, and are able to exercise different degrees of agency against these constraints in different contexts of their lives.

Their socio-culturally mediated capacity to engage in everyday *tactics*[16] (De Certeau 1984), however, varies in the different social settings where these children negotiate their emerging sense of belonging. A crucial focus of this book is how Moroccan immigrant children negotiate belonging and difference through everyday discursive and interactional practices, as these practices are differentially configured through the structural constraints and affordances of different social fields. To capture this, I draw inspiration from the children's lifemaps and offer the reader a *tour* (De Certeau 1984) of the everyday landscapes of Moroccan immigrant childhoods in Vallenuevo.

1.4 Theoretical Paradigms for Understanding Difference and Belonging

As debates about the failure of integration gained momentum in Spain, as well as in many other European countries,[17] notions of *acculturation* and *assimilation* of immigrants into dominant society polities have been one of the leading heuristics through which institutions and politicians, increasingly concerned about national integrity and cultural cohesion, have attempted to address the dynamics of immigrants' processes of settlement. The dominance of these assimilationist constructs, such as *integración social*, is particularly visible in the area of public policy, in spite of competing discourses of *interculturalidad* (inter-culturality) and of a new *convivencia* (living-together).[18] It may be surprising how older models of immigrant incorporation have persisted and resurfaced[19] in European discourse, given the ways in which these paradigms have been critiqued in the last few decades in academic discourse.[20] This assimilationist tendency has become more prominent in debates over membership after 9/11 and after the attacks in Madrid, 2004, and in London, 2005 (Brubaker 2010).

In this book, I consider how Muslim and North African immigrants in Spain have come to be viewed as *unassimilable*, focusing on how this affects Moroccan immigrant children's opportunities to develop commonality of belonging to their multiple communities in the immediate contexts that constitute their everyday existence. I am concerned with the politics of difference and belonging and how it is negotiated, contested, and politicized in quotidian sites of social life. Therefore, while the book offers a multilayered account, attempting to integrate local histories, discourses, debates in the public sphere, and the globalizing forces of late capitalism that brought Moroccans to Vallenuevo in the early 1990s, the focus is on how Moroccan immigrant children in this rural community navigate the politics of difference and belonging in their daily interactions with teachers, peers, family members, friends, doctors, coaches, and religious figures. This book emphasizes the importance and the complexity of what have been called "the informal aspects of the politics of belonging" (Brubaker 2010, pp. 65–66). I outline the dynamics of processes of categorization and identification and of practices of inclusion/exclusion in everyday, seemingly innocuous and mundane encounters. I focus espcially on these dynamics as refracted through the lenses of ethnopragmatically-informed linguistic anthropology.

In providing theoretical and ethnographic specificity to these *informal aspects of the politics of belonging*, this work attempts to complement the body of contemporary scholarship that has been devoted in the last few years to *formal aspects of the politics of belonging*, such as forms of citizenship and political rights for immigrants and other transnational populations (e.g., Brubaker 1989, 1992; De Genova 2005; Ong 1996, 1999, 2003, 2006; Rosaldo 1994, 1999). After all, the ways in which immigrant groups are treated, accepted, and recognized (or not) in their daily social life, can often belie and be at odds with codified forms of membership. In this sense, everyday social relationships can be as important and consequential for the wellbeing of individuals and communities as the more formal aspects of the politics of belonging, at the very least phenomenologically and experientially.

A key dimension of the informal aspects of the politics of difference and belonging are the notions of *identification* and *commonality*, insofar as they represent the emergent and historically-situated nature of processes through which individuals categorize themselves and others (Brubaker and Cooper 2000). Identification refers to the processes through which people come to experience a sense of commonality or difference. Identification involves acts carried out by agentive subjects, as well as people and objects who undergo the act of being identified. Commonality refers to the affective sense of belonging or to the affiliative feeling of being connected to a group. This perspective is complementary to my analytic lens focusing on Moroccan immigrant children's situated negotiation of belonging and difference because this paradigm captures the contingent, emergent quality of how processes of categorization, similarity, membership, and difference are made relevant in everyday social interactions and practices.

Thinking about how Moroccan immigrant children navigate the informal aspects of the politics of belonging, brings me to address one of the most popular exegetic keys to interpret the experience of immigrant children and youth: the metaphor of *in-betweeness*. Tropes of *caught in between two cultures* or *existing in between two worlds* have been commonly used to explain the sociocultural, psychological, and educational lives of immigrant children of the so-called 1.5 (brought to the receiving country at an early age) and second (already born in the receiving country) immigrant generations. The more I became involved in the children's lives and the more I have thought about my observations of them and our interactions and conversations together over the last few years, the less helpful I have found these tropes from both an ethnographic and a theoretical point of view, at least to capture the lifeworlds of the Moroccan immigrant children in Vallenuevo.

Theoretically, as an enduring legacy of acculturation and assimilation models, these metaphors contain the residue of linear and teleological developmental narratives by which immigrants will integrate themselves into the "mainstream" culture over the course of the generations. Ethnographically speaking, I believe that these analogies privilege excessively the perspective of adult researchers, like me, who arrive in a community to study immigrant children, and recognizing areas of discontinuities between practices and expectations across contexts, map the analytic experience of their own discernments onto the lived experiences of immigrant children. While understanding that all academic metaphors have limitations and that complete identification with an emic perspective is an impossibility, it seems to me, however, that children do not experience these differences with the same sense of rupture and disjuncture than outside observers do, but rather within the situational fabric of their daily lives.

More resonant with the contradictory positionalities that Moroccan immigrant children often inhabit, especially when it comes to negotiating difference and commonality of belonging, is having to navigate these politics from the position of being both *insider* and *outsider* at the same time. That is in some ways children are positioned by others (or position themselves) as more or less outsiders or insiders in given social domains, but very often they have to contend with both poles of the membership/marginality continuum simultaneously. In thinking about this framework, I have been influenced by concepts emanating from contemporary political philosophy, particularly that of Agamben's zone *of indistinction or indifference* (1998, 2005), as it intersects with Deleuze's notion of *zone of indiscernibility* (1981, and Deleuze and Guattari 1980). Although there are clear differences between these two notions,[21] what I find powerful about them is how both of these types of *zones* are considered to be ontological realms in which dichotomies that have come to be understood not only as distinct but also as opposites are seen to coincide or overlap – for my purposes here, dichotomies about membership, such as sameness/difference and exclusion/inclusion. Most evocatively, Deleuze discusses these zones as primordial domains for becoming. Also, both Deleuze and Agamben think of these zones as the underlying ontological logic that persist beneath fields that we have ordered around relational opposites, including, I think it is safe to assume, those systematic taxonomies that are produced around the identification, categorization, and social sorting of individuals, in this case immigrant children.

Although these notions have been helpful to me in thinking through these issues, there are some crucial differences between the ways in which I describe children's lives and participation in ontological-social domains of simultaneous exclusion and inclusion and Deleuze's *zone of indiscernibility* and Agamben's *zones of indistinction*, particularly the latter. Agamben (1998) developed the notion of "a zone of indistinction, between outside and inside, exception and rule, licit and illicit . . ." (pp. 170–171) around extreme cases where exceptional sociopolitical relations have become rule and individuals are almost devoid of power, such as prisoners in concentration camps or refugees in contemporary nation-states. Even if it is possible to say that some aspects of the problematization of Muslim and North African immigrants in contemporary Spain are reminiscent of sociopolitical *abnormalization* as discussed in Agamben's (2005) analysis of post-9/11 events, clearly, Vallenuevo is a far cry from any of the draconian sociopolitical conditions found in concentration camps or in places like Guantánamo. Moroccan immigrant children in Spain today obviously do not suffer the indignities of such extreme human conditions. Yes, Moroccan immigrant children experience historically-informed discrimination and everyday *microaggressions*, but even in the settings where they encounter most constraints, they are sometimes able to assert themselves and counteract how they are being characterized.

In spite of these important and significant differences, I want to suggest that this idea of being both outsider and insider at the same time, experiencing both exclusion and inclusion simultaneously (Agamben 1998, p. 181) might be very fruitful in understanding people's everyday lives in less extreme, contemporary sociopolitical conditions like of Moroccan immigrants in communities such as Vallenuevo, or, more generally, of (un)documented immigrants and their families, permanent-resident card holders, and other denizens of modern nation-states whose de facto status and rights are often uncertain and imprecise.

Across the social contexts of immigrant children's everyday lives, I explore what negotiating participation and belonging may mean in contexts where Moroccan immigrant children experience themselves as being both insiders and outsiders to varying degrees. In proposing that the development of immigrant children's sense of membership is dependent on having to negotiate the boundaries of their simultaneous inclusion/exclusion in the social spheres of their everyday life, what I am trying to capture is how this group of children bargains for commonality of belonging within domains where sameness and difference are sometimes muted, but are sometimes *marked* and made socially distinctive.

Moroccan immigrant children in Vallenuevo, who are either born in Spain or brought to the country by their parents when they are toddlers, cannot be considered as Spanish citizens, according to Article 17 of the Spanish Civil Code, by which only children of Spanish nationals are considered citizens by origin (*españoles de origen*). Moroccan immigrant children can only become citizens by residence, or *españoles por residencia*, through a process that requires one to 10 years of legal residence in the country (depending on whether they were born in Spain) and that can only be initiated by them when they reach 18 years of age, or by their immigrant parents after they reach 14. Yet, educational laws in Spain recognize the right to a free public education and provide for the full inclusion of immigrant children until the age of 16, regardless of their parents' legal status. Other social policy follows this same reasoning, providing medical and social services to immigrant children, who for most purposes are accorded the same rights as their native-born peers at least until their late teens. The enormous contradictions of being institutionally treated like insiders, but being legally and ideologically considered outsiders reverberate throughout the social interactions I analyze in subsequent chapters of this book, as children make sense of different aspects of membership and belonging to their multiple communities.

1.5   A Linguistic Anthropological Lens on Negotiating Difference and Belonging

Linguistic anthropology is helpful in understanding the everyday politics of Moroccan immigrant childhoods in Vallenuevo because of its focus on how the variety of cultural- and group-specific subject positions that people enact or attribute to others inheres in social interaction and is an "outcome of cultural semiotics that is accomplished through the production of contextually relevant sociopolitical relations of similarity and difference" (Bucholtz and Hall 2004, p. 382). Within linguistic anthropology, along with related disciplines, such as sociolinguistics and conversation analysis, much scholarship has been devoted to theorizing how social actors enact and construct categories for themselves and others in the midst of social activities, and otherwise position themselves as interactions unfold (e.g., Agha 2007a; Benwell and Stokoe 2006; Goffman 1981; Gumperz 1982; Mendoza-Denton 2002; Ochs 1992, 1993, 2002; Sacks 1992; Schegloff 1991, 1992). Such work has also demonstrated how everyday micro-level interactions, like the ones with which this book is mostly concerned, are consequential for the subject positions individuals come to occupy in the world and for larger social and political issues related to collective identifications, distribution of power, and representation (e.g., Baquedano-López 2000; Bucholtz 2001; Chun 2001; Eckert and McConnell-Ginet 1995; Klein 2009; Mehan 1996; Mendoza-Denton 2008; Reyes 2007; Rymes 2001; Shankar 2008).

In trying to understand how Moroccan immigrant children make sense of their lives and negotiate their social relations, I take an ethnopragmatic and ethnomethodological-informed approach that privileges the analysis of everyday language use and interactions in both its most immediate communicative and its larger sociocultural contexts (Duranti 2007; Duranti and Goodwin 1992; Ochs and Schieffelin 1984, 2012). This book draws heavily from these approaches in linguistic anthropology to delineate the microgenesis of membership and belonging for Moroccan immigrant children in Vallenuevo, paying particular attention to how difference, (mis-/non-) recognition, and inclusion/exclusion are discursively constructed in quotidian social encounters. The analysis in this book underscores, on the one hand, how difference and commonality of belonging are, at its most primordial level, products of everyday practices and interactions. On the other hand, it also emphasizes how immigrant children's everyday social encounters involve micro-discursive and interactional aspects of participation and membership as they intersect with larger sociocultural categories of identity and belonging.

A particularly helpful paradigm for this study is the body of work by scholars of language socialization, who for the last 25 years have been documenting and theorizing children's daily lives and participation in communities and institutions, including attention to children's language use in their own peer cultures (e.g., Goodwin 1990a; Heath 1983; Schieffelin and Ochs 1986a, 1986b; Ochs 1988; Schieffelin 1990), and to children's everyday interactions within the historical, economic, and sociopolitical contexts of families and communities (e.g., Kulick 1992; Zentella 1997). Language socialization researchers have also been paying increasing attention to how contested sociopolitical histories shape childhoods in contexts where children grow up having to negotiate multiple languages and/or the consequences of rapid language and culture shift, such as among formerly colonized nations and populations (e.g., Garrett 2005; Meek 2011; Minks 2013; Moore 2006; Paugh 2012; Reynolds 2008; Riley 2007), as well as in immigrant and diasporic communities (e.g., Baquedano-López 2004; Ek 2005; Fader 2009; García-Sánchez and Orellana 2006; He 2000; Klein 2009; Lo 2009; Mangual Figueroa 2011; Zentella 2005a). Indeed, research conducted in contexts that have undergone or are undergoing large-scale language and culture contact is one of the most vital strands of contemporary studies of language socialization.

This book builds on and elaborates a number of important foci in this rich body of scholarship, namely how children and youth in these contact areas negotiate sometimes disconnected familial and institutional settings, cope with conflicts in religious and secular social identities, manage their multilingual subjectivities, deal with differential forms of citizenship and belonging across and within immigrant generations, and learn the subtle but politically important indexicality involved in the use of different linguistic codes. The language socialization paradigm offers a nuanced and flexible to approach to the complexities of Moroccan immigrant childhoods at multiple levels of analytic scale and across different social contexts because of its attention to "the tensions between macro-political and micro-interactional social phenomena" (Baquedano-López and Mangual Figueroa 2012, p. 541) and because of its integrated, cross-context ethnographic perspective (Garrett 2006).

A second body of scholarship that I draw upon in this book is devoted to how language is involved in *racialization*, or "the processes through which any diacritic of social personhood –including class, ethnicity, generation, kinship/affinity, and the position within fields of power- comes to be essentialized, naturalized, and/or biologized" (P. A. Silverstein 2005, p. 364).[22]

Since the earliest studies on discrimination,[23] language has always been considered central to the processes by which immigrants and other minorities are racialized as *outgroups* and excluded from participation in many areas of social life. Certain forms of discourse have been deemed to play a pivotal role in symbolic means of domination, (re)production of racial/ethnic prejudice, as well as (non-) recognition and articulation of *otherness*.[24] In contemporary scholarship, the linguistic production of social *markedness* or difference is viewed as a form of symbolic violence, and perhaps one of the most insidious varieties of the processes "by which people become marked as exemplars of racial imaginaries" (Urciuoli 2011, p. E113).

An important focus of theoretical elaboration has been everyday and institutional ways of talking about and representing immigrants as racialized *Others* in a variety of ethnographic contexts and social settings. Although political and policy discourse has undoubtedly received the most systematic attention (e.g., Dick 2011; Martín-Rojo 2000; Mehan 1997; Van Leeuwen and Wodak 1999; Wodak and van Dijk 2000; Wiley and Lukes 1996; Woolard 1989, 1990; Wright 2005), other kinds of public discourse, such as mediatized forms and artistic performances, have also figured prominently (e.g., Reyes 2011; Santa Ana 1999, 2002; van Dijk 1991, 1993, 2000; Wirtz 2011). This work has established the interdiscursive relations between overt forms of racialized discourse, namely slurs, and covert forms, namely mock varieties and code words, and has outlined how representations of immigrants and minorities move across social space and time (e.g., Alim 2005; Bucholtz 1999; Chun 2009; Hill 1998, 2009; Rokin and Karn 1999; Wortham, Mortimer, and Allard 2009). The investigation of racialization processes in ordinary conversation and educational talk has been less common, however (but see Edwards 2003; Myers 2005; Pagliai 2009, 2011; Urciuoli 2009; van Dijk 1984; Verkuyten 1998, 2001).

A major contribution of this body of scholarship has been the systematic description of the ideological tenets and discursive strategies of the so-called *new, neo-, modern,* or *symbolic* racism, which is characterized by a discourse of denial of prejudice and a focus on cultural differences as the basis for abnormalization and rejection (Balibar 1991; Barker 1981; Bonilla-Silva 2003). Since racism has increasingly become associated with political extremism and cultural backwardness, those expressing negative views about immigrants or other minorities face a threat to their presentation of self. In delineating the anatomy of the denial of prejudice, social psychologists, critical discourse analysts, and linguistic anthropologists have repeatedly shown how speakers legitimize their negative views about immigrant and minorities, while still managing to convey a positive self-image and avoid charges of racism, by either presenting their views as reasonable or by presenting them as harmless jokes (Billig 1988; Billig et al. 1998; Hill 2008, 2009). By identifying a range of ideological practices (Hill 2008) and discourse strategies (see Augoustinos and Every 2007 for review) used to accomplish the naturalization of modern racism, this work has also shown that language does not have to be visceral or overtly racist to (re)produce conditions of discrimination and social exclusion.[25]

This book contributes to this body of work on language and racialization by addressing an aspect that has been very little explored to date: how daily situated talk in interaction between members from majority-dominant groups and members from immigrant minority groups is a primordial semiotic locus for the production of *social markedness*. Surprisingly, most previous scholarship has centered on racialized institutional, political, and everyday ways of talking *about* the *Other* – an *Other* that is rarely a participant, or even present, in these interactions being examined. And yet many minority and immigrant groups have reported experiencing feelings of exclusion and discrimination not only by how they are represented or (mis-/non-)recognized, but also by how they are differentially *treated* in everyday ways, or what critical race theorists have called *microaggressions of race* (Solórzano 1998; Solórzano, Ceja, and Yosso 2000; Solórzano, Allen, and Carroll 2002). My intent is to contribute to this body of work on language and racialization by uncovering the semiotic architecture of these microaggressions and the micro-genesis of racialized exclusion in the everyday practices of individuals as situated within historically-constituted cultural ideologies and social structures.

Understanding the interactional and discursive architecture of everyday racializing encounters is of critical importance, given the serious sociopolitical consequences for how immigrant children are able to negotiate membership and commonality of belonging. Through an examination of daily naturally-occurring social encounters of young Moroccan immigrant children in Vallenuevo, I trace how a racialized *Other* is effectively created in everyday, seemingly mundane interactions by focusing on how social actors make value-laden distinctions between different subjectivities and ways of being in the world. As an important counterpoint, however, I also analyze how Moroccan immigrant children are able to negotiate, counteract, and contest the different subject positions to which they are sometimes relegated. In this sense, my ethnography of Moroccan immigrant children in Vallenuevo also contributes to the burgeoning literature in linguistic anthropology that explores minority responses to forms of racism, as well as to ethnic youth's creative use of their multiple linguistic repertoires to resist racialization and to create their own local forms of identification (e.g., Bucholtz and Skapoulli 2009; Chun 2012; Mendoza-Denton 1999, 2008;

García-Sánchez 2013; Tetreault 2008, 2010; Rampton 1999, 2009; Reyes 2007; Reynolds and Orellana 2009; Roth-Gordon 2007; Shankar 2009; Zentella 2005b).

1.6 The Chapters in this Book

Following the introduction, this book consists of eight chapters. Chapter 2 starts by reviewing the literature on Moroccan immigration into Spain, in general, and into the area of Vallenuevo, in particular. The second part of the chapter illuminates how contemporary discourses about Moroccan immigration in Spain are produced at the juncture among anti-immigrant sentiment and contemporary anxieties about religious fanaticism and security in relation to Muslim immigrants as they intersect with historical, racialized images of the dangerous Moor invaders, *los moros*, of centuries past. I also elaborate on the analysis of these discourses by showing the vitality of the processes of entextualization by which the figure of *los moros* has permeated mytho-historical narratives, contemporary political discourse about Muslim and North African immigrants, and even everyday discourse about Moroccan immigration in Vallenuevo.

Chapter 3 offers an overview of the sites and methods of data collection in relation to how I negotiated my positionality in these contexts. In so doing, I consider details of research implementation as they intersect with the human and ethical dimensions of ethnographic research with Moroccan immigrant children in Vallenuevo. I focus on aspects of ethnographic reflexivity and examine some of the issues I faced as a Southern Spanish woman, perceived by locals as having turned foreign expatriate, doing research with Moroccan participants in a Southern Spanish town. I also reflect on how the specific linguistic ethnography I was conducting, heavy in technical gear, confronted me early on with the sensitive local politics of a town that increasingly resented outsiders' focus on Moroccan immigration.

Chapter 4 provides a panoramic view of Moroccan immigrant childhoods in Vallenuevo. I first present portraits of the children with whom I had the privilege to work more closely. I hope that these portraits will help readers get a better sense of the individuals that will appear in many of the interactions that are analyzed in subsequent chapters. In a second part of Chapter 4, bringing together my own observations with interview data, I discuss how different sociocultural domains shape, and are shaped by, Moroccan immigrant childhoods in Vallenuevo, placing special emphasis on how the children themselves understand and discuss their lives in these different social spheres.

Chapters 5 through 8 delve into individual social contexts of the children's lives and comprise the linguistic and ethnomethodological section of the book, where children's communicative practices and social interactions are analyzed. These four chapters are organized relative to the degree of autonomy for action that the children have in different contexts, moving from social spheres where children have less autonomy, such as in the public school and in Arabic language classes at the oratory-mosque, to those with more opportunities for action, such as in the clinic where they act as language brokers and in their neighborhood play groups.

Chapter 5 examines the subtle practices of exclusion that were a constitutive part of the relational fabric of Moroccan immigrant children's social life at school, in spite of the public discourse of inclusion, interculturality, and respect for diversity that constituted the school's official curriculum. Through detailed analysis of the daily interactions between Moroccan immigrant children with their Spanish peers and teachers at school, the chapter describes the micro-genesis of *social markedness* and racialized exclusion as the product of everyday practice and as it is constructed in social interaction.

In Chapter 6, I consider how notions of what it means to be a Moroccan and a Muslim are played out in the teaching of the Arabic language to younger generations of Moroccans in Vallenuevo. Because these children attend Arabic language classes at the public school and after-school religious classes at a small oratory run by a Islamic cultural association, I pay particular attention to the internal dynamism of the Moroccan immigrant community and address similarities and differences between these two contexts in the manufacturing of ethnoreligious identifications for the younger generations of Moroccans. Across both contexts, however, I highlight the crucial role of linguistic and literacy practices in the production of diaspora identities.

Chapter 7 discusses the sociocultural, ethical, and interactional paradoxes that Moroccan immigrant children manage when they act as linguistic brokers and sociocultural mediators between their families and members of Spanish institutions. I emphasize how children manage these varied paradoxes through the translation filters and subtle modifications they use. In mediating institutional encounters, the children exhibit a discerning ethical sophistication about their dual roles as agents of the institution and as representatives of the families, successfully building constructive bridges among their families and healthcare professionals.

In Chapter 8, through an investigation of Moroccan immigrant children's codeswitching practices in play, I focus on how children themselves are making sense of various aspects of the politics of belonging. In pretend-play, Moroccan immigrant girls explore some of the meanings and implications of the barriers they encounter in their present life and in their potential futures. As they imagine possible selves and futures, the girls' actions-in-play, particularly in their subversive, tactical nature, involve both the reproduction and change of some of the sociocultural formations with which they contend on a daily basis. Chapter 9, the conclusion, ties together the central themes of the book. The book's main concern – how Moroccan immigrant children negotiate the politics of difference and belonging in the quotidian sites of their social life at a time of heightened problematization of Muslim and North African immigrants – is revisited in light of the data presented in Chapters 4 to 8.

Notes

1 The name of the town, as well as the names of all the people, are pseudonyms to protect as much as possible the privacy and the anonymity of the people who, directly or indirectly, participated in this study and are featured here.

2 In the months that followed these events, several Spanish newspaper articles actually echoed these grim reports of alienation among North African and Muslim immigrant youth in several European countries. For example, in a March 2006 article (*El País*), the writer discussed how, according to a 2006 Official Report by the Dutch Central Office of Statistics, second generation Turkish and Moroccan Immigrants (born and raised in the Netherlands) felt less at home there than their own parents, who immigrated to the country as adults. Similarly, in an August 13, 2006 article (*El País*), a commentary by the prestigious British journalist Timothy Garton Ash was fully translated and expanded upon. The focus of this piece was the growing irritation of British Muslims, particularly young British Muslims, who, again, according to the latest statistics released in the United Kingdom, felt more distanced and excluded than their parents' generation; a feeling, the article continued to say, that is more acute and pervasive than that of the French youth who had so violently rioted in the housing estates outside France's major cities in fall 2005.

3 For a fuller critique of this idea, see Y. Samad and S. Kasturi (2007).

4 Literally *Moors*. The sociocultural and historical meaning of this expression in contemporary Spain will be taken up more fully in Chapter 2 of this book.

5 These points of contention have been well documented by Spanish scholars. See Arango Vila-Belda (2002); Barbolla Camarero (2001); Carrasco (2003) Castaño Madroñal (1997); Chacón Rodríguez (2003); Checa (1998); Checa et al. (2001); López García and Berriane (2004); Goytisolo and Naïr (2000); Martín Muñoz et al. (2003).

6 See V. R. Dominguez (1994) for a general discussion of how immigrant groups have increasingly become anthropology's exotic *Other* and P. A. Silverstein (2005) for a more specific discussion of how immigrants have come to occupy racialized subject positions within the academic history of European migration studies.

7 In addition to P. A. Silverstein (2005), see the volumes Prum et al (2007); Samad and Kasturi (2007).

8 See, for example, Alexander (2007); Levidow (2007); Samad and Kasturi (2007); Turner (2007); Werbner (2005).

9   See, for example, Barrett (2007); Gandy (2006); Levidow (2007); Turner (2007); Prum et al. (2007).

10 In addition to 9/11, the London 2005 subway bombings, and the March 2004 train bombings in Madrid (the largest-scale terrorist attack to date on Spanish soil), it is important to add other local events that although less well-known outside of Spain have, nonetheless, affected perceptions of Moroccan immigrants, such as the January 2000 pogrom-like attack on the Moroccan population of the southeastern Spanish town of El Ejido. This attack that was legitimated and rationalized as the inevitable consequence of the irreconcilable cultural differences between the Moroccan and Spanish populations of the town.

11 For a more extended treatment of the implications of this regularization process, please see, María P. López (2007) "Immigration Law Spanish-Style: A Study of the Regularización of Undocumented Workers in Spain."

12 For some prime examples of this scholarship see the work of Hall (1995) among Sikh youth in Great Britain and the work of Lee (2005) and Pease-Álvarez and Vásquez (1994) among Hmong youth and Latino children in the United States, respectively.

13 Much recent work has emphasized the importance of scholarship devoted to providing this holistic understanding, see, for example, Gutiérrez (2008); López (2003); Orellana (2009); Portes and Rumbaut (2006); Suárez-Orozco, Suárez-Orozco, and Todorova (2008); Valenzuela (1999).

14 See Appendix 2 for Arabic Transliteration Symbols used in transcription.

15 Although I did not collect lifemaps from Spanish children in the town, my own observations, as well as scholarship documenting the role of children in contemporary Spanish families, indicate that most Spanish children have very few responsibilities, if any, in their households. The notion of childhood in Spain has changed dramatically over the last 50 years. This change has been well-documented by American anthropologist Jane Collier (1997) and by Spanish sociologist Amando de Miguel (2000). Both Collier and de Miguel discuss how Spanish families have increasingly become child-centered; family life revolves around children's needs and education. One of the consequences of this shift is that children's involvement in family responsibilities has declined significantly. Primacy is given to children's responsibilities in school to the point where parents now do most things for their children in the household.

16 De Certeau's (1984) examination of the operational logics of the adaptations performed by individuals caught in the nets of structured forms of power illuminates the multitude of clandestine, creative everyday practices of resistance to dominant culture, economy, and politics. In discussing people's everyday practices, De Certeau has distinguished between strategies and tactics. *Strategies* are practices or everyday ways of acting that proceed in accordance with the power-legitimized order of things. These normative practices organize institutions and structured-power, and implicate authority and relations of power. *Tactics* are everyday ways of acting through which individuals transform and subvert technocratic structures to fit their own needs and interests. They involve individuals' manipulations of the system and are organized outside the gaze of power and authority. While tactics tend to remain minor and concealed, they are integral to the fabric of society.

17 See for instance P.A. Silverstein's description of tropes of immigrant assimilation in France (2004), and in general within European migration studies (2005).

18 *Convivencia*, "living-together," is also a historical ideology that emphasizes how Muslim, Christian, and Jewish communities in Medieval Spain were supposedly able to live together harmoniously. This point of view also highlights how this peaceful coexistence yielded a

productive syncretism that, in turn, produced some of the most positive and uniquely-Spanish cultural achievements of this period. *Nueva Convivencia* ("New Living-Together") has been used as a trope in both general discourses about immigration in Spain, as well as in scholarly analysis (see e.g., Erickson 2011 and Suárez-Navaz 2004).

19   The terms *acculturation* and *assimilation* emerged in the fields of anthropology and psychology through the work of Redfield, Linton, and Herskovits (1936) and Graves (1967) as analytic concepts to explain the patterns of cultural change that occur when groups of individuals from different cultural backgrounds come into continuous first-hand contact with one another. Redfield, Linton, and Herskovits (1936) focused on group-level phenomena, while Graves (1967) concentrated on individual-level processes. The concepts soon found their way into descriptive paradigms of the immigrant experience, such as Gordon's (1964) model of assimilation of immigrants into American life. Contemporary sociological reframings of immigrant incorporation emphasize the dialectic interaction of multiple scale factors (e.g., Portes and Zhou 1993). One of the most useful and influential theoretical paradigms of immigrant assimilation has been the segmented assimilation model (Portes and Rumbaut 2001; Rumbaut and Portes 2001). This model has addressed many of the criticisms leveled at previous models of assimilation in that it stresses the interplay of multiple factors and the internal variability within both the immigrant population and the dominant society itself.

20   For an extended review of anthropological critiques of acculturation/assimilation models, see, for example K. Hall (2002, and particularly, 2004). On the one hand, assimilationist paradigms have been problematized for failing to address the ideological tenets that position immigrants as specific kinds of subjects, often as abject subjects, against symbolic representations of the nation as an *imagined community*; and, on the other hand, these models have also been critiqued for leaving unquestioned how the cultural logics of these forms of classification organize social practice and structural relations as well as forms of cultural domination, misrecognition, and social exclusion.

21   See Gilson (2007) for a thorough exposition of the differences between these two concepts, as well as areas of complementarity, in Agamben and Deleuze's philosophy.

22   In most contemporary scholarship of language and racialization, race is viewed as a cultural category of difference that is locally produced as naturalized and commonsensical against a normalized and normative field. Therefore, most definitions of racialization, in addition to P. Silverstein's above, emphasize constructed distinctiveness. See for instance, Urciuoli's definition: "racialization can be understood as one of many linked processes of social marking, including processes of gender, ethnic, class and other modes of markedness, all operating against an unmarked background of what social actors perceive as normative" (2011, p. E113), or Wodak and Reisigl's "the dynamic, and dialectical representational processes of categorization and meaning construction in which specific meanings are ascribed to real or fictitious somatic features" (1999, p. 180).

23   Allport's (1954) seminal study of prejudice and interethnic relations was one of the first to focus our attention on the importance of language in the stigmatization and exclusion of minority groups. He identified five categories of behavior associated with prejudice that naturalize the positioning of minorities as outgroups and legitimize acts of discrimination and violence as ethically acceptable: antilocution, avoidance, discrimination, physical attack, and extermination. Antilocution is perhaps the most critical for the present discussion. Allport defined antilocution as the use of language to articulate antagonism and "otherness." In his view, extreme and/or socially-organized forms of discrimination and violence against

minority groups need to be understood alongside softer forms of rejection and exclusion in which language plays a crucial role.

24 See e.g., Blommaert and Verschueren (1998); Hill (1998); Mehan (1997); Santa Ana (1999); M. Silverstein (2003); Urciouli (1996); van Dijk (1984, 1987, 1993); Verkuyten (1998, 2001); Zentella (1996); Wodak and Reisigl (1999).

25 The ideological and discourse practices that have been identified in this literature can be grouped in four broad categories: first, arguments, that are inherently discriminatory, are organized and justified around democratic and liberal principles, such as freedom, equality, national legal codes, and individual rights (e.g., Blommaert and Verschueren 1998; Martin Rojo 2010; van Dijk 1993; Verkuyten 1998; Woolard 1990). Second, in Hill's (2008) *folk theory of racism*, she traces how individuals of the majority group perpetuate the idea that the racism that persists is just the remnants of bygone times upheld by small fringe and radical groups, rather than a more pervasive and contemporary structural practice upheld by all members of society. This is accomplished through two types of language ideologies, that of personalism and referentialism. *Personalism* is deployed to cast speakers as *intentionally* racist, whereas *referentialism* is invoked to argue that even though speakers might have sounded racist because the words they used have racist connotations, they are not really racist because this was not intentionally done, such as in commonly called *gaffes* and *slips of the tongue*. Third, forms of negative categorization have been documented to play an important part in discursive processes of *othering*. Negative descriptors of minority groups are, for example, accompanied by positive characterizations of the majority group. Contrast structures in the deictic field, such as "us vs. them," accentuate inter-group differences. Additionally, explicit racial/ethnic categories tend to be attenuated or simply eliminated in favor of categories such as dress code, alien traditions, and culture (e.g., Bonilla-Silva 2002; Mehan 1997; Pollock 2004; Urciuoli 2009; van Dijk 1987, 2005). Finally, story-telling is a primordial means of creating distant, different, and distorted models of personhood for immigrant groups, as well as a powerful means for the circulation of these models across communicative networks and discursive chains (e.g., Bucholtz 1999; van Dijk 1984; Verkuyten 2001; Wortham, Allard, Lee, and Mortimer 2011). In telling stories about immigrants and ethnic minority groups, speakers present events as factual and common rather than as subjective and individual narratives of personal experience. The use of details, vivid description, and reported speech are common devices endowing events with a halo of objectivity.

2

Moros en la Costa: The Moroccan Immigrant Diaspora in Spain

Es que cuando yo estaba en segundo, en tercero, y en cuarto
los niños– los de mi clase me querían mucho, me abrazaban–
me abrazaban todos y sólo vino Malika y muchos marroquines y ya está.
Y estaba SIEMPRE jugando con las españolas y cuando ya vino Malika
y más chicas, ya está. Me empezaron a odiar. No sé por qué.

It's that when I was in second, in third, and in fourth grade
the [Spanish] children – the ones in my class, loved me very much;
they would hug me – all of them would hug me,
and then Malika came and lots of Moroccans and that was it.
And I was ALWAYS playing with Spanish girls and when Malika and
more [Moroccan] girls already came, that was it. They [Spanish children]
started to hate me. I don't know why.

(Manal, age 11, interview fragment)

Moros en la costa is part of a popular and colloquial expression in the Spanish language, "(No) hay moros en la costa," roughly equivalent in meaning to the English saying "the coast is/is not clear." Historically, the meaning of this expression harks back to the late Middle Ages and early modern period, when Mediterranean coastal towns, particularly those situated between the modern regions of Valencia and Murcia, were objects of raids by small groups that settled along the northwest African coast. As a defensive measure, many of these towns built special watchtowers, called *atalayas*. When raiding ships were spotted, the lookout would usually light up a big torch and shout

Language and Muslim Immigrant Childhoods: The Politics of Belonging, First Edition.
Inmaculada Mª García-Sánchez.
© 2014 John Wiley & Sons, Inc. Published 2014 by John Wiley & Sons, Inc.

"Moros en la costa," literally "Moors on the coast," to warn the town's population of the presence of raiders. The expression has continued to be used in both Peninsular and Latin American varieties of Spanish. Over time, its meaning has evolved to indicate situations in which we can or cannot proceed because a potential danger we fear is either present or not. I use it in the title of this chapter in a pun-like manner to evoke for the reader primarily two issues. I want to make reference, on the one hand, to the pernicious Moor/Moroccan slippage, with which part of this chapter is concerned, and which structures much public discourse about Moroccan immigration in Spain. I also want to address, on the other hand, some of these discourses head-on by highlighting the widespread impression among a large part of the Spanish population who believe, regardless of actual statistics to the contrary, that most Moroccan immigrants arrive illegally on Spanish coasts in ramshackle boats called *pateras*. In the first part of this chapter, I indirectly address these and other stereotypes, by offering a socio-logical account of the Moroccan immigrant community in Spain, in general, and in Vallenuevo, in particular. In the second part of the chapter, I discuss discourses about Moroccan immigrants more directly. I highlight how these discourses are produced at the complex intersection of anti-immigrant sentiment, contemporary concerns about security and religious fanaticism attributed to Muslim immigrant groups, and historical anxieties aroused by Orientalist and racialized images of the dangerous Moor invaders of centuries past.

2.1 A Brief History of the Moroccan Immigrant Diaspora in Contemporary Spain

Morocco has undergone profound demographic changes in the last five decades, particularly, a decrease in birth rate and mass migration from rural to urban centers. This internal migration eventually channeled itself to other countries.[1] As a result, the depopulation of many rural areas in Morocco has become very significant in the last few years (Kerzazi 2004). The shift from this first migration to Moroccan urban centers, as well as other international destinations, predominantly in Europe, began to take shape early in the twentieth century. More specifically, the beginning of Moroccan migrations to Europe date back to the First World War, when France encouraged and facilitated the massive arrival of Moroccan immigrants to replace the large number of French workers who were called up to fight on the front. Because of this long history of international migration, Moroccan communities are among the most dispersed and flourishing immigrant diasporas in Europe, with significant communities in France, the Netherlands, Belgium, Germany, Spain, and Italy. In fact, in the 2002 elections – the first ones which took place during the reign of Mohammed VI – the number of Moroccan citizens residing abroad had already reached over 2 million people.[2]

In the long evolution of Moroccan migratory flows into Europe, Spain did not begin to figure in the minds of most Moroccans as a potential immigration destination until the beginning of the 1980s, following the economic crisis of 1974. The oil crisis had a profound impact on the economies of many European countries (e.g., Germany, France, and the Netherlands) that had traditionally absorbed, until then, the lion's share of Moroccan immigration into the continent. The governments of France, Germany, and the Netherlands, started to see these migratory processes with growing concern. As a consequence, Europe closed its borders, and the only viable way for Moroccans to continue to have legal access to these countries was through family reunification policies. It was due to these difficult economic circumstances that the Moroccan population was forced to open new migratory paths towards the only two permeable spaces in Europe before the Schengen Agreement[3] was put into place: Italy and Spain.[4]

In Spain in particular the economic prosperity of the country during the construction bubble of the 1990s and 2000s gave rise to an unprecedented increase in the number of Moroccan immigrants in the country, as well as immigrants from other areas of the world, namely Romania, Ecuador, and Colombia.[5] By the 1990s, Spain, which during the 1960s and the 1970s had exported thousands of immigrants to the industrialized areas of Europe, was itself becoming an important destination of immigrants and country of reception. By 2005, it was among the top 10 countries in the world with the largest numbers of international migrants[6] and one of the biggest immigration rates worldwide, a trend that has continued until 2011 when the absolute numbers of immigrants in the country decreased, by roughly 37,000, for the first time in more than two decades.

With regard to the Moroccan diaspora in Spain, in particular, the size of this community in 1991 was that of 30,000; at the beginning of 2004, when I had barely started building the foundations of this ethnographic project, the Moroccan immigrant population had soared to 333,770, which constituted a tenfold increase in less than 15 years. In addition to that number are, of course, the thousands of undocumented Moroccan workers who do not feature in official census data. The latest statistics show that the number of Moroccan immigrants in the country has continued to increase rapidly. By December 31, 2011, the Moroccan diaspora community in Spain had reached 801,690. This makes the Moroccan community the largest immigrant community of *el régimen general*, which includes immigrant communities from all areas of the world except from countries of the European Union; the rights of immigrants from the latter are regulated by the so-called *régimen comunitario*. In absolute terms, including immigrant communities from both *el régimen general* and *el régimen comunitario*, the size of the Moroccan immigrant community in Spain is second only to the Romanian immigrant community, totaling 912,526. The numerical figures in the Southwestern region of the Spain where I conducted this ethnography, closely mirror migratory and demographic trends at the national level, with the number of Moroccans being the highest for those immigrants in *el régimen general* (8,350), barely surpassed, in absolute numbers of immigrants, only by the Romanian community (9,046), regulated by *el régimen comunitario*.[7]

The history of the evolution of the Moroccan immigrant diaspora in contemporary Spain can be summarized in three or four distinct phases, depending on different scholarly descriptions of the phenomenon.[8] Losada-Campo (1993), for instance, talks about a first pre-1967 period, characterized by the slow, but steady arrivals of Moroccans into the *autonomous* cities of Ceuta and Melilla.[9] The vast majority of the Moroccans who arrived in these two cities at this time came from the most impoverished areas of the old Spanish Protectorate.[10] Most authors also discuss a second period between 1967 and 1974. This involved the arrival of small groups of Moroccan immigrant workers to Catalonia. The so-called *industrial belt* surrounding Barcelona, in particular, was the most industrialized region in the country and underwent a spectacular economic surge during this period. This small contingent of Moroccan immigrants, however, did not spread to any other areas of the country that suffered, at that time, from a depressed economy. The third period (mid–1970s to beginning of the 1990s) is unanimously considered to be the first migration phase that had a real demographic impact on both Spain as a country of reception and on shifting trends in Moroccan migratory patterns. As I already mentioned above, in the context of the history of the Moroccan diaspora, Spain did not start to play a significant role until the mid– to late 1970s, when the other European countries imposed severe restrictions on their immigration policies, and Spain increasingly became a new geographical destination for migrants originating from Morocco. During the late 1970s, Spain was, for many Moroccans, still *a country of transit* from Morocco to other European countries, and the impact of Moroccan immigration on Spanish society was minimal. The 1980s, however, witnessed a steady increase in the Moroccan community in all areas of Spain. While Moroccan immigrants initially tended to concentrate in larger urban areas, such as Madrid, Barcelona, or Valencia, they soon after started to settle in a wide variety of Spanish regions. A similar process occurred in Morocco. Although most of the immigrants initially came from the Rif and other areas of influence of the old Spanish Protectorate (see Note 4), such as Nador, Alhoceima, and Tétouan, these migratory patterns soon became more geographically diversified to include other regions that had been historically under the area of French colonial influence, such as Oujda, Berkane, Jerada, or Taourirt. By the beginning of the 1990s, Spain had become one of the most important European destinations for Moroccan immigrants.

The fourth phase of the history of the Moroccan diaspora in Spain was inaugurated by the regularization process that took place in 1991, which provided a status of legal residence to four-fifths of the 30,000 Moroccans who were then living in the country mostly in the precarious conditions that sometimes accompany undocumented situations (López García 2004). This regularization process became a necessity due to the rapid growth that the Moroccan immigrant community had undergone in little over a decade. This growth would continue during the 1990s and the 2000s. By 2003, the number of Moroccans had reached 333,770; the community not only increased in number, but also in geographical range, diversifying its presence in almost all the provinces of Spanish national territory. Even though the Spanish government began to implement more and more restrictive immigration laws starting in the late 1990s and particularly in 2000 (many of which discriminated against Moroccans in particular, as will be discussed below), the community has continued to grow at a vibrant pace in the last few years, due mainly to the number of births,[11] and to policies of family reunification. Since 2003, Moroccan children have been the second largest immigrant student body in Spanish schools (Martín Rojo 2010 Mijares 2004b), a trend that has continued to grow in the last few years, and that illustrates how the Moroccan immigrant community is developing increasingly strong intergenerational roots in the country (García Ortiz and Díaz Hernández 2004). Also, although the borders have increasingly become policed and *secured*, unauthorized immigration between Morocco and Spain still continues to be a source of newcomers into the country (Lahiou 2004). The latest statistics estimate that there are 801,690 Moroccans in the country, which makes the Moroccan diaspora in Spain one of the largest immigrant communities in the country and with the longest history of settlement. Moreover, around 40% of Moroccan immigrants in Spain have already acquired status as permanent residents, which also reinforces the trend towards permanence across generations that has already been observed in other European countries with longer histories of Moroccan immigration (Izquierdo Escribano 2004).

Although the Moroccan diaspora community in Spain is extremely diverse, there are a few macro-sociological characterizations that have been made about the evolution of its demographic composition and processes of settlement. In terms of the demographic composition, the most important generalization is that the Moroccan immigrant diaspora in Spain is eminently young and of working age; indeed, in 2003 one in four Moroccans in Spain was below the age of 18 (López García 2003), a trend that still continues today. Nevertheless, as the processes of settlement have evolved, so has the demographic make-up of the Moroccan community. For instance, although Moroccan immigrants initially tended to be single, young male workers in agriculture and construction,[12] in the last 15 years, there has been a progressive feminization in the migratory patterns.[13] This shift has not only been due to family reunification processes. Throughout the 1990s, more and more Moroccan women arrived in Spain not only to be reunited with their husbands, but as immigrant workers in their own right. Although many Moroccan mothers still tend to remain in the home as primary caregivers, by 2003, one in three Moroccan women in Spain were fully integrated in the labor market and worked outside the home.[14]

Another instance of how the migratory patterns have become progressively feminized has to do with the ratio of males to females in post-secondary education (16 to 20 years old). During the 1990s, there was a noticeable predominance of male students, particularly at more advanced levels of education. A prejudiced explanation of this phenomenon – having to do with the assumption that Moroccan adolescent girls were abandoning their education in droves due to cultural and religious reasons – was exposed when educational data was compared with general census data. There were more Moroccan young men than women in schools during this time because the Moroccan migratory pattern in general was heavily masculinized. As more women have become involved in the process of migration, the prevalence of Moroccan male students in post-secondary levels of education has also disappeared. In recent years, the presence of young Moroccan women in higher levels of education is 14 percentage points higher than that of their male counterparts.[15]

Finally, another shift that the Moroccan immigrant community has undergone during the last decade is related to their increased involvement in tertiary economic sectors. While agriculture and construction have continued to be important sources of employment for the Moroccan immigrant community, increasingly more Moroccans have sought and occupied jobs in service-related sectors of the economy.[16] In terms of *integration patterns*, the Moroccan immigrant population in Spain has been said to vary along a continuum from isolation from non-Moroccans to integration in the dominant society at all costs, even if it means abandoning cultural, religious, and linguistic practices rooted in their communities of origin.[17] This multifaceted heterogeneity contrasts with the perceptions of Spanish institutions and communities, which tend to hold a homogeneous view of the Moroccan immigrant community. This homogeneous image is mass-mediated and deficit-oriented, often blaming Moroccans for their supposed lack of willingness to integrate, and associating them with rising crime rates, violence, and religious fanaticism, an issue that will be taken up more in depth below.

2.2   The Moroccan Immigrant Community in Vallenuevo

Vallenuevo is a small rural town with a surface area of 103.8 square miles located approximately 125 miles southwest of Madrid. With a total population of 10,815, Vallenuevo has been a major settlement area for Moroccan immigrants since the early 1990s, when Moroccan immigration into Spain started to take off demographically. Vallenuevo has had a long history of Moroccan immigration relative to many other areas in the country. It has been an important destination for Moroccans almost from the inception of these migratory movements to Spain, attracting large numbers of Moroccan immigrants even before 1991. The importance of Vallenuevo as an immigration destination is further emphasized by the fact that 33% of the migrant population that has settled in the two provinces that make up this region of the country is tightly concentrated in the area of Vallenuevo and its neighboring communities.[18] The total immigrant population of Vallenuevo is estimated to range between 3,975 and 4,573 people, a significant number that makes up approximately 37% of the total population of the town. Except for a handful of Latin American families, the bulk of the immigrant population – approximately 93% of this 37% – is overwhelmingly of Moroccan origin.[19]

At the beginning of the so-called *immigration boom* of the 1990s, Moroccan immigrants in this town were mostly single males in their late twenties to early thirties. Soon after that, however, many married males also started to come to Vallenuevo, being followed slowly, but steadily, by their wives and children. The processes of settlement of these young men during the first decade of Moroccan immigration in this town, from 1992 to 1996, have been documented in depth in previous studies. These studies focused, in particular, on their living and working conditions in the fields, as well as on the perceptions of the Spanish local population of Moroccan immigration into the area.[20] The "extraordinary regularization process" (*proceso de regularización extraordinaria*) passed by the Spanish government on December 30th, 2004, barely eight months before I moved to Vallenuevo, was extremely important in the consolidation of the family-oriented migratory patterns that had already started in this area a few years earlier. As more and more families started to settle in the area, a number of establishments, from specialty grocery stores to oratories, were opened to fulfill the needs of the growing Moroccan community in Vallenuevo.

At the time I conducted this ethnography, there were four stores run by Moroccan families, three of them grocery stores specializing in Moroccan imports (such as traditional food and spices, daily-baked flat bread, ceramic tagines and other cooking ware, as well as some traditional clothing). Most importantly for the Moroccan community, these shops were the sources of *halal* meat, which is meat from animals who are slaughtered by having their throats slit so as to drain the body of blood and impurities, and bearing the official inspection stamp indicating the slaughter was supervised by an imam.[21] In the diaspora Moroccan community of Vallenuevo, having access to *halal* meat is of utmost importance, since its consumption is crucial to daily, observant religious practices. There were also two Moroccan coffee shops, where Moroccan men gathered in the evenings to drink tea and share daily events with their compatriots. An oratory-mosque, run by the local Islamic cultural association, Assalam, was also established in a former warehouse to serve the religious needs of the community, particularly Friday prayers and the religious education of the new generations. Qur'anic and Classical Arabic after-school classes for Moroccan immigrant children were held in one of the rooms of this building.

Finally, there were also three *locutorios* in the town, two run by Moroccan families and the third run by a Spanish family. *Locutorios* are public telecommunication establishments with independent, enclosed phone booths and computers with Internet access. Since many Moroccan families did not have a landline phone in their houses, these facilities were crucial not only for Moroccan immigrants to keep in touch with their loved ones living in Morocco or in other European countries, but also for the maintenance and strengthening of transnational networks among the Moroccan diaspora. In addition, lured by the prospect of relatively inexpensive Internet access, these establishments attracted a large number of Moroccan adolescents and young adults, who frequently gathered there in the afternoons and spent long hours in front of the computer screens emailing their friends in Morocco or *visiting* popular chat-rooms among the Moroccan transnational, diasporic youth.

The economy of Vallenuevo is based mostly on agriculture; the most common crops being tobacco, pepper, asparagus, cherries, and raspberries. Since, with few exceptions, these crops continue to be harvested manually, they are particularly demanding in terms of the human labor required not only during their harvest, but also in the initial stages of produce processing. Many Moroccan immigrants started settling in this town pre-cisely because of the overwhelming need for seasonal farm workers. Also, the fact that the harvesting of some of these crops occur simultaneously, while the others are consecutive in the agricultural harvesting calendar means that there is both abundance of work, and, more importantly from the perspective of seasonal farm workers, work over longer periods of time during the year. These harvesting requirements facilitated family settlement in Vallenuevo, unlike in many other areas of the country, where production concentrates solely on one or two crops. As the main source of seasonal farm workers, Moroccan immigrants were very much responsible for the vast amounts of wealth that has been generated in this area in the last two decades. Few locals in Vallenuevo would be willing to admit this fact, however, and the interethnic relations between Moroccan immigrants and a big part of the Spanish local population were delicate and precarious, despite their daily economic interdependence. Since most Moroccans in Vallenuevo were economic migrants, with a large percentage performing seasonal manual labor, they also tended to occupy subaltern and marginal positions both socially and economically, as well as in the political and cultural life of the town.

Although some Moroccan families have attained a relatively stable and comfortable way of life, particularly among those with longer histories of settlement, most Moroccan families I came in contact with still faced much financial hardship, poor housing conditions, and long hours of double-shift work in the fields. The financial responsibilities that many families had for their relatives in Morocco, to whom they sent monthly allowances to amel-iorate their living conditions, added an additional level of economic stress to these constraints. Previous studies done in this area documented, for example, that 27.3% of Moroccan households in the town did not have running water and 38% did not have electricity. In addition, approximately 43% of Moroccan households were occupied by more than five people.[22] While some of these living conditions have to do with the fact that, often-times, several families opt to live together to help out with the cost of rent, the reality is much more complicated than that. Choice of housing for Moroccan immigrants in Vallenuevo is extremely limited, not only because of economic circumstances, but also, mainly, because many locals refused to let their empty houses and apartments to Moroccan families. Housing dis-crimination was rampant in Vallenuevo. The only houses that locals are often willing to rent to Moroccan families are in the oldest and most decrepit buildings in the town. A telling example of this common situation is the reaction of my landlady when she learned of the nature of my fieldwork in Vallenuevo. Although I did not have a problem finding a suitable apart-ment to rent, my landlady became increasingly concerned when she realized that I was going to be working with Moroccan children, and we had several arguments about the access that *los moros* were going to have to my apartment. A fairly embarrassing situation regarding housing also occurred when Rashid, the new public school Arabic teacher sent by the Moroccan Ministry of Education, moved to Vallenuevo, about the same time as I arrived in town. When Rashid and his wife, Amina, started looking for a house, they were denied access to the nicest houses they inquired about, and were only shown a few decrepit houses. Eventually, the principal of the school, Carlos, had to intervene and intercede with the local real estate agency, so that the Arabic teacher and his wife could rent a modern house in good condition. Unlike the Arabic teacher and his wife, however, most immigrants coming to the town did not have these outside resources to help them. Most of the households I was familiar with did have both electricity and running water. Nevertheless, in some cases the physical and structural conditions of the houses themselves were poor with basic furniture and few electrical appliances. A couple of the households of my focal children, however, those of Kamal and Wafiya, were not actually apartments or houses, but rather commercial properties that were being used as living spaces. These properties were poorly maintained by the landlords. Other focal children, although also living in relatively modest households, did not have to endure the material hardship these two families did, as I will explain in subsequent chapters.

2.3   Communities of Origin of the Moroccan Immigrant Community in Vallenuevo

The vast majority of the Moroccan immigrant community in Vallenuevo comes from the Northeastern area of Morocco, particularly from the regions of Oujda, Taourirt, and Jerada. Although emigration processes from the Northeastern region to international destinations did not intensify until the late 1970s – relatively late in comparison with many other areas of Morocco – this area has now become one of the largest *exporters* of Moroccan immigrants to Europe. During the last decade, Spain has been one of the most important destinations for immigrants originating in the Northeastern area, which is not only the community of origin of most Moroccan immigrants in Vallenuevo, but also of a sizable amount of Moroccan immigrants in other areas of the country.[23]

Politically and administratively speaking, the Northeastern region is composed of the provinces of Berkane, Taourirt, Nador, Jerada, Figuig, and the prefecture of Oujda-Angad. Precipitation levels in this area tend to be low, and the region becomes increasingly desertic towards the south, with a rough, arid climate and low population densities. The main economic activities in the region have traditionally been agriculture, semi-nomadic cattle-herding (especially in the south), coal mining, and smuggling (given its proximity to Algeria).

In the last few decades, however, the region has suffered from a deep economic crisis. Demographically, this has translated into a staggering depopulation of rural areas, in particular. The main causes of this economic crisis have been, on the one hand, the successive closing of many of the mining facilities in Jerada, and, on the other hand, insufficient water resources for sustainable irrigation and cattle-herding. In addition to these adverse economic conditions, the area also suffers from a scarcity of basic social services, such as health and post-elementary education.

As a consequence, rising unemployment and lack of economic, social, and educational opportunities has forced much of the population to emigrate to large Moroccan urban areas first, and, then, to international destinations, such as Spain. Migration has indeed had a profound impact on the demographic and social changes that this area has experienced in the last two decades. International migration, for example, has contributed to the increased urbanization of the Northeastern area, since most of the immigrants who have returned have settled in the major cities, such as Oujda, rather than returning to the small rural villages where they originally migrated from.[24] In relation to the migrants who come to Vallenuevo from this Northeastern region, it is important to note that the majority of them come from the most rural areas from within this region. Before coming to Vallenuevo, most families were involved in the main economic activities in the region, especially seasonal harvesting of agricultural products and semi-nomadic cattle-herding. Because the literacy rates in these areas are very low, particularly among women, many of the immigrants who have settled in Vallenuevo have very basic levels of formal education.

2.4   Contemporary Discourses About Moroccan Immigration in Spain

The problematization of Moroccan immigrants in Spain shares many features with the prejudice and mistrust that Muslim immigrant groups face in other European contexts (e.g., Bowen 2007, 2010; Ewing 2008; Mandel 2008; P. A. Silverstein 2004). Certainly, this problematization partakes of both what Werbner (2005) has called a wider discourse of Islamophobia, as well as of Asad's (2003) discussions of secularism as the ideological underpinning of the misrepresentation and exclusion of Muslims in Europe. Even the briefest review of the literature on contemporary Moroccan immigration in Spain will suffice to establish the fact that Moroccan immigrants are the group that focalizes most of the popular, political, and media, debates over integration and assimilation.[25] In this sense, Moroccans have come to embody the *social visibility* of the recent immigration phenomenon in Spain, and have become the main protagonists in the much-discussed *crisis of integration models*. Moreover, the dominant discourse about Moroccans' integration in Spain blames them for not making enough of an effort to assimilate, and they are widely perceived as resisting assimilation. Indeed, in both public opinion polls and research surveys about immigration, as well as in scholarly work about racism and xenophobia in Spain, Moroccan immigrants, particularly Moroccan males (Rogozen-Soltar 2012a), are invariably the most rejected and ill-regarded group. They are the group that arouses the lowest levels of sympathy among all immigrant groups in the country, evoking images of religious fanaticism, violence, sexism, dirtiness, criminality, mistrust, inferiority, and difference.[26]

Terren (2004, p. 442), for example, using a terminology that is reminiscent of Werbner's (2005) *Islamophobia* but socioculturally and historically grounded in the Spanish context, maintains that there is a deeply rooted *morofobia* (literally, phobia of the Moor) that has translated itself into higher levels of exclusion for Moroccans in all spheres of social life. Along the same lines, López García (2006) and Bravo López (2004) have both claimed that the Moroccan community in Spain has come to represent the body of the immigrant population which, in the public imagination, is considered to be *inasimilable* (unassimilable). Bravo López (2004), in particular, has argued that postmodern *culturalist* brands of racism have provided the mechanisms by which perceived cultural differences between the Moroccan immigrant population and the Spanish local population are discursively exacerbated until they become in effect insolvable: the integration of Moroccan immigrant populations becomes impossible because their Islamic culture, religion, and identity is irreconcilable with Spanish (and European, in general) culture and identity. Adding an interesting layer to this argument, Dietz (2005) and Rogozen-Soltar (2012b) have both highlighted how Islamic religious fanaticism, as opposed to ideals of secular humanism, is often emphasized in discursive constructions of Muslim immigrants in Spain. Moroccan communities in Spain are thus regarded as constituting a problem of integration because they are seen as posing a threat to a Spanish national identity strongly aligned with Europeanism; an identity that many regions of the country have worked hard to achieve and to project.

At the policy level, one of the most consequential outcomes of this supposed threat to Spanish national identity was a discriminatory immigration policy during the late 1990s that blatantly favored Latin American and Eastern European immigration to the detriment of immigration from North African, Islamic countries.[27] Within a few years, Ecuadorians, for example, who until then had had a minimal presence in the country, became in 2003, the largest immigrant community in Spain, surpassing for the first time the number of Moroccan immigrants, who had been, theretofore, not only the largest immigrant community, but also the immigrant group with the longest history of migration to Spain. The role of cultural bias in immigration policy and in the differential treatment of immigrant groups has been documented to explain this rapid shift in migratory trends.[28] Unlike Moroccans who are constructed as *too foreign* and with different cultural traditions, Latin Americans, and even Eastern Europeans, such as Romanians, are seen as belonging to *very* similar cultural traditions with close cultural, religious, and linguistic ties to Spain. Given the close historical ties that no doubt exist between Spain and Morocco, other scholars have gone further in identifying the obvious irony and racist foundation of the *culturalist* argument, positing that *cultural compatibility* is a convenient euphemism in order to favor a Christian immigration of lighter skin (Flesler 2008; Goytisolo and Naïr 2000).

Because perceived Islamic radicalism plays such a prominent role in how Muslim immigrant communities are constructed as cultural outsiders, this *cultural threat* has been relatively easy to conflate, particularly in the press and political discourse, with the terrorist attacks of September 2001, and, of course, the Madrid train bombings in early 2004. Because of this routine conflation, Moroccan communities in Spain have increasingly become to be seen under a security paradigm (Moreras 2004). In this respect, Barbudo (2004, p. 27) has argued that some of these events brought about another radical change in Spanish institutional approaches to immigration. In addition to the new restrictions imposed on Moroccans and the discriminatory immigration policies described above, immigration stopped being considered a *social phenomenon* to become increasingly treated as a *problema policial* (police or security problem). Racialized discourses about Moroccan immigrant communities in Spain can be thus summarized as twofold. On the one hand, they are considered a threat to a presumably distinct and homogeneous Spanish character and identity, and, on the other hand, they are also considered as a potential threat to Spanish national security. The problematization of Moroccan immigrants in Spain on these two counts is similar to the experience of Muslim immigrant groups in other parts of Europe, where they have also been positioned in a very distinctive category of exclusion regardless of country of origin and settlement and other contextual differences.

Beyond the current geopolitical climate of suspicion surrounding Muslim and North African immigrants, however, it is also important to look at how these contemporary discourses may be historically informed, particularly in those parts of Europe, such as Spain, that have had a history of encounters with Muslim populations during the medieval and early modern periods. Gingrich (1998, 2010), for example, has explored the case of Turkish immigrants in eastern Austria, in relation to the historical Turks of the Ottoman Empire, and through the prism of what he calls *frontier orientalism*. Like its classic counterpart (Said's *Orientalism*, 1978), *frontier orientalism* refers to a constellation of sociocultural representations, artifacts, and practices, including linguistic ones, that construct a racialized *Other* (*they/them*) that enters in hierarchical relation to a homogeneous and normative *we/us*. Unlike in classic *Orientalism* (Said 1978), the racialized *other* produced in *frontier orientalism*, however, is not in some far-away colonial location, but in our backyard. What makes contemporary immigrant groups susceptible to be viewed through the distorting lens of *frontier orientalism*, particularly those who can potentially be seen as descendants of past Muslim invaders to European territories, is that *frontier orientalist* discourses "selectively relate a territorial present to a mytho-historical past, and vice-versa, imbuing the landscape of the present with the myths of the past" (Gingrich, 2010, p. 78). The *longue durée* of spatiotemporal frameworks sustaining *frontier orientalism* makes the identity slippage particularly harmful to contemporary immigrant groups, particularly when those historical narratives in circulation positions *them* as violent and dangerous invaders whom *we* had to fight back.

Frontier orientalism, as described by Gingrich, has indeed many analogous features to an Iberian-grown kind of orientalism. A brief example of these parallelisms can be seen in the expression, *moros en la costa*, which makes up the first part of the title of this chapter: an expression whose seemingly harmless nature, as well as widespread social acceptance, can foster among Spanish speakers the association of *moros* with a fearsome danger. Another case in point is how, in spite of strong scholarly objections by many Spanish historians and philosophers,[29] school-age children in Spain, even today, continue to learn the word *reconquista* (literally, reconquest) to refer to the historical process lasting approximately 800 years,[30] through which the Christian kingdoms of the Iberian peninsula sought complete peninsular control by occupying those territories in the hands of Islamic rulers. The word *reconquista*, however, is far from a neutral description of historical events. Rather, it projects a Christian and Eurocentric perspective and carries a strong ideological foundation that legitimizes those military campaigns as part of defending and recovering something that legitimately belonged to *us*, while driving *them* (*los moros*) back to where they belong, thus saving Spain and Europe from the dangers of Islam. While many people in Spain today would at times recognize these ideological underpinnings as inappropriate and inaccurate, nevertheless, the circulation of these ideologies and discourses also persist below the surface in unacknowledged ways, often taking a life of their own. Related to this, Martín Rojo (2000) has discussed, for example, how the trope of Spain as the outer wall of the European fortress was at work in Spanish parliamentary debates about immigration policy, particularly immigration coming from Africa. As these quick examples demonstrate, this Iberian version of *frontier orientalism*, that structures discourses about North African Muslim immigrants in Spain, emanates from the historical, cultural, and geographical particularities of the Spanish context and its close relationship with North Africa, throughout 1,300 years.

In the remainder of this chapter, I explore some of these particularities in two ways. First, I summarize recent scholarship that has examined how racialized and gendered constructions of Moroccan immigrants in Spain as *inasimilable* (unassimilable) and potentially dangerous are deeply anchored in Spanish history itself.[31] Second, I focus on the ambivalent responses to Moroccan immigration to Spain in relation to the circulation of discourses about *los moros*, as Moroccan immigrants are pejoratively called in Spain. I highlight how contemporary racialized meanings of this linguistic and cultural form, *moros*, are the product of historical processes of entextualization and interdiscursivity (Bauman and Briggs 1990; Silverstein and Urban 1996) across cultural texts, genres, artifacts, and other forms of representation. Central to how these semiotic processes of entextualization move diachronically across interdiscursive webs of meaning, is understanding how *los moros* function as a chronotopic figure (Agha 2007b, elaborated from Bakhtin's 1981 novelistic chronotope); or, in other words, how *los moros* function as a package of space-time-personhood, to which contemporary social actors orient to make sense of Moroccan immigrants, and which anchors Spanish people's ambivalent reaction to current Moroccan immigration. Certainly, I cannot fully trace here the diachronic inter-linkages of the diverse communicative chains that yield the chronotopic figure *moro* as a social category and model of personhood (Agha 2007a) for contemporary Moroccan immigrants – a topic I feel would deserve a book of its own. Nevertheless, I will offer some examples of the vitality of these semiotic processes in mytho-historical literary narratives and contemporary political speeches. In connection to this, I also explore how the diachronic phenomenal textuality of discourses about *los moros* affect the currency of everyday life of Moroccan immigrant children. In this regard, I analyze both everyday and political discourses surrounding the construction of a mosque and an Islamic cultural center, and the ways in which this event was constructed as a threat in Vallenuevo.

2.5   Between New "Convivencia"[32] and New "Morofobia"

Although Spain may have a short history as a *country of immigrants*, the cultural, religious and historical links between the Iberian Peninsula and North Africa date back to the very beginning of the Middle Ages. Moroccan immigrant children growing up in Vallenuevo, as well as their families, are inextricably caught up in this web of historical echoes, rancid ideologies, popular beliefs and hostilities that goes beyond their presence in the country as immigrants alone.

Flesler's (2008, p. 91) analyses on contemporary Spanish responses to Moroccan immigration in relation to Spanish history and in light of 1,300 years of cultural representations of past encounters with *the* Moor, have focused on what she calls "the Moroccan/*Moor* slippage" to explain the powerful feelings that Moroccan immigration stirs in Spain; feelings that go beyond a mere anti-immigrant sentiment alone. One of the most interesting aspects of Flesler's argument is her analysis of how historical encounters with *the Moor* become even more acute because of the ways in which they both destabilize and reaffirm Spain's own ambivalence to its own national, regional, ethnic, and cultural identities, particularly the question of Spanish identity in relation to Africa. As she thoughtfully discusses, Spain's current uneasiness with regard to Moroccan immigration is inextricably linked to the fact that this migratory process began to take shape precisely at the time when Spain was accepted as a full-fledged member of the EU in 1986. It was then that Spain eagerly attempted to emphasize its "Europeaness," not only abroad, but also domestically. Against this backdrop, Moroccan immigration reaffirms, on the one hand, Spain's European identity, since the fact in itself that Spain has to deal with the much touted *immigration problem* is indexical of her belonging to first-world Europe. On the other hand, however, Moroccan immigration confronts Spain with the issue of its own cultural and ethnic formation as a nation. In other words, Moroccan immigrants become an embodied reminder of the non-European, African, and Oriental aspects of Spain's national identity and cultural heritage. Thus, "Moroccans turn into a 'problem' not because they are different, as many argue, but because they are not different enough" (Flesler 2008, p. 9).

Flesler's (2008) argument further explores the cultural and socio-psychological mechanisms by which the average Moroccan immigrant is transformed into the figure of the Medieval Moorish invader. She illustrates how the stereotype of the violent, invading Moor has haunted the Spanish imagination for centuries in a number of cultural traditions. These specters and stereotypes were re-awakened in early contemporary history when insurgent General Franco used mercenary Moroccan troops to fight on the rebel side in the Spanish Civil War (1936–1939). The public imaginary often positions these mercenary Moroccan troops as having been involved in some of the worst atrocities in the war, such as the massacre of Badajoz. Paradoxically, old ghosts are also often revived, as López García et al. (1993) have pointed out, due to the fact that in an ironic twist of fate many of the current economic migrants have settled into the same geographic areas (such as the region of Valencia or the province of Granada) where *moriscos* lived in vibrant communities before their expulsion in the seventeenth century.[33] "In the specific context of Moroccan immigration to Spain, what we find is a mechanism by which immigrants are seen as the return of the imaginary returning Moor who was the 'owner' of Al-Andalus [. . .]Obviously, nothing could be further from the realities of their daily struggles for economic survival and social integration. The language of hospitality quickly turns into a language of military defense against a potential enemy" (Flesler 2008, pp. 56–94). While the discourse of hospitality that dominates contemporary discussions of immigration in Europe has been critiqued more generally for its inaccuracy and for how it obscures more complex power relations (e.g., Rosello 2001), the close, but not always smooth ties that Spain and Morocco have maintained throughout many centuries creates an even greater ambivalence between the current positions of *host* and *guest* that is full of old prejudices, and not-easily-solved anxieties.[34]

Flesler (2008) cogently posits how these cultural and psycho-social processes leave an enduring residue in Spanish collective consciousness. She has traced how these historical anxieties have endured through time in recurrent stereotypical images of the violent, invading *moro* that still persist today in both religious traditions and secular festivities, such as *Moros y Cristianos* (Moors and Christians), or *El Día de la Toma* (The Day of the Taking) in Granada, also recently examined by Rogozen-Soltar (2007). In addition to these psycho-social processes, however, there are also some discursive and semiotic mechanisms that have not been emphasized as much, but that are crucial to enlighten our understandings of how historically-informed forms of racialized exclusion, social markedness, and discrimination are (re)created. Collective forms of discourse, such as narratives and other textual resources involving the historical past, have, after all, been identified as crucial for the perpetuation of certain types of prejudice (e.g., Wertsch 2002). Central to these discursive mechanisms in the case of Moroccan immigrants in Spain, is the mostly unproblematic and routine naming of the Moroccan diaspora itself as *los moros*, and the rhetoric of invasion that usually goes along with it. It is important to recognize the intertextual or interdiscursive phenomenology by which the chronotopic figure *moro*, which originally referred to North African Muslim armies and then to the population of mixed Arab and Berber origin who settled in the Iberian Peninsula during the Middle

Ages, has become a naturalized, albeit pejorative, category to refer to contemporary Moroccan immigrants. *Moro* is now a widespread, everyday way of referring to people who have crossed the Strait of Gibraltar for either economic or political reasons, sometimes risking their lives, many of whom end up working in the construction and service industries and as day-laborers in farming communities, such as Vallenuevo.

How, then, has *moro*, as a chronotopic figure, moved and changed through historical space-time and across narratives and discourses so that the models of personhood indexed by it have *congealed* (M. Silverstein 1992), at the semantic level, or have become consistently associated with contemporary Moroccan immigrants, including school-age children? The notion of cultural chronotope is helpful to grasp the intricate semiotic layers of the socio-historical category *moro*, because it allows us to capture that, beyond its temporal dimensions, historical representations are also about types of people that inhabit specific places and forms of social organization. Furthermore, while most cultural chronotopes involve some temporal displacement (Agha 2007b), I argue that the sketch of personhood-in-time-and-place formulated in *los moros* as a chronotopic depiction is particularly palimpsestic, in that it simultaneously denotes the historical Moor and the contemporary Moroccan immigrant, along with a host of racialized connotations, that mutually reinforce each other in a *frontier orientalist* fashion. In this sense, as the examples discussed below will show, it dislodges the frontier orientalist *they-here-then* into an all-encompassing and more immediate *they-here-now*, just like *then*. This is especially the case when it comes to national identity and security, the two main counts on which Moroccan immigration is problematized.

Understanding *moro* as a palimpsestic chronotopic depiction also allows us to enlarge the historical present to consider how the socio-historical category *los moros* became an extractable text that was subsequently decon-textualized and recontextualized (Bauman and Briggs 1990), in Christian and Eurocentric frontier orientalist mytho-historical narratives. These recon-textualizations provided additional meanings and ideological-laden semantic interpretations. It can thus be said that *los moros* have undergone a series of authoritative entextualization processes in the mass-mediated public space of a dominant Christian majority, particularly in those historical discourses linked to the formation of Spain as an *imagined community* (Anderson 1983). In these entextualization processes, *los moros*, as a palimpsestic figment of chronotopic forms of personhood, are portrayed as diametrically opposed in meaning to authentic *Spanish-ness*. Its semantic dimensions are characterized simultaneously by an extension of its meaning as an ethnic category to include any Moroccan, North African, Muslim, or even Arab, and by a reduction of its affective value to index increasingly negative affect and pejorative characteristics about the people who are constituted as inhabiting this category. The diachronic narrative links and interdiscursive webs of the socio-political and economic indexicality of the chronotopic figure *moro* are long and complex. Nevertheless, I would like to give an example of the dynamism and contemporary currency of the processes I have just posited, by tracing the movement of entextualized elements in mytho-historical narrative poems from the Spanish oral tradition to more recent public speeches by prominent Spanish politicians. In order to discuss the interdiscursive links of racialized narratives about *los moros*, as a palimpsestic chronotopic figure, in Table 2.1 below, I reproduce a fragment of an oral-tradition poem about the Battle of Clavijo,[35] and a fragment of a lecture delivered by José María Aznar, Prime Minister of Spain from 1996 to 2004, at Georgetown University,[36] only months after the 2004 Madrid train bombings.

I have chosen the narrative poem of the Battle of Clavijo, whose first few stanzas are reproduced here, for two reasons. First, because as a *romance popular* (poem from the oral tradition), minstrels and other street performers have recited it innumerable times across the centuries in public squares in towns and villages all over Spain. Second, this poem is also important because it offers a mytho-historical, nativist account of one of the inaugural, and better known, battles of the *reconquista*, by which the Christians rulers started the restoration of *their* country to its *rightful* owners and to its *true* religion. According to this account, when King Ramiro I of Asturias refused to pay a tribute of 1000 maids to Caliph Abderramán II of Córdoba, Christian and Muslim armies confronted each other near Clavijo, in the present-day region of La Rioja, in the year 844. Although outnumbered and defeated at first, King Ramiro I was urged to continue to wage war on *los moros* the following day by the Apostle St. James, patron saint of Spain, who appeared on the battlefield riding on a white horse to lead the Christian armies to victory, hence the legend of *Santiago matamoros*, or *St. James The Moor-slayer*.[37] Because this poem features the legend of how St. James aided the Christian armies, it is also fairly well-known among the pilgrimage poems that were sung by pilgrims on their way to Santiago de Compostela (alleged resting place of St. James), particularly during Jubilee years.

The first few stanzas of the poem define *los moros* as chronotopically configured social types. As figures of personhood, the poem delineates and foregrounds *los moros* as cruel, war-mongering, and merciless people. This is important because the representation of *los moros* as it is entextualized in this poem, and the popular legend that it captures, becomes a frame of reference for subsequently ideologically-saturated texts that formulate this chronotopic figure. Each rendition of the poem reinforces this frame of reference, in that the performers reanimate the authoritative voices of tradition, posing as history. Moreover, through a series of deictics of personal reference (*nuestro rey* – "our king"; *nuestra España* – "our Spain"; *los nuestros* – "our people"), audiences participating in the performance frame of the poem are asked to

Table 2.1 *Los moros* and its entextualization from epic poems to political speeches.

Fragment of popular poem about the Battle of Clavijo	Fragment of José María Aznar's lecture at Georgetown University
Los Moros que son gente bárbara y fiera A la España pusieron en injusta guerra. Rodrigo, nuestro rey fue vencido, por ellos en el primer combate. Este infeliz suceso fue por el año de setecientos once del siglo octavo. Rendida toda la Andalucía Toledo donde la corte entonces estaba por el General Muza fue conquistada. Doscientos mil crueles mahometanos corren por todas partes con sable en mano, robando y sin piedad matando, inundan nuestra España de sangre, los nuestros a los montes se acogen de terror llenos.	Se darán cuenta de que el problema que España tiene con Al Qaeda y el terrorismo islámico no comienzan con la crisis de Iraq. De hecho, no tiene nada que ver con las decisiones del Gobierno. Deben retroceder al menos 1.300 años, a principios del siglo octavo, cuando España, recientemente invadida por los moros, rehusó a convertirse en otra pieza más del mundo islámico y comenzó una larga batalla para recobrar su identidad. Este proceso de reconquista fue largo, unos 800 años.
The Moors who are barbaric and fierce people. Waged an unjust war on Spain. Rodrigo, our king was defeated by them in the first battle. This unhappy event was around the year 711 in the eighth century. All of Andalucía surrendered; Toledo, where the Court was then, was conquered by General Muza. Two thousand cruel Muslims run everywhere, sabre in hand, stealing and killing without mercy, they flood our Spain with blood. Our people, full of terror, took shelter in the mountains.	You'll realize that the problem Spain has with Al Qaeda and Islamic terrorism did not begin with the Iraq crisis. In fact, it has nothing to do with government decisions. We must go back no less than 1,300 years, to the beginning of the eighth century, when Spain recently invaded by the Moors refused to become just another piece in the Islamic world and began a long battle to recover its identity. This process of reconquest was long, about 800 years.

align, or take up a position, towards the heroic (almost martyr-like) Spaniards and towards the violent, bloodthirsty *moros*. It is also important to notice that *los moros* are constructed not only as non-Spanish, but also as enemies of the Spanish people. In this sense, the poem locates participants present at the time of the performance in determinate social relations with mytho-historical people. Participants encounter, for instance, the chronotopic figure of *los moros* waging war on a mytho-historical Spain. The fact that, in the temporal frame of the events narrated by the poem, Spain did not exist as a socio-political entity and that it would not exist as political reality in the form of a modern nation-state until the end of the fifteenth century, seven centuries later than the supposed occurrence of the Battle of Clavijo, remains irrelevant. This, as well as the fact that many aspects of modern Spanish identity and cultural forms are the product of syncretism and contact between Christian and Islamic cultures, including the Spanish language itself which has significant Arabic linguistic elements, is rendered invisible in the historical narrative upheld in the poem. The poem is an emblematic cultural artifact of frontier orientalism (Gingrich 1998) in how it depicts *los moros* as figures of person-hood, violent and distinct from Spaniards, and in how it contributes to ideo-logical processes of erasure (Irvine and Gal 2000) by promoting exclusively a Christian, Eurocentric perspective.

This mytho-historical Spain constructed in the poem about the Battle of Clavijo is, arguably, the same as José María Aznar is invoking when he claimed in the lecture he delivered at Georgetown University in the fall of 2004 that "at the beginning of the eighth century Spain was invaded by los moros and had to begin a long battle to recover its identity." The dialogic quality and intertextual links between a poem and a lecture separated in time by several centuries are, I think, hard to miss. The Madrid train bombings, to which he indirectly refers at the beginning of the paragraph, when he mentions "the problems that Spain has had with Al Quaeda and with Islamic radicalism," are thus framed in the historical nativist discourse of the *reconquista*. The here-and-now is an extension of the past: *los moros* have returned; and the "war on terror," which the former prime minister so adamantly supported, becomes one more military campaign of the *reconquista*, in which Spain had to defend herself from the dangers of Islam to preserve her identity and security. It is in this chronotopic displacement that we see Gingrich's *frontier orientalism* at work more strongly. Mr. Aznar is also using this form of chronotopic dis-placement to absolve himself and the government over which he presided of any responsibility of having put Spain in the crosshairs of Al Qaeda by endors-ing and participating in the Bush administration's war on Iraq; an involvement that was massively protested by Spanish people on the streets and one of the reasons why his party was defeated in the general election of May 2004. The temporal dislodgement that frames Mr. Aznar's lecture also brings to bear the palimpsestic nature of *los moros* as figments of chronotopic forms of personhood. These figments can have a powerful grip on the public imagination, particularly when most of the on-the-ground-perpetrators of the Madrid 2004 bombings happened to be Moroccan nationals. The former prime minister of Spain, thus contributes to cement the image of contemporary Moroccans, and Muslims in Spain more generally, as the natural descendants of the mytho-historical Moors.

The semiotic sedimentations of the socio-historical category *moro* in present-day Spain, much like an archeological palimpsest, can be interpreted by contemporary social actors from both its entextualization processes and as a product of them. It is this asymmetrical field upon which the current positions of *host* and *guest* are predicated, and it is these funhouse mirrors through which contemporary Moroccan immigration in Spain is sometimes framed through a confrontation with the Medieval Moors. This hegemonic discourse of violence, invasion, and defense is often used to justify the rejection and exclusion against many Moroccan immigrants in the country. The racialized models of personhood that these discourses promote also impinge upon the lives of Moroccan immigrant children in complex and consequential ways, as I will show in subsequent chapters of this book, particularly in the ways in which some of their Spanish peers position them in what Trouillot (1991) has called the *new savage slot*.

Because of its derogatory nature as a socio-historical category and as an ethnic slur, the problematicity of using *moros* to refer to Moroccan and other North African Muslim immigrants, has in fact been the object of linguistic activism by individuals and groups of people in Spain who are committed to a more tolerant society. Anti-racism watchdog and pro-immigrant rights organizations, for example, have produced educational literature to raise people's metapragmatic awareness (Silverstein 1976/2001) of the negative ideological implications of using *moro*, along with other controversial metaphors used to talk about immigrants and immigration. Figure 2.1, below, reproduces one of the pages of an educational pamphlet distributed by a Spanish NGO devoted to the rights and welfare of immigrants.[38]

These linguistic awareness campaigns have usually focused on indicating to speakers how expressions like *inmigrante ilegal* (illegal immigrant) or *clandestino* (clandestine immigrant), and words like *invasión* (invasion) or *avalancha* (avalanche), which taken together foster a rhetoric surrounding immigration based on criminality and fear, are not neutral, but rather politically charged and ideologically saturated. Similarly, when insisting that speakers use actual geographical or national origin to refer to immigrants from different ethnoracial groups instead of slurs such as *moro, sudaca,*[39] or patronizing euphemisms such as *persona de color* (person of color), these efforts also attempt to disrupt semiotic processes like the one I have been describing and by

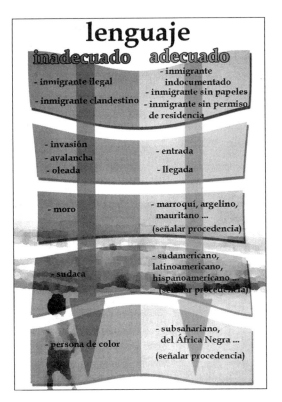

Figure 2.1   Suitable language.

which immigrants get categorized and racialized. While the parts of the pamphlet not reproduced here make these arguments in narrative form, the graphic representation summarizing these points, reproduced as Figure 2.1, makes more vivid the ideological saturation of the everyday discourses that problematize the figure of the immigrant. This extract from the pamphlet is divided into two columns, entitled respectively *lenguaje inadecuado* and *lenguaje adecuado*, (inappropriate and appropriate language). The juxtaposition of inappropriate terms, such as *inmigrante ilegal* (illegal immigrant), *invasión, avalancha, oleada* (invasion, avalanche, and massive wave), and *moro* next to their more neutral counterparts, such as *inmigrante indocumentado* (undocumented immigrant), *entrada, llegada* (entrance, arrival), and *marroquí, argelino* (Moroccan, Algerian), can be analyzed as an attempt to disrupt racializing regimes of language (Kroskrity 2000). Alternatively, it can also be seen as an attempt to substitute such regimes of language for another regime that is considered more neutral or ideologically benign. The contrast strategy used also constitutes an eloquent visual representation of to what extent ideologies and stereotypes about immigrant groups, such as Moroccans, have become ubiquitous and naturalized.

2.5   Welcome to "Vallemoro": Myths and Realities about Life in the Community

Vallenuevo is a town simultaneously conscious and self-conscious of its new character as a multiethnic, multicultural, and multilingual community, with a complicated relationship with the new demographic changes that have significantly altered the fabric of what, until recently, was a fairly homogenous and tightly-knit rural community. This complicated relationship can be seen from the moment you turn into the main access road that leads you to the main street of the town: a huge roadside sign that used to read "Welcome to Vallenuevo" has now been vandalized and defaced with "Welcome to *Vallemoro*." *Vallemoro is* a pun on the name of the town itself (Vallenuevo) and the socio-historical slur *moro.* Although it is probable that the road sign was initially vandalized by those opposed to the presence of Moroccan immigrants in the area, ironically the word "Vallemoro" has also now been appropriated by many people in the Moroccan community who often use it tongue-in-cheek to not only to refer to the town, but also to their strong demographic presence in it. This is actually one of the most common instances in which I heard members of the Moroccan community used the term *moro* to refer to themselves. This instance shares many aspects with other examples of subversive appropriation of racializing speech by members of minority communities to whom such racializing speech is usually directed (Chun 2009[40]): Moroccans can use *Vallemoro*, without symbolically crossing the membership line, and every time I heard them doing so was always in a jocular or sarcastic vein. For example, I usually heard them use it in conversational contexts with other Moroccans to index the socio-economic importance and visibility of their community in the town, as well as to index the strong intergenerational roots that the Moroccan community was developing in Vallenuevo. This use of *Vallemoro* can thus be seen as a critique of those ideologies that would position them as outsiders who are taking over the town. By signaling how thoroughly they are embedded in the fabric of life of this community, they are able to decontextualize the term *moro* and destabilize the non-belonging aspect of this identity.

Vallenuevo, indeed, has had a long history of Moroccan immigration in comparison to many areas of the country. In the late 1990s and beginning of the 2000s, the town caught the attention of the Spanish national press, particularly for the seemingly lack of ethnic tensions surrounding the integration of immigrants into the life of the town. Vallenuevo has been featured in a significant number of articles in national newspapers and magazines, which hailed the town as an example of tolerance and successful social integration of immigrants. Representing the town as *interculturality at its best*, some of these articles described the town as a small miracle of tolerance. In fact, apart from the large percentage of Moroccan families concentrated in Vallenuevo, these characterizations of the town were one of the main reasons why I decided to conduct my fieldwork there. At first glance, it is easy to see how the town was depicted in these terms; and I would also hasten to add that, in some respects, its reputation for tolerance is well deserved: local authorities, social services, and many locals in the town have been extremely proactive in working towards harmonious integration between the communities. In addition, throughout all these years, there has not been one single episode of open racist or violent conflict in the town. The reality of daily life in Vallenuevo is, however, much more complex than this image of tolerance and diversity might convey to outsiders.

Previous studies carried out in this area– when the number and visibility of the Moroccan community was not as high and as conspicuous as it was in 2006 – had already reported some ambivalent feelings towards the presence of Moroccan immigrants in the town.[41] In the early to mid–1990s, while most locals' perceptions of Moroccans were generally positive, there were already slight underlying attitudes of *needed but not necessarily wanted*. Or, in other words, although they welcomed Moroccan immigrants for the great need of seasonal farm work labor in the area and reported having no problems with them and their families living in the town, at the same time, some long-established Vallenuevo residents admitted that their presence could become *problematic* in many ways, especially from a *linguistic* and *cultural* point of view.[42] As I was able to ascertain during the time that I spent in Vallenuevo, the current economic crisis that the agricultural sector has been experiencing in the area, coupled with the increased social visibility and the strong roots that the Moroccan community has established in the town, has accentuated these ambivalent feelings towards Moroccan immigrants in Vallenuevo in the last few years.

This is where the perspective provided by Manal, the Moroccan immigrant girl whose quote opens this chapter, is particularly illuminating. With the candidness that usually only a child displays, Manal tells us about how some of her Spanish classmates changed their attitude towards her from the time when she arrived in Vallenuevo with her family, and the percentage of the Moroccan population was smaller, to a later time when the demographic impact of Moroccans had become more visible. She experienced going from feeling welcomed and appreciated by her Spanish peers to feeling unwanted and left out, as more Moroccan families arrived and more children enrolled at the public school. Manal was not the only one who discussed with me how attitudes may have changed over time and how she experienced the limits of the community's tolerance for immigrants, or what Blommaert and Verschueren (1998), have called a "threshold of tolerance." In what was possibly one of the most surprising exchanges that I had while in Vallenuevo, my landlady also talked to me about the settlement of Moroccan immigrants in the town from her perspective as a Spanish local, born and raised in the town. This conversation took place towards the end of the study; she made it clear to me that she was worried that perhaps I had got the wrong impression about the local people. When I reassured her about the many friendships I had made among local Spanish people and asked about what she might be referring to more specifically, she expressed her concerns that I might be too naïve, and that because I had spent so much time with Moroccans, I did not understand how things really were. She then went on to tell a story, which is in some way the mirror image of Manal's quote. In my landlady's words, when Moroccans started settling in Vallenuevo, the whole town opened their hearts and minds to receive them: "Al principio, cuando llegaron aquí, todo el pueblo se volcó" (**At the beginning, when they got here, the entire town bent over backwards**). In her view, some frictions started to develop when Moroccan immigrants proved to be excessively stubborn and rigid about their ways of living, and things changed when their numbers increased and Moroccans opened their own shops and establishments. It is in the intersection between Manal's quote and my landlady's story that the subversiveness and the ironies of Moroccans using *Vallemoro* to refer to the town can be fully appreciated.

Indeed, although the local authorities and representatives of social services I met with when I first arrived in Vallenuevo still continue to advocate this image of tolerance, it became apparent to me early on that there were fairly complex dynamics between the Spanish and Moroccan populations of the town. In one of my first reflections about the town at the beginning of fieldwork, I wrote that I was getting the impression that Vallenuevo was *"una balsa de aceite"* (a large flat container of oil). This Spanish expression refers to a situation in which things appear very calm on the surface, and certainly things can remain calm if handled with care; yet, the situation is, intrinsically, extremely flammable. The longer I lived in this town and the more I participated fully in everyday situations in many different contexts, it was easy to see that there were two overlapping realities: the *official reality* – the utopic view of Vallenuevo as a model of integration and as pioneers in addressing the issues of inclusion raised by massive immigration- and the *everyday reality*, fraught with, sometimes unexpressed, tensions, anxieties, and fears on the part of both populations. My initial impression of these overlapping realities was confirmed in subsequent months, as the later chapters of this book will make apparent.

Many Spanish locals were careful about how they expressed themselves about Moroccans in front of me, particularly as my involvement with the Moroccan community increased and the particularities of my research became general knowledge. Nevertheless, I was still able to document how the long-held prejudices, historical stereotypes, and fears about *los moros*, discussed earlier in the chapter, were alive and well in Vallenuevo. Expressions such as "*Los moros son muy traicioneros*" (**"The Moors are very treacherous"**); "*Los moros son muy guarros*" (**"The Moors are very dirty"**); or "*Los moros son muy vengativos*" (**"The Moors are very vengeful"**), were common around me, particularly coming from older locals who seemed more threatened by the settlement of Moroccan immigrants in the town, and who were less guarded in expressing these thoughts and feelings to me. They often did so in the context of wanting to warn me in relation to my work with the Moroccan community. In this vein, I was even warned about the school children I was working with: "*Ten cuidado que estos niños están muy espabilados*" (**"Be careful because these children are very precocious"**).

The initial discussions that I had with one of the neighbors in my building soon after I settled into the community are also illustrative of the circulation of racializing discourses about Moroccan immigrants in Vallenuevo, in addition to being fairly representative of the attitude that most locals had towards the Moroccan population. When I asked her about the most convenient places to do my weekly shopping and about general safety in the town after dark, she responded:

Hay una tienda ahí arriba. Bueno, hay otra más cerca- en frente de dónde fuiste a tomar café el otro día, pero es de moros. Eso no quiere decir nada, pero nosotros los del pueblo vamos a comprar a la otra tienda que la lleva gente del pueblo. En fin, a veces, vamos a comprar alguna que otra cosilla a la tienda de los moros, pero carne no! Porque a mi me da como asco.

There is a shop all the way up there. Well, there is another shop closer by - in front of where you went to have coffee the other day - but it belongs to the *moros*. That doesn't mean anything, but we, the people from the town, we do our shopping in this other shop that is run by people from the town. Well, sometimes, we go to buy some little

```
item in the moros's shop, but no meat! Because it
kind of disgusts me.
```

Regarding my safety at night, she said:

```
Aquí en el pueblo no vas a tener ningún problema.
Esta calle es muy tranquila. Luego, dos calles más
abajo, ahí ya- viven muchos moros. No es que te
vayan a hacer nada, pero bueno . . . Además, se
quedan hasta las tantas en la calle.
```

```
Here in this town, you're not going to have any
problems. This street (meaning the one on which
we both lived) is very quiet. Then, two streets
down, there already - a lot of moros live there.
It's not that they are going to do anything to
you, but, well . . . Besides, they stay out on
the streets until the small hours.
```

This last comment referred to the fact that it was customary for Moroccan men to gather in groups on streets, in the main square, and/or in the Moroccan coffee shops in the afternoon and evenings to chat with their friends. Some locals were frustrated by their conspicuous presence on the streets, claiming that they were "taking over" the public spaces of the town. Another interesting aspect of these two examples of everyday discourse is how in both cases my neighbor insinuates something negative about the shop and the street because they are, respectively, run or inhabited by *moros*. In both cases, however, she stops short of going on record with an overtly prejudicial characterization of Moroccans, and instead hedges and claims that she does not mean anything critical by these remarks. These hedging moves, although somewhat nullified by later remarks in which she expresses a negative opinion of Moroccan immigrants' lifestyle, allow her to issue some sort of warning that remains implicit. In this way, she provides herself with plausible deniability against any charge of blatant discrimination, while at the same time inviting me, an interlocutor who shares her linguistic and cultural background, to fill in what is left underspecified with historical and sociocultural stereotypes about *los moros*.

In addition to how racializing discourses and cultural representations of Moors/Moroccans surface in informal conversations in Vallenuevo, the current geopolitical climate of suspicion surrounding Muslim and North African immigrants also interacts powerfully with the dynamics between Moroccan immigrants and locals in this community. These tensions become particularly visible around certain points of cultural contention. In particular,

Figure 2.2   Pamphlet against the construction of a mosque in Vallenuevo.

towards the end my fieldwork, some of these unexpressed anxieties and fears reached their climax when the local council approved a request by the local Islamic association, *Assalam*, to build a mosque and an Islamic cultural center that would replace the small oratory that had been precariously serving the religious needs of the Moroccan community for a number of years. Prior to, during, and after the town council decision-making, there were strong reactions from the Spanish population, ranging from less to more aggravated, including heated arguments in public town-hall forums, death threats to the mayor, and public demonstrations against the mosque. I reproduce as Figure 2.2, one of the pamphlets that were handed out during one of the anti-mosque demonstrations that took place in the fall of 2006. The evident tensions surrounding these events also unraveled the myth of Vallenuevo in the national press; an article published in one of the most widely read newspapers in September 2006 had as a headline "Un centro islámico hace peligrar la convivencia en Vallenuevo" (An Islamic center endangers *convivencia* in Vallenuevo),[43] making reference to the epithet with which the same newspaper had praised the town three years earlier.

Discursively, what is interesting about the text of the pamphlet is that it encapsulates the two main arguments discussed earlier in this chapter,

through which Moroccan immigrant communities are routinely problematized: (1) Moroccans as a threat to Spanish cultural identity, and (2) Moroccans as a potential threat to national security. The following translation of
the first page of the pamphlet illustrates this point:

> Mezquita No! Por un pueblo *seguro* y habitable. Por la *defensa* de *nuestra*
> *identidad*. Por el *control de la inmigración*.

> No mosque! For a habitable and *safe* town. For the *defense* of *our identity*. For
> *immigration control*..

Beyond the typical anti-immigrant sentiment, which also reverberates
strongly in the text, the construction of a mosque and Islamic cultural center
is depicted as both a threat to the traditional character and identity of the
town and as a threat to the safety and security of the Spanish population,
which requires defensive measures. The main text of the second page of the
pamphlet conflates the mosque with Islamic radicalism, terrorist violence,
and with the 2004 Madrid train bombings.[44] I offer a full translation of the
second page of the pamphlet in Note 44.

The mayor and other local politicians, in an effort to calm the waters
and minimize the fallout of these events, claimed that extreme-right groups
distributed these pamphlets during the demonstrations,[45] as well as being
responsible for the death threats. They further maintained that, therefore,
these views could not be taken as being representative of those of most
people in Vallenuevo. In fairness, there is some currency to this version: it
is true that the pamphlet I have reproduced here, in particular, was distributed by extreme-right groups during the demonstration that took place in
September 2006. It is also true that many local businesses in Vallenuevo
remained open on the day of that demonstration, in spite of the fact that
the organizers had called for a general strike that would have included the
closing down of stores, shops, and other public establishments. It would,
then, be tempting to take comfort in the fact that, these views are not
representative of, in words of Blommaert and Verschueren (1998), "the tolerant majority" of the town. When I returned to Vallenuevo for a short visit
in the summer of 2007, just after local and regional elections were held in
May, however, a newly formed party called Asociación Para los Derechos
Cívicos de Vallenuevo, or Association for the Civic Rights of Vallenuevo,
whose main, perhaps I should say exclusive, platform was stopping the
construction of the mosque, was elected by the majority of the population.
It was in the complex political atmosphere that culminated in these events
that I conducted this study on Moroccan immigrant childhoods in
Vallenuevo.

Notes

1 See, for instance, Kerzazi (2004); López García (2002); Munárriz (1995), Ramírez (1995).

2 See López García (1993, 2003, 2004).

3 The Schengen Agreement (signed in the town of Schengen Luxembourg on June 14, 1985) began the gradual abolition of border controls for citizens (and goods) of European nation-states included in the agreement (also known as the Schengen Area). Migrants and other international travelers, however, must still contend with fairly tight border controls to enter any of the countries in the Schengen Area.

4 Berriane (2004a); López García (2003).

5 Arango Vila-Belda (2002); Chacón Rodríguez (2003).

6 Source: United Nations, Trends in Total Migrant Stock, the 2005 Revision. http:// www.migrationinformation.org/. Migration Policy Institute.

7 The source for the figures on immigrants registered (or with residence card) at the national level is the latest statistical report published by Observatorio Permanente de la Inmigración (Ministerio de Empleo y Seguridad Social. Secretaría General de Inmigración y Emigración). Publication date: February 29th, 2012. (Accessible online: http://extranjeros .empleo.gob.es/es/Estadisticas/operaciones/con-certificado/index.html). At the regional level, the source for the figures is latest statistical report published by Observatorio Permanente Para la Inmigración (Consejería de Igualdad y Empleo). Publication date: January 1st, 2009. (Accessible online: http://igualdadyempleo.juntaex.es/observatorioInmigracion/index .php?option=com_content&view=article&id=60&Itemid=56).

8 See, for example, Berriane (2004a); Losada-Campo (1993); López García (1993, 2003, 2004).

9 Ceuta and Melilla are two cities on the North African coast that have territorially belonged to Spain since the seventeenth and sixteenth centuries, respectively. Under the current legal and territorial organization of Spain, these two cities are considered neither regional communities nor provinces. They enjoy an *autonomous* status as cities (that is, they do not depend on the government of any other province or regional community), as well as certain special political and legal rights.

10 The Spanish Protectorate in Morocco was established in 1912 and lasted until 1956, when both Spain and France recognized Moroccan independence. It consisted of the strip of land in Northern Morocco between the cities of Ceuta and Melilla. The capital of the Spanish protectorate was Tétouan.

11 According to the laws that regulate Spanish citizenship, children born of Moroccan parents are considered Moroccan nationals regardless of whether they have been born in Spain or in Morocco. Therefore, second- generation children born in Spain of a Moroccan father and a Moroccan mother are regarded as Moroccan nationals in official census data and statistics. See Código Civil Español (1889) for a more detailed description (online). Available from: http://noticias.juridicas.com/base_datos/Privado/cc.html.

12 See Checa (1998); Martín Díaz (2001); Pumares (1995).

13 For a thorough discussion of these trends, see Dietz (2002); Ramírez (2004).

14 See López García (2003); Ramírez (2004).

15 See Colectivo Ioé (2004); Mijares (2004b).

16 See López García (2003, 2004); Losada-Campo (1993).

17 See Castién (1995); Castaño Madroñal (1997); Checa (1997); Gregorio Gil (1995).

18 See Campesino Fernández and Campos Romero (2004); Mora Aliseda et al. (2003).

19   Sources for these population figures include local census data collected during my ethno-
     graphic study, as well as the following references: Barbolla Camarero (2001); Campesino
     Fernández and Campos Romero (2004); Mora Aliseda et al. (2003).

20   See in particular the study carried out in the area by the sociologist Barbolla Camarero
     (2001).

21   In spite of this, there were some lingering doubts among members of the local Moroccan
     community about how *halal* the meat sold in these shops truly was, and some shops were
     considered, in this respect, more trustworthy than others. Nevertheless, in a potentially
     morally contaminating non-Muslim Spanish context, most members of the community
     agreed that it was safer to consume meat purchased in these shops than in regular Spanish
     supermarkets.

22   See Barbolla Camarero (2001, pp. 124–125).

23   See, for example, Agoumy (2004); Berriane (2004b); Laouina (2004).

24   For a more in-depth treatment of these processes, see Kerzazi (2004); Laouina (2004).

25   Checa et al. (2001); López García et al. (1993); Martín Muñoz (2003).

26   See for example, Aramburu (2004); Bravo López (2004); Granados (2004); Terren (2004);
     Petit Caro (2001); Romero (2001).

27   See Barbudo (2004); Bravo López (2004); Izquierdo Escribano (2004); López García (2003).

28   See, for instance, Wingo's (2004) study of migratory trends in Spain during the 1990s and
     early 2000s.

29   In his work *España Invertebrada: Bosquejo de Algunos Pensamientos Históricos* (originally pub-
     lished in 1921), Ortega y Gasset famously said "Y a ello respondo ingenuamente que yo
     no entiendo como se pudo llamar reconquista a una cosa que dura ocho siglos" (And to
     that I naively respond that I do not understand how something that lasted eight centuries
     could have been called *reconquista*) (Translation mine]).

30   The *reconquista* is usually said to have began around the year 722 with Don Pelayo's rebel-
     lion and to have ended in 1492 with the taking of Granada, the last Muslim stronghold in
     the Iberian Peninsula.

31   See, for example, Flesler (2008); Flesler and Pérez Malagosa (2003); López García et al.
     (1993); Rogozen-Soltar (2007); Terren (2004).

32   *Convivencia*, "Living-together," is a historical ideology that emphasizes how Muslim, Chris-
     tian and Jewish communities in Medieval Spain were supposedly able to live together
     harmoniously. This point of view also highlights how this peaceful coexistence yielded a
     productive syncretism that, in turn, produced some of the most positive and idiosyncratically-
     Spanish cultural achievements of this period. Nueva Convivencia (New Living-Together)
     has been used as a trope in both general discourses about immigration in Spain, as well as
     in scholarly analysis (see e.g., Erickson 2011 and Suárez-Navaz 12004).

33   In exploring regional identity narratives in areas of the country, such as Andalucía, whose
     idiosyncratic regional distinctiveness depends to a large extend on the deployment of his-
     torical Muslim/Arab identities, Rogozen-Soltar (2007, 2012b) and Dietz (2005, 2004) have
     both pointed out how this process is fraught with ironies that encourage the highly con-
     trolled mobilization of safe aspects of Mulism/Arab identity, while suppressing and distancing
     from other expressions of this identity that are considered undesirable and dangerous.

34   See also López García et al. (1993).

35   A full version of the poem can be found in Panizo Rodriguez (2000).

36   From "La Lección de Aznar en Georgetown." El Siglo de Europa, no 618, October 4th,
     2004. Translation: Cintia Escadell http://www.elsiglodeuropa.es/siglo/historico/politica/
     politica2004/618Aznar.htm.

37   Although very few people would give historical credence to the narrative propagated by the legend, influential historians such as Sánchez Albornoz maintain that there might have been a real Battle of Clavijo that would have taken place later than 840 (probably around 860) and that would have been fought between Ordoño I of Asutrias and the Muslim military leader Musa Ibn Musa. The importance of this battle might have rested on the fact that Clavijo was strategically important for travel routes and communication. Clavijo town hall maintains a very useful and informative website with many different historical, literary, and artistic resources about the real and the mytho-historical battles of Clavijo. In addition to this poem, the Battle of Clavijo has been featured in plays, religious iconography, and more recently in movies (http://www.ayuntamientodeclavijo.org/La-Batalla-de-Clavijo.1817 .0.html).

38   I personally collected this pamphlet from one of the branches of the NGO *Andalucía Acoge* in Sevilla when I was doing pilot fieldwork, prior to this study, in the summer of 2004.

39   *Sudaca*, literally means somebody from the South plus the negative/pejorative suffix -aca. This slur is often used to refer to immigrants from South America, and even sometimes to immigrants from sub-Saharan Africa.

40   For a fuller discussion of subversive appropriation and ideologies of legitimacy about who can use racializing speech, how and when, see E. Chun (2009).

41   See, for instance, Barbolla Camarero's (2001) 1992–1996 study.

42   Barbolla Camarero (2001, pp. 261–306).

43   The actual headline has been slightly modified in this ethnographic account.

44   Translation of the second page of the pamphlet: "Spain has become one of the main targets of Islamic radicalism. Even as we still have fresh in our memories the terrible images of March 11, we continue to see Islamic terrorists being captured on a daily basis. Our politicians, far from taking preventive measures, facilitate and subsidize the expansion of Islam in all our cities and towns. Now it is the turn of our town. With the new mosque, our town will become a place of concentration and proselytism for all Muslims in the area. Do we want that for our town? How long will it take for us to see on television the arrest of Islamic radicals in our own streets?"

45   Indeed, the pamphlets were printed by the neo-fascist political group *Democracia Nacional* (National Democracy), whose members attended the demonstration and handed out these and similar pamphlets.

3

Learning About Children's Lives: A Note On Methodology

When I was a little girl growing up in Southern Spain, my grandmother, who was a font of knowledge on Spanish oral traditions, liked to teach me about the complexities of life and other important things that, as she used to put it, I was not going to learn at school. One of the ways in which she used to do this was by teaching me *refranes* (proverbs and popular-lore aphorisms), but always with an ironic twist or addition of her own that would make it clear that there are always different points of views for any given situation. Perhaps because there is nothing like the ethnographic process to highlight the perspectival dimension of experience, rarely have I found myself remembering my grandmother's *refranes* and quips more than during the time I spent in Vallenuevo. And at a time when I often worried about how I was perceived, and should or could be, perceived by others in this fieldwork town, I could hear my grandmother saying, *el hábito no hace al monje* (the habit doesn't make the monk), to which she always added with a tongue-in-cheek, yet earnest expression, *pero ayuda a reconocerlo* (but it certainly helps to recognize one).

With this in mind, I made it a point from the beginning to go into the community with all my research equipment in tow, as much as possible and as often as possible, with the hope that eventually I would come to be seen as a fixture of the place, equipment and all, and accepted as an established researcher. As an ethnomethodologically- oriented linguistic ethnographer, however, that meant walking around the town, going into public buildings and into people's houses, not only with a notebook and pencil in hand, but also with audio- and video- recoding equipment, as well as a tripod and a still camera. I did this even when I knew that I was not going to be using any or most of these tools, again hoping that over time, I would become identified with my equipment, and that, when the time came to use it,

Language and Muslim Immigrant Childhoods: The Politics of Belonging, First Edition.
Inmaculada Mª García-Sánchez.
© 2014 John Wiley & Sons, Inc. Published 2014 by John Wiley & Sons, Inc.

people would not find it so strange or off-putting. I also did this because I wanted to confront as early as possible people's reactions, questions, and doubts about who I was and what I was doing in their town.

I decided that the best way to let the community start getting to know me would be while I was also getting to know every corner of the town where I was going to spend at least the next 12 months. During the first few weeks of fieldwork, in addition to formal introductions and networking visits to a variety of institutions and social services, I made it a habit to take long walks around the town, taking pictures of buildings and street signs; talking to retired people perched on benches in the town's main square about the beautiful sixteenth-century church; marking sites of interest on commercial or self-sketched maps; engaging groups of mothers in the park in casual conversation about the best places to go shopping or to get an afternoon coffee, and so on. Needless to say, everyone also had plenty of questions for me. Not everything about initially introducing myself to the community, however, went as smoothly. There were also challenges that I had to overcome, but in working through those challenges I learned valuable lessons not only about managing my ethnographic positioning in a community that was hyper-aware of its own prominent place in regional and national discourses about Moroccan immigration, but also about some of the tensions that from time to time would bubble up to the surface.

I can still recall vividly, for instance, people's looks, ranging from mildly amused and curious to slightly wary, vis-à-vis my own sense of awkwardness, the first couple of times I went out in full gear for these long walks around the town. I was often approached by groups of children, probably daring one another, who, while giggling and exchanging furtive glances with each other, would finally gather up the courage to ask me "Eres de la tele?" ("Are you from TV?"). My misrecognition as a reporter happened most frequently during the first months of fieldwork, but it remained a common occurrence throughout my stay, especially when I encountered people who did not know me. While some of my recording equipment might have helped locals place me in that identity category, Vallenuevo, as I have already mentioned in Chapter 2, had been the object of national media attention for its seemingly successful integration of a heavy concentration of Moroccan immigrants in a relatively short period of time. Once the town had become "a story," many journalists, as well as scholars and researchers, such as myself, did in fact continued to come to Vallenuevo, intrigued by these favorable reports, wanting to investigate further how processes of immigration were evolving here. Just in the time I spent in Vallenuevo, the town was visited by two national television crews, one radio program, and one team of reporters who published an in-depth extended article in a national newspaper, in addition to being the object of dozens of short news stories in both the national and regional press. This was indeed a high degree of interest in a rural town with less than 11,000 people.

A second related aspect that these initial walks revealed was that this attention in itself constituted a problem for a handful of Spanish locals who resented outsiders' focus on Moroccan immigrants. For this reason, whether or not a real journalist, I, as an outsider who came to the town to study Moroccan immigrant children, also had to contend with some of these negative reactions. The most intense encounter I had happened the third week after I moved to Vallenuevo. I was taking one of those long walks, and found myself at a junction near the main park, as I tried to figure out how to get to a small *librería-papelería* (bookstore and stationery shop) that I had found on a previous outing. I approached a middle-aged woman with two bags full of groceries who was waiting for a traffic light to change, and asked her for directions. Although she told me how to get to the shop, it was obvious that she was regarding me with some suspicion, and at some point, asked me directly whether I was a journalist. I told her that I was not, but before I had a chance to say anything else, she continued: "En el pueblo estamos hartos de periodistas que vienen aquí a grabar a los moros" ("In this town, we are sick of journalists who come here to record *los moros*"). As the traffic light changed, she walked away still fulminating, while I remained on the corner a bit startled and without knowing how to react. Such angry outbursts, although few and far between, tipped me off early during fieldwork about the existence of complex dynamics brewing below the surface. This was particularly important at a time when most people had yet to show any willingness to speak to me on the record about Moroccan immigration beyond safe platitudes. It also allowed me to see clearly that studying Moroccan immigrant children in Vallenuevo was going to involve more than gaining the trust of the children and that of their caregivers; namely, that my success learning about the children's lives was also going to depend, to a large extent, on how gracefully I would negotiate my ethnographic positioning in the community and on how carefully I would navigate very sensitive local politics. In this chapter, I discuss the methods of data collection and analysis that I used to investigate Moroccan immigrant children's lives. In doing so, I place special emphasis on how I negotiated my own position in the different social contexts where I observed the children.

3.1 A Methodological Overview

This study is based on a total of 16 months of fieldwork in the town of Vallenuevo (12 consecutive months between September 2005 and September

2006, and four months in the summer of 2007[1]), during which, I participated as fully as possible in the daily lives of the children and the community.[2] Data collection for this project included various ethnographic methods: (1) participant observation; (2) ethnographic interviewing with children, teachers, and caregivers; (3) video-recording of children's naturally-occurring interactions with their parents, teachers, peers, siblings, doctors, and other community members; (4) transcription of video- and audio-recorded data; (5) collection of lifemaps produced by the focal children; (6) collection of site texts and documents concerning education, language, and social services; and (7) collection of newspaper and magazine articles featuring the community of Vallenuevo from the mid-1990s until 2007. To investigate how Moroccan immigrant children negotiate the racialized politics of difference and belonging in their everyday lives, it was crucial to observe and record these children's participation in linguistic and social practices, as well as in everyday routines across a wide variety of contexts. As Schieffelin (1990, p. 1) has argued, the study of children's "speech activities that organize and give meaning to [their participation in] the give and take of everyday life" is key to understanding how "through language, they create social relationships between themselves and others."

Children's points of view were also documented through longitudinal, ethnographic interviews. This method was used to illuminate Moroccan immigrant children's emergent understandings of their own lives, as well as their sense of developing processes of identification. These interviews were critical to my own understanding of just how aware children were of the processes of exclusion and racialization that I document in this study, as well as of the varied situational expectations that others had of them. The combination of interviews and interactional data is a powerful way of grounding the meanings of sociocultural processes in both the realm of participants' subjectivities, as well as in social processes of interaction among individuals. As Sapir (1949, p. 515) reminds us, "the true locus of culture is in the interaction of specific individuals and, on the subjective side, in the world of meaning which each one of these individuals may unconsciously abstract for himself from his participations in these interactions." Furthermore, the concurrent implementation of interviewing methodologies and recording techniques of naturally-occurring activities permits, on the one hand, the examination of beliefs about practices versus how those beliefs and practices are enacted in social action, and on the other hand, the examination of how participants position themselves through narratives about their lives vis-à-vis how they position themselves and are positioned by others as they go about their daily routines. In this sense, comparisons of observed communicative practices with interview data allow the researcher to illuminate the tensions that surface between immigrant children's perceptions of their realities and the sociocultural and linguistic fabric of their daily lives.

Finally, when conceptualizing this study methodologically, issues of scale and scalarity had to be seriously considered. In documenting the lives of immigrant children of the Moroccan diaspora in Spain, it was critical to account for private and public; local, global, and transnational; historical and contemporary forces, which, in combination, impinge upon these children's emerging identities in crucial ways. As Hall (2004, p. 118) has noted, ethnographers seeking to understand immigrant children and youth processes of identification and incorporation in modern nation-states beyond traditional models of immigrant assimilation, should implement "a shift in ethnographic vantage point from an exclusive focus on everyday worlds to the broader historical and cultural processes in which these worlds are embedded." Two different approaches allowed me to establish the macro cultural logics through which representations of the Moroccan community were produced, circulated, and organized in social practice: (1) my ongoing informal conversations with a variety of public figures in Vallenuevo, as well as my ethnographic engagement with social agencies and in socio-political events of the community and at the national level; and (2) the collection and study of site documents (related to educational practice and policy, as well as to public policy) and media articles.

This chapter provides an overview of data collection sites, as well as outlining the implementation of research methods explaining their significance in the formation of an integrated, multilayered, ethnographic data corpus.

3.2   Sites of Data Collection and My Ethnographic Role

As a Spanish woman in my early thirties, originally born and raised in a city three hours away from the small town where I conducted my fieldwork, one could easily assume that my positionality relative to the local Spanish population was easier to negotiate than my positionality with the Moroccan community. In some regards, this was true; and my "insider status" accounts for the fact that from the beginning of the study, many local institutions facilitated my arrival and settling-in. In many other regards, however, my relationship with the larger Spanish community of Vallenuevo was somewhat ambivalent and, in a few cases, difficult. In addition to the fact that I was originally from a larger city, I was perceived as a foreign-educated expatriate who had spent the last 10 years living in the United States. But, most importantly, from some people's point of view, I was in the town solely to study Moroccan immigrants, a concern I alluded to in my opening vignette. Given the complex interethnic relations in this town, that fact did not win much sympathy for my cause among a small group of Spanish locals. Some locals began to identify me as *la amiga de los moros* (the friend of *los moros*). I know that many people who used this epithet did so in a tongue-in-cheek way, trying to tease me or get a reaction out of me, since some of them were also people who were trying to help me. I also know, however, that some others had less than these benign intentions.

Despite the political complexities of studying immigration in such a small, tightly-knit community, the vast majority of Spanish locals did not display any negativity towards my presence in this town, and some of them were extremely hospitable and welcoming, such as Pepa, vice-principal of the school, and her colleagues Paco and Teresa. Pepa, for instance, invited me to join her aerobics class, and introduced me to some single Spanish women with whom I went out for coffee every now and then during weekends or special local celebrations, when they often invited me to a variety of events. These friendships were very helpful in establishing rapport with the Spanish locals, as well in managing my own reputation as a married woman, while working and living alone in the community. As is the case in small communities in many parts of the world (e.g., Besnier 2009), gossip was a major source of information and form of social control in Vallenuevo. As an outsider, I was aware that both the Moroccan and Spanish communities were scrutinizing my behavior. The extra layers of evaluation did, of course, make sense, given that everyone wanted to make sure that someone who worked closely with their children was safe and trustworthy. Another way in which I cultivated my ties and relationships with the local Spanish population throughout the study was to continue to frequently visit those institutions and organizations that had originally facilitated my entry into the community. I would stop at the town hall and the health center a few times a week to greet the employees, the local police, and, particularly, social services which provided assistance to the Moroccan community. I often participated in and volunteered my time for community events throughout the course of the study, such as *talleres interculturales* (interculturality workshops) and *foros por la tolerancia y la convivencia* (thematic conferences about immigration, emphasizing tolerance and living-together), many organized jointly by NGOs and the regional and local governments.

The Moroccan community considered me a "local" Spanish woman, and therefore initially saw me as an outsider. However, I was unlike most Spanish people that the Moroccan community in this town had come into contact with. What set me apart from most Spaniards, in their view, was that I was a very serious student of both Moroccan and Standard Arabic, with a certain command and fluency in both languages. In addition, I had spent time living in Morocco and was, therefore, familiar with many cultural traditions and some of the habitual ways of doing things in the community. From that standpoint, I was a *nice* rarity and a novelty. I heard several people refer to me as "the friendly woman who speaks good Arabic" (referring to Modern/ Standard Arabic). Those facts also helped me establish rapport with Moroccan immigrant families and overcome some initial guardedness about my research, although, among some members of the Moroccan community, those feelings of mistrust continued for several months. After this initial period of wariness, many families soon extended their hospitality to me and regularly invited me for tea, meals, and celebrations (such as naming ceremonies, the breaking of the Ramadan fast, and 'Eid-al-Kabir). While the curiosity that I aroused among many Moroccan families was partly the reason for many initial invitations, I continued to receive them throughout the study (and not just from the families of the focal children) because in their perception, I was not only interested in *recording and interviewing them*, but also genuinely interested in spending time with them outside of my "*official*" role as a researcher. They would tell me that they were pleased that I joined them for daily family events and special celebrations in their households because Spanish people in Vallenuevo did not usually show interest. Indeed, I did enjoy spending many social afternoons, talking over coffee and pastries or Harša (a sweet flatbread made from semolina), with many of the Moroccan women I was getting to know, such as Worda's elder sister and mother, Kamal's mother, and Amina, the wife of Rashid, the Arabic teacher at the public school.

In addition, many Moroccan families showed much enthusiasm about the fact that I had spent time in Morocco and they would often ask me many questions regarding my stay in their country and about the places where I had been. Apart from my research, the families were curious about me personally, especially those aspects of my life that were different from their expectations, such as the reasons why I did not have children or why I lived so far away from my family. When I would briefly relate some of my life circumstances, they very often felt sorry for me. While they could certainly understand having to move for a variety of reasons, including work, most Moroccans I talked to saw this as a hardship, particularly the fact that I lived alone and did not even have any immediate family with me, since the family unit is still a crucial source of social status and identity among Moroccan immigrants in this town. Very often, their immediate reaction was to say, "*muskina*" (Moroccan Arabic for "poor little thing"), and to wish that God would grant me children and a family in the future.

Initially, the children did not know what to make of me. Because I would spend long hours observing them at the public school at the beginning of the study as well as spend time in some of their homes and observe them during the track-and-field team training sessions (where most of the children were of Moroccan origin), they were unsure of my possible status as a teacher. They would often come up to me and ask my name and what I was doing in their town. After those first two and a half months of fieldwork, however, I was rarely questioned by either the children or the parents. As my ongoing involvement with the children, their families, and the community became greater, an increasing feeling of informality developed in our daily interactions, conversations, video-recordings of everyday activities, and video-recorded interviews.

I collected my data in three institutional settings, namely the public school, the health center, and the oratory-mosque. At the health center, the head of pediatrics was immediately supportive of this research project, which she considered important. Therefore, she granted me permission to be at the clinic with a video-camera, provided that I got informed consent from each individual Moroccan family that I was to record. Access to the other two institutional settings was a bit more difficult to negotiate. During the first three months of fieldwork, I was not allowed to enter or undertake any video-recording in the oratory-mosque where the children attended Qur'anic and Classical Arabic classes. I had to meet several times with the leaders of the local Islamic association Assalam, that ran the oratory, before I was granted permission to video-record these classes. At those meetings, I was thoroughly questioned about the purpose and objectives of my research project, about other sites where I was collecting data, about how the data was going to be used in the future, and about my knowledge and opinion about Islam. Through regular discussions with these leaders, they became better acquainted with me and my research, and I was eventually given access to the classes held in the oratory in December. Following the religious protocol of respect in this sacred environment, I wore a headscarf covering my hair and loose pieces of clothing which covered my arms up to my wrists and my legs down to my ankles while video-recording at the oratory.

As Carlos, the principal of the school, told me when he met me, the public school was no stranger to researchers coming and wanting to conduct research with their student population. Consequently, it did not take me long to obtain administrators' permission to observe the children. However, unlike other researchers who had made observations at the school for a couple of months and/or distributed questionnaires to the students, my research involved weekly visits to a number of settings at the school throughout the academic year, and additionally, with a video-camera. Once these particulars were known, and despite the principal and vice-principal's steadfast support, at the beginning of the study, some teachers were uncomfortable and apprehensive of my research methods, which they considered to be very intrusive. Through both formal meetings and informal conversations with teachers and administrators, I was able to ascertain that the root of their uneasiness had to do with two facts: (1) some teachers were worried that the presence of a video-camera would create havoc among the students and would become a bothersome distraction that would prevent them from accomplishing their pedagogical goals in the classroom, and (2) others were worried that, although I said I was there to document the sociocultural lives of the children, some part of my study might have included teachers' evaluations of some kind. This second worry disappeared over time as more and more teachers learned that the school was only one among many sites for data collection in my study, and that I was also carrying out observations and recordings in children's homes, the health center, the oratory, and the track-and-field club. With regard to the first concern, and to minimize the impact of the video-camera in the normal functioning of classroom activities, I developed a schedule that consisted of two months of daily observations (so that the children would get used to my presence), at the end of which, I began to gradually introduce the camera. Contrary to some teachers' expectations, and to my relief, when I started to videotape regularly, the camera did not cause major excitement or rumpus among the children. Ironically, although teachers, were initially anxious anticipating my video-recording in the classroom, I later learned that the actual video-recording, made them less anxious than when I had sat at the back of the classroom taking notes during the first two months of fieldwork. A couple of the teachers whose classes I videotaped most told me one afternoon over coffee that this was because the quiet note-taking made them wonder what I could possibly be writing about or taking an interest in, while they perceived the subject of the videotaping to be completely obvious and transparent. In addition, apart from the times I visited the school to observe and videotape, I offered my services to the teachers to do substitutions, to help with art projects and special school events that were very taxing on teachers' time, and to accompany teachers on fieldtrips when extra adults were welcomed to supervise the children. I also regularly joined the teachers at social gatherings and celebrations outside the school context. This assistance and conviviality were very much appreciated by the staff, and, certainly, by me as well.

The children's own peer groups were the contexts in which my positionality as a researcher was most difficult to negotiate. Because I wanted to document children's lives as much as possible from the perspective of the children themselves, the peer group was a crucial locus of ethnographic inquiry. It was also the context in which my status as a foreign adult, however, was more conspicuous since I was observing and recording inter- actions that usually took place without adult supervision. As Christensen and James (2000, p. 5) have posited, it is in these contexts, when generational issues are bound to take center stage both at the ethical and practical levels, that researchers need to be particularly reflective and mindful of "the ways in which they are being accepted by the children as a particular kind of presence in their normal everyday lives." For this reason, before I actually did any video-recording of peer-group activities, I spent many afternoon hours during the first four months of research, hanging-out with the chil- dren in the park or in the street so that, little by little, they would become accustomed to my presence in these settings, gradually introducing my practices of note-taking and photographing their activities. Even though I would converse with the children during these periods of "hanging-out," I established a practice of *non-intervention* in peer-group activities, whether ludic or adversarial.

I followed and documented a group of focal children's everyday routines and activities across a wide variety of institutional and familial contexts and social situations that were central to their lives, including the public school, mosque-oratory, households, peer group, health center, and the track-and- field team. To ascertain similarities and variability in communicative prac- tices across social situations and whether the meanings of such practices change depending on context, it was essential to follow participants in a number of different settings, and with different levels of involvement – from observer to participant – (Duranti 1997). Examining *how* Moroccan immi- grant children manage languages and social practices to establish social relationships and to negotiate difference and commonality of belonging was central in this study. It was also crucial to study the co-occurrence of fea- tures in various sites; particularly, the co-occurrence of features both in communicative practices and in children's social engagements, as well as how they relate to each other and to the larger context. As Bateson (1972) argues, for meaningful patterns and processes to arise in people's lives, a certain degree of *redundancy* should hold between settings and social situations.

3.2.1   The Public School

The town public school, *colegio de educación primaria* (primary education includes both elementary and middle school), was a key site of data collec- tion due to the fact that, except for weekends and vacations, the children spent a significant amount of their day in this context, interacting with one another, with their Spanish peers, and with teachers. The public school was also a crucial site because it had come to occupy a prominent role in the achievement of a high degree of peaceful and stable *convivencia* (living-together) in the community. The principal Carlos, a very strong leader and also a very astute politician in his own right, was very aware of this important role, and always considered both carefully, the educational and political ramifications of every decision that was made in the school, including, of course, whether or not to authorize my research. While the principal was always amenable to my project, among the major concerns that he had about my presence in the school was the issue of how to best secure the informed consent of the parents. When I explained that my research would not interfere with the children's regular activities and that, furthermore, I would implement measures to ensure the confidentiality of their children's identity, the principal responded that the biggest problem was how to explain my presence in the school to the local Spanish parents. He further suggested that we might want to explain my research goals as neutrally as possible and to background the fact that I was in the school to investigate primarily Moroccan immigrant children. Bewildered by his response, he proceeded to explain: "Sí, porque los padres protestan y dicen que aquí todo lo que se hace, se hace por los moros. Y no queremos más problemas de los que ya tenemos" ("Yes, because parents protest and say that everything that is done here, is done on behalf of *los moros*. And we don't want more problems than the ones we already have"). He wanted to make sure that my research was not going to be perceived as something special that the school was doing for the sake of the Moroccan students. On the contrary, and if at all possible, he wanted my larger involvement with the school, beyond my specific research goals, to be perceived as something that could potentially be beneficial to all students, Spanish and Moroccans.

After my research in the school was authorized, and before selecting one main classroom in which to do my research, I visited the school's four fourth-grade classrooms. One of the four classrooms was eventually chosen for three reasons. In consultation with Carlos, the principal, I learned that most of the Moroccan children in this classroom had a very low record of sojourning, that is, their families usually stayed in the town for the duration of the academic year and would rarely travel for long stays in Morocco outside official school vacation periods. This was important to minimize participants' attrition during the study. In addition, I had already established positive initial contact with several families whose children were in this particular classroom, which could facilitate my access to the children's lives in out-of-school contexts. The third reason was that the teacher in this classroom was an experienced teacher who was amenable to this research study and who did not show as many signs of discomfort with my presence and the presence of the camera as some of the other teachers had shown.

The total number of students in the focal class was 24, out of which, seven were Moroccan immigrant children: **Sarah**, Miriam, **Wafiya**, **Karim**, **Mimon**, Jalal, and Yimad.[3] As I will elaborate in Chapter 5, the school had had a long history of addressing the incorporation of Moroccan immigrant children into the Spanish educational system and had received several awards for their work towards social inclusion and program development.

The initial two-month period of observation allowed me to become familiar with the children's schedules and activities, as well as with routine workings of the institution itself. This time also helped me identify the types of classes that I needed to record to obtain extensive documentation of what a typical school day looked like from the point of view of Moroccan children, as well as the venues where video-recording could be complicated. For example, due to the size of the school's three playgrounds and because children were physically very active during recess, I made the decision not to video-record on a regular basis during these leisure periods. However, I did make ongoing observations and take fieldnotes during recesses, focusing on the activities of the focal children. Towards the end of the academic year, however, I was able to videotape a few of the games played by a group of my focal children with their classmates. Some of the Moroccan children in the study followed the regular curriculum along with their Spanish peers in all classes (Miriam, Mimon, and Yimad). Others (Sarah, Karim, Jalal, and Wafiya), however, followed the regular curriculum along with their Spanish peers for only some of the classes, and were withdrawn from their regular classroom for several hours a day for Spanish Literacy and Math enhancement classes. School officials called this *Programa de Educación Compensatoria* (Compensatory Education Program), but colloquially both teachers and children routinely refer to it as *la clase de apoyo* (the support class). For these reasons, I decided to record four types of classes: (1) classes in which only completely mainstreamed Moroccan children were present with Spanish children (Math, Social Studies, and Language Arts); (2) classes in which all Moroccan children (mainstreamed and recent immigrants) were present with Spanish children (Music, and Dance and Performing Arts); (3) the Spanish Literacy and Math enhancement class from the Compensatory Education Program that the four non-mainstreamed Moroccan children attended; and (4) the Arabic Heritage Language class that all seven Moroccan children attended once a week, while their Spanish peers had religious education.

In Vallenuevo, there were two main sites for Moroccan immigrant children to receive instruction in the Arabic language: children attended Arabic language classes in the Spanish public school and in after-school religious classes in a makeshift oratory-mosque run by the local Islamic cultural organization Assalam. As part of the LACM Program, all Moroccan children in this study attended Arabic language classes once a week at the public school, while their Spanish peers attended Catholic religion classes. The LACM Program[4] (*Programa de Enseñanza de Lengua Arabe y Cultura Marroquí* – "Arabic Language and Moroccan Culture Teaching Program") is a relatively new educational initiative jointly funded by the Spanish and Moroccan governments. Spanish schools' participation in this program is voluntary. The public school in Vallenuevo had been participating in the LACM program for several years. Under the provisions established as part of the agreement, the Spanish government offers logistical support (classroom, office space, etc.) for Arabic language classes to take place in those public schools that apply for it, and the Moroccan government is responsible for the curriculum, as well as for selecting, providing and paying for Arabic language teachers, who, with very few exceptions, come from Morocco. Both the Spanish and Moroccan governments are responsible for designing instructional materials and offering professional development training programs to participating teachers.

3.2.2   The Oratory-Mosque

The small oratory that served the religious needs of the Moroccan community of Vallenuevo was also the setting where Moroccan immigrant children attended after-school Qur'anic classes in the afternoon. The classes were held in a small, separate room at the back of the oratory with a separate exit to the street. Therefore, the children and I never entered through the main door that gave access to the more sacred space[5] of the oratory-mosque, but through the back door on the other side of the building. The classes were divided into two groups: a class for adolescents and older children that met on Mondays, Wednesdays, and Saturdays from 5:00 to 6:00 p.m., and a class for younger children that met on Tuesdays, Thursdays, and Sundays from 5:00–6:00 p.m. This is the class that all of the focal children in the study attended, except for Kamal. No classes were held on Fridays, the mandatory holy day of prayer for Muslims. Since during the weekdays, I was usually busy either at the public school or at the health center, I tended to visit the oratory-mosque during the Sunday lessons. Once I obtained permission to record these classes, I videotaped in this setting every other Sunday. Occasionally, however, I went more or less frequently, depending on whether I traveled to track-and-field meets with the children.

The classroom itself was in state of disrepair: small pieces of the wall were flaking off, the room had only one electrical outlet, and the ceiling leaked in various places when it rained. At the beginning of my recordings, the classroom was furnished with only a few old rugs and a half-broken board that hung precariously from the wall until second-hand desks were eventually donated. Also, the teachers often did not have enough instructional materials for all the children who attended. I contributed notebooks, pens, and pencils, and a small heater, since the facility got extremely cold during the winter months. The local *fqih* (religious teacher), Bilal[6] and his wife, conducted the classes.

3.2.3   The Health Center

The local public health center is a small-scale clinic that covers the basic medical needs of the town's population. For more serious conditions, births, and surgical operations, patients were referred to specialists in a larger hospital situated in a larger town approximately six miles away from Vallenuevo. At the time, this study was conducted, healthcare in Spain was public, government-run, and free. This included basic healthcare for undocumented migrants, as well as pre- and post-natal care for immigrant pregnant women and minors until age 18, independent of their legal status. All documented immigrants had access to the free public health care system.[7]

Through informal conversations with children, parents, and community members, I soon learned that Moroccan immigrant children often translated for their families, particularly at the local health center. At the health center, attitudes among healthcare personnel towards children's roles as translators were mixed. On the one hand, the staff valued children's efforts, and how much children's work as interpreters facilitated their work as healthcare professionals. On the other hand, and mirroring popular beliefs towards language brokering, doctors and nurses would also tell me that they disliked this practice because they felt it was putting too much responsibility on the children. In fact, they tried to eliminate it by hiring a professional interpreter in the mornings. There was no interpreter available in the afternoon or in the evening hours, however, when the local health center and its emergency unit was still operative. This was when Moroccan children would often accompany their families and neighbors to perform interpreting services. When, after four months in the field, I approached the clinical staff and requested permission to record medical visits involving Moroccan children who translated in the afternoon hours, they were very supportive of my study. Doctors were particularly interested in knowing whether or not children felt uncomfortable performing these tasks and the difficulties they had doing translations.

Working with one pediatrician, Rocío, and her nurse in particular, I went to the health center once every two weeks. The pediatrician and her nurse were extremely generous in informing me in advance about which day of the week they would have more appointments with Moroccan families. This set of data, however, is the least systematically-recorded, and due to several reasons, it involves a large number of non-focal Moroccan children. This was due partly to the unpredictability of medical needs and/or children's availability to act as language brokers in these encounters. There were also other constraints, such as the fact that I had to obtain the permission of each individual family before recording the medical encounter. Since I started recording at the health center after being in Vallenuevo for four months, many families already knew me personally or knew of my research. These families almost always granted me permission to record their interactions. There were a number of families, however, who either did not know me at all (particularly those who came from nearby small villages) or who were uncomfortable with me recording their interactions. As a result, I was sometimes unable to videotape even a single medical consultation at the clinic, whereas other times, I was able to make recordings of several families in one visit. I sometimes missed a recording because families did not always attend their scheduled visits.

The clinic's staff had actually developed a theory as to why families missed their appointments so frequently. They guessed that because medical care in rural parts of Morocco was probably limited and expensive, many immigrant families had developed *una mentalidad de supervivencia* (a survival mentality) regarding health. Doctors often told me that they needed to help the families change this survival mentality into one more compatible with preventive health care and regular visits to the clinic. Although I do not dismiss the doctors' hypotheses, I also suspect that some Moroccan families missed appointments for other reasons, including tiring, double shifts during the harvest seasons. Appointments were also probably missed because some families had trouble reading letters from the clinic. Often during my study, I observed parents asking their children to help them decipher such letters, since the household was another site where language brokering occurred on a regular basis. Many times, parents would also bring out these letters for me to translate during visits to focal children's homes, in the hope of getting me to tell them exactly when they had to take their children to the doctor, for what reason, and what paperwork they needed to bring with them. Although observing how families worked together to translate these letters was part of the interactional dynamics that I was hoping to capture, I could not, of course, refuse to help with translation when families had so graciously welcomed me into their homes.

3.2.4   The Households

I usually visited the households of all focal children once a week. Initially, I was treated as a high status guest. Therefore, it was very difficult to determine the normal routines of the household that the children participated in. However, after spending a few months with them, families began to relax during my visits, conducting themselves in a more casual manner. It was then when I was able to document children's involvement and participation in the homes. Key practices, in which children, particularly girls, participated included doing house chores (such as cleaning, washing clothes, cooking), and translation of letters and documents.

One of the most difficult aspects of videotaping in the homes was video-recording family meals and afternoon teas without directly being asked to participate in them. For the Moroccan families I spent time with, it was extremely embarrassing to have me present in the room and to not have me join in on the meals and interactions. It took many months in Vallenuevo and weekly contact with focal families for a few of them to agree to such recordings, and for them not to insist during those recordings that I take part in the activity. For some Moroccan families the idea of having me in the household without participating in the meals or celebrations continued to be an unthinkable notion, bordering on the absurd. Such being the case, on certain occasions, I actually decided to record these activities with me as one of the participants, to which the families did not object as long as I joined for lunch, tea, or whatever was being served. This technique also allowed me to see whether or not there was any difference in families' behavior and practices between these meals and the meals in which I was videotaping the families alone. This comparison, however, had limitations in that it involved different families. Similarly, many families found it strange that I wanted to videotape when mothers and girls were working together preparing the food or tidying up the house. They would asked me, genuinely perplexed, whether it would not be better to *take pictures* or *make a video*, as they often referred to my videotaping activities, once the house was already clean and the food ready for presentation. Whether videotaping or not, I always wrote extensive notes as soon as I finished with each of the home-visits.

Eventually, in addition to regularly observing these activities, I was able to videotape at least a few instances of all of the practices I have just described, namely girls' participation in chores; translation events; sibling interactions; family meals; and afternoon teas. Video-recording in the homes of the focal children was, however, uneven. For example, I was only able to video-record activities in the homes of four of the focal children, those of Sarah, Worda, Karim, and Kamal. Wafiya's family never gave me permission to video- or audio-record them. Every time I asked for their permission to record, Wafiya's parents and elder siblings would talk with embarrassment about the precarious conditions of the lower-level garage in which they lived. And they would add that, if they lived somewhere else or if they managed to move to a better house, I would be welcomed to record. These situations were not uncommon. When I first established contact with Kamal's family at the beginning of the study, they lived in what used to be the business premises of an old local butcher's shop. While this space was barely fit for a family of four to live in, Kamal's mother could not afford to rent anything else. Often, when I visited this family during the first few months of the study, we had to sit around a table having tea or dinner by the light of several candles. A few months later, thanks to a subsidy and two part-time cleaning jobs that Kamal's mother was able to secure, the family was able to move to a spacious apartment where I was able to visit often and to videotape. Mimon's family was always very reluctant and uncomfortable with the presence of a video-camera or any kind of recording device in the household, even though, unlike Wafiya's family, they lived in a very nice townhouse. Although they were always very cordial to me, they specifically told me that I had permission to record Mimon at school, at the mosque, and outside the home, but not inside.

3.2.5 The Peer Group

Given the amount of out-of school-time that Moroccan immigrant children in Vallenuevo spent playing and interacting with other children, peer-group communicative and social activities were crucial in this study. Although I started documenting and observing peer-group practices from the very first weeks of study, for reasons I have mentioned above, I did not videotape these activities until four months into the project. This initial period of observation allowed me to get a general sense of the importance of peer-group cultures in these children's lives: I studied the sociocultural organization of peer-group activities, as well as the compositions of the groups; I learned about their favorite games and how they were played, and in general about peer-group routines and the children's most common meeting places. Specifically, there were three types of places in the town where focal children would concentrate for their games: on the street near their houses, in the local park, and in a couple of vacant lots of land scattered around the town. This last piece of information proved to be crucial when I began systematically recording the peer-group activities. Although as the study progressed, I would ask the focal children in the school whether and where they were going to play on a given afternoon – and often they would let me know where they were going to be playing – many times the chosen location was unpredictable. And I spent many afternoon hours wandering around the town until I would find the location where the children were playing, especially at the beginning of the study. Once I established a recording schedule, I videotaped peer-group activities once a week, alternating between the different peer groups to which the focal children belonged.

This alternation mostly meant that I followed the extended peer networks of two of the most sociable and well-liked focal girls (Worda and Wafiya), on the one hand, and the networks one of the most charismatic focal boys (Kamal), on the other hand. Their convivial demeanor and large number of friendships allowed me to connect to a large number of children and their interactions, including other focal children (such as Sarah), and children that I had the opportunity to get to know in other contexts (such as Yimad, Jalal, and Manal).

Unlike other sites of data collection (such as the school, the mosque, the households, or the clinics), where children were (and expected to be) under adult "supervision," my presence in peer-group games and activities stood out more conspicuously. At the same time, however, my daily presence in so many other contexts of their lives, and my lack of directly interfering with the children's routine activities in these other contexts, also helped to normalize somewhat my observations and recordings of peer-group games and practices. During the course of the recordings, I adopted the role of observer and minimized my participation in any of the activities that the children themselves organized in the context of their interactions with peers; for instance, I never elicited any speech or form of language use. Also, I never directed or made decisions regarding peer-group games or activities, even though, particularly at the beginning, the children would ask for my input or invite me to take part in their games quite frequently. While it is not uncommon for children to want adult researchers to participate in games or to act as an arbiter in their disputes, children also tried to involve me in their activites in a way that I had not anticipated before I undertook this study: during the first couple of video-recordings, when children were trying to confront other children's alleged game rule violations, they turned to me and asked whether they could review the violation in question to determine who was at fault, if anyone. The first time this happened, it created a comically awkward moment for me, not only because the children caught me off guard, but also because, although I had to deny their request, I could not help but visibly delight in the cleverness of their idea. As the process of data collection went along, however, all these behaviors began to disappear. This was mainly due to two facts: (1) the focal children grew accustomed to my daily presence and my recording of their everyday activities; so, even the novelty of the camera lost its initial appeal; and (2) the focal children also began to trust my promise of confidentiality, when they realized that I was not reporting any of their peer-group activities to any of their adult caregivers, particularly those activities the children *could get more in trouble for*, such as fights, use of *bad* language, *inappropriate* gossip about adults, or play conversations fantasizing about adult–like topics, such as going out to night-clubs or having girlfriends/boyfriends.

On a few occasions, however, some children participating in these activities, particularly friends of the focal children who were not as used to my presence and systematic observation, continued to try to recruit my intervention in games and ongoing interactions. This happened especially when conflict and disagreement erupted among themselves, but, sometimes, also for ludic purposes. Even for this handful of occasions, I reminded the children that I was interested in knowing how they played and learned together, and I did not intervene in any subsequent course of action that children took, including those involving fights. More interestingly, in these few occasions, the focal children themselves reprimanded the other children for trying to involve me in their games and disagreements, telling them to leave me alone and reminding them that, when I was recording with my video-camera, I was *an invisible ghost*, a trope that I had previously used with the children in the initial stages of my interactions with them during data collection.

Although children's activities during the track-and-field training sessions cannot be considered *per se* peer-group activities, since they are supervised by adults, namely two male coaches and several parents who would accompany the children on and off to some of the most geographically removed competitions, children also enjoyed free, relatively unsupervised periods during the training sessions, bus journeys, and in between competitions. Unlike the local soccer and indoor soccer clubs whose membership was dominated by Spanish children, Moroccan immigrant children made up the majority of the local track-and-field team. Given the international record of success that Moroccan athletes have attained in track-and-field competitions, it is not surprising that so many Moroccan children in the town were interested in the sport. I suspect, however, that the appeal of this club for Moroccan immigrant children had much to do with the fact that one of the coaches, Félix, had a strong commitment to fairness and equality and was a passionate advocate of the benefits of sports for children. He strongly encouraged the Moroccan immigrant children to join the track club, even going to great lengths to find sponsors for those children who could not afford the equipment and travel expenses.

Given the large number of Moroccan immigrant children who were part of this athletic club, I asked the coaches of the team whether I could observe the children at practices. Although both coaches were very helpful from the beginning, Félix was particularly enthusiastic about my study, sensing, I think, that he had found another person who shared his concern about the welfare and education of children. I began attending training sessions once a week almost from the beginning of the study. My involvement became more intense when I discovered that three of the children who eventually became focal children in the study (Worda, Wafiya, and Kamal) were members of this club. By the beginning of winter 2006, I also started traveling on the weekends with the team to many of the athletic competitions that occurred during the year. As my involvement with the team grew, I became a volunteer helper to the coaches, helping to supervise the children's training, cheering the children on during competitions, photographing the team with their winning medals, and in general, doing whatever I could to facilitate the club's activities. I made a deliberate choice to minimize my videotaping in this context. I did this in part because training and competitions did not easily lend themselves to videotaping, given that both children and accompanying adults were literally doing much running around, but also because I wanted to develop a more informal and intimate type of relationship with the children during these recreational activities. Indeed, my ongoing presence on the team allowed me to develop a very close bond with the three focal children and their teammates, and to establish excellent rapport and trust with many other Moroccan children and families in the town. Of course, I did take extensive fieldnotes of children's activities and interactions, but I usually wrote these up in the quiet of my apartment after the practices and competition trips. On a number of occasions, however, I did videotape activities that I thought were representative of peer cultures in the track and field club, such as unsupervised interactions during practice or between races. This allowed me to develop at least a partial video record of the track-club activities that I could add to my general corpus of video-recordings.

3.3   Participant Observation and Recording of Naturally-Occurring Interactions

Bernard (2002) has identified participant observation as the foundational method of any anthropological endeavor, which he defines as being "both a humanistic method and a scientific one. It produces the kind of experiential knowledge that lets you talk convincingly from the gut . . . It also produces effective, positivistic knowledge" (pp. 322–323). Participant observation can range on a continuum from complete observer to complete participant. In this ethnographic study, I adopted the mixed role of participant observer: at times, I was fully taking part in some aspects of the community and children's lives going on around me, such as my involvement at the track-and-field club. At other times, I adopted a more distanced role, recording practices and events as they unfolded without my active participation, such as when I was behind the camera videotaping lessons or visits to the doctor. In this sense, participant observation was a fluid process that led me to reflect on how my dual role might have affected the research context and the data collected in the process. During observations and recordings, there were moments when I definitely thought that my presence was affecting the behavior of those around me. For instance, during my initial visits to the children's homes, I was always treated as an *honored* guest. Consequently, the families stopped the normal routines of the households and all interactions and activities centered upon my presence in the house. Oftentimes, the families would go to great lengths to enact an appropriate reception, wearing their best garments and preparing elaborate meals. Although these initial visits were critical to establish close bonds with the children and their families, my active social participation in these social gatherings, as well as the way I was being positioned by the families, preclude me from using these interactions in most of my analyses of family practices, except for those having to do with cultural practices of hospitality. At other times, in the midst of videotaping, I had to stop being an "observer" and become an important "participant," such as the time when a child injured himself seriously during play or when, on one occasion in the health center, a child was translating the wrong dose of antibiotics to be given to a sick baby.

Video-recording was crucial to this study for several reasons.[8] The video-recording of social practices facilitates a multifaceted analysis of linguistic practices enriched by kinesic details and material environments that are essential for the examination of face-to-face interaction (e.g., Goodwin 1993). Video-recordings allowed me to investigate the interactional achievement of social and linguistic practices, and to identify and contrast patterns within these practices at a level that would not have been possible otherwise. In addition, I supplemented the video-record with site documents, field notes, and my own ethnographic diaries collected and written throughout the study. In these field notes and diaries, I recorded my daily observations and informal conversations with various members of the community. A total of 86 hours of video-recorded data were collected. The number of hours and categorization of the data according to the social setting in which they were collected are summarized in Table 3.1 below.

Video-recorded data and transcription are central to the ethnomethodological analysis that I have conducted in Chapters 5, 6, 7, and 8 of this book. In Appendix 1, I describe how I worked with this type of discourse data and how I constructed the transcripts. In Appendix 2, I provide a list of the symbols I used to transliterate Arabic speech into the Roman alphabet.

Table 3.1   Number of hours of video-recording.

Social Settings	Number of Hours
Public school	28
Mosque	12
Households	13
Peer group	11
Health center	3
Track-and-field and other social settings	4
Interviews	15
Total number of hours of video–recordings	**86**

3.4   Ethnographic Interviews

I used two different types of interview methods in this research study. The first kind was the semi-structured interview conducted with the focal children's parents and some teachers at the public school, namely the head teacher of the fourth-grade class, Guadalupe, whom I followed and recorded throughout the academic year, as well as Rashid, the Arabic heritage language teacher at the public school. These semi-structured interviews yielded important insights about attitudes, values, and ideologies surrounding the linguistic and sociocultural practices that I was observing and recording. As Duranti (1997, pp. 103–104) reminds us, however, ethnographers need to be particularly mindful of the cultural ecology of interviews, since "reactions to the researcher's questions will vary, depending on [. . .] the extent to which the interview format fits into local practices of obtaining information." This consideration was critical in my study because, whereas teachers seemed to be very comfortable with the interviews and, in many ways, expected to be interviewed in the context of my research study, Moroccan parents seemed ill at ease and more awkward about responding to my questions in formal interview situations. In contrast, Moroccan parents were more relaxed during our informal conversations, answering my questions, providing information, and often discussing with me, even without being prompted, difficult and problematic aspects of their lives, of their relationships with their children and with the community at large (both Spanish and Moroccan). Even though I conducted these semi-structured interviews during the later stages of the research to ensure a maximum degree of trust between the parents and me, during formal interview situations, many of them still appeared stiff, nervous, and, even a little apprehensive of going "on the record" to discuss topics that they had already shared willingly and unselfconsciously in informal conversations with me. To my surprise, some parents even contradicted themselves in these semi-structured interviews, going to great lengths to depict rosier characterizations of situations that they had previously discussed as challenging, and trying to minimize the impact of events that, on other occasions, they had described as being the source of a great deal of pain and distress. Because of the awkwardness that formal semi-structured interviews caused, I made the decision that the best way to obtain information from parents was to continue to hold informal conversations with them during my weekly visits to the households, and to write extensive notes about these conversations as soon as possible after my visits had ended.

Because an important aspect of this study was to investigate how the children themselves portrayed and made sense of their lives, the second interviewing method I used was an open-ended *person-centered approach*. This approach allows participants themselves to steer the interview process and to provide accounts of how they experience their lives, moving beyond treating participants as mere cultural informants (Levy and Hollan 1998; Hollan and Wellenkamp 1996; Hollan 2001). Unlike other interview methodologies, in the person-centered approach, individuals who are interviewed take on a more agentive role in the ethnographic process. As Hollan (2001, pp. 48–49) has noted, since a main focus of person-centered interviewing is on how an individual's subjective experience both shapes, and it is shaped by, sociocultural processes, "an effort is made to represent human behavior and subjective experience from the point of view of the *acting, intending,* and *attentive subject*, to actively explore the emotional saliency and motivational force of cultural beliefs and symbols (rather than to assume such saliency and force), and to avoid unnecessary reliance on overly abstract, experience-distant constructs" (emphasis mine).

Because very close and ongoing contact is necessary before people are willing to take part in the kind of frank and meaningful interviews that the person-centered approach advocates, I did not start this kind of interviewing with focal children until I had been in the field for six months. In addition, this method questions the role of the ethnographer and emphasizes the importance of rethinking the dynamics of the interview in the ethnographic process. These factors are critically important in my study since, unlike other studies where person-centered interviewing had been implemented (e.g., Klein 2007), participants in my longitudinal, in-depth interviews were young children. Mayall (2002), for example, has discussed at length how power differential and generational issues can be of great consequence when holding any kind of conversation or interview with children. In my case, I had to think through these issues carefully and closely review past interviews for self-monitoring purposes, especially given the agentive role that children were supposed to take in person-centered exchanges (where the interviewer is dissuaded from shaping participants' talk or nominating subjects for discussion), and given that children were being asked to offer their reflections of, emotions about, and moral perspectives on their everyday lives and activities.

To lessen power disparities and to allow the children to take as much control as possible during the interview process, I often started the interviews by replaying for children some of the recordings that I had made with them in previous weeks, or by asking general questions about certain events of their lives for which I was not present (i.e. a training session, a class, a special celebration). Also, at the beginning of the interview series, I encouraged the children to draw *lifemaps*, a method adapted from Orellana (2001), which consists of a combination of drawings and brief text captions produced by the children. In addition to tapping into children's views of how their lives could unfold, *lifemaps* are also powerful artifacts of self-representation. Often, I would use these *lifemaps* as a springboard to move discussions along during interviews. Because successful person-centered interviewing entails high levels of meaningful and voluntary involvement from participants, I did not implement this methodology with all focal children. Although all focal children were interviewed at least once throughout the study, only those who expressed genuine interest in participating in a long-term series of interviews were selected for this segment of the study. Person-centered interviews were conducted with Kamal, Sarah, Worda, and Wafiya over a period of five months. In addition to these four focal children, I also interviewed children of other families that I became close to for shorter periods of time. In particular, I want to highlight the contributions of Manal and Abdelkarim to this interviewing process, both of whom were extremely articulate and forthcoming, and whom I quote in several parts of this book.

As part of the methodology, interview materials were mined for recurring themes, points of continuity and contradiction, and issues that materialized as significant for the children. Even though I privilege children's quotidian practices and social interactions as the keystone of my ethnomethodological analysis, interview materials are crucial in several respects. First, one of the premises that underpin this book is that the Moroccan immigrant community in Spain is positioned in a very specific category of exclusion informed simultaneously by anti-immigrant sentiment, contemporary geopolitical discourses about Muslim populations, and historical discourses of *Moorish* invasions. The interviews were a powerful record that revealed just how much Moroccan immigrant children are aware of the racialization of their own immigrant community and how they make sense of this exclusion on a daily basis. Second, interview materials also proved to be invaluable to determine to what extent those interactional processes that I, as an analyst, was identifying as meaningful in children's everyday social engagement, were also salient to the children themselves, and if so, what aspects were more significant to them. Third, and finally, because I was hoping to develop as holistic a picture of the children's lives as possible, the interviews allowed me to better understand the depth of children's emotional reactions to daily occurrences. This level of understanding would not have been possible by attending to the interactions alone, since rules of social conduct often require that we stifle our depth of feelings about particular situations. In this same vein, through interviews, I was also able to obtain personal information about the children and families that enabled me to have a deeper understanding about the way interactions would unfold in certain cases. For example, one of the children's fathers had been involved in illegal activities, and indirect references to this situation came up in a couple of aggravated fights I observed between the children in a way that directly affected my understanding of the meaning of the interaction for the children participating in the fights.

3.5   Collection of Site and Press–Media Documents

While in the field, I obtained many locally available documents that provided information about the lives of the Moroccan diaspora community in Vallenuevo. For instance, from the regional government, I obtained a copy of the *Plan Integral para la Integración Social de Inmigrantes* (Comprehensive Plan for the Social Integration of Immigrants). From the local authority, I was able to gather actualized census population figures in the town, by both age and national origin. From numerous social services in town, I collected a handful of Spanish-Arabic bilingual brochures advertising institutional campaigns and forms of social assistance available, as well as training booklets for social workers who were being trained to provide services to local immigrants. The brochures were helpful in examining how sociocultural institutional knowledge and norms were presented to the Moroccan community. The booklets were informative of institutional ideologies underlying local construction of immigrants' needs and rights, in addition to providing information about kinds of cultural knowledge about Moroccan immigrants that social workers were expected to have and enact in their dealings with their immigrant clients.

The public school principal, Carlos, generously allowed me to photocopy several of the school's curricular guides and documents pertaining to the internal structure of the school and its vision. These documents were instrumental, for instance, for me to recognize the schism that existed between official curricular statements and policies about inclusion, and the social dynamics that I observed among Spanish and Moroccan children at the school on a daily basis. Several teachers also allowed me to photocopy instructional materials from books and handouts that were used during many of the classes that I recorded, and which I used to supplement the video-record. These materials provided useful information about teaching methodologies, the skills, knowledge, and values to be taught, and the ideologies organizing knowledge and values. In addition, I consulted the newspaper archives in the local library of a nearby larger town to retrieve articles published about Vallenuevo in the local and national press from the mid-1990s to 2007. I used these materials to ascertain how life in the town and Moroccan immigration had been characterized and portrayed. They were also a valuable source of information for learning what some of the public figures whom I knew (i.e. the school principal, the town mayor, and several social workers) had told the press about the Moroccan community and the town. Very often, I used these articles and statements as starting points for informal conversations with these figures to probe their views and/or shifting perceptions about the social and demographic changes in the town.

I have, thus, used a variety of methodologies and approaches to capture as completely as possible the complexity of Moroccan immigrant children's everyday experiences and concerns in Vallenuevo. Although the following chapters usually focus on only one of the social contexts of children's lives, it is important to note that my analyses of these specific social settings are always informed by the larger body of data as a whole.

Notes

1   The first 12 consecutive months of research were funded by a Wenner–Gren Foundation Individual Dissertation Research Grant (Grant # 7296), and the four months in summer 2007 by funding from a Harry and Yvonne Lenart Foundation Graduate Research Travel Grant, and by a UCLA Center for European and Eurasian Studies Summer Dissertation Research Grant.

2   In addition, during the summer of 2004, I conducted a preliminary pilot study that was designed to lay the groundwork for this research. This preliminary research had three purposes: (1) to identify a suitable site, (2) to make initial contact with the community with which I would be doing my research and (3) to gather ethnographic information on the lifeworlds of recent Moroccan immigrants from the perspective of educators and social workers who interact closely with the children and their families. The preliminary study consisted of ethnographic interviews of teachers and social workers, and observation of several meetings of Arabic heritage language instructors in several areas of Southwestern Spain. This

preliminary study was crucial in order to identify (a) institutional reflections on Moroccan immigrant children's attempts to manage multiple cultural and linguistic expectations, (b) their possible roles as cultural brokers and interpreters for their households, and (c) the challenges that they face in different settings (i.e. household, peer group, educational institutions). Whereas this pilot fieldwork focused on institutional and adult perspectives of Moroccan immigrant children's lives in Vallenuevo, the later research focused on these children's life-worlds from the perspective of the children themselves and their caregivers.

3   The names of the children bolded and italicized are those children who eventually became the focal children of this study. As for the other two focal children, Worda was placed in another fourth-grade group, and Kamal attended sixth grade at the same school. On a couple of occasions, I was granted permission by the teachers of these classrooms to record a few classes in which Worda and Kamal were present.

4   The LACM Program was first implemented in the 1985–1986 academic year. Although the impact of this program is still limited, currently, schools from roughly 25 provinces (out of the 52 Spanish provinces) participate in this program, offering Arabic Language and Moroccan Culture classes either during regular school hours or as a formal after-school enrichment program. For more information about this program, visit http://www.educacion.es/cide/jsp/plantillaAncho.jsp?id=inn07.

5   This area was reserved for prayer and Friday services.

6   Unlike the previous *fqih* (whom I met only once during a Ramadan dinner), who was said to be harsh and have a proclivity towards physical punishment, Bilal was an extremely patient man and kind to the children. Although some of the focal children discussed with me their reticence about attending the classes for fear of physical punishment, I never observed any instance of physical punishment during my recordings. Bilal explicitly told me that he was against it, and the children never complained about him physically punishing them as they had done when talking about their previous teacher. Bilal was always very friendly to me during the recordings and informal conversations.

7   In 2012, the Spanish government implemented a reform of the public healthcare system such that, while pregnant women and minors still receive medical care independent of their legal status, undocumented immigrants no longer have access to basic health care and can only use the public health system in emergencies. In addition, documented immigrants must also pay a supplement for their medicines and certain medical services like any other Spanish resident.

8   I used a medium-sized, three-chip, digital video camera, enhanced by a powerful shotgun microphone, and at times, by a wireless microphone placed in strategic locations, for most of the video-recordings of naturally-occurring interactions. In a few environments however, where the use of this camera proved to be very cumbersome, I used instead, a smaller digital camera that I otherwise used for photographic documentation. In the public school, the oratory-mosque, and the health center, I used a tripod, while I recorded outside activities of the peer group or the track-and-field team training sessions using a monopod. The monopod was much more portable and allowed me to follow more easily (yet steadily), children's high mobility during games.

4

Moroccan Immigrant Childhoods in Vallenucvo

> The landscape of contemporary childhood includes three major sites – families, neighborhoods, and schools.
>
> Each of these worlds contains different people, patterns of time and space . . .
>
> (Barrie Thorne 1993/1995, p. 29)

This chapter is concerned with the landscapes of Moroccan immigrant childhoods in Vallenuevo. In an effort to trace such landscapes in a way that both represents the histories and particularities of the children who let me into their lives, but that can also teach us more general aspects of how Moroccan immigrant children in rural areas may be able to negotiate their commonality of belonging and, I first present a snapshot of the children whom I got to know more intimately. In the second part of the chapter, bringing together my own observations from my interviews with the children, I discuss the contexts of their lives. Moroccan immigrant children's lifemaps (see Chapter 1) resonate with Thorne's observation that contemporary childhood is shaped most prominently in three sites – families, neighborhoods, and schools. As Moroccan immigrant children move across these domains, however, the contextual boundaries may present some qualities that are specific to their experiences as immigrant children. In capturing these nuances and salient features in Moroccan immigrant childhoods, Thorne's insight to pay attention to the people and patterns of time and space that develop in each of these worlds becomes more important than ever. While subsequent chapters of this book address Moroccan immigrant children's interactions with other people who populate different domains

Language and Muslim Immigrant Childhoods: The Politics of Belonging, First Edition. Inmaculada Mª García-Sánchez.

of experience, I focus in this chapter on the (temporal) unfolding of these children's everyday lives across (spatial) contexts.

4.1   Snapshots of the Focal Children and their Families

While I could not know in advanced which children would eventually become focal in my study, I had some methodological and theoretically-motivated ideas about the kind of children I wanted to work with. My first concern was to identify Moroccan children who were relatively recent immigrants to Spain (ideally, between one and six years, but no more than 10 years of residence). A second guiding principle was age: I wanted to work with children around age 10 (+/− two years) because middle-childhood and pre-adolescence have been identified as crucial periods in child development in which children begin to sort out their own identities, as they start navigating their own ways through societal structures and institutions.[1] Basic information about focal children, along these parameters, is summarized in Table 4.1.

Also, as much as possible, I strived to select children in households that included siblings of both genders since previous research on Moroccan immigrant children in Spain had described gender as a significant factor in the types of activity settings in which they are routinely engaged and the roles they take therein. For example, household chores and sibling care is a common responsibility of girls.[2]

Before moving on to the portraits of the focal children and their families, I want to consider briefly what I mean by *focal*. During my time in

Table 4.1   Focal participants.

Name	Gender	Age (beginning of study)	Age (end of study)	Approximate Time Living in Spain (by the end of study)
Worda	F	9	10	7 years
Wafiya	F	9	10	7 years
Sarah	F	8.5	9.5	1 year
Karim	M	8.5	9.5	4 years
Mimon	M	9	10	6 years
Kamal	M	11	12	6 years

Vallenuevo, I met and spent time with many Moroccan families and their children. Similarly, during the many hours a week I spent in school, in the mosque, and in the health center, I got to know and regularly talked to many Moroccan children, not only those in the fourth-grade class I would videotape consistently. Certainly, the knowledge I gained through these conversations and acquaintances inform this ethnography; and in some cases, interactions involving non-focal children are featured in the analysis. In fact, and especially during the first few months of the study, it was not easy for me to distinguish, among the many acquaintances I was pursuing, those who were focal from those who were not. Over time, however, my contact with some children and families became steadier, whereas with others it remained erratic. In addition to deeper intimacy and trust, this greater frequency of contact also allowed me to follow and videotape these children in more social contexts. These are the group of Moroccan immigrant children whom I considered to be focal to this study, even if, in some cases, I was not able to videotape all focal children in all the social contexts I investigated. Often, this was because the children themselves did not take part in these activities. For example, Karim and Kamal rarely, if ever, would attend Qur'anic classes at the mosque; Mimon almost never participated in neighborhood peer play in the afternoons; and Sarah, Karim, and Mimon did not belong to the track-and-field club. Other times, however, this was because the children's families, such as Wafiya's and Mimon's, gave me limited observational access inside their households (see Chapter 3). Table 4.2 shows in which contexts I was able to follow and videotape the focal children on a regular basis.

Below I present brief portraits of each of these six focal children. Although they share a number of life experiences, as well as familial, linguistic, and sociocultural characteristics, I would also like to give readers a flavor of the uniqueness and individuality of each child.

Table 4.2   Observation-videotaping contexts and focal children.

	School	Mosque	Home	Neighborhood Play	Track-and-Field Club	Longitudinal Interviews
Worda	✓	✓	✓	✓	✓	✓
Wafiya	✓	✓	✗	✓	✓	✓
Sarah	✓	✓	✓	✓	✗	✓
Karim	✓	✗	✓	✓	✗	✗
Mimon	✓	✓	✗	✗	✗	✗
Kamal	✓	✗	✓	✓	✓	✓

4.1.1 Worda: The Responsible and Reliable One

Worda was born in Jerada, although her parents were building a house in Oujda at the time I met them. She came to Spain with her mother and her siblings when she was approximately two years old. Her father had already been working in Spain for a few years before their arrival. Her household was composed of eight members who shared a rented two-storey townhouse on a Vallenuevo street that was mostly inhabited by other Moroccan immigrant families. She had two elder sisters. The eldest of the two, Nada, was 16 years old and was finishing high school. She wanted to become a professional translator/interpreter, but she often became frustrated with the language requirements of professional translation programs, where applicants had to show high-intermediate proficiency in three languages to be considered for admission. Although Nada was bilingual in Spanish and Arabic and had been studying English at school for several years, Arabic was not among the languages certified by these professional schools. Worda's second elder sister, Salma, was 12 years old. Even though she was two years older than Worda, Salma was in the same class and grade level as her sister due to a hearing impairment. Salma had suffered a serious ear infection as a baby. As a consequence, she had lost most of her hearing and could not speak. Worda also had an 11-year-old brother in sixth grade, and a four-year-old younger sister. In addition to her parents, her maternal grand-mother also lived with the family after becoming a widow the previous year. Both of her parents worked outside the home as seasonal farmworkers and as temporary night guards at a cherry-holding warehouse. Because of the long hours of work that both her parents put in, Worda's mother relied on her and her adolescent sister for most household chores. Worda was a proficient cook and was often in charge of taking care of her four year-old sister, Dunia, whom she often took with her during neighborhood peer play. In addition, Worda sometimes translated for her parents, a responsibility she shared with both her 16-year-old sister and her 11-year-old brother, mostly at the health center and the social services office in Vallenuevo.

Worda was completely mainstreamed academically and followed the general curriculum. She was doing well in her classes, and her favorite subjects were Math and Language Arts. Her teachers thought very highly of her. She was also a successful runner on the track-and-field team and enjoyed sports. Some of the afternoons when she did not have to train, Worda attended Arabic and Qur'anic lessons in the small oratory-mosque. Although not as consciencious and enthusiastic about these classes as Wafiya was, Worda was a responsible participant who took the lessons seriously. Worda said that she did not go every single time because sometimes she preferred to pray at home with her mother and elder sister, who were most involved in her religious education. Unlike her mother and her sister Nada, and unlike many girls her age, Worda never used a headscarf when she went to these lessons because her mother and sister had told her that she was still too young, and Bilal, the *fqih* at the oratory-mosque, had told children that wearing a headscarf was optional for younger girls like her. In fact, Worda was very articulate when explaining to me her own understanding about the practice of wearing headscarves. Worda believed that wearing headscarves was not really mandatory, only something good that women and older girls should do, particularly if males who were not close relatives were present. One time, she also confessed to me that, unlike her elder sister Nada who had decided to start wearing a headscarf two years earlier, she did not plan to wear a headscarf when she was older because it made her feel a little embarrassed wearing one in the town. Worda had many friends and was very welcoming of others. For example, when Sarah had newly arrived in the town that year, she was the first to include her in her extended peer group. Worda was also a very even-tempered child and mature for her age. When conflict erupted in neighborhood peer play, Worda would often be the one trying to mediate between the parties and asking the other girls to stop fighting so that they could continue with their game. Worda's best friend, Manal, was a sixth-grader who lived close-by and whose mother was Worda's mother's best friend. In the previous year, Worda had also started to get close to Wafiya, who like her, participated in the track-and-field team and was in fourth grade at school.

4.1.2   Wafiya: The Firecracker

Wafiya was born in Taurirt and she also came to Spain at around two years of age. Like Worda, Wafiya's mother and her siblings had followed her father after he had been working in Spain for 12 years. Wafiya's household was composed of seven members, and she was the youngest child in the family. Wafiya had three elder sisters. One of them was 18 and the other two were already in their twenties. She also had an elder brother in eighth grade who, like Wafiya, was also an active member of the track-and-field team. They lived in a large, rented garage-like structure on the lower level of a multi-storey building, located towards the outskirts of the town and near the small oratory-mosque. The living space was maximized to meet the basic needs of all the members of the family, but the household had very few creature comforts and almost no electric appliances. Her parents and elder sisters all worked as seasonal farm workers, although the youngest of the elder sisters also attended Spanish- as-second-language afternoon classes for adult immigrants at the local branch of the Red Cross. Wafiya's parents often traveled around the country, following the harvest calendar in various parts of Spain.

Wafiya and her brother were sometimes left in the care of her elder sisters for months at a time. This was the reason why Wafiya was heavily involved in households chores. She would wash her own clothes by hand, as the household had no washing-machine, and like Worda, she was already a proficient cook. She was indeed a very self-reliant and resourceful child who on numerous occasions showed that she could take care of herself and others very well. For example, during weekend athletic competitions for which the children had to travel outside Vallenuevo, she would promptly get ready by herself and, then, would turn to help the younger children get ready as well. Sometimes, Wafiya also translated for her family, although oftentimes, if her elder brother was available, he took the lead, in particular translating official letters that the household received, since Wafiya found those difficult to translate.

Although Wafiya had been in Spain for the same amount of time as Worda (seven years), she was not completely mainstreamed in school, and she was withdrawn from her regular class for several hours a week to attend the *support class* for Spanish Literacy and the Math Enhancement Program. Wafiya was enthusiastic and volunteered often in her regular class, however. As a result, her teachers, who thought that she was very bright and quick to learn, usually included her in as many activities of the regular curriculum as they thought Wafiya would be able to handle. Her favorite subjects were Math, Social Studies, and Physical Education. She had a little bit of a reputation for being mischievous and badly behaved in class, in particular for being too talkative. After months of close contact with her, I began to suspect that some of her acting up in class could be due to boredom with some of the assignments she was given in the *support class*. Wafiya was supposed to work on these assignments in her regular class, while the rest of the class participated in other activities that were deemed by her teachers too academically demanding for her. In my careful observation, these were times when Wafiya was most likely to misbehave and interrupt the ongoing activity. Wafiya would often tell me how much she liked going to school and studying, and in spite of her reputation for being slightly disruptive, I did come to believe that she genuinely enjoyed learning. Another instance of her interest in school-related activities was how very responsible she was about attending Qur'anic classes at the oratory-mosque in the afternoons when she did not have track-and-field practice. Unlike some of the other children, she would rarely skip these classes, and when called upon by the *fqih* Bilal, she would recite with eagerness, even if she often got some verses wrong and needed to be corrected. Wafiya often attended these lessons wearing a headscarf. She had a stronger and more rigid understanding about wearing a headscarf than Worda, and sometimes the girls would argue about whether and when wearing a headscarf was mandatory. In spite of this, being the hyperactive and boisterous girl that she was, the headscarf did not usually stay long on her head, and, by the time the lessons were over, she would often be playing with it in her hands.

Like Worda, she was also a successful runner in the track-and-field team, and enjoyed sports and all kinds of physical activity. She was an extremely social, active, and outgoing child. Wafiya had a strong personality and a quick temper, and I often referred to her affectionately in my fieldnotes as *a little firecracker*. In neighborhood peer play, she would be the first to call out what she perceived to be cheating or foul play. When fights broke out, if Worda was often the pacifier, Wafiya would most often be in the thick of things arguing or confronting other girls or boys.

4.1.3   Sarah: The Newcomer

Sarah was born in Oujda, and when I met her, she had been in Vallenuevo only a few weeks longer than I had. Even though her father and elder siblings, as well as most of his father's family, had already been in Spain for a few years, Sarah had just come to the town with her mother and her three-year-old brother, Anuar. Sarah's household was more complex because there were three nuclear families living together: her own and those of her father's brothers. The three families shared a rented apartment on the fourth floor of a building near the old center of town, where many Moroccan immigrant families lived, and not too far away from Worda's family's house. This living arrangement was not uncommon among Moroccan families in Vallenuevo, who sometimes used this strategy to make the rent more affordable. In addition to her younger brother, Anuar, Sarah had an elder sister, Naima, who had just turned 17. Naima had finished high school the previous year. The more I got to know the family, however, the more I suspected that Naima, given how much she still struggled with written and oral Spanish, had just *aged out* of the system, rather than graduating.[3] During the harvest in Vallenuevo, Naima worked in the fields along with her father in the morning, and in the afternoon attended Spanish classes for immigrants at the local branch of the Red Cross. In addition, Naima had many responsibilities inside and outside the household, as she routinely walked her younger siblings to school and took them to the doctor. Sarah also had a 14-year-old brother in high school, Musa, who had a very bad reputation among other youths and adults in the community for being very feisty, combative, and a *troublemaker*. Sarah told me that she was afraid of him because he often physically disciplined her when, in his opinion, she misbehaved. In fact, a couple of times, I witnessed an altercation between Musa and his mother, in which the latter reprimanded him for being disrespectful to her and unnecessarily harsh to his younger siblings.

During the study, Sarah's mother was pregnant with her fifth child, and she gave birth to another boy in May 2006. Like Wafiya's family, Sarah's father and elder sister also traveled to other areas of the country looking for seasonal work in agriculture. Because of this and her mother's pregnancy, Sarah took over many household responsibilities that routinely would have been performed by Naima, including being left in charge of her younger brother, Anuar, whom she often brought along with her during neighborhood peer play.

Since this was her first year in the country, Sarah was not mainstreamed and spent many hours of the school day in the support class in the *Compensatory Education* building. In addition, she had many problems following regular classroom activities in which she participated. Her teachers often relied on Mimon, Wafiya, or Miriam to translate for her in class until Sarah's proficiency in Spanish improved. She was considered to be very shy and well-behaved in class, however, and all the teachers strived to make as many allowances for her as possible during these activities. I suspect that some of her shyness was due to her limited proficiency in Spanish and to the newness of her social and educational environment, in general. Although always on the reserved side, when she was interacting with her cousins or with me, she was definitely more talkative and outgoing. At first, Sarah had difficulties making friends, and, at the beginning of the study, she spent much of recess sitting alone on the steps overlooking the playground. She would tell me that she felt very sad and lonely and that she wanted to go back to Morocco because she missed her friends and her school very much. It also took her quite a few months to find friends with whom she could hang out after school. I do not think this was only because she was a newcomer. During games, Sarah would get easily frustrated playing with other girls and would often choose to leave, rather than try to work things out and continue playing. As the study progressed, she became closer to Wafiya and Worda, who like her were in fourth grade, and began to join their group of friends regularly. She also started hanging out with Jalal's female cousins and her group of friends, who were slightly younger, but who, like her, had moved recently from Morocco to Vallenuevo. Sarah excelled in the Arabic Heritage Language class, and the teacher tried to challenge her as much as he could, even though it was noticeable that Sarah still found these classes basic and unchallenging. Indeed, Sarah's knowledge of Standard Arabic was very high compared to that of most Moroccan immigrant children I knew. As Sarah's mother liked to remind people with obvious pride, Sarah had studied four years of Classical/Modern Standard Arabic in Moroccan schools before coming to Spain. In spite of this, Sarah was not assiduous about attending the after-school Qur'anic and Arabic lessons. One time, she told me that she thought they were very noisy and that she did not like them very much. So, often, she stayed home helping her mother or going out to play with her new friends.

4.1.4 Karim: Always in Trouble

Karim was born in Taurirt. He came to Spain when he was approximately five years old. Because of the age at which he was brought to Spain by his parents, Karim first went to school in Morocco. His memories of school in Morocco, however, were dim; what he remembered the most was sitting in front of erasable wooden tablets, learning the alif baa – the Arabic alphabet –and reciting the Qur'an with other children. He had five siblings, two elder brothers in their twenties, an elder sister in high school, a younger brother in second grade, and a baby sister who was born during the course of the study. His father and elder brothers jointly ran a local Moroccan grocery store with another Moroccan family in town. His mother stayed home taking care of the children and did not work outside of household. Like Sarah's mother, she was also pregnant during the study and gave birth to a baby girl a few weeks after Sarah's mother. His family lived in a rented single-storey semi-detached house towards the southern outskirts of the town. Although there was a small pocket of Moroccan immigrant families who lived in this area of Vallenuevo, this part of the town was heavily populated by the Roma minority. Karim's favorite way of helping out was running errands on his bike, either for his mother at home or for his father and siblings at the store. Otherwise, Karim's responsibilities in the household were fairly minimal. The vast majority of chores were done by his elder sister, Jalila, whose responsibilities at home increased as her mother's pregnancy progressed. Jalila was also in charge of most of the translation needs of the family, whether in institutional settings or for the letters and documents sent to the house. Once I became a regular visitor to their household, however, Karim's mother started saving these official documents for me to read and translate when I visited their home. Karim was rarely involved, any translation tasks. As their mother explained to me, this was not only because Jalila was older, but mainly because Jalila's command of Spanish was much better than Karim's. In fact, when Jalila was not available, Karim's mother often called on neighborhood children to accompany her to the clinic.[4]

At the Spanish public school, Karim was not mainstreamed and was withdrawn from his regular class every day for a certain amount of time to attend Spanish Literacy and Math Enhancement classes. Academically, he was not doing well, and his teachers were concerned about his lack of progress. The only subject that he genuinely seemed to enjoy was Plastic Arts. Often, Karim did not do his homework, and his assignments were messy and in disarray. Even though he was a friendly and sweet boy, he often got in trouble with his teachers due to what was discussed as his lack of attention and erratic behavior in the classroom. The Arabic Heritage Language teacher, in particular, did not have a lot of patience with him because of Karim's goofy and frequent disruptions during the Arabic class, a subject with which he was also struggling. He was not diligent in attending Qur'anic classes at the local oratory either, often skipping them. In addition, although he was not an overtly aggressive boy, he did seem to end up in the middle of many schoolyard altercations with other boys. This certainly did not improve his standing with teachers and led to him being frequently grounded. He would sometimes complain that other boys provoked him or blamed him unfairly. Whether this was true or not, it is hard to know. In my observations, however, I noticed that, while he certainly did not have many close friends in or out of school and that other children often treated him badly, at the same time, Karim frequently exhibited poor judgment negotiating conflict with his peers. Many of the squabbles he was involved in occurred during soccer games, a sport that Karim loved to watch and play. In fact, it was common to see him playing soccer with different groups of children both during recess and around town during the afternoon. When he was not playing soccer, he would often be riding his bicycle alone throughout the town.

4.1.5   Mimon: The Computer-game Wiz

Although Mimon was born in Taurirt, and that was the area of Morocco where most of his relatives were from, Mimon's family is an excellent example of the geographical dynamism of the Moroccan immigrant diaspora, and of how Moroccan immigrant family networks often spanned several countries. Both his grandparents had initially immigrated to France. Mimon's father, for example, was born in France and lived there for 21 years before returning temporarily to Morocco, where he married Mimon's mother. Mimon's father later decided to migrate to Spain, where the rest of the family joined him when Mimon was approximately three years old. Indeed, Mimon had few relatives left in Morocco. Most of his extended family either lived in other areas of Spain or in France. Mimon's family often went to Paris on vacation to visit his paternal uncles and cousins, of whom Mimon would often speak fondly and with obvious affection. Mimon had two elder sisters in their early twenties. His father had a permanent job working at a tobacco-processing factory and was also involved in business with some of his relatives who owned stores elsewhere. Mimon's mother and his sisters did not work and stayed at home. In fact, they rarely left the household, except to visit close friends, to go to the weekly outdoor market, where I would often run into them, and in joint family outings to nearby cities where other family members lived. Mimon's family lived in a semi-detached two-storey townhouse in the newer area of Vallenuevo, where most of the buildings were of recent construction. While I was never able to ascertain whether they rented or owned the house, what I do know is that not very many Moroccan immigrant families in Vallenuevo could afford to live in this area of town.

Mimon was completely mainstreamed at the public school, and did well academically. His teachers all thought that he was very intelligent, although they believed that he did not work hard enough. Consequently, his grades were lower than what his teachers believed he could achieve. Sometimes the teachers became frustrated with him, when they thought he was selling himself short, and encouraged him to perform better. Nevertheless, he was well-liked by his teachers, perhaps because he was very participative and amiable in class and would often raise his hand enthusiastically when his teachers asked for volunteers. Like Wafiya, he assiduously attended Qur'anic classes at the local oratory where he was one of the star students. Certainly, his knowledge of the Qur'an was superior to that of any of the other children. When asked to by the *fqih*, Mimon always recited with confidence and very rarely had to be corrected. Although his family was no more outwardly observant of Islamic religious practices than other families that I got to know, they had spent a lot of time on their children's religious education. Mimon's father told me that, since Mimon was very little, he had sat with him every day to teach him how to pray and to recite Qur'anic suras. In fact, Mimon had already memorized significant parts of the Qur'an. Not surprisingly, towards the end of the study, Bilal told him that he should stop attending the classes for younger children and attend instead the Qur'anic class he ran for adolescent boys. He also excelled in the Arabic Heritage Language classes at the public school. His performance in Rashid's class was only surpassed, and not often, by Sarah's. This was indeed quite an accomplishment, since, unlike Sarah, Mimon had not received formal education in Modern Standard Arabic in Morocco, having left Morocco when he was just a toddler. Rashid, the Arabic teacher, often held Mimon as an example for the rest of children in his fourth-grade class, particularly for Karim, who struggled the most. Arabic Language, along with Social Studies and English were Mimon's favorite school subjects. In addition to Arabic, Mimon's second passion was the computer and computer games. He had real expertise with computers and knowledge of the Internet. He loved it when teachers would take the class to the computer room to finish an assignment, or when they would let them all play as a reward for the last few minutes of class. During these times, rather than play the often repetitive educational games already installed on the computers, he would ask permission to access game websites instead. And he definitely knew what the most popular and fun web-based games were. He would often tell me about the games he liked to play with his cousins or about the latest game he had challenged himself to finish. Unlike most Moroccan immigrant children in Vallenuevo, Mimon rarely spent any time playing on the street; he preferred to stay home playing with his computer, either alone or with friends who were invited to the house.

4.1.6   Kamal: The Athlete

Even though his mother was from the Marrakesh area, Kamal was born in Oujda. He came to Spain with his mother when he was approximately six years old. Like Karim, he had also attended school in Morocco for a little over a year. What he remembered most about his early childhood in Morocco was playing with his classmates. He still maintained some of these friendships and played with some of the same boys when he visited Morocco in the summer. Kamal's was the smallest household of all of the focal children. He had an elder brother, Hussein, in high school, and a younger brother, Hisham, in first grade, who was born in Spain. His parents had also had a daughter who had been born years before Kamal, but who died of a liver disorder in infancy. Kamal's mother was divorced, and his father lived in Morocco, where he had remarried. The three children would see their father once a year, usually when they visited Morocco. One time during the study in the summer of 2007, however, the father came to visit and spent a couple of months in Vallenuevo with the children. Kamal's mother had regularly worked in the fields as a seasonal farm worker, but when she was not working on the land and for most of the time I was in Vallenuevo, she was a part-time cleaning lady for one of the Moroccan-run *locutorios* in town and had other hourly cleaning jobs she was called to do here and there. These jobs and a small subsidy from the town social services allowed her and her children to move from the run-down business space where the family lived at the beginning of the study to a larger apartment on the third floor of a building on the main street of the town. Once they moved to this apartment, Kamal's maternal uncle also came to live with the household, and acted like a father figure for the children. Towards the final months of my stay, however, he decided to move to a bigger city to look for better job prospects. He had been trained as a journalist in Morocco but was having a lot of trouble finding a job in Spain that did not involve manual labor.

Kamal's older brother, Hussein, was only home on the weekends; during the week, he stayed at the boarding facility of his high school in a nearby town. Kamal, however, was able to see Hussein on Tuesdays and Thursdays when both brothers went to track-and-field practice at the sports complex in the larger town where Hussein attended high school. On the weekends, and beyond the sports competitions in which they both participated, the brothers liked to hang out together at home watching TV or playing with a used Playstation they had been given. Kamal and his elder brother often helped their mother with household responsibilities. Kamal was most involved in household chores, since, unlike Hussein, he was at home every day. He routinely helped to set the table and wash the dishes after meals, as well as take out the trash. Sometimes he also folded clothes and performed heavier tasks, such as cleaning the windows at the apartment. While Kamal was more involved in household work than the other boys I observed, it was still less than what focal girls performed. For instance, unlike Sarah and Worda, Kamal was rarely left in charge of his younger brother, Hisham. Instead, his mother would instruct Kamal to take Hisham to an older cousin who also lived in Vallenuevo. Also, although both Kamal and, particularly his brother Hussein, had sometimes translated for their mother in previous years when their mother was still learning Spanish, it was no longer a large part of what they did. This was partly because, even when Kamal's mother's command of Spanish was lower, she always liked to find other adults who were able to help her with her translation needs. During the time I was in Vallenuevo, for example, and even though her communicative Spanish was quite good, Kamal's mother would ask me to accompany her to social service offices, and go with her to several parent-teacher planning meetings in Hisham's classroom because she wanted to get more involved in school projects, such as helping with the children's costumes for the Carnival jamboree. Throughout the study, Kamal's mother would also ask me to translate the letters sent to the household for her. In addition to his mother's preference for finding adults to help, I know that Kamal did not like having to translate for adults very much. He would say that there were many words in Moroccan Arabic he did not know. So, he tried to dodge that bullet whenever he could.

Kamal was not only the eldest child in the study, but also the only one who was not in fourth grade; he attended sixth grade at the same public school as the other focal children. He was mostly mainstreamed, but still had to attend the *support class* for a few hours a week for Spanish Literacy Enhancement, since he still struggled with language arts in particular. In spite of this, he did well academically. His favorite subjects were Music, Plastic Arts, and Physical Education. His teachers thought he was very intelligent and spoke highly of him. In addition, he rarely got into trouble. Kamal, too, liked the school staff and most of his teachers, with whom I would often see him joking. Kamal was social, charismatic, and had many friends in and out of school. He was a gifted athlete and devoted to his track-and-field training. Every afternoon at 4:30 p.m., he would attend practice religiously; he would train three times a week in Vallenuevo, and twice a week in a nearby town. He had a special bond with Félix, the main track-and-field coach, whom he respected immensely. Kamal did not attend after-school classes in the mosque-oratory, preferring instead an active sports training schedule. His mother was not very religious either, even though the family followed some Islamic religious traditions, such as eating always *halal* meat and celebrating special festivals. Moreover, towards the end of the study, Kamal's mother started to consider converting to Christianity, when she was befriended by a young Dutch-Moroccan missionary couple who had settled in Vallenuevo, hoping to start an Evangelical Christian community.

These six children provided the main windows through which I learned about Moroccan immigrant childhoods in Vallenuevo. There was another group of children who also inform this study in important ways, however, even though I observed them less systematically and knew them less intimately. These were Moroccan immigrant children who either attended the same fourth-grade class as most of the focal children, were active participants of the track-and-field club, translated at the health center, or were neighborhood friends of the focal children. My observations of them collectively gave me a better sense of the contours of children's lives in this rural community. Out of this larger group of children, there are a few that I would like to highlight here whose names also appear throughout the book. Miriam, Jalal, and Yimad were classmates of most of the focal children. Miriam came new to the school after winter break when her parents moved to Vallenuevo from another region of Spain. Although Miriam was new to the school, she had been living in Spain since she was a toddler, and was at greater ease with her new surroundings than Sarah. For instance, Miriam was not deemed to be in need of the *compensatory education program* and, like Mimon and Worda, was academically mainstreamed. Jalal and Yimad, however, attended the daily *support class* with Karim, Wafiya, and Sarah. Yimad had been in Spain for three years, and he was a fairly quiet child who usually kept to himself. Most of the time, he would hang out with his two brothers, one slightly older and the other one younger than he was, but he also loved playing soccer with other children. Jalal, who had been in Spain for six years, was a very small child, with a real passion and gift for drawing. He usually kept a small notebook with his drawings under his schoolbooks, and he liked to work on them in class when his teachers were not looking. Jalal was fairly introverted; once in a while, however, he would come out and join Kamal's extended network of neighborhood friends, particularly if they were playing games of skill and aim, such as marbles, at which he was excellent. Jalal's elder sister, Malika, was known for being a very good dancer and she was usually asked to perform at school festivals. Malika was in the same sixth-grade class as Manal, Worda's best friend.

Beyond her prominence in Worda and Wafiya's network of friends, Manal became one of the most insightful participants in the longitudinal interviews that I conducted. Manal was academically mainstreamed and doing well in school, even though she struggled a little with Math and English. Manal disliked household work and was more than happy to leave those tasks up to her two elder sisters, while she used the time to do her homework or to play with her dolls. Wafiya and Worda, particularly the latter, jokingly chided her for what they saw as a little bit of laziness and irresponsibility on Manal's part. What Manal enjoyed doing and was very good at, however, was translating for Moroccan adults in Vallenuevo. In spite of being the youngest, she did most of the interpreting in her household and beyond, since neighbors and acquaintances of her parents often came looking for her help. In addition to Manal, Sarah, and Worda's sisters Salma and Dunia, there were a number of other girls who were part-time members of this peer group, participating on and off in different games and activities. Among the most important was Houriya, age 11, who was a member of the local track-and-field team and trained with Worda and Wafiya; Lamia, age eight, Worda's next-door neighbor; and Leila, age eight, a distant relative of Wafiya's family who also attended the track-and-field training sessions from time to time.

Finally, it is also important to mention Abdelkarim and his siblings. Abdelkarim was also an articulate participant in the longitudinal interview series and someone whom I got to know during my many visits to his household. Abdelkarim's father, Mustafa, worked for a national union and often acted as an informal liaison officer between many members of the Moroccan immigrant community and different social services in Vallenuevo. Mustafa's eldest son, Abdelkarim, was a bright fifth grader, and like Manal, had a knack for translation. He not only took care of his mother's interpretation needs when Mustafa could not accompany her, but neighbors and acquaintances of his parents' also sought him out. Abdelkarim had twin siblings, Fouziya and Khalid, who were in third grade. All three children were academically mainstreamed and doing well in school. The family also had a fourth, three-year-old son, Abdelgani, of whom his siblings would say "cuando sea mayor va a ser más español que nosotros porque ha nacido aquí" **(When he grows up, he is going to be more Spanish than us because he was born here)**.

4.2   The Contexts of Children's Lives

If in the previous section, I have given a sense of children as individuals, to complete the landscape of Moroccan immigrant childhoods in Vallenuevo, I turn now to how different sociocultural domains shape, and are shaped by, these childhoods. Following De Certeau in his *Practice of Everyday Life*, I highlight the polyvalent character of these contexts and discuss them as both *places* (the objective configuration of elements) and *spaces* (as lived in and *practiced* by the children). Thus, I sketch the basic organizational features of these contexts, as well as how the children understand and talk about them. In tracing how Moroccan immigrant children navigate boundaries across these contexts, and in keeping with Thorne's quote, which encourages us to capture *patterns of time and space*, I aim to offer a *tour* (in De Certeau's sense, 1984) of Moroccan immigrant children's everyday lives, as a narration of children's movement through the unfolding of what could be considered a typical day in their lives. In narrating how Moroccan immigrant children move and often *bridge* the boundaries of cultural domains of experience, I pay particular attention to the *itineraries* that produce the sociocultural, linguistic, and communicative practices that will be the focus of subsequent chapters.

4.2.1   School Contexts

Like many places in the world today, children in Vallenuevo spend the majority of their waking hours either in school or preparing for school. In the public elementary school that the children attended, classes were held from 9:00 a.m. to 2:00 p.m.. These were followed by a lunch period from 2:00 to 3:00 p.m. that was attended either by children who qualified for government-sponsored free lunches or by children whose families decided to pay for this service, usually due to parental work schedules. Out of the focal children, only Kamal and Wafiya qualified for free lunches and stayed in school after class. They both told me that they enjoyed their lunches at school very much because, unlike many other schools in the area, this school offered *halal* menu choices to accommodate Muslim dietary constraints. Other families I knew, such as Sarah's, had also applied for this service, and her parents were hoping that she would qualify for these free lunches the following year.

The public elementary school in Vallenuevo had received a great deal of attention since the mid-1990s. At this time the immigrant population in the school soared due to processes of family reunification among the mostly male immigrants who arrived in the town in the early 1990s. The numbers of Moroccan immigrant children in the school continued to increase in the following years, and in the 2005–2006 academic year, 251 children out of a total of 678 students were immigrant children of Moroccan descent. This amounts to 37% of the student body of the school, one of the largest percentages not only in the southwestern region where Vallenuevo is located, but also in the whole country. The large number of Moroccan immigrant children that the school served gave this institution a very special character and positioned it uniquely in the midst of regional debates about immigration and schooling. Even the most unwitting visitor to the school could readily notice not only this special character, but also how aware the school's administrators were of the school's unique positioning. The first thing that welcomed visitors into the school was an immense panel that featured newspaper clippings, pictures of awards ceremonies, interviews, and mementos of other events publicizing the school's involvement in migrant education. A map of Morocco hung prominently on the wall of the entrance hall to the administrative offices and was surrounded by several national symbols of both Spain and Morocco. Similarly, the walls of the classrooms on the ground floor that were adjacent to the administrative facilities were decorated with a collage of statistics and charts about the school's diverse population and levels of educational attainment. There were also memorabilia of students' participation in a variety of intercultural events. The door signs of the different school facilities, even those of the administrative personnel, appeared in both Spanish and Arabic.

Precisely because of the large numbers of Moroccan immigrant children, the school launched a major revision of its curricular programs in 2000, standardizing and systematizing the practices that they had been developing and implementing since approximately 1994, when the number of Moroccan immigrant students increased greatly.[5] Table 4.3 reproduces an abridged version of the preamble to the revised curriculum of the school. As Table 4.3 illustrates, the issue of the "new diversity" of the school takes central stage, reverberating in most curricular objectives and principles. Thus, the main tenets of the school curriculum centered around creating a strong sense of community and a spirit of tolerance and respect for the cultural and linguistic heterogeneity of the student body. In practice, these goals translated into four main actions that were gradually executed in the subsequent years: (1) the implementation of a *compensatory* education program that emphasized Math and Spanish Literacy skills for immigrant children who were academically *behind* and/or whose Spanish language academic skills were not at an acceptable level;[6] (2) a Performing Arts program funded with a grant from a private foundation to promote cooperation among students;[7] (3) an Arabic Heritage Language Program for Moroccan immigrant children during the school day funded jointly by the Spanish and Moroccan Ministries of Education; and (4) the annual implementation of

Table 4.3 Curricular objectives and principles.

Objetivos Curriculares (Curricular Objectives)	Principios Curriculares (Curricular Principles)
Mejorar las relaciones interpersonales en el Centro.	La formación en el respeto a los derechos y libertades fundamentales y en el ejercicio de la tolerancia y la libertad dentro de los principios democráticos y de convivencia.
(Improve interpersonal relations in the school.)	(Educate (children) to respect fundamental rights and freedoms and to exercise tolerance and freedom within democratic principles of coexistence.)
Respetar las diferencias de cualquier índole.	La formación en el respeto de la pluralidad cultural y lingüística de España.
(Respect differences of any kind.)	(Educate (children) to respect the cultural and linguistic plurality of Spain.)
Crear un clima de trabajo y respeto adecuado en el aula.	La formación para la paz, la cooperación y la solidaridad entre los pueblos.
(Create an adequate working environment of respect in the classroom.)	(Educate (children) for peace, cooperation, and solidarity among peoples.)
Fomentar en todas las actuaciones que se den en el Centro, un espíritu comunitario y de solidaridad.	
(Promote a spirit of community and solidarity in all activities undertaken in school.)	

schoolwide activities, such as the celebration of Interculturality Day or the International Day of Peace, that were designed to advocate the core curricular principles of tolerance and respect.

The school also instituted a set of core civic values – such as dialogue, friendship, and cooperation – intended to regulate the academic and social life of the school. These were enacted through schoolwide activities and through classroom practice. The values were prominently displayed on walls, classrooms, and public areas of the school. Special schoolwide celebrations were also taken as opportunities not only to uphold the official values that the school tried to promote among the student body, but also to celebrate the school's diversity. These celebrations ranged from traditional Spanish national holidays and festivities, such as Carnival, Christmas, or the End-of-Year-Festival, to more specific events, such as Interculturality Day, or the International Day of Human Rights or of Peace. Although these celebrations were very different in nature, a common thread running through the way in which diversity was incorporated in these events was the essentialization of superficial and folkloristic manifestations of Moroccan traditions. Thus, these schoolwide activities could also unwittingly identify Moroccan immigrant children as culturally different, exotic, and alien. In these festivities, cultural differences, rather than similarities or common historical and artistic legacies, were emphasized. Moreover, a reified and static notion of *culture* was understood to be a property only of those students different from the majority group: a property of Moroccan immigrant children and other minorities in the school, such as Roma children. Thus, Moroccan children's ethnic identities become associated with difference and social markedness.

Interculturality Day, for instance, is a prime example of how *culture* was usually regarded to be embodied in the *Other*. In spite of the prefix *inter* (in *Inter*culturality Day), the activities performed during this celebration were fairly one-sided, consisting of demonstrations of henna body decoration, sampling of traditional Moroccan dishes, or watching a video about Morocco among others.[8] These forms of multicultural education have been amply criticized precisely because they perpetuate ethnic stereotypes and further mark Moroccan immigrant children's identities as the *Other*.[9] Elsewhere, I have also discussed more fully the larger implications of some of the negative unintended consequences that these forms of inter/multiculturalism, as realized in actual classroom practice, could have on Moroccan immigrant children's sense of *cultural citizenship* (Ong 1996; Rosaldo 1994). I have also argued that these unintended consequences may be difficult to avoid, even by the most thoughtful and well-intentioned educators, insofar as most schools in Spain still work within a hegemonic ideological field of *homogenism* (Blommaert and Verschueren 1998), or the belief that a homogenous society is the norm, and diversity is a *problem* to be overcome (see García-Sánchez 2013).

Nevertheless, it is important to point out that some of the school programs and pedagogical practices did have a positive impact in terms of the community values of respect and tolerance that the school curriculum advocated. The Physical Education Program of the school, for instance, as well as the Performance Arts Program funded by the Yehudi Menuhin

Foundation, emphasized cooperation and interdependence among students to achieve a common goal.[10] Instead of the usual focus on competition that often characterizes sports and artistic endeavors, the activities in these classes were designed to maximize team effort, trust, synchronicity, and physical contact among students of different ethnic backgrounds. The beneficial impact of these programs could also be seen in the strong average scores of Moroccan immigrant children's performance in areas like Language Arts and Math. According to the school's own statistics, amply displayed in information bulletins on the wall, Moroccan immigrant children's academic achievement at the school was higher than regional and national averages. Equally as important, however, was the constructive impact of these policies of inclusion in Moroccan's immigrant children's overall positive attitude towards the school and most of its teachers. While sometimes they would tell me about small grievances, they mostly spoke highly of their teachers, with a few exceptions, and often admitted to me when they had done something to warrant a teacher's reprimand.

In spite of these programs and of the children's general positive attitude towards school, they also felt that they were not completely accepted by many of their Spanish peers. They complained about how they often felt that they were being treated differently, and sometimes outrightly mistreated, particularly when the teachers were not looking. Manal perhaps put this sentiment in words more strongly than other children when she once told me:

Mira, delante de los maestros son ángeles y detrás de los maestros son diablos (.) a ver- que se portan con nosotros bien cuándo estamos con el maestro o algo y al fin- y al final- cuándo se va el maestro o algo están hablando de nosotros y todo. Hablan de nosotros mal. Dicen que somos sucios y todo y yo me ducho siempre por la noche.

Look, in front of the teachers they are angels and behind the teachers they are devils (.) let's see- they do behave well with us when we are with the teacher or something and at the end- and at the end- when the teacher leaves or something, they are talking about us and everything. They talk about us badly. They say we're dirty and everything, and I always take a shower at night.

Children reported that the mistreatment often took the form of ethnic slurs, and among these, all focal children reported situations in which they were called *moro/mora*. In addition, focal children who had a darker complexion, such as Kamal, also reported receiving other insults of an obvious racialized nature, the most frequent being *negro* (black) and *mono* (monkey). Many of them also complained about being beleaguered by their Spanish peers when they were overheard speaking Moroccan Arabic at school, or in Wafiya's words "Nos dicen por qué hablais en marroquí, hablad es español que esto es España y no Marruecos" **(They ask us why do you speak in Moroccan. Speak Spanish that this is Spain and not Morocco)**. Classmates' language ideologies contrasted with those of most teachers and school staff. The use of Moroccan Arabic at school, although not necessarily encouraged unless the teacher needed one Moroccan child to act as translator on behalf of another, was for the most part tolerated. I never witnessed or heard of a Moroccan child being reprimanded by the teachers for speaking Moroccan Arabic at school. The exception to this were the teachers in the Spanish Literacy Enhancement classes, who had a Spanish-only (or at least Spanish-as-much-as-possible) policy in these classes to support and accelerate Moroccan children's Spanish language development.

Moroccan immigrant children's narratives of ethnic bullying at school during interviews coincided with one of my earliest observations that was quite disturbing to me: that name-calling and other overt exclusion sometimes occurred when teachers and other school professionals were absent, and when Spanish children were not cognizant that I or other adults at the school were observing them. While the interactional architecture of the everyday forms of racialized exclusion I observed at school will be the focus of the next chapter, the resonance of children's stories helped me understand the deep emotional impact of these daily occurrences. Hearing children's accounts of these episodes was also a powerful experience to realize just how conscious they were, even at their relatively early age, of their own racialization and of the politically-charged nature of appellatives, such as the chronotopic figure *moro*. The following interview fragment, in which Worda, Wafiya, Sarah, and I were participating, reveals Moroccan immigrant children's perspectives on *negative recognition* and their experience of *difference* and lack of *commonality of belonging*. Prior to this excerpt, we had been discussing a recent school trip to the Madrid zoo. The girls were telling me about it, what they had done, and what they had liked most about it.

1. INMA: Y:: hay algo de la excursión que nos
os gustó[11]
**And is there something about the trip
that you didn't like**

```
        o que os sorprendió o-?=
        or that surprised you or-?
2.  WAFIYA:  =Sí:: en- en el autobús y en clase
        lo de- que no nos
        =Yes on- on the bus and in class
        that- that we do not
        sentábamos con los ma- con los
        españoles y tal y tal
        sit with Mo- with Spanish (children)
        and so on
3.  SARAH:  Y tal y tal= ((laughing))
        And so on= ((laughing))
4.  INMA:  =Y tal y tal. A ver. ¿Qué pasa [con
        eso?
        =And so on. Let's see. What's going
        on [with that?
(.  .  .)
5.  WAFIYA:                     [Pero ellos-
                               [But they
        pero ellos que no queriban que
        sentados con nosotros=
        but they (it's them) that did not
        want to sit with us=
        =porque dicen que somos sucios
        y-y-y- moros=
        =because they say that we are dirty
        and-and-and "moros"=
        =y- y asina=
        =and- and like that=
6.  WORDA:  =Y no les gusta el pan que nosotros
        comemos.
        =And they do not like the bread we
        eat.
7.  INMA:  A ver ¿c que- ¿cómo es eso que dicen
        que sois sucios
        Let's see how that- how is that they
        say that you are dirty
        (.) ¿Qué es eso?
        =dirty? (.) What's that?
8.  WAFIYA:  Pos Karim el otro día- no sé qué día ha-
        So Karim the other day- I do not
        know what day has-
        ha vení sucio.
        has come dirty.
9.  INMA:  Sí.
        Yes.
```

10. WAFIYA: ¿Karim- Karim Mezyan? (.) y-y-y-y- y
              ellos creíban=
              Karim- Karim Mezyan? (.) and-and-and-
              and and they thought=
              =que som to- todos los marroquines.
              =that we'r- al- all the Moroccans.

11. INMA: Sí.
             Yes.

12. WAFIYA: Y-y lo han creído eso y estaban todos
             [(xxx)
             And-and they have believed that and
             they were all [(xxx)

13. SARAH: [Y otro día=
                                     [And other day=
             =me dice Mónica **VENGA, VENGA** ducha.
             =Monica says to me COME ON, COME ON,
             take a shower.

14. INMA: ¿Mónica te dice eso a ti?
             Monica says that to you?

15. SARAH: ((nodding)) ¿Un día estaba donde el
             Hanut?
             ((nodding)) One day I was where the
             shop?

16. INMA: La tienda, sí.
             The shop yes.

17. SARAH: Sí y-y::: estaba jugando y me ha
             dicho mi madre ve a
             Yes and-and I was playing and my
             mother says to me go=
             =comprar una cosa? y me ha dicho
             VENGA Sarah,=
             =buy something? and she has said to
             me COME ON, Sarah=
             =venga, ducha.
             =come on, take a shower.

18. INMA: ¿Pero quién te ha dicho eso?
             But who has said that to you?

19. SARAH: Mónica.
             Monica.

20. INMA: ¿En la tienda?
             In the shop?

21. SARAH: ((nodding)) Sí, donde la tienda.
             ((nodding)) Yes, where the shop.

Children's reflections in interviews emphasize their awareness of the exclusion, negative social markedness, and routine problematization to which they

and Moroccan immigrant communities are subjected. An aspect that I find compelling is Wafiya's grasp of how categorization and stereotyping of ethnoracial groups often work, as illustrated in her story of how an individual instance of one Moroccan child coming to school dirty is generalized to the rest of Moroccan children (lines 8 through 12). It is also important to note that there are disturbingly resonant interdiscursive links between the discrimination experiences narrated by the children in the previous interview regarding their supposed dirtiness (Wafiya and Sarah's stories), or locals' dislike of their traditional foods (Worda, line 6), with, for instance, my Spanish neighbor's refusal to buy meat in Moroccan-owned stores because "it disgusted her." This reverberates with the way Moroccans are presented as "dirty" in the shared racialized imaginary of many Spanish people as discussed in Chapter 2.

I sometimes suspected that this ongoing feeling of not being completely accepted might have had something to do with Moroccan immigrant children's lack of participation in the after-school program, or *Programa de Actividades Extra-escolares*. I never received, however, direct confirmation of this in the interviews. While the school closed briefly at 3:00 p.m. immediately after lunch, it reopened every day for several hours in the afternoon with a quite ambitious after-school program of academic support and enrichment. *El Programa de Actividades Extra-escolares* consisted of homework tutoring supplemented by study-skills sessions. They also undertook craft projects, and a dance group had been formed where children learned and rehearsed traditional dances from the region. Carlos, the principal, was very worried about Moroccan immigrant children's lack of interest in a program that he considered would be extremely beneficial for their academic development and socialization. Indeed, of all the Moroccan children I met during the study only Mustafa's children, Abdelkarim and his twin siblings, attended the after-school program. These children also confirmed for me that they were among only a handful of Moroccan children who had signed up for it.

During the hours of the after-school program, the focal children and many other children I knew, went either to track-and-field practice, to Qur'anic classes at the oratory-mosque, or were engaged in other forms of work and play either at home or in the neighborhood. The school's staff main contention was that Moroccan children did not come to *extra-escolares* because the Qur'anic classes at the oratory-mosque from 5:00 to 6:00 p.m. fell right in the middle of the after-school program schedule. This issue had indeed been a source of tension for quite some time between school staff and representatives of Assalam the local Islamic cultural association that ran the oratory. The school staff wanted these Qur'anic classes to be offered either later in the evening, or only during the weekends. Neither of these options was acceptable to the representatives of Assalam who saw these classes as critical in safeguarding Moroccan children's religious and linguistic heritages, and who thought that, as it was, children did not get nearly enough of them. While their role as the guardians of Moroccan cultural heritage was largely self-appointed, a significant number of Moroccan families had ratified their legitimacy by sending their children to these classes. There were indeed many children who regularly attended with alacrity, such as Mimon and Wafiya. School staff's counter-arguments, that during the week, Moroccan children already attended Arabic Heritage Language classes at school with Rashid, did not take them very far in solving the scheduling conflict. The reason for this was that, as I explore in Chapter 6, most people involved in Assalam did not believe that the school Arabic program went far enough in the cultivation of religious and cultural values in relation to the Arabic language.

4.2.2   Family Contexts

Except for Kamal and Wafiya, most focal children went home for lunch when the regular school day was finished at 2:00 p.m. Family meals were ethnographically interesting because, particularly during the seasons other than harvest, these were moments when the extended family unit usually came together, and when there was a high degree of interaction between parents and children, as well as between siblings, and other relatives. Other moments that involved extensive family interaction included times when female neighbors and friends visited each other, especially in the afternoons, or when the family was relaxing watching television together in the evenings. During afternoon visits, the hostesses offered tea and refreshments to the visiting party, and then the entire group would sit around the table to talk about personal problems or pass on gossip that had been circulating around the town. It was a common practice for mothers to instruct their children to assist in setting up these afternoon refreshments, and to help welcome family friends and visitors appropriately. Most importantly, children were almost always present for these afternoon teas. Children's direct participation was not encouraged, and they were sometimes reprimanded for "interfering" in adult affairs when they volunteered comments, particularly if these comments were somewhat sassy and suggested that children were acting what parents thought to be beyond their age. Nonetheless, the children were welcome to join in the afternoon meal, and they would observe and listen attentively to everything the adults said.

An aspect of family interactions that I did not expect when I first started hanging out in children's homes was how much Spanish was spoken in the households. Perhaps my initial mindset was influenced too much by the traditional academic framework that dichotomizes immigrant children's heritage languages (Moroccan Arabic and Amazighe[12]) as *home languages*, and target-country language (Spanish) as *school language*. While this dichotomy might have some analytic validity, it does not reflect the sociolinguistic matrix of Moroccan immigrant children in Vallenuevo. Children sometimes used Moroccan Arabic at school in their dealings with other Moroccan classmates. At homes, while Moroccan Arabic was often used with parents and other adult relatives and neighbors, Spanish was prevalent in interactions among siblings. Various degrees of codeswitching between Spanish and Moroccan Arabic was often the communicative code of choice in many households, and not just between siblings, but also between parents and children. Also, because of the multilingual character of Moroccan communities, other languages could often be heard in the household, such as French, particularly in the homes of Mimon and Abdelkarim. On some occasions, children would also try to use their limited knowledge of Amazighe to communicate with elderly relatives, such as Worda with her grandmother. Most children expressed an affinity for both Moroccan Arabic and Spanish, and enjoyed being able to speak both. A few of them, such as Abdelkarim and jois siblings, decidedly said that they preferred to speak Spanish "porque tenemos más amigos españoles, hablamos más español" **(because we have more Spanish friends; we speak Spanish more)**. Even if they were proficient in Moroccan Arabic, sometimes children felt more comfortable speaking Spanish. For Kamal, for instance, literacy skills made the difference in his overall feeling of accomplishment in both languages. He felt more at ease in Spanish because there were some words he was unable to say in Moroccan Arabic and because "no sé leer ni escribir el árabe y el español, sí" **(I can neither read or write in Arabic, and in Spanish, I can)**.

In addition to interacting with their families, when they got home from school, Moroccan immigrant children also contributed significantly to the needs of their families by doing quite a bit of household work. In many homes of the Moroccan diaspora in Vallenuevo, children were expected to engage in a significant amount of daily chores from an early age, such as sibling care, running errands, cleaning, washing clothes, and cooking. It would be an oversimplification to explain children's work as a result of the economic constraints faced by many of these working-class immigrant families. Rather, it is important to understand how these practices are also linked to notions about children's appropriate sociocultural, moral, and civic development among the Moroccan diaspora.[13] In the focal households, as well as in many other Moroccan homes that I visited frequently, there was an ethos of generational interdependence and a strong expectation that children also had to contribute their share to the sustainability of the household. This strong ethos was visible, for example, in terms of task-initiation, with children regularly carrying out household chores without having to be told explicitly by parents. Furthermore, when I discussed these issues with the families, mothers emphasized that it was both necessary and important for children to learn how to do these chores. In fact, Moroccan parents in Vallenuevo would shame and reprimand children who resisted or complained about these chores, worrying that this refusal – perceived by parents as lack of respect and obedience – would lead to negative future outcomes for the child. Moroccan parents were concerned that children who resisted helping out with these tasks were not turning out "the right way." The belief that doing your share at home was related to both respect for one's parents and appropriate moral character, could also be seen in how girls like Worda and Wafiya often jokingly chided girls like Manal, who avoided housework as much as possible, for her supposed laziness and selfishness.

As some of the earlier portraits already suggest children's responsibilities were mostly organized according to two main factors, gender and age, with most of the household responsibilities falling progressively on the eldest female siblings, or on the eldest male in the absence of females.[14] In both interviews and lifemaps, girls in particular discussed at length what a major part of their daily lives household responsibilities were. In the following interview excerpt, Worda and Wafiya are telling me how they help at home:

1. WORDA: Algunas veces cuando está mi madre trabajando yo hago la comida
   Sometimes when my mother is working, I prepare the meal.

2. INMA: ¿Sí? Y qué haces?
   Yes? And what do you prepare?

3. WORDA: Mira e:::::h primero hacemos- cortamos cebolla, hacemos sal-=
   Look, a:::::h first we do- we chop onions, we put salt-=
   =hacemos s- hacemos sal un poco de aceite y: carne
   =we put s- we put salt- a little bit of oil a:nd meat

4. INMA: Sí
   Yes

[. . .]

5. WORDA: Hacemos unos pimientos-
   We put a few peppers-

[. . .]

6. WORDA: Y luego tiramos- cortamos las patatas=
    **And then we throw- we cut the
    potatoes=**
    =los tiramos ahí. Echamos agua=
    **=We throw them there. We pour on
    water**
7. WAFIYA: Y otra vez sal
    And salt again
8. WORDA: Sí- otra vez sal. Y luego hacemos el
    pan
    **Yes- salt again. And then we make
    bread**
9. INMA: ↑Ah también ¿sabes hacer <u>pan</u>?
    ↑Oh You also know how to make <u>bread</u>?
10. WORDA: No(.)pero algunos dí- algunas veces me
    dice mi madre=
    **No (.) but some day- sometimes my
    mother tells me=**
    =que vengas a hacer
    =to come over and do ((Puts one hand
    on top of the other and starts making
    kneading motion with her hands))

This lengthy extract from an interview, in which Worda and Wafiya list the dishes they cook either by themselves or with their elder sisters, continues with a description of the most effective ways to wash clothes by hand to minimize creases and to make sure that the stains come off. The way in which both girls co-construct the narratives of how they perform household chores (see line 7) is an indication of their familiarity with the tasks. Another interesting aspect that the interview makes relevant is how parents gradually introduce their children to these chores by breaking their participation in manageable tasks. For instance, although Worda does not know how to make a loaf of bread by herself yet, she is already involved in the process of bread-making in her household.

A distinctive responsibility that many Moroccan immigrant children have in Vallenuevo is acting as language brokers for their parents and other Moroccan and Spanish adults in a variety of familial and institutional con-texts. The ways in which children acted contextually in these interactions will be the focus of Chapter 7. An important point to make here, however, is that, while translating for adults may be a responsibility particular to immigrant childhoods, it still needs to be understood in the ecological context of family life – that is, how sociocultural and generational-specific notions of childhood and of appropriate sociocultural development organize the distribution of rights, obligations, and responsibilities among family members. Elsewhere I have examined in depth language brokering in rela-tion to the range of responsibilities displayed by and expected of many Moroccan immigrant children in Vallenuevo (García-Sánchez 2010a). Given the organization of responsibilities that I have just discussed, translating work can be seen as an extension of the expectations of many Moroccan parents about children's appropriate contributions to the household. Children's involvement in language brokering on behalf of their families is congruent not only with conventional roles of children in homes of the Moroccan diaspora in Vallenuevo, but also with the collaborative ethos observed in the vast majority of the households.

In light of the many points of cultural continuity that language brokering shares with the family practices described above, it is not surprising that most Moroccan immigrant parents and children that I had the opportunity to talk to about this issue viewed and experienced language brokering as normal and appropriate. Rather than a reversal of family and generational hierarchy and power, Moroccan parents would complain if, after being asked, children refused to translate. Moroccan parents in this study interpreted these refusals as their children being inconsiderate and disobedient.[15] When considered in relation to the larger ecological context of family life and relationships, children's willingness to perform and provide help with trans-lation tasks when asked upholds, in many ways, community-specific notions of childhood and of appropriate development (or what being a "good," "moral," and "respectful" child means in many households of the Moroccan diaspora in Vallenuevo). For these reasons, and contrary to widespread popular beliefs,[16] it may also help maintain family structural arrangements and bonds of generational interdependency among Moroccan immigrant children and their parents. Children who often translated for their parents and other people and who admitted enjoying this task, like Abdelkarim, specifically mention that one of the main reasons they enjoyed doing it, was "sólo para ayudar en la casa" **(only to help at home)**. A similar feeling of self-satisfaction or self-accomplishment was also described by Manal, who like Abdelkarim was also recruited by many adults to help with this task. When I asked her once why she enjoying translating so much, she responded: "Siento como que estoy trabajando- como- como- a ver- siento como relajada" **(I feel like I am working- like- like- let's see- I feel like I am relaxed)**.

Children's work as translators had been even more widespread before I arrived in Vallenuevo. Parents, children, school staff, and many other community members confirmed that two or three years earlier, it was extremely common to see Moroccan immigrant children in the town hall, at the banks, and in the offices of different social services helping their families take care of official matters. Because the business hours of many of these establishments coincided with when the children were required to be in school, educational authorities in the town were concerned about what they perceived to be the habitual absenteeism of a high number of Moroccan students who performed these translation duties regularly. They strongly lobbied for the town hall and public social services to hire translators during school hours. Carlos, the public school principal noted that he did not necessarily mind children using their bilingual skills to help their families; it was the fact that they were doing so during school hours that was, in his view, a serious problem. Although it was still possible to witness occasionally Moroccan children translating for their families in some privately run businesses (i.e., banks), immigrant children's language brokering in the public sphere during school hours had been almost completely eradicated by the time I began conducting this study.

Nevertheless, Moroccan immigrant children continued to have a critical role as linguistic brokers and sociocultural mediators in their communities. In particular, I documented children translating in three different settings: first, in their homes, where they sometimes translated official paperwork and letters for their parents and neighbors; second, in the public school, where Moroccan children were often unofficially recruited by teachers to translate directions for newly-arrived Moroccan classmates, such as Sarah. At school, however, Moroccan immigrant children were never asked to act as translators in more formal situations, such as parent-teacher conferences.

The school had a policy that children could not be present during these interactions between parents and teachers. In contrast to the principal's earlier statement, school administrators felt that it was not appropriate for children to assume translation responsibilities. The Arabic language teacher and other community volunteers provided translation in these contexts. Finally, I was also able to record Moroccan immigrant children's role as translators at the local health center. The health center had a translator in the morning and early afternoon hours. The health center was also open during late afternoon and evening hours, however, and there was no staff translator during these times. Because children were not in school at these times of the day, parents (particularly, mothers) would continue to take their children with them in the afternoons to perform interpreting tasks in this setting.

Unlike other responsibilities where the division of labor by gender tends to be fairly distinct, language brokering responsibilities cross gender boundaries. As suggested in the portraits, families negotiated translation tasks based primarily of who was available, and who, among those, had the best language proficiency to carry out the tasks. Yet, consistent with the assignment of most household tasks to females, girls would often end up in charge of executing translation tasks in the actual occurrences that I was able to observe. Language brokering also had to be considered in relation to other needs in the family, such as childcare. This also influenced who ended up going to the doctor. This is the reason, for instance, why Worda had to be the translator for most of her own medical needs: "Alguien se tiene que quedar en la casa para cuidar de (.) mi hermana pequeña" **(Someone has to stay at home to take care of (.) my younger sister)**. Very often she was the one who stayed at home to take care of Dunia, while her elder sister Nada accompanied her mother. When Worda was in need of medical attention herself, Nada would have to stay home in charge of the rest of the siblings and Worda would go to the doctor with her mother: "Por ejemplo yo- yo me tengo que ir al médico a hacer una vacuna y- y yo- no puede ir conmigo nadie sólo mi madre y yo tradujo- traduzco porque- como sé español" **(For example, I- I have to go to the doctor to get a vaccination and- and I- no one can come with me, only my mother and I translate because- since I know Spanish)**. Another common pattern that I observed in these interactions was that children usually translated for mothers, and very rarely for fathers. In fact, when fathers were present during the medical visit, fathers usually took the initiative since, in general, they tended to have a better command of Spanish than mothers.

4.2.3   *Neighborhood Contexts*

In the afternoons, when children were not training, helping out their parents, or attending Qur'anic lessons, most of them could be found on the street, playing with friends. From an early age, many Moroccan immigrant children in Vallenuevo spent an average of three hours daily playing and interacting with school friends, neighborhood children, siblings and other children in their extended families, an amount that increased during holidays and school breaks. Most Moroccan parents I knew in Vallenuevo did not consider the household an appropriate domain for children to engage in ludic interactions and usually did not allow their children's friends into their homes. Home and street/park were clearly delineated spaces not only by physical boundaries, but also by the activities that routinely took place in them. The home was restricted for household and other adult-dominated activities, while children's games were seen as an interference[17] to those activities. This distinct delineation of space allowed Moroccan children to carry out their peer-group activities with little interference from adults.

With very few exceptions, peer groups were distinctly divided along ethnic and gender lines in this community. Moroccan girls played with Moroccan girls and Moroccan boys played with Moroccan boys; Spanish girls played with Spanish girls and Spanish boys with Spanish boys. Small boys were sometimes present in Moroccan female peer groups, like Sarah's younger brother Anuar, because, starting in middle-childhood, Moroccan girls were often assigned the responsibility of caring for younger siblings. If girls like Worda or Sarah went out to play with friends they brought their younger siblings with them. Young boys, like Anuar, rarely participated in the focal activities of the female peer group, remaining on the sidelines either as observers or engaging in their own forms of play.

Although similar gendered-segregated arrangements have been described in children's cultures and peer groups across a wide range of settings and speech communities (Goodwin 1990a; Thorne 1993/1995), what is striking about the organization of peer groups in this town is the pervasive lack of multiethnic children's groups in informal settings[18]. This absence of multiethnic playgroups can be seen as a reverberation of larger processes of racialized exclusion in this community, as well as an extension of the pervasive practices of negative social marking that Moroccan immigrant children are subjected to by their own Spanish peers at school.

Moroccan immigrant peer groups in Vallenuevo were usually composed of children of different ages who often possessed varying degrees of expertise and experience in Spanish and Moroccan cultures and languages. A peer group may include a child who had been born in Spain (e.g., Dunia), a child who had spent most of his/her childhood in Morocco and had just recently arrived in Spain (e.g., Sarah), and a child who came to Spain when s/he was just a toddler (e.g., Kamal, Wafiya, or Sarah). In other work (García-Sánchez 2010b), I have investigated how the intergenerational, mixed-expertise character of Moroccan immigrant children's peer groups can facilitate sociocultural learning in powerful ways, in that this mixed expertise allows for an original range of possible types of participation as experts and/or novices that blur the age distinctions usually associated with these roles. This characteristic, along with the minimal adult supervision of peer-group activities, also emphasizes the importance of the peer group as an autonomous arena for action in which immigrant children can act as agents of language socialization into communicative practices and sociocultural norms; an issue that I will also revisit in Chapter 8.

Moroccan immigrant children's peer groups were usually fluid in their composition. While membership of peer groups remained fairly stable throughout the study, there was also an ebb and flow of participants present at any given peer group interactions. Often different neighborhood children, cousins, or siblings would join in the play activities. The size of a peer group could range from three to eight children, and even sometimes more, although this was not very common. In the context of their peer groups, Moroccan immigrant children engaged in a wide variety of activities, such as pretend-play, marbles, soccer, hopscotch, jump-rope games, singing nursery rhymes and traditional and popular songs, clapping rhymes, tag and other chasing games. Children's discursive practices were also varied and included: word play, arguing, negotiating, reciting, gossiping, and explaining game rules. The prevailing feature of these activities is their hybrid nature. These activities are characterized by a high incidence of codeswitching between Spanish and Moroccan Arabic, particularly among girls who tended to codeswitch to a greater extent than boys.

Whether traced through portraits of individual children or through narrative *tours* of the everyday contexts of children's lives, the landscapes of Moroccan immigrant childhoods in Vallenuevo offer a glimpse of the sociocultural and linguistic complexities that these children have to traverse as they form social relationships across these spaces. The following chapters turn to the quotidian interactions that unfold in each of these contexts, and through which Moroccan immigrant children establish these relationships with others, as they negotiate difference and belonging. In trying to capture the daily communicative intricacies of these processes, particular attention will be paid to the constraints and affordances that children face in each of these contexts, as well as to how multiple categories of identity – ethnic, religious, national, gender, age, class – are claimed, marked, muted, legitimized, contested, or appropriated by either the children or other social actors that are part of the children's lives.

Notes

1 See e.g., Blos (1962); García Coll and Szalacha (2004); García Coll and Kerivan Marks (2009); Kroger (2004); Lerner (1993).

2 See, for instance, Franzé (1995); Gregorio Gil (1995).

3 Public education in Spain is mandatory up to age 16. This means that public high schools cannot turn away any student younger than 16 who wants to attend school. During my time in Vallenuevo, however, I heard several reports of older Moroccan immigrant students, who not having started their schooling in Spain until age 14 or 15, being expelled from the system once they turned 17 , even if they had not met graduation requirements.

4 Two of the interactional examples analyzed in Chapter 7 focuses on visits to the doctor involving Karim's mother, a neighborhood girl, and Rocío, the pediatrician, in an exchanges about Karim's newborn baby sister.

5 It was not uncommon, particularly around the early 2000s, for a small-town school like the one in Vallenuevo to undertake reforms to address changing social, linguistic, and demographic circumstances. How concerted these reform efforts were with other schools in the area, the province or the regional community really had to do with how many other schools were in similar circumstances. Sometimes, these efforts were coordinated at the provincial, and even at the regional, levels, and a large number of schools were involved. In some cases, however, like in the one being studied, the coordination level remained fairly local. There are two aspects of the Spanish context that made these small-scale reform efforts possible: one has to do with educational administration and the second with immigration policy. Administratively-speaking, education in Spain is quite decentralized, and mostly managed by the governments of each of the regional communities. The state only establishes the minimum number of hours that need to be devoted to each subject for each educational cycle, and it only interferes if the basic educational rights of citizens are being compromised. There are high levels of regional and local control when it comes to curriculum and instruction. These levels of local control are even higher when it comes to deciding extra-curricular activities and supplementary programs offered by schools. The variable levels of coordination between regional communities, and sometimes, even among different provinces within the same regional community, also has to do with Spanish migration's policies, which, at every level of government, can be characterized as being reactive rather than planned and designed. As a consequence, many of these types of reforms were undertaken in different places at different times, and depending on different variables related to immigrant settlement processes. Nevertheless, it is possible to find quite a few commonalities among reform efforts, such as a strong philosophical ethos of *interculturality* underlying the reforms, or the implementation of the supplementary Spanish literacy enhancement in the form of *programas de educación compensatoria* (compensatory education programs), *aulas de apoyo* (support classess), or *aulas de enlace* (bridge classes) among others.

6 In spite of the best efforts of the school professionals and administrators, often these pedagogical practices had unintended consequences that helped create and perpetuate the image of Moroccan immigrant children as the alien *Other*. For instance, the supplemenary Compensatory Education Program was designed to maximize Moroccan immigrant children's physical placement with their same-age Spanish peers and to gradually mainstream immigrant children to follow the regular curriculum as quickly as possible. Hence, Moroccan immigrant children were never withdrawn from their regular class for more than two hours

a day, and it was mandatory for them to participate along with their Spanish peers only in subject areas that did not require a sophisticated level of Spanish academic language skills, such as Physical Education, Music, and the Performing Arts program. In practice, this meant that, once the children returned to their regular classes from the Compensatory Education building – a building that furthermore was separate from the main school facilities, many Moroccan immigrant children spent most of the school day physically present with their Spanish peers in their regular classes, but cognitively, behaviorally, and emotionally disengaged from the regular activities that were taking place in subject areas such as Math, Language Arts, Science, Social Studies, and English – subjects that comprised the lion's share of the children's academic schedule. During the time in which these subjects were being taught, Moroccan immigrant children who were not completely mainstreamed did not participate in the regular activities of the class. Instead, they were supposed to study independently at their desks, filling out the pages of their computations and basic literacy workbooks that had been assigned as homework by their Compensatory Education teacher. In addition, the number of mainstreamed Moroccan immigrant students was not very high in comparison to the total number of Moroccan immigrant children in the school. Of the focal children in fourth grade, only three (Mimon, Worda, and Miriam) followed the regular curriculum. Wafiya, Karim, Sarah, Jalal, and Yimad spent most of their school day sitting at their desks, disengaged not only from their schoolwork, but also from their teachers and peers. This physical presence, but psychological and academic absence, was consequential in marking Moroccan immigrant children as different or, even worse, as deficient.

7　MUS-E Programs are funded with grants from the Yehudi Menuhin Foundation. The MUS-E Program started being implemented in Europe in 1994. Since then, many schools, particularly schools with high percentages of minorities and immigrant population, have benefited from it. The following passage is an excerpt from the website of the Yehudi Menuhin Foundation in Spain that explains the goals and principles of the program:

> La finalidad del Programa MUS-E es el fomento de las Artes, especialmente de la música, el canto, el teatro, la danza y las artes plásticas, en el ámbito escolar como herramienta que favorece la integración social educativa y cultural de niños y niñas, previene la violencia, el racismo y fomenta la tolerancia y el encuentro entre las distintas culturas, desde el respeto a la diversidad. El MUS-E hace hincapié en la importancia del diálogo y la interacción entre las diferentes culturas así como el desarrollo de la creatividad y la imaginación en la práctica de las disciplinas artísticas como base de la educación.
>
> (http://www.fundacionmenuhin.org/programas/muse1.html)

> The goal of the MUS-E Program is to promote the Arts, especially, music, singing, theater, dance, and plastic arts, in school environments as tools to aid the social, educational, and cultural integration of boys and girls; to prevent violence and racism; to promote tolerance and the encounter of different cultures, respecting diversity. MUS-E emphasizes the importance of dialogue and interaction between different cultures, as well as the development of creativity and imagination in the practice of artistic disciplines as foundations of education.

8　Another example is the way in which the school's *diversity* was made part of traditional Spanish holidays, such as Christmas or Carnival. The school went about these celebrations as usual, for instance, with the traditional Christmas Carol Concert or the Costume Parade. After the regular program of events was over, a traditional Moroccan dance was usually performed by a group of Moroccan girls in the higher grades almost as an encore or an after-thought detail, but not as part of the mainstream culture of the school.

9 See e.g., Lee (2005); Nieto (2000).

10 The contact theory of prejudice has long maintained that increased interaction between different ethnic, racial, or religious groups is likely to decrease tensions between them, since the conventional view among social psychologists was that prejudice was largely an outcome of the lack of knowledge about a different group of people. However, more recent scholarship has demonstrated that only certain kinds of interactions have the desired effect of reducing antagonism between different groups, those that require people to become interdependent and work as a team towards the fulfillment of a common objective (Levin and Rabrenovic 2007). The Physical Education and the Performance Arts programs at this school were based on these principles of teamwork, collaboration, and mutual aid.

11 In all transcripts, `Spanish` is shown in `regular font`; ***Moroccan Arabic*** is shown ***bolded and italicized***; and the **English** translation is shown **bolded**.

12 Because of my lack of knowledge of Amazighe, the families I worked with in this study were mostly Arabophone or bilingual speakers of Moroccan Arabic and Amazighe. Therefore, my observations of Amazighe use remain anecdotal. I was able to document how Moroccan Arabic was the *lingua franca* for most social and communicative purposes in the Moroccan community in Vallenuevo, even among Amazighe speakers. The use of Amazighe was, for the most part, restricted to private, family communication, and it was mostly used by the older women in the households. Moroccan immigrant children's knowledge of Amazighe was either passive (i.e., had varying degrees of language comprehension, but not production abilities), or very basic. There are concerns about the survival of Amazighe among Moroccan immigrant communities in Spain , particularly among second-generation members (Tilmatine 2002). In Morocco, Berber or Amazighe is still spoken as a primary language of communication by approximately 40%–50% of the population, although attitudes towards Berber in Morocco are often mixed and derogatory (Crawford 2002; Hoffman and Crawford 2000; Hoffman 2002a; Hoffman 2002b; Ennaji 2005). In the last decade, however, there have been significant efforts to revitalize Amazighe, including the development of linguistic and educational programs in these languages, as well as the professional development of teachers for the implementation of such programs in Moroccan schools (Ennaji 2005; Mijares and López García 2004).

13 Recent literature on children's responsibilities across cultures, such as Cohen (2001); Fasulo et al. (2007); Klein et al. (2008); Ochs and Izquierdo (2009); Such and Walker (2004), highlights that, beyond their contributions to household economy and sustainability, the tasks children perform for themselves and for others are inextricably interwoven with sociocultural understandings of the moral status of childhood and parenthood and constitute an essential aspect of child socialization and human development. In other words, responsibilities are organized by the ecological contexts of social situations and of cultural notions about child development.

14 Fernea (1995) and Schaefer Davis and Davis (1995) have also documented a high degree of children's involvement in household responsibilities in Morocco. Like in many Moroccan households in Spain, in Moroccan households in Morocco the division of chores is remarkably distinct. Both researchers coincide that most households they studied displayed a strong division of labor by sex. Girls typically have many daily chores that are not expected at all of boys, and, in addition, girls also start to perform these chores at an earlier age. Fernea (1995) and Schaefer Davis and Davis (1995) have described that boys become an extension of the father outside the home and girls become an extension of the mother inside the home, whether they are or not in school. Moreover, as in the households I documented,

an exception to this strong division of labor according to gender occurred in those families in which there were no girls. In those cases, these responsibilities fell on the eldest brother.

15   See also the Latino families documented by Orellana (2009) who felt that children have "too much" power when they were not willing to help and/or translate for parents when needed.

16   In spite of the fact that, to date, no study has reported negative effects resulting from immigrant children's engagement in language brokering activities (see Orellana 2009: 149 for a review of this literature), immigrant children's role as translators has attracted quite a bit of media attention in the last few years. This media attention has often focused on the supposed children's *parentification* or role reversal within the family system, and the presumed anxieties and distress that these *adult-like* responsibilities may cause among immigrant children (e.g., Flores 1999). Many of these assumptions and beliefs tend to be ethnocentric in that they are often based on contemporary and normative Western views on what it means to be a child and on what should be expected of children (see e.g., Zelizer 1985, 2005 for a description of some of these contemporary ideologies).

17   Paugh (2005) has also discussed the significance of place and spatial restrictions on children's language use in her study of children's multilingual play in Dominica. See also, Schieffelin's (2003) discussion of language and play in children's worlds.

18   The only out-of-school context in which both Moroccan immigrant children and Spanish children of mixed genders came together in a socially shared space of action was the track-and-field team. In this arena, boys and girls of multiple ethnicities participated jointly in weekly training and weekend competitions. However, these endeavors cannot be considered peer group activities *per se* since they are supervised by adults, namely two male coaches and several parents, who would sometimes accompany the children in some of the most geographically distant competitions. In addition, even in these contexts, I was able to document a tendency for Spanish children and Moroccan children (again, segregated by gender) to cluster separately during training breaks or down-times before and after the competition. Certainly, during the often long bus rides ferrying the children to different competition venues, Moroccan and Spanish children rarely sat together.

5

The Public School: Ground Zero for the Politics of Inclusion

Un día que me – estaba con Malika – Un día que estaba en el servicio
hablando con Malika en marroquina. Que yo no sabe mucho español!
Y ha dicho Cristina: "Eh, venga, no se habla, venga, venga."
y luego nos vamos a clase y lo dice a la seño.

One day that I – I was with Malika – One day that I was in the bathroom
  speaking to Malika in Moroccan [Arabic]. That I don't know very much
  Spanish!
And Cristina [a Spanish classmate] has said:
  "Eh, come on, it's not spoken, come on, come on."
And then we go back to class and she [Cristina] tells Miss (the teacher).[1]
                              (Sarah, age 9, interview fragment)

Si nos insultan, yo no me quiero quedar ahí en esa escuela [. . .]
pero Luis, mira, dice que todos somos iguales y que si te insultan
que eres un moro, me lo vienes a decirmelo, ya verás lo que hago yo.

If they insult us, I don't want to stay there in that school [. . .]
but, Luis [a teacher], look, he says that we are all equal and
that if they insult you that you are a "moro," come to tell me
and you'll see what I do.
                              (Kamal, age 11, interview fragment)

The hubbub of laughter and shouting coming from school playgrounds
and playing fields was almost deafening, and Paco, one of the fourth-grade

Language and Muslim Immigrant Childhoods: The Politics of Belonging, First Edition.
Inmaculada Mª García-Sánchez.
© 2014 John Wiley & Sons, Inc. Published 2014 by John Wiley & Sons, Inc.

teachers who was in charge of supervising the midday recess, and I had to walk close together so that we could hear each other's conversation over the students' noise. I never videotaped during recesses on the days of the week when I was in the school. I would have had to contend with the technical difficulties involved in covering the sizable yard, where two playgrounds and a large playing field were next door to one another, and through which the children moved with impressive fluidity. In addition to these issues, I was always a little afraid of the commotion that the presence of a videocamera would cause among the large student body, who converged on the playgrounds at that time of the day, particularly for those children who did not know me.[2] Nevertheless, I made a habit of being outside during all recesses, rather than in the staffroom, taking notes, making observations about children's playful interactions or talking to students who often sought me out, especially at the beginning of my stay in Vallenuevo when the novelty of my school visits had not yet worn off. Teachers at the school rotated recess supervision according to a schedule developed by the administration. It was always nice when one of the teachers I knew or one I had struck up a friendship with was on duty because we could spend some time chatting about upcoming school events, about how my study was going, or about what we had done the previous weekend. But it was a real treat when my visits coincided with Paco's turn. I would look forward to a half an hour of engaging conversation walking alongside Paco, who simultaneously surveyed the fields, occasionally joking with or scolding children, sometimes mockingly, sometimes more seriously. Paco and his wife Teresa, who was also a teacher at the school, had taken to me, which was also mutual on my part, and befriended me in and out of school. They were two of the most experienced teachers and had taught at this school for many years; they were also among the small group of teachers who actually lived in Vallenuevo. Most of the teachers lived in a bigger town approximately six miles away, and some others stayed in Vallenuevo only during the school week in rented accommodation. Paco was a decent and a kind man, both in actions and demeanor; a quintessential "good guy," and he was very popular and appreciated by his students. Not surprisingly, children often looked for him when there was a dispute or when a child was hurt, even after they had moved on to higher grades and no longer had him as a classroom teacher. Although his was not the fourth-grade class that I videotaped and followed more intently, he often invited me to visit and observe as soon as he learned that I was following Worda in out of school contexts, since Worda and her eldest sister Salma happened to be his students.

On that day, Paco and I had just finished going around the perimeter of the main schoolyard and were standing next to the steps of the northwest entrance to the school. A group of Spanish girls was playing jump-rope a few feet away from where I was conversing with the teacher. Mouna, a Moroccan immigrant girl whom I often recorded in *Compensatory Education* classes along with Sarah and other children of the fourth-grade focal class-room, approached this group of girls and asked them whether she could join in the game. Although it was hard to hear everything that was being said, it was obvious that Mouna was not allowed to join in. After a second negative response from other girls in the group, Mouna tried to get in line for jumping, nonetheless, but was physically pushed out. At that point, all the Spanish girls who were in the line waiting to jump stood closer together so as not to leave even the shadow of a gap in which Mouna could fit. It was clear that there was no room for Mouna in this game, but just in case Mouna had any doubts, one of the girls shouted aloud: "¡Vete ya!", **(Now go away!)**, as she clenched her arms and torso against the back of the girl who was in front of her.

With divided attention, I was trying to carry on my conversation with Paco, while following attentively everything that was going on in the girls' group with the corner of my eye, wondering whether there was something I could or should do about it. I decided that I would at least bring what was happening to Paco's attention and take it from there. When I was about to start telling him, Paco, who also happened to be Mouna's classroom teacher, excused himself for a few minutes and started walking towards the group of girls asking if he could join in the game and making a big show of himself wanting to play jump-rope. Once in line, he immediately reached out to Mouna, who was still on the sidelines looking at the other girls sadly and dejectedly, and invited her to get in line immediately before him. Mouna jumped up with a big smile on her face and got in line with alacrity; none of the Spanish girls stopped her from joining the game at that point. Paco played with the girls for a couple of rounds, countering mock defiantly the jokes the students were making about his age. After a few rounds, however, he admitted to the girls with feigned reluctance that they were right about him being too old to play jump-rope, and stepping out of the line, continued his conversation with me. Paco did not say a word to me about what had just happened and he appeared as if he was not giving any thought to it at all, but I did notice that on that day we did not resume our walk around the playgrounds. We stayed close by, next to where all the girls, Mouna included, were playing jump-rope uneventfully until the end of recess.

This vignette crystallizes in a snapshot the complex politics of inclusion in schools with which this chapter is concerned. The public school is perhaps the most appropriate starting point of this exploration of the social lives of Moroccan immigrant children in Vallenuevo, since, as discussed in the previous chapter, children spend much of their waking hours in this environment. In addition, as one of the first institutions involved in the settlement processes of immigrant families, schools all over Spain have become one of the major battlegrounds in the politics of inclusion. Educational institutions do not work in isolation from larger societal forces, and therefore, are not immune to the sociocultural ideologies, forms of representation, and discourses examined in Chapter 2. In this sense, they do not only reflect the tensions and makeup of the wider society, but also have a very decisive role in the construction of new social relations and dynamics. It is precisely because of this Janus-like nature of educational institutions – in that they are simultaneously agents of social reproduction (Bourdieu and Passeron 1977; Collins 2009), but also agents of social change – that schools all over the country have become so emblematic in the contested debates surrounding immigration and the politics of inclusion.

Spanish educational and immigration laws clearly state that all children under the age of 16 have a right to free state education regardless of their parents' legal status. Therefore, the points of contention generated by the increasing levels of cultural and linguistic heterogeneity in the country, coupled with the anxieties provoked by the Muslim background of a large percentage of the newcomers have become, in the last few years, particularly salient in the educational arena. Indeed, most of the scholarly work devoted to immigrant children in Spain has focused on the sociocultural and linguistic controversies that the increasingly visible presence of these children in public schools has engendered: from documenting schools' management of multilingualism and cultural diversity (Martín Rojo 2010; Mijares and Relaño Pastor 2011; Relaño Pastor 2009) to describing the obstacles that both schools and immigrant children have to overcome to achieve meaningful inclusion and educational success (García Castaño and Carrasco Pons 2011; Gibson et al. 2012; Martín Rojo 2003).[3]

Vallenuevo schools have been at the forefront of many of these points of contention. Since 1994, when the immigrant population in the school increased significantly, the local elementary and high school have had to manage carefully well-publicized issues such as the use of the headscarf, the teaching of Arabic to Moroccan immigrant children at the school, or the accusation by local Spanish parents' that the presence of immigrant children was negatively affecting their children's levels of educational achievement. They have also taken consequential decisions about less mediated, albeit no less important issues, such as appropriate training and professional development for their teachers, as well as the design and implementation of programs for the gradual mainstreaming of immigrant children whose first language was not Spanish. Some of these decisions have been the objects of tension among the population of the town, particularly in the early to mid-2000s, when antagonism between some Spanish locals and the Moroccan immigrant community became more evident. School officials have thus become important mediators in the community, regulating both educational decisions and social life in the school, and also to some extent, regulating peaceful *convivencia* (living-together) in the town. As Carlos, the principal of the elementary school told me once, he had always proceeded with the awareness that any incident in the school could potentially jeopardize the balance of everyday life in Vallenuevo.

Although the importance of educational policies and practices is undeniable, this chapter examines the politics of inclusion as it is forged in the daily social life of school and in students' relationships. The importance of positive and resonant relationships with peers has emerged in the last few years as a key theme in educational research focusing specifically on ethnic minority and/or immigrant children (Gil Conchas 2006; M. Suárez-Orozco, C. Suárez-Orozco, and Todorova 2008). It is becoming increasingly apparent that there is a strong relationship between having *peer social capital* (Gibson, Gándara, and Koyama 2004), and related notions of positive *peer social mirroring* (C. Suárez-Orozco 2000, 2004), and immigrant children's patterns of academic achievement, feelings of belonging, and educational enfranchisement. In sociolinguistics and linguistic anthropology, there is also a vigorous tradition of scholarship documenting the importance of everyday interaction for participation in the peer social order and for dealing with opposition and conflict within the social world of peers, both in high school contexts (Eckert 2000; Bucholtz 2011), as well as in elementary- and middle-school settings (M. H. Goodwin 2002, 2006; Kyratzis and Guo 2001; Kyratzis 2000; Sheldon 1990). Linguistic anthropological studies of the inclusion of children with marginalized identities, in particular, such as children with autism and economically disadvantaged students, have emphasized that, beyond laws and educational programs, members of the school community, namely teachers and peers, are crucial agents in the successful inclusion of marginalized children into the social life of the school (Goodwin 2006; Ochs et al. 2001). Positive relationships with peers, in particular, have been shown to be essential in the successful inclusion and socialization of those children most vulnerable to social ostracization: "Successful inclusion depends upon recipiently designed procedures for maximizing participation and understanding [. . .] the practice of inclusion rests primarily on unaffected schoolmates rather than teachers, who typically are occupied monitoring academic progress and disciplinary transgression across a range of children" (Ochs et al. 2001, pp. 400–401). Looking closely at the everyday social life of schools and classrooms becomes even more crucial since this previous linguistic and educational anthropological research has suggested that on the one hand, a schism may exist between institutional ideologies about inclusion and children's actual behavior towards their peers with marginalized identities (Goodwin 2006), and on the other hand, that even in schools that seem well integrated from the outside, there may sharp divisions between immigrant students and their native-born peers (Suárez-Orozco et al. 2008).

Although there was variation in the behavior of individual children, the relations between local Spanish children and their Moroccan immigrant peers at the elementary school in Vallenuevo were characterized by a systematic pattern of avoidance. School professionals were aware of this hostility, and, preventing fights was an important concern of teachers and administrators. As in many other school environments characterized by the risk of conflict, the typical intervention approaches observed in this school focused on preventing physical forms of aggression and overt ethnic victimization (e.g., Nishina and Juvonen 2005). The principal and several teachers remarked during the course of my research that in previous years, fights and verbal harassment between Spanish and Moroccan children were so prevalent that they had to prohibit temporarily playing soccer and other recreational activities during recess, as they were susceptible to degenerating into fights. The children also discussed this atmosphere of fights and insults during our interviews. Kamal, for instance, who regularly played soccer at recess explained to me that part of the problem was that children used to organize these games along national lines, pitting the Spanish kids versus the Moroccan kids as if it were an international soccer competition. In this environment, the normal competitive interactions of a sports game would sometimes quickly turn into ethnic name-calling. Kamal reported having often been called, "puto moro" (equivalent to **fucking Moor**), and himself calling Spanish children in retaliation, "payo rojo" (literally, **red payo**). *Payo* is a slightly pejorative adjective that the Spanish Roma population routinely uses to refer to Spanish people who are not ethnic gypsies. Semantically, the word itself can carry connotations of being fair-skinned and of being a simpleton. As a consequence, Kamal added: "En el recreo todos los días tenía que suceder una pelea" **(During recess, a fight had to happen every day)**.

Teachers were hyper-vigilant regarding violent and abusive behavior, either physical or verbal. When soccer and other competitive activities were allowed again in the playgrounds, for example, the administration made it known that only ethnically and nationally-mixed teams of children would be permitted to play. The proactive attitude of the school staff also comes through in the interview quote by Kamal that introduces the chapter. In this quote, Kamal, while describing some of the problems that he still encountered in the daily social life of the school, was also telling me about a group of adults whom he felt really cared about the well-being of the Moroccan immigrant children at the school. Among them, Kamal told me about Luis, a teacher he particularly admired. Kamal was grateful for Luis's, and other teachers' sensitivity, and for their willingness to make clear that they were not going to tolerate any kind of ethnic slurs and other explicit forms of victimization.

The consistent actions of the school professionals had helped to ameliorate the general atmosphere at the school. By the time I arrived in the town, physical fights and overt forms of racial hostility were no longer part of daily life in the school. On the contrary, they were somewhat exceptional. Along these same lines, many teachers were also quick to react whenever they witnessed other kinds of peer harassment and microaggressions of race (Solórzano, Ceja, and Yosso 2000), such as blatant exclusion from games or other school activities, as Paco did in the vignette that opened this chapter. Such forms of blatant exclusion often took place during recess, when it was easiest for the children's actions to escape the watchful gaze of their classroom teachers. Even in these spaces of the school where children's behavior was most likely to escape the teachers' control, teachers were often sensitive to these overt forms of exclusion.

Although instances of overt forms of exclusion were very rare in the videotaped classroom data, I have recently examined two extended examples of everyday discriminatory practices that were recognized as forms of exclusion in the official classroom space, insofar as teachers intervened to prevent the exclusion of Moroccan immigrant children from taking place (García-Sánchez 2012a). Like in the vignette that opens the chapter, where Mouna was not being allowed to join in a game of jump-rope during recess, a common thread running through these overt forms of exclusion was Spanish children's attempt to exclude their Moroccan immigrant peers from participating in activities. There was an important difference between these overt forms of exclusion, in which Spanish students were reprimanded for having crossed the line, and the more subtle microaggression that was pervasive in the data, and with which this chapter is centrally concerned: in the latter, rather than excluding Moroccan immigrant children from taking part in a given activity, the collective actions of Spanish children can be seen as constituting an attempt to exclude their Moroccan peers from symbolic membership in the social group.

These forms of exclusion speak to the everyday ways in which a pattern of avoidance and rejection was usually enacted by most of the Spanish children at the school towards their Moroccan peers, in spite of the public discourse of inclusion, tolerance, and respect that constituted the school's official policy. The Spanish children were aware of the values of friendship, cooperation, and respect that the school was trying to promote; they were also sensitive to the consistent message sent by the school administration that violence, insults, and overt exclusion would not be tolerated. In response, the Spanish children engaged in subtler forms of avoidance, rejection, and exclusion of their Moroccan immigrant peers. Given that this subtler exclusion was a constitutive part of the relational fabric of children's social life in the school, it is fair to say that the relative lack of fights and of overt forms of exclusion were more indicative of Spanish children's formal compliance with school policies, rather than symptomatic of improved interethnic relations at the school, or of an prevailing ethos of tolerance. This observation is resonant with findings that, as social taboos against the overt expression of prejudice and racism have become prevalent, social actors have developed an array of more sanitized and inconspicuous discourse strategies that nonetheless continue to negatively position out-groups, such as immigrants and ethnic minorities (Hill 2008).[4]

Although teachers were often not aware of these subtler forms of exclusion, they were cognizant of a systematic pattern of avoidance that sometimes interfered with the regular progress of class activities or with play activities during recess. Most obvious was Spanish children's reluctance to have physical contact with their Moroccan immigrant peers. This was often problematic in Physical Education and Performaning Arts classes, where physical contact was not only unavoidable but also emphasized in curricular goals and pedagogical practices (see Chapter 4). Unlike physical fights and blatant forms of exclusion, the teachers rarely intervened directly to address this problem. Although they were troubled by this avoidance, teachers often found themselves hesitating about the best course of action to take to address these situations.

One morning, as I was preparing my equipment in the teachers' lounge to record one of the Performing Arts classes, I witnessed a telling exchange between the fourth-grade Physical Education teacher and one of his colleagues in the Performing Arts program. Because there were many similarities in the curricular goals of both classes, communication between these two teachers was particularly important. In this conversation, the Performing Arts teacher was describing to the Physical Education teacher the program of activities that he had designed for that term. At some point, he explained that since one of the main objectives of the Performing Arts program was for children of different ethnicities to become comfortable interacting with each other, he had planned activities that involved a lot of physical contact among the children. Then, he added: "porque no se tocan ni de casualidad" **(because they don't touch each other, not even by chance)**. The Physical Education teacher responded: "¡Dímelo a mi! En educación física cada vez que los pongo en pareja- bueno un español y un marroquí- tiene que ser obligao" **(Tell me about it! In Physical Education every time I pair them up- well, a Spanish child and a Moroccan child- I have to make it mandatory)**.

This pattern of avoidance was also manifest in the prevailing seating arrangements at the school. As Duranti (1994) has noted, "spatial distinctions seem to reverberate claims and rights assigned through linguistic means and tend to support a particular social order" (pp. 6–7). In this school, teachers had different approaches to seating arrangements. As illustrated in the charts below, some preferred to assign the seats themselves, whereas others preferred to let the children choose their own seats. In the first framegrab, taken during a Performing Arts class, children were distributed by the teacher in such a way that there were no ethnic or gender clusters. In the second framegrab taken during a Music class, where the teacher did not assign seats, however, we find two very distinct ethnic clusters of children, with Moroccan and Spanish children sitting on different sides of the U-shaped table. The two diagrams below illustrate how different semiotic modalities are involved in the architecture of the social organization of inclusion/exclusion (Figures 5.1 and 5.2, respectively). This spatial pattern of seating arrangements will echo the interactional and linguistic practices that will be discussed in the following pages.

Along with these more or less subtle instances of rejection and avoidance, the behavior of Moroccan immigrant children in the school was constantly monitored, not necessarily by the teachers but by their Spanish peers. In the fourth-grade class that I observed on a weekly basis, Moroccan immigrant children were often the targets of tattles and policing. Within these practices, immigrant children were regularly treated differently and ascribed negative characteristics. The linguistic and interactional features of negative differential positioning reveal not only how Spanish peers construct

 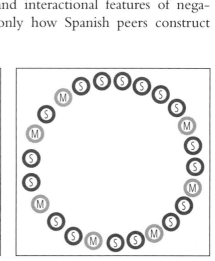

Figure 5.1 Seating arrangement at a Performing Arts class.

 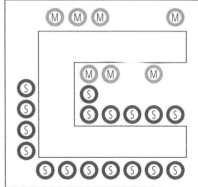

Figure 5.2   Seating arrangement at a Music class.

marginalized social identities for Moroccan immigrant children, but also the everyday microgenesis of the racialized exclusion of Moroccan immigrant youth within the mainstream culture of the school and dominant society. The cumulative effect of these negative daily experiences with peers may be consequential to Moroccan immigrant children's development of a pervasive sense of alienation and marginality. A sense of belonging to a particular social group depends to a large extent on the treatment received by others in public domains of social life, specifically whether one is allowed to assume and develop social identities that are ratified by others as compatible with sanctioned membership in a social group (Ochs 2002).

5.1   The Microgenesis of Social Markedness and Racialized Exclusion

Through the examination of the daily naturally-occurring interactional practices of very young Moroccan immigrant children with their Spanish peers and teachers during the school day, this chapter documents how language is involved in racialization processes of exclusion at the most primordial level of social life in a community, that of social interaction among its members. As Hallam and Street (2000) succinctly noted: "The Other is never simply given, never just found or encountered, but made" (p. 1). The systematic analysis of Moroccan immigrant children's relations with local Spanish children and teachers in Vallenuevo reveals how, through routine participation in, and the cumulative effect of, the exclusionary everyday interactions described in this chapter, a *new savage slot* (Trouillot 1991) is interactionally constructed for Moroccan immigrant children. Moroccan immigrant children are constructed as the racialized *Other* through a complex architecture of exclusionary practices in which they are consistently put into positions for being treated differently.

This social markedness may be consequential in the long run, since immigrant children's developing sense of who they are, as well as their developing sense of membership and belonging in this rural Spanish community, depend not only on their interactions in private life, but also on their interactions in school and other institutions.[5] The examination of children's daily school-life is a window that allows us to catch a glimpse of how Moroccan immigrant children in Spain may grow up with a feeling of not-belonging and a heightened sense of alienation. Additionally, it provides ethnographic evidence of how some of these processes of exclusion and alienation start in early to middle-childhood – a crucial age in child development in which children start to navigate their own ways through societal structures and institutions (Garcia Coll and Szalacha 2004). The following analysis attempts to capitalize on the analytic richness of everyday interaction in discerning the emergent, moment-to-moment creation of social life and social relations. By laying out the complex architecture of exclusionary interactions, and by describing Moroccan immigrant children's socialization into marginalized identities, this chapter considers the origins of the experience of racialized exclusion as a social interactional achievement.

While the pattern of avoidance described above was visible from my earlier observations at the school, the close analysis of 18 videotaped hours of classroom interactions uncovered a series of practices of monitoring and policing that characterized a significant amount of the interactions between the Spanish and the Moroccan children. Focusing more specifically on the surveillance that the Spanish children in the class exercised over their Moroccan peers, I found three inter-related interactional practices in the videotaped data.[6] These three practices are *acusar* (tattling), *mandatos* (peer directives), and *echar leña al fuego* (fueling the fire). These practices in and of themselves do not constitute practices of social exclusion. In fact, many of them, such as tattling, are indigenous to children's cultures in many communities around the world.[7] Tattling, for instance, takes place even among Spanish children and Moroccan children in this school. There are, however, numerical differences in how often these practices are initiated by Spanish children targeting their Moroccan peers. Figure 5.3 below captures these numerical differences. The distribution of the three practices among the different ethnic combinations of students is represented on the x-axis, and the total number of examples found for each practice in the videotaped data is represented on the y-axis.

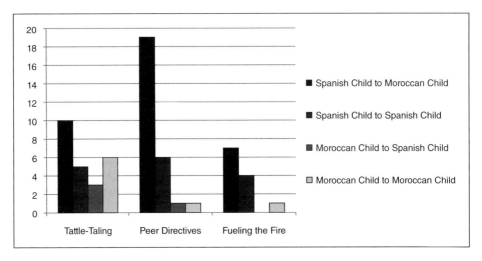

Figure 5.3   Instances of *acusar, mandatos,* and *echar leña al fuego.*[8]

As this figure illustrates, the number of examples found in the video record shows that, in all of the practices, Spanish children target Moroccan immigrant children more frequently than other Spanish children. These numerical differences are most visible in the practice of *mandatos* (peer directives), which is perhaps the most aggravated of the three practices. Most importantly, however, and in addition to these numerical differences, there are also differences in the way in which these practices are enacted in actual interaction that turn these practices of policing into practices of social marking and racialized exclusion.

To distill the distinct web of indexical relations between acts, stances, and participant roles that are constitutive of these differences, I have identified three key linguistic and interactional dimensions. These features are critical in understanding how these everyday practices play a major role in the construction of a pervasive sense of social exclusion and marginalization among Moroccan immigrant children:

(1) *Linguistic Resources:* The role of grammar and linguistic encoding in the formulation of one's own and other people's actions is critical in the constitution of degrees of personal agency, responsibility, and ethical worlds (Duranti 2004). In this sense, the recontextualization of target-children's past actions as either wrongdoings or as accidental, for instance, is vital to the construction of these children's identities and personal moral characters. In addition to grammar, namely morpho-syntactic and semantic resources, other linguistic means such as pitch and intonation, in combination with gestural semiotic channels, are important resources in the construction of positive and negative stance.

(2) *Interactional Positioning:* The architecture of participation frameworks (Goffman 1981b; Goodwin 1999b) is crucial in understanding the differential ways in which targeted Moroccan or targeted Spanish children are positioned by others. Participation frameworks also structure children's differential access to claims and rights in the larger social order.

(3) *Alignment:* Whether the teacher and the rest of the peers align themselves or not with the action performed towards the targeted child and the way in which this alignment is displayed (positively or negatively) is important in the (re)production or subversion of social identities and relations. Alignment is crucial because whether or not the negative identities ascribed to Moroccan immigrant children do indeed take hold depends, to a large extent, on whether other interlocutors ratify with their participation the speaker's attempt to construct Moroccan children's identities in this fashion.

5.2   *Acusar* (Tattling)

The practice of tattling can be generally characterized as the public or private reporting of a peer's infraction, or violation of institutional and ethical codes of conduct, to a teacher, an adult, or any person in a hierarchically superior position to both the perpetrator of the tale and the victim of the accusation. Tattling, as a cultural practice, is prevalent in the social organization of many children's groups, particularly in early to middle-childhood. In spite of being common, children soon learn that tattling is a socially frowned-upon activity. By subverting the values of trust and solidarity, this practice jeopardizes the social cohesion of the group and, moreover, subjects it to the unwelcome, and often problematic, intrusion of adult authority figures. In Spanish, for instance, children who often engage in this practice are designated by the disdainful term *acusica*, a compound noun formed by the combination of the verb *acusar* (to accuse) and the scorn-laden negative-affect suffix *-ica*. The negative consequences for the social face and status of the tattler can be so serious that even in severe cases of peer harassment and victimization, as the literature on bullying has documented (Juvonen and Galván 2008), children are reluctant to report these behaviors to teachers and other school officials for fear of being deemed a *tattler*. Therefore, since informing teachers about other students' violations can be socially detrimental for the tattler, children in this fourth-grade class were highly strategic about this practice. They resorted to it either in extreme circumstances, or in situations in which the social status of the child-target was so low that there was really no danger of negative social consequences for the tattler. In these cases, the initiator of the tattle was usually a *popular* student of higher status in the social organization of the class.

As illustrated in Figure 5.3 above, in the randomly videotaped school interactions analyzed, Spanish children were twice as likely to tattle their Moroccan immigrant peers than other Spanish children. Furthermore, those Spanish children who were the victims of tattles were often children with *spoiled identities* (Goffman 1963), namely children who had been held back from a grade promotion and were doing badly academically, or children who were overweight and, otherwise, not very popular. This pattern not only holds for instances of tattling, but also for the other two practices that will be discussed in this analysis, namely *mandatos* (peer directives) and *echar leña al fuego* (fueling the fire). In addition to Moroccan immigrant children being the target of tattles more often than even Spanish children with marginalized identities, there were interactional differences that made the tattles against Moroccan children more severe and aggravated. These differences will be illustrated in the following two examples. These two particular examples were chosen because they are simultaneously compact in length and fairly representative of the way in which tattling practices would typically unfold in the context of this classroom. In the first example, students are individually reviewing the homework that they were supposed to have completed at home. The target of the tattle is a Spanish student named Ana and the tattler is her classmate Rosa, another Spanish student.

Example 5.1
Participants: Rosa, Ana, Teacher, Mimon

1. ROSA: Ana no sabe hacer el ejer- el dos de
             la:::-dos~de~la~ficha
             **Ana doesn't know how to do exr-number
             two of the- two in the handout**
2. TEACHER: ¿Qué no sabe hacer el dos de la ficha?
             **That she doesn't know how to do
             number two in the handout?**
3. ANA: Sí   [sé, Rosa
             Yes I [do, Rosa
4. ROSA: [No::::
                    [No::::
5. TEACHER: Vamo' a ver, Rosa. Y TÚ ¿por qué me
             dices que ella no sabe hacerlo?
             **Let's see, Rosa. And why do YOU tell
             me that she doesn't know how to do it?**
6. ROSA: Porque lo estaba haciendo mal
             Because she was doing it wrong
7. MIMON: No te importa
             It's none of your business

8. TEACHER: Ana, ahora te lo veo yo y te lo explico
             **Ana, I'll look at it now and I'll
             explain it to you**

In the second example, children are individually working on a Math handout. The target of the tattle is Karim and the tattler is Gloria, a Spanish classmate.

Example 5.2
Participants: Gloria, Teacher, Karim, and Cristina

1. GLORIA: ¿Maestra?
            Teacher?
2. TEACHER: ¿Qué?
            what?
3. GLORIA: Karim no está haciendo los deberes. Se está t-se está pintando con los rotuladores en la cremallera=
            Karim is not doing his homework. He's t-he is painting on his zipper with markers=

4. KARIM: =°¿En qué cremallera?
            =°On what zipper?
5. GLORIA: No:: mira
            No:: look
6. TEACHER: Karim, Karim=
            Karim, Karim

7. GLORIA: =Está así
            **=He's doing
            like this**
8. TEACHER: ¿Tú comprendes que la ropa está para pintarsela con rotuladores?
            Do you think that clothes are to be painted on with markers?
9. TEACHER: KARIM (2.0) Karim.
            Mírame~que~te~estoy~ha [blando

```
           KARIM (2.0) Karim.
           Look at me I'm talking to you
  10.  CRISTINA:            [¡Qué desastre!
                            [What a disaster!
  11.  TEACHER: Hoy vienes un poco tonto (1.5) ¿U::mmm?
                Today you're acting a bit foolish
                (1.5) Hu::mm?
  12.  TEACHER: Karim, venga, a trabajar y deja de
                tontear ya
                Karim, come on, work and stop fooling
                around now
```

In analyzing the two previous examples according to the three key dimensions that I identified earlier (linguistic encoding, positioning, and alignment), the first striking difference can be found in the grammatical structure of the tattle itself. Whereas in the first tattle example (Spanish child to Spanish child) we have the structure, **X Doesn't Know Y**, "Ana no sabe hacer el ejer-el dos de la:::-dos~de~la~ficha" **(Ana doesn't know how to do exer-number two- two in the handout)** (Example 5.1, line 1), in the second tattle example (Spanish child to Moroccan child) the grammatical structure is: **X Doesn't Do Y X Does Z**, "Karim no está haciendo los deberes. Se está t-se está pintando con los rotuladores en la cre-mallera" **(Karim isn't doing his homework He's t-he's painting on his zipper with markers)** (Example 5.2, line 3). "Y" refers to what the child should have been doing (his homework), while "Z" refers to a violation of normative behavior and rules of self-comportment in this community (he's painting on his zipper with markers).

As Duranti's (2004, 2005) analysis on agency in language has demonstrated, grammatical choices are not irrelevant. The role of grammar is crucial in the moral characterization of people and in constituting varying degrees of responsibility, as well as in the formulation of different versions of reality. Moreover, by unpacking the grammatical framing of speakers' versions of events, it is possible to ascertain participants' stances to those events, to other participants, and to social values and relations important in the community. In these particular examples, the semantic and syntactic structures of the verbs "to know," "to paint," and "to do homework" require an actor. However, in the first example, this participant role cannot be filled by an agent but by an experiencer, since there is no DO in the semantic structure of the verb to know (Van Valin and Wilkins 1996). The powerful combination of syntactic and semantic resources in the linguistic encoding of the tattle is an important building block in the interactional construction of social actors as more or less ethical, responsible, and worthy: whereas the targeted Spanish child is positioned as a passive experiencer that has, at most, epistemic responsibility, the targeted Moroccan child is positioned as an active agent and, therefore, assigned full moral responsibility for the infraction.

The negative characterization of the event as a *wrongdoing* and of the Moroccan child a fully responsible agent in the second example is further underscored by the tattler's deployment of multimodal sentences (M. H. Goodwin, C. Goodwin, and Yaeger-Dror 2002), consisting of linguistic prompting – "Está así" **(He is like this)** – and embodied demonstrations of the infraction (see framegrabs reproduced above). When Karim attempts to defend himself and denies the accusation in line 4, "En que cremallera?" **(On what zipper?)**, the Spanish girl responsible for the tattle, Gloria, initiates a number of interactional moves in lines 5 and 7 (Example 5.2) that render Karim's denial of the infraction ineffective. In line 5, Gloria directs everyone's attention to the zipper with an amplified-pitched response cry (**No:::**), and the command, "mira" **(look)**, while simultaneously leaning over in Karim's direction and pointing directly at Karim's jacket zipper with her pen. Thus, through the interplay of language and gesture, these multimodal sentences convey a *negative affective alignment* and a *negative oppositional stance* not only toward the actions of the Moroccan boy, but also toward the Moroccan boy himself (Goodwin 1998, 2000; Ochs 1993). Moreover, in line 7, the tattler reproduces Karim's infraction for the teacher and for the rest of the children to (**He's doing like this** + while moving her pen up and down her sweater), showing that her tattle is the result of a norm-oriented evaluation of Karim's behavior. Through the use of these embodied performances, the tattler is then able to replay the Moroccan child's violation in such a way that claims to have had visual access to the infraction, while simultaneously orienting to a certain notion of objectivity, morality, and normative behavior.[9]

As Table 5.1 below illustrates, this distinct grammatical pattern of unmitigated vs. mitigated agency, depending on whether the target of tattles are Moroccan or Spanish children, is not only constitutive of ethical personae in these two examples being analyzed, but it also holds across an overwhelming number of instances in this corpus. In this sense, the role of syntactic and semantic resources in the construction of *facts* and personal character of their *agents* is not only a moral commentary on how different social actors organized around local norms and values, but also political statements organized around the differentiation of out-group and in-group membership. In other cases in which the grammar of blaming has been investigated, the mitigation of agency is the norm. Studies of blaming in talk-in-interaction have highlighted that the direct, negative, and unmitigated mention of the *agent-referent* (found in all of the examples of tattles directed against Moroccan immigrant children) is, indeed, very rare. In her conversation analysis on reports of unhappy events and subsequent attributions on responsibility among

Table 5.1 Attribution of responsibility in tattles.

Spanish (tattler) – Moroccan (target) *Unmitigated* Agency and Attribution of Responsibility	Spanish(tattler) –S panish (target) *Mitigated* Agency and Attribution of Responsibility
X Does Y + Z Maestra (.) Mimon se ha sacado el chicle y se lo ha metido en el bolsillo **(Teacher (.) Mimon has removed his chewing-gum and put it in his pocket)** After the teacher has asked Mimon not to chew gum in class.	**X Doesn't Know Y** María no sabe tocar eso **(María doesn't know how to play that)**
X Doesn't Do Y Si no la hecho, seño **(He hasn't even done it, Miss)**	**X Doesn't Have Y** Seño, Teresa* no tiene hecho el cinco **(Miss, Teresa does not have number five done/complete)** Although Teresa (the target of the tattle) is positioned as the grammatical subject of the sentence, the morpho-syntactic and semantic structure the verbal form *tener (tiene)* + *past participle (hecho)* makes this sentence a passive construction also known as *pasiva analítica de proceso* (See Note 10). Therefore, the grammatical subject of the sentence "Teresa" is not the agent-actor of an active sentence, but the subject of a passive construction that emphasizes process. Agency and attribution of responsibility are, therefore, also mitigated in this case.

Table 5.1 *(Continued)*

Spanish (tattler) – Moroccan (target) *Unmitigated* Agency and Attribution of Responsibility	Spanish(tattler) –S panish (target) *Mitigated* Agency and Attribution of Responsibility

X Does Y

Seño, ella tiene un abrigo
 ((pointing at Sarah))[10]

**(Miss, she's wearing a
 coat))**

The teacher had asked all students to
 remove their coats after entering the
 Performing Arts classroom.

X Does Y

Mimon solo ha unío uno

**(Mimon has only paired up
 one)**

*Part of a lengthier exercise that
 students were supposed to have
 completed at home

X Does Y

Wafiya está haciendo
 plastica*

**(Wafiya is doing Plastic
 Arts)**

*During Math class

**Pointing + Calling Everyone's
 Attention to a Violation in
 Progress**

Mira la Wafiya, mira la
 Miriam

**(Look at Wafiya; look at
 Miriam)**

These two Moroccan girls were
 whispering to each other after the
 teacher had repeatedly asked the
 children to be quiet.

X Does Y

Wafiya, me está haciendo
 burla

**(Wafiya is making fun of
 me)**

X Doesn't Know Y

Ana no sabe hacer el
 ejercicio dos de la
 ficha

**(Ana doesn't know how
 to do number two
 on the handout)**

middle-class Americans, Pomerantz (1978) has established that, as is often the case when performing delicate social actions, there is a strong preference for the mitigation of the actor-agent's degree of responsibility. This mitigation of agency is often accomplished either by not incorporating an actor-agent, or by shaping the blameworthy actions as reports of events that happened, rather than actions performed by a specific social actor. While this description is strikingly similar to the way in which agency is mitigated when a tattle is directed against a Spanish peer, the opposite process can be traced when the tattle is directed against a Moroccan peer.

Finally, there is also a difference in alignment towards the action of *acusar*. In the first example, when the victim of the tattle is another Spanish girl, both teacher and peers align negatively with the tattle. In line 5 (Example 5.1), the teacher scolds the tattler: "Vamo' a ver, Rosa. Y TÚ ¿por qué me dices que ella no sabe hacerlo?" **(Let's see, Rosa. And why do YOU tell me that she doesn't know how to do it?)**. The dissaffiliation stance with both the action of tattling and with the tattler herself is further marked by the increased amplitude in volume and pitch with which "TÚ" **(YOU)**, which refers in this case to the tattler, is pronounced. Then, in line 8, the teacher addresses Ana, the victim of the tattle, in a reassuring way: "Ana ahora te lo veo yo y te lo explico" **(Ana I'll look at it now and I'll explain it to you)** (Example 5.1). In addition, one of the classmates also aligns negatively with the tattle, boldly disapproving of the action: "No te importa" **(It's none of your business)** (Example 5.1, line 7).

I want to highlight in this example that the classmate who negatively aligns with the action of tattling is Mimon who, like the rest of Moroccan children in the class, is also often the target of these practices. Mimon's indignant reaction is significant because, beyond expressing a negative stance towards the actions of tattler, he also questions in a public and unmitigated manner Rosa's right and authority (rather, her lack thereof) to be doing such reporting. Mimon's move can be viewed as both an indication of his own vexation when he himself is the target of these practices, but also as a form of retaliation towards the Spanish girl by insisting on her inappropriate behavior, after the teacher has already reprimanded her for it. In this sense, Mimon's action can be seen akin to the practice of *echar leña al fuego* (fueling the fire) that will be discussed below.

In the second example (Example 5.2), however, when the target of the tattle is one of the Moroccan immigrant children in the class, both teacher and peers align positively with the tattler. The teacher scolds Karim (lines 6, 8, 9, 11, and 12 of the transcripts above). This scolding not only sanctions the action of the tattler and ratifies the negative moral identity that has been ascribed to the Moroccan child, it also characterizes the child as careless, irresponsible, and lacking work ethics. Moreover, although negative assessments are dispreferred and, therefore tend to be mitigated in conversation (Pomerantz 1975, 1984; Goodwin and Goodwin 1992), in line 10 (Example 5.2), in the midst of the teacher's telling-off, one of the Spanish classmates produces an upgraded negative assessment of the Moroccan child: "¡Qué desastre!" (**What a disaster!**). With this assessment, the classmate also ratifies the negative moral character of Karim and sanctions the actions of the tattler. This type of assessment, furthermore, is more in line with what an adult may tell a child who has, for instance, an untidy bedroom than with the type of negative assessment that a peer might tell another peer. Table 5.2 summarizes the analysis of the tattling practices carried out in the preceding pages:

Table 5.2   Tattling.

	Acusar Spanish Child to Spanish Child	Acusar Spanish Child to Moroccan Child
Linguistic Encoding	**X Doesn't Know Y** "Ana no sabe hacer el ejer-el dos de la:::- dos~ de~la~ficha" **](Ana doesn't know how to do exr- number two- two in the handout)**	**(K Doesn't Do Y) K Does Z** "Karim no está haciendo los deberes. Se está t-se está pintando con rotuladores en la cremallera" **(Karim isn't doing his homework He's t-he's painting on his zipper with markers)**
Positioning	Experiencer **Epistemic Responsibility**	Volitional Agent **Moral Responsibility**
Teacher's Alignment	**Teacher's Negative Alignment** "¿Y TÚ por qué me dices que ella no sabe hacerlo?" **(And why do YOU tell me that she doesn't know how to do it)**	**Teacher's Positive Alignment** "Tú comprendes que la ropa está para pintarsela con rotuladores?" **(Do you think that clothes are to be painted on with markers?)**

(Continued)

Table 5.2   (*Continued*)

	Acusar Spanish Child to Spanish Child	Acusar Spanish Child to Moroccan Child
Other Peers' Alignment	**Other Peers' Negative Alignment** "No te importa" (**It's none of your business**)	**Other Peers' Positive Alignment** "¡Qué desastre!" What a disaster!

5.3   Mandatos (Peer Directives)

Although the use of imperatives has sometimes been documented among people of equal status, particularly when there are close personal bonds of trust and cooperation between them (Celce-Murcia and Larsen-Freeman 1999), in pragmatics, directives are also associated with negative politeness, and most importantly, with an indexical feature of hierarchical and unequal social relations of power (Brown and Levinson 1978, 1979; Levinson 1983). Indeed, directives in educational settings, such as classrooms, are usually the prerogative of teachers, administrators, and other adults in the school. The directives that I analyze here, however, are characterized by being commands and other bold, aggravated forms of corrections among children themselves: a child is the initiator of the correction that is always directed against another child in the classroom, hence *peer directives*.

As was the case with *acusar* practices, the vast majority of these directives targeted the Moroccan immigrant children in the classroom. As illustrated in Figure 5.3 above, Moroccan peers were over three times more likely to be the victim of these forms of correction than their Spanish counterparts. In this section, I present the in-depth analysis of two examples (Examples 5.3 and 5.4) that are representative of these sequential, linguistic, and affective differences.

Before the sequence starts in Example 5.3, students had been learning about rhythmic patterns in a Music class, and the teacher had asked students to individually compose a rhythmic scheme containing the elements they had just studied. After finishing their compositions, the teacher had asked for volunteers to come up to the front of the class and perform the rhythmic scheme they had just composed, using only hand-claps and the syllables *ta* and *ti*. The rest of the class had to be attentive to the performance, since at the end they were supposed to identify the specific rhythmic pattern underlying their classmates' composition. If, after the performance, the selected student in the audience offered the right rhythmic pattern, then he/she also had the opportunity to go to the front of the class and perform his/her composition. Since these types of activities were fairly popular among the children, there was often fierce competition for the floor. Because of the problems this competition generated, the teacher had enforced a rule that those students who wanted to be considered and selected to volunteer the answer must raise their hands first. If someone happened to blurt out the answer right at the end of the performance without raising his/her hand, that student would have to forfeit their chance to be the next performer. It was, therefore, important to raise a hand as quickly as possible after the completion of the classmate's performance, since usually those students who raised their hands first had more opportunities to be selected. In the next sequence, Estrella is performing her rhythmic scheme for the class. As soon as Estrella has finished the first part of her composition, Roberto raises his hand conspicuously. Gloria, another Spanish student who also wanted to participate, sees Roberto's actions and issues a command directing Roberto to lower his hand.

Example 5.3
Participants: Gloria, Teacher, Roberto, Estrella

```
1.          ((Roberto raises his hand in the
            middle of Estrella's performance))
```

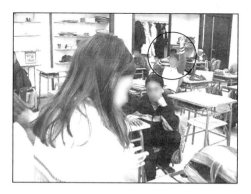

```
2.  GLORIA:  No más ha dicho una o sea que baja
             la mano ((To Roberto))
             She has only said one so lower your
             hand
```

    3. TEACHER: Muy bien, Gloria,   [¿eh? Te voy a
                  poner aquí conmigo
                  **Very nice, Gloria, [ah? I'm going to
                  put you here with me**
    4. ESTRELLA: [Ta-ta-ta-ta-ti ((While clapping
                            her hands))
                            [Ta-ta-ta-ta-ti

Example 5.4 is also extracted from one of the Music classes. In this instance, a Moroccan student named Miriam is performing a musical scale task and is discovered by her classmates to be chewing gum. The target of the peer directive is Miriam and the initiator of the command is one of her Spanish peers, Margarita:

Example 5.4
Participants Miriam, Teacher, Margarita, and Susana

    1. MARGARITA: Tira ese chicle, Miriam
                    Throw away that chewing-gum, Miriam
    2. TEACHER: Miriam ese chi:::cle
                    Miriam that chewing-gum
    **((Miriam continues to perform the musical scale
    task))**
    3. SUSANA: Miriam, el chicle
                    Miriam, the chewing-gum
    4. MIRIAM: Vale::
                    OK

    ((After completing her task, Miriam gets up and
    throws the chewing-gum away while being
    scrutinized by two of her peers to make sure that
    she had actually thrown the chewing-gum away in
    the trash can))

Before proceeding with the analysis according to the three dimensions identified above (linguistic encoding, positioning, and alignment), there is also an important sequential difference between these two examples that must be addressed. The directive in Example 5.3 is germane to the activity in that the interaction occupies the business of the class, "No más ha dicho una o sea que baja la mano" **(She has only said one so lower your hand)** (Example 5.3, line 2). In this sense, Gloria's directive cannot only be considered sequentially relevant, but also an appropriate next action to Roberto raising his hand. Moreover, there may be strategic reasons for Gloria's deployment of the directive, since, if Roberto continues with his hand raised until Estrella completes her scheme, he, instead of Gloria, might be selected to provide the answer and perform next. The directive in Example 5.4, "Tira ese chicle, Miriam" **(Throw away that chewing-gum, Miriam)** (Example 5.4, line 1), however, is completely extraneous to the focal activity that is at that point being carried out in the classroom, namely the performance of musical scales. In addition to the sequential non-relevance of this directive, it is important to add that Miriam's chewing gum, unlike Roberto's raising his hand, does not impact, in any way, the other children in the classroom.

Pragmatically, performing a directive in interaction can be quite a delicate undertaking, since bald imperatives can threaten the social face of all participants involved, namely speaker, intended recipient, and other hearers. A number of politeness strategies have been documented as being employed by social actors to perform such actions in as little a face-threatening way as possible (Brown and Levinson 1978). In fact, speakers usually do a significant amount of facework when directing imperatives, orders, and commands to other participants in order to soften as much as possible the *illocutionary force* of these utterances. The linguistic encoding of the directive in Example 5.3, "JUSTIFICATION + DO X," is an example of one of the ways in which that softening or mitigation is accomplished, "No más ha dicho una o sea que baja la mano" **(She has only said one so lower your hand)** (Example 5.3, line 2). The directive proper **("Lower your hand")** is preceded by a justification **("She has only said one")**. The fact that the justification occupies the turn-initial position is significant because, in this way, the issuing of the directive within the boundaries of the turn is delayed as much as possible. This deferral of the directive speaks in itself to the dispreferred nature of this kind of social act. In addition to mitigating the directive, the justification provides a reason that socially validates Gloria's claims and rights to subsequently perform such a bold action. The rationalizing function of the justification is further underscored by the phrase "o sea que" **(so,**

therefore, thus . . . etc.) between the justification and the directive proper. As Table 5.3 below shows, another politeness strategy Spanish children used to mitigate the directives they issued to Spanish peers is phrasing the directives as questions, for example "Juan, ¿te quieres estar quieto ya?" **(Juan, do you want to be still now?**, or, **Do you want to stop fidgeting now?)**. Thus, taking the form of quasi-requests, locutionary acts also cushion the illocutionary force of these directives (Austin 1962).

In Example 5.4, however, the basic grammatical form is "DO X" with the name of the child either preceding or following the directive, "Tira ese chicle, Miriam" **(Throw away that chewing-gum, Miriam)** (Example 5.4, line 1). This kind of unmitigated directive, which has been termed *bald on-record*, is one of the most aggravated, negative-affect-laden, and face-threatening social acts that can be performed in interaction. According to Brown and Levinson (1978), a speaker performs baldly on record without redress when the speaker (S) is hierarchically vastly superior to the hearer (H), or when the speaker is certain to be able to enlist audience support to destroy H's face without losing his own. Therefore, this type of directive can be seen as indexically consequential in the interactional construction of hierarchical social relations, as well as in the constitution of firm boundaries of in-group and out-group membership in this community.

As illustrated in Table 5.3, this pattern of grammatical and pragmatic aggravation is present in the vast majority of examples of directives targeting Moroccan immigrant children. In many cases, the aggravation is made more pronounced by placing in front of the directive the emphatic particle *qué*, as in "¡Qué os calléis!" **(Will you shut up!)** or by placing the preposition *ya* (now) at the end of the directive, as in "Estate quietecita ya" **(Now be still)**. In addition, the forcefulness of the directive is often accentuated by producing it with increased volume, vowel lengthening, and an amplified pitch contour, as in "¡CÁLLATE:::!" **(SHUT U:::P!)** (see Table 5.3). Such phonological markers have been amply discussed as being of critical importance in constructing conflict, disagreement, and exclusion, as well as in exaggerating oppositional stances and negative affect in children's peer groups' talk-in-interaction (M. H. Goodwin 1984, 1990a and b, 1995, 1998, 1999a, 2002, 2006; C. Goodwin and M. H. Goodwin 2000). Furthermore, the phonological aspects of how directives are delivered are crucial to the social meaning of directives in this fourth-grade class. While many *bald on-record* strategies directed at Moroccan children are phonologically salient and aggravated, phonological mitigation is used when Spanish children use directives with other Spanish children, particularly if the directives are

Table 5.3   Aggravated peer directives.

Peer Directives (Spanish Child to Moroccan Child) Unmitigated Directives	Peer Directives (Spanish Child to Spanish Child) Mitigated Directives
BALD ON-RECORD – **Do X + Name** Cállate ya, Karim **(Shut up now, Karim)**	**Phrasing Directive as Question/** **Request** ¿Os queréis callar? ¿Os queréis callar ya? **(Do you want to be quiet?** **(Do you want to be quiet now?)** Cristina says this to a group of Spanish students who are making noise during individual silent reading time.
BALD ON-RECORD – **Name + Do X** Mimon baja la mano, ¿eh? **(Mimon lower your hand, eh?)**	**Justification + Directive** Na más ha dicho una, así que baja la mano **(She's only said one so lower your hand)**
BALD ON-RECORD – **Name + Do X** Wafiya, tira el chicle **(Wafiya, throw the chewing-gum away)**	**Name + Phrasing Directive as Question/Request** Juan, ¿te quieres estar quieto ya? **(Do you want to be still now? –or, Do you want to stop fidgeting now?)**
BALD ON-RECORD and **Phonological markedness –** **Name + Do X + Name** Karim, quítate. ¡Kari:::m, Kari:::::m! **(Karim get out of the way. Kari:::m, Kari:::m!)**	**Phonological and Paralinguistic Mitigation – Name + Do X** Roberto, estate quieto **(Roberto, be still –** **or, Roberto, stop fidgeting)** Margarita says this softly and in private to Roberto.

(Continued)

Table 5.3 (*Continued*)

Peer Directives (Spanish Child to Moroccan Child) Unmitigated Directives	Peer Directives (Spanish Child to Spanish Child) Mitigated Directives
BALD ON-RECORD – **Name + Do X** Wafiya qué te calles que tú tienes tu instrumento **(Wafiya, will you shut up.** **You already have your** **instrument)** [11]	**Phonological and Paralinguistic** **Mitigation** ° Estaros quietos **(Be still – second-** **person plural – or,** **Stop fidgeting –** **second-person singular)** Gloria says this softly and in private to a few Spanish boys who were sitting right in front of her and who were fidgeting excessively, presumably interfering with her ability to focus.
BALD ON-RECORD and **Phonological Markedness –** **Do X** ¡Cállate:::! **(Shut u:::p!)**	
BALD ON-RECORD – **Do X + Name** Qué tires el chicle, Miriam **(Will you throw the** **chewing-gum away, Miriam)**	
BALD ON-RECORD – **Do X** Estate quietecita ya **(Be still now)**	
BALD ON-RECORD – **Do X + Name** ¡Y habla en español, Wafiya! **(And speak Spanish, Wafiya!)**	
BALD ON-RECORD – **Do X** ¡Qué os calléis! ((To Karim, Jalal, Yimad)) **(Will you shut up!) ((To** **Karim, Jalal, Yimad))**	

syntactically unmitigated. This is the case, for instance, in the last two examples presented in Table 5.3. Both directives "Roberto, estate quieto" (**"Roberto, be still"**, or, "**Roberto, stop fidgeting"** – second-person singular) and "°Estaros quietos" (**"Be still"** or, **"Stop fidgeting"** – second-person plural) use unmitigated imperative verb forms. In both cases, however, these directives are uttered in a low voice, almost a whisper, particularly the second example. In addition, both of these directives are delivered in a non-public manner, that is, they are said privately to the interested parties, so as not attract the attention of the teacher or of other peers.

Following the pattern already described in tattling practices, there is also a significant difference in the way in which other participants align with the peer directive in Examples 5.3 and 5.4. Although at first glance it may seem that the teacher aligns positively with Gloria's directive to Roberto, a closer analysis of the turn reveals that, in fact, the teacher not only disaligns, but also that, embedded in the disalignment, there is a subtle rebuke of Gloria's behavior: "Muy bien, Gloria, ¿eh? Te voy a poner aquí conmigo" (**Very nice, Gloria, ah? I'm going to put you here with me**) (Example 5.3, line 3). After the apparent praise that initiates the turn (Very nice, Gloria), the teacher makes a comment that effectively questions and undermines Gloria's authority to reprimand her classmates by means of a directive (I'm going to put you here with me). By stating that he's going to put Gloria by his side, that is, *in the position of the teacher*, he is also insinuating that it is not Gloria's prerogative to monitor peers' behavior and, then, engage in admonitions and other forms of correction. Thus, Gloria's directive is both non-ratified interactionally and treated as non-appropriate.

In Example 5.4, however, we find positive alignment of both teacher and other peers towards the *mandato* targeting Miriam. Following the peer's directive in line 1 ("Tira ese chicle, Miriam" **Throw that chewing-gum away, Miriam**), the teacher sanctions the peer's action of reprimanding and correcting Miriam as appropriate, publicly validating the directive in the official space of the classroom by repeating an elliptical version of the command in line 2, "Miriam, ese chi:::cle" (**Miriam, that chewing-gum**). Although the imperative form is elided in this shortened version, the indexical meaning of the act and stance of the teacher is congruent with that of the peer who issued the directive, since the focus of the teacher's repetition is the emphatically-produced noun phrase, "ese chi:::cle" (**That chewing-gum**), which highlights the cause of Miriam's infraction and upholds the negative social identity ascribed to Miriam by her fellow-student as someone who does not comply with the norms of behavior of the community. Similarly, Daniela, another Spanish peer, echoes both the original peer directive and the teacher's recasting of it, by reiterating the command in line 3: "Miriam, el chicle" **(Miriam, the chewing-gum)**. It is important to note that the directive is adamantly repeated by peers and teacher alike until finally in line 4 Miriam acquiesces verbally, "Vale:::" **(OK)**, and, then, complies by getting up to throw away the chewing-gum. It is also significant that, even when Miriam gets up to throw the chewing-gum away, her behavior is closely monitored by two other Spanish girls in the class who follow Miriam attentively with their gaze to verify that she has indeed thrown the chewing-gum in the trash can (see framegrab reproduced above), since, often, children in the class would only pretend to throw the chewing-gum away in similar situations. In this way, the Moroccan child's marginal social positioning is positively ratified by both the teacher and peers, who insist on the *mandato* when Miriam, instead of immediately getting up to throw the chewing-gum away, continues to perform the Music task.

The following table (Table 5.4) summarizes the analysis of the practices of mandatos:

Table 5.4   Peer directives.

	Mandatos Spanish Child to Spanish Child	**Mandatos** Spanish Child to Moroccan Child
Linguistic Encoding	**MITIGATED DIRECTIVE** **Justification + Do X** "Na más ha dicho una, así que baja la mano" **(She's only said one so lower your hand)**	**BALD ON RECORD** **(Name) Do X (Name)** "Tira ese chicle, Miriam" **(Throw that chewing-gum away, Miriam)**
Positioning	Unfair classmate	Uncouth/Ill-bred classmate Non-member of the community
Teacher's Alignment	**Teacher's Negative Alignment** "Muy bien, Gloria. Te voy a poner aquí conmigo" **(Very nice, Gloria. I'm going to put you here with me)**	**Teacher's Positive Alignment** "Miriam, ese chi:::cle" **(Miriam, that chewing-gum)**

Table 5.3   (*Continued*)

	Mandatos Spanish Child to Spanish Child	Mandatos Spanish Child to Moroccan Child
Other Peers' Alignment		**Other Peers' Positive Alignment** "Miriam, el chicle" **(Miriam, the chewing-gum)**

Peer directives, in that they amount to aggravated forms of correction and public shaming, position Moroccan immigrant children in a very precarious and delicate position in the social structure of the school. Certainly, language socialization research has established that censure and shaming routines are an integral part of novice members' socialization into the conventional expectations of any given community (Brown 2002; De León 2005; Fung 1999; Lo and Fung 2012; Ochs 1988; Schieffelin and Ochs 1986a; Schieffelin 1990). In discussing how shaming socialization routines serve to include children in the larger community rather than to set them apart, two crucial elements have been identified cross-culturally: (1) a playful affective key achieved through the deployment of linguistic resources or the horizontal structuring of the participation frameworks, and (2) the lack of negative consequences for children following these routines. As the analysis has already made obvious, neither of these features are, however, present in the practices of *mandatos*, nor in the tattles or fueling-the-fire practices. Not only are negative disciplinary consequences likely to befall Moroccan immigrant children as a result of these practices, but also the affective key of these interactions is characterized by being severe, oppositional, and disapproving.

With these directives particularly, when censure is repeatedly voiced by classroom peers in an unmitigated, public, and direct way that overwhelmingly targets Moroccan children, we have a socialization routine in which children are positioned not only as uncouth classmates, but also as non-members of the community. They are positioned as persons who have to be consistently reminded of rules and other norms of social behavior. Unlike shaming routines of young children by family members documented in other socialization studies, the shaming practices that Moroccan immigrant children encounter in school on a daily basis serve to exclude, rather than include, them from symbolic membership in the social group. Rather than a means of socialization into identities that are congruent with competent membership in the community, such practices realize Moroccan immigrant children's socialization into marginalized, deviant, and negative identities.

5.4 *Echar Leña al Fuego* (Fueling the Fire)

The practice of fueling the fire can be described as an aggravated variant of tattling in that fueling the fire is intended to call teachers' attention to the inappropriate or non-normative behavior of another peer, and in that it is deliberately intended to get the teacher to enact disciplinary measures for the targeted child. Unlike tattling, however, *echar leña al fuego* is not designed as an accusation. In fact, in fueling-the-fire practices, the sequence initiator is never the child-perpetrator, but the child-target. In this sense, fueling the fire sequences are invariably initiated by the child who will eventually become the target of this practice with either an announcement of a problematic event to the teacher (e.g., a child announcing that s/he has forgotten the homework at home or that s/he was not given the handout the day before) or with a particularly sensitive request to the teacher (e.g., asking to borrow the teacher's books or materials). Given that these sequences are delicate, in these announcements and requests, actions are strategically formulated in as neutral or benign a way as possible. In my analysis, what characterizes these sequences as fueling the fire is that these announcements and requests are followed by inflammatory comments from other children to the teachers. Often these comments are deployed as soon as the child-target has made the announcement or request, without the teacher even having a chance to react. These inflammatory comments constitute attempts at subverting the neutral, benign, or accidental character with which the original speakers have imbued their formulations of actions. Therefore, as in the case of *acusar*, it is also important to pay analytic attention to the grammatical encoding of agency and differential degrees of responsibility in the recasting of formulations of action found in *echar leña al fuego* sequences.

As illustrated in Figure 5.3 above, Moroccan immigrant children are almost twice as likely to be victims of these types of inflammatory remarks as other Spanish peers. Also, in line with the analysis of the other two practices, the extent of the severity and aggravation of these remarks in actual interactions is mitigated and diminished when the target of fueling-the-fire practices is another Spanish child in the class, as the analyses of the following examples, 5.5 and 5.6 respectively, will show.

Example 5.5 is extracted from a Music class. On the day of this recording, the children were going to rehearse a composition with half of the class playing instruments and the other half singing. In order to decide which children would get the instruments, the teacher carried out an impromptu oral review of the main concepts that they had been studying in class. Only those children who responded with two questions correctly were initially given instruments. However, at the end of the review, there were still a few instruments to give out. When the teacher is trying to decide the best way to hand out those instruments, Marta, a Spanish student, approaches him to request one, telling him that she has also answered two things correctly: "(también) he dicho dos cosas bien" **(I have (also) said two things correctly)** (line 1).

Example 5.5
Participants: Marta, Teacher, and Ramón

1.	MARTA:	(xxx) (también) he dicho dos cosas bien=
		(xxx) (also) I have said two things correctly=
2.	TEACHER:	¿Has dicho dos cosas bien?
		You have said two things correctly?
3.	MARTA:	((Nods)) Cuando has dicho tú [(xxx)
		((Nods)) When you said [(xxx)
4.	RAMÓN:	Sí pero no – no ha terminao de- de [cirlas
		Yes but she didn't – she didn't [finish saying them
5.	TEACHER:	[No has rematao, Marta=
		[You didn't finish them off, Marta=
6.	TEACHER:	=Venga coge un instrumento
		=Come on, pick up an instrument

The teacher responds in line 2 by repeating Marta's claim with rising intonation, "¿Has dicho dos cosas bien?" **(You have said two things correctly?)**, thus questioning the veracity of Marta's statement, and interactionally signaling the problematicity of Marta's implied request for an instrument. When Marta proceeds to offer an account of these two occasions in an attempt to convince the teacher that she deserves an instrument: "Cuando has dicho tú" **(When you said)** (line 3), Ramón intrudes in the middle of her turn with a fueling-the-fire comment directed at the teacher that is designed to persuade him of the opposite, namely that Marta does not deserve the instrument after all, "Sí pero no – no

ha terminao de decirlas" **(Yes but she didn't - she
didn't finish saying them)** (line 4). Although the turn is initially
shaped to display positive alignment with the insertion of the agreement
token "sí" **(yes)** at the beginning of the turn, the "pero" **(but)**
that follows already foreshadows what is indeed a negative reformulation of
Marta's claim, namely that she has not provided two correct answers, but
only partially correct answers. The upshot is that she has not fulfilled the
conditions for being granted an instrument. Ramón's own initiation of the
turn with an agreement token, and his hesitation, as evidenced by his cut-off
hedging of (**"but she didn't - she didn't finish saying
them"**), may mark his awareness of the socially-dispreferred, tattle-like
nature of what he is about to do, as well as Ramón's own struggles with
how to formulate his turn without getting himself in too much trouble.

In terms of alignment, the teacher initially displays agreement with
Ramón's comment by recasting it in line 5, "No has rematao, Marta"
(You didn't finish them off, Marta). The teacher's positive
alignment, however, also has to be understood in the context of the teacher's
own initial reaction to Marta's request in line 2, when he questioned the
validity of Marta's claim of having given two right answers. In fact, the
teacher starts his turn in line 5 before Ramón has finished saying his in
line 4. In spite of his agreement with Ramón's comment, however, almost
immediately the teacher continues in line 6 with "Venga, coge un
instrumento" **(Come on, pick up an instrument)** (Example
5.5). By nonetheless granting Marta an instrument in line 6, the teacher
renders ineffective Ramón's likely attempt to prevent Marta from obtaining
an instrument, and thus disaligns with the fueling-the-fire practice.

Example 5.6 is extracted from Math class. Before this exchange takes
place, students are getting ready to correct the homework that they were
assigned the day before. The sequence initiator is Mimon, who announces
that he has forgotten his homework at home in line 1, "Seño (.) Seño
el ejercicio me lo he olvidao en casa" **(Miss (.) Miss
I forgot the exercise at home)**. Even before the teacher proceeds
to scold him, his peers start making inflammatory comments.

Example 5.6
Participants: Mimon, Ramón, Estrella, Karim, Margarita, and Cristina

1.	MIMON:	Seño (.) Seño el ejercicio me lo
		he olvidao en casa
		Miss (.) Miss I forgot the exercise
		at home
2.	STUDENTS:	Aahhg Aahhg
		Aahhg Aahhg

3.   RAMÓN:

> Pos ya sabes lo que dijo la otra
> semana la señorita que el que no
> trajera los esos se iba pa casa
> **Well, you already know what Miss said**
> **the other week that whoever didn't**
> **bring the things would go home**

4.   TEACHER: ¿Qué hacemos, Mimon?(1.0) ¿Te mando
a tu casa?
What do we do, Mimon?(1.0) Do I
send you home?

5.   TEACHER: ¡Hombre!
Please!

6.   KARIM: No~te~rías
Don't~laugh

7.   ESTRELLA: Seño siempre se le olvida algo
Miss he always forgets something

8.   TEACHER: Bueno, los demás también callaros,
¿vale?
Well, the rest of you be quiet, too, OK?

9.   TEACHER: Mimon, ¿qué hacemos? (3.5)
Mimon, what do we do? (3.5)
No, explsícame (2.0)
No, explain it to me (2.0)
¿Cuándo va a venir tu padre o tu
madre a hablar conmigo?
When is your father or your mother
going to come to talk to me?

10.   MIMON: °No sé
°I don't know

11.   MARGARITA: °¿No sabes?
°You don't know?

12.   TEACHER: Hace ya mucho tiempo que te lo
estoy diciendo

                    I've been telling you for a long
                    time

13.   CRISTINA: Pos [de:::sde – desde el año pasao
                    Well [si:::nce – since last year

14.   TEACHER: [¿Ummm?
                    [Hummm?

15.   TEACHER: Sí:::
                    Yes

16.   RAMÓN: Es verdad desde el año pa[sao
                    It's true since last [year

17.   TEACHER: [Y tú en vez de arreglar las cosas
                        y portarte – y trabajar. . .
                        [And you instead of fixing things
                        and behave – and work. . .

18.   TEACHER: Mimon, ¿así no podemos seguir, e:h?=
                    Mimon, we can't go on like this, eh?=
                    =Te voy a prestar el material yo
                    hoy pero así no podemos seguir.
                    =I'm going to lend you the materials
                    today but we can't go on like this.
                    ((Mimon nods repeatedly))

19.   TEACHER: NO. Sí pero SÍ, no sí para que me
                    calle, ¿VALE?
                    NO. Yes means YES, not yes so that
                    I keep quiet, OK?

20.   TEACHER: ¿ENTENDIDO?
                    UNDERSTOOD?

21.   TEACHER: Mañana martes tengo yo e::h tutoría.
                    Tomorrow, Tuesday, I have e::h
                    tutoring day
                    =Así que dile a tu papá o a tu
                    mamá que vengan a hablar conmigo
                    mañana, ¿vale?
                    =So tell your dad or your mom to
                    come to talk to me tomorrow, OK
                    (.)¿Vale, Mimon?
                    (.)OK, Mimon?

22.   TEACHER: Déjame tu agenda que [te lo voy a
                    apuntar
                    Let me have your planner that [I'm
                    going to write it down

23.   CRISTINA: [Seño, no tienen muchas
                                        ganas de hablar contigo
                                        [Miss, they are not too
                                        eager to talk to you

24. TEACHER: Sssss (A Cristina)
                Shhhh (To Cristina)

As soon as Mimon announces that he has forgotten his homework, there is a series of scandalized exclamations performed in a choral, polyphonic manner by many of Mimon's peers "Aahhg Aahhg" in line 2. These exclamations lay the foundations for the escalation that is to come in the following turns, since they are designed to draw other participants' attention (including, of course, the teacher's) to Mimon's infraction as a serious violation worthy of a stern reprimand. Then, one of Mimon's Spanish peers, Ramón, produces the first inflammatory comment in line 3, "Pos ya sabes lo que dijo la otra semana la señorita que el que no trajera los esos se iba pa casa" (**Well, you already know what Miss said the other week that whoever didn't bring the things would go home**). This first comment is interesting not only due to its inciting nature, but also because of its grammatical structure vis-à-vis its delivery. In particular, the gaze direction of the child speaker while delivering this utterance is crucial for escalation. Although this sentence is produced with Mimon as the grammatical addressee, as is clear by the second-person singular of the verb "sabes" (you know) and the reference to the teacher in the third person "lo que dijo la otra semana la señorita" (**what Miss said the other week**), Ramón, the speaker, is looking directly at the teacher and not at Mimon when he produces it (see framegrab reproduced above). The gaze direction then ratifies the teacher as the intended recipient of this utterance, which is in effect an attempt to get the teacher to suspend Mimon. In addition, with the verb form "sabes" (**you know**) and the preposition "ya" (**now**), the Moroccan child is cast as a cognizant actor who is aware of both class rules and consequences, and who has broken those rules knowingly.

The negative identity ascribed to Mimon is both ratified and amplified by another inflammatory comment produced soon after by another Spanish classmate, Estrella. This comment in line 7 does directly address the teacher: "Seño, siempre se le olvida algo" (**Miss, he always forgets something**). By the use of the intensifier adverb, "siempre," (**always**) the classmate effectively questions the accidental nature indexed by the verb "forget" with which Mimon had characterized his own action. The use of modalizing forms, such as *always*, to modify descriptions and formulations of action characterizes *extreme case formulations*, and their use is prevalent in accusations and attributions of blame (Pomerantz 1986). Extreme case formulations are a polarizing way of linguistically framing one's own or, more commonly, other people's actions by including adverbs and other modalizing terms such as *always, never, all the time* . . ., and so on. Interestingly, in research on how minorities are discussed by members of the dominant population, extreme case formulations are one of the most common discursive means for constructing the behavior of immigrants and other minorities as deviant in everyday interactions (e.g., Augoustinos and Every 2007; Verkuyten 2001). With the extreme case formulation of Mimon's behavior, the second classmate not only aligns positively with the inciting comment of the first classmate, but also manages to increase the escalation of the interaction by rendering ineffective Mimon's attempt to present his own action as an isolated accident and by characterizing him as essentially a bad student, irresponsible and careless.

This is not, however, the only instance of other peers' positive alignment with the action of *echar leña al fuego*. Other classmates continue to intervene and deploy inflammatory comments until the end of the sequence, in spite of the teachers request in line 8, asking them to be quiet, "Bueno, los demás también callaros, vale?" **(Well, the rest of you be quiet, too, OK?)**. In line 9, for instance, the teacher asks Mimon when his parents are going to come and talk to her, and Mimon responds that he does not know **"No sé"** (line 10). Immediately after this response, a third classmate, Margarita, repeats Mimon's response with a rising intonation, "¿No sabes?" **(You don't know?)** (line 11). The questioning, slightly ironic, tone of the repetition casts doubt over Mimon's response, and also helps to construct a negative moral identity for the Moroccan child. Furthermore, when in line 12 the teacher reminds Mimon that she's been telling him for a long time that she wants to talk to his parents, another classmate, Cristina, comes in specifying exactly how long it has been, "Pos de:::sde-desde el año pasao" **(Well si:::nce- since last year)** (line 13). Then, Ramón comes in to bear witness to the veracity of what, Cristina, the previous speaker, has said, stating "Es verdad desde el año pasao" **(It's true since last year)** (line 16). Throughout these instances of escalation, the Moroccan child and his parents are targeted and constructed as a certain kind of moral personae: the child is portrayed as a liar and as an irresponsible student who ignores class rules and his teacher's requests and recommendations; the parents are portrayed as people who do not have any interest in the education of their son. This is made clear by the last inflammatory comment deployed by Cristina, implying that Mimon's parents did not want to come and talk to her, "Seño, no tienen muchas ganas de hablar contigo" **(Miss, they are not too eager to talk to you)** (line 23).

Unlike the clear positive alignment of other peers, the teacher's position in this interaction is much more ambivalent than in previous examples. Certainly, the severity of the teacher's reprimand increases throughout the sequence and is congruent with the escalation trajectory of the children's inflammatory comments. However, although eventually Mimon is given a parental note with a request for an extraordinary parent-teacher meeting, in the end he is allowed to continue to work in class with replacement handouts and materials. In addition, on two occasions the teacher tells the rest of Mimon's peers to be silent, once in line 8, as discussed earlier, and another time in line 24 "Sssss" **(Shhhh)**. Although these examples are small in number, there are a handful of instances in which the teachers display ambivalence in aligning positively with the practices of *acusar* (tattling), *mandatos* (peer directives), and *echar leña al fuego* (fueling the fire) targeting Moroccan immigrant children, particularly when there are high levels of aggravation in the enactment of these practices, as in this last example. Teachers tended to respond negatively and swiftly not only to physical aggression and overt racial insults, but also to blatantly deliberate cases of Moroccan children's exclusion from participating in games and class activities, as described earlier in the chapter. It would then make sense that the more aggravated *acusar*, *mandatos*, and *echar leña al fuego* became, the more likely teachers would be to disalign.

A key point that I would like to emphasize, however, is that the architecture of social exclusionary practices experienced daily by Moroccan immigrant children in this school setting may be far more subtle and complex than blunt cases of verbal or physical abuse and rejection. As the previous examples show, constructing exclusion is a complex social act in terms of participation frameworks and the participants' alignments with respect to the speaker, the practice, and the target of such practice. In particular, when the target of the three practices analyzed is a Moroccan immigrant child, the participation frameworks and alignments that sustain them can be summarized as follows:

In *acusar*, the intended recipient and addressee is always the teacher. Due to its public character, however, it is meant to be overheard by the Moroccan child and by other Spanish peers, who usually then ratify the actions and the stance of the tattler.

In *mandatos*, Moroccan immigrant children are the main addressees. Yet, like tattling and fueling the fire, *mandatos* are designed to get the teacher to take disciplinary action. Therefore, teachers are crucial overhearers of the mandatos. As in the case of *acusar*, teachers as well as other Spanish peers regularly align positively with the speaker of the directive. In *echar leña al fuego*, teachers are most commonly the intended recipients of the comments, although sometimes Moroccan children can be addressees. This action, however, requires the participation of other Spanish peers who, although initially participating as overhearers, very often become active co-constructors of the action.

In thinking about the complex architecture involved in the constitution of exclusionary practices through language use in interaction, social exclusion cannot be reduced to a directive or an accusation targeting a Moroccan child. Rather, social exclusion as an interactional achievement is accomplished through the ratification of the acts and stances of the original speaker by other participants in these interactions, namely teachers and other peers. In this sense, the only one who is consistently excluded from these alignments and differentially positioned in the participation frameworks of these interactions without mitigation of any kind is the Moroccan child.

An important point to add to this discussion is that the peer policing and surveillance of Moroccan immigrant children's behavior described throughout this chapter went beyond the boundaries of the classroom proper. Sarah's interview fragment at the beginning of the chapter, about how she was once reported to the teachers for speaking in Moroccan Arabic with another Moroccan student in the bathroom, makes clear that Moroccan children's behavior was also monitored in many other settings in school, even those that we would consider more private. The violations, or perceived violations (speaking in Moroccan Arabic was, after all, not against school rules), that Moroccan immigrant children incurred in the hallways, the playgrounds, and even in the bathroom, were also the object of Spanish children's tattles and fueling-the-fire sequences. In this sense, the active surveillance of Moroccan immigrant children's behavior by their Spanish peers echoes, in many ways, the intense scrutiny to which the Moroccan immigrant community as a whole has been subjected at national and local levels.

In addition, while this fourth-grade class was the group that I followed and videotaped systematically, I found evidence that this linguistically mediated surveillance and racialized exclusion also took place in other classrooms and grades in the school. During the course of our interviews, Kamal and Manal, both in sixth grade, spoke candidly and shared stories that were very reminiscent of the kinds of exclusionary practices that I had been observing among the fourth-grade students. The following interview excerpt is particularly poignant in that Manal not only shares how Moroccan children in other grades of the school become the targets of these types of practices, but also that Moroccan immigrant children themselves interpret these interactional practices as being exclusionary and harmful. In this excerpt, I was having a group interview with some of the focal girls of the study: Worda, Wafiya, Manal, and Sarah. Sarah's toddler brother, Anuar, was also present in the interaction. The girls started talking about their impression of how Spanish children did not like them. At that point, half facetiously, I asked the girls: "How do you know they don't like you? Do they come and tell you that?" Probably annoyed by my tongue-in-cheek tone, Manal started shaking her head emphatically.

INMA: Tú dices que no con la cabeza, ¿qué pasa Manal?
**You say no with your head, what is going
on Manal?**

MANAL: Qué no [que lo dice:::n a sus amigas=
No ((emphatic)) they say it to their friends
((Anuar starts whimpering and there is a brief
interruption))

INMA: ¿Cómo que lo dicen a sus amigas?
How is it that they say it to their friends?

MANAL: Miran una mirada - por ejemplo yo (a:/
ahora a) ti-
**They look a look ((meaning= they give you a
look))- for example now I to you ((meaning
she is= going to give me that kind of a look))**
tú eres una marroquina y yo una española.
You're a Moroccan and I a Spaniard

Te miro
**I look at you ((Rolls her eyes
shakes her head))**

y- y cogen a su amiga y están así
**and- and they grab her friend and they are
like this ((Turns to Worda and pretends to
whisper things in her ear))**

((Anuar starts
crying and
I turn to
tend to him))

Manal starts reporting this microaggression (Solórzano, Ceja, and Yosso 2000) by asserting that "`lo dice:::n a sus amigas`" **(They say it to their friends)**. Interestingly, however, rather than quoting the speech of the Spanish girls – that is, what they presumably say to their friends about Moroccan immigrant children – Manal quotes instead the behavior of the Spanish children, by demonstrating with embodied displays (Clark and Gerrig 1990) how Spanish children position their Moroccan peers as intended overhearers of their negative remarks about them. Moreover, by offering embodied demonstration of Spanish children's looks, headshakes, eye rolls, and secretive whispers as part of her reporting (see framegrabs above), Manal manages to convey powerfully the contemptuous affect and emotional stance with which Spanish children's critical remarks are delivered (Goodwin, Cekaite, and Goodwin 2012). An important aspect of Manal's quotations is that, while these transmodal stance-taking practices are usually produced by their original authors with a high degree of stylization (Goodwin and Alim 2010), Manal animates her reported demonstrations of these practices in a markedly non-stylized manner. Her containment in representing these transmodal practices imbues her narrative of microaggressions with great gravitas and authenticity. After a brief interruption in which I turned to tend to Sarah's little brother, who had started crying, Manal continued with her narrative by addressing directly the practices of *acusar* (tattling) and *mandatos* (peer directives), particularly the latter:

```
MANAL: una cosa, es que se me ha olvidado antes
       decirte-
       Something that I forgot to say earlier
       que::: se ponen- se ponen- a ver (.)
       that they do- they do- let's see (.)
       que cuando están hablando las chicas
       españolas=
       that when the Spanish girls are talking=
       =nosotros no decimos na'
       =we don't say anything
       y ellos cuando estamos hablando pues eh-
       dicen=
       and they when we are talking then eh- they
       say=
INMA:      [Ah en clase- en clase
           [Ah in class- in class
  ((Manal nods))
```

=`"PERO QUEREIS
CA- CALLAR"` (.)
**=BUT DO YOU WANT TO
SH- SHUT UP**
así gritán[donos
((Frowning))
**Like that yell
[ing at us**

INMA: O sea que cuando están hablando- montando
escándalo=
So that when they are talking- being rowdy
=los chicos españoles vosotros no decís
nada=
=the Spanish kids, you don't say anything=
Pero cuando [(inaudible)
But when [(inaudible)

MANAL: [y chicas españolas
              [and Spanish girls

INMA: Y cuándo estáis hablando vosotros ¿qué
pasa?
And when you are talking, what happens?

MANAL: Qué dicen CALLAROS (.) así gritándonos
**That they say SHUT UP (.) like that
yelling at us**

WAFIYA: Y también lo hacen en mi clase=
And they also do it in my class=

INMA: ((To Wafiya)) =En tu clase lo he visto yo
hacer eso (.) Sí
**=In your class I have seen that being done
(.) Yes**

WORDA: A nosotros también
       They do it to us, too
  INMA: ¿Sí?
       Yes?
((Worda nods))

Manal continues her description of daily microaggressions with a narrative of how tattling and peer directives are directed at Moroccan immigrant children in her class. Although Manal is a sixth-grader, she could have well been *replaying* (Goffman 1974) many of the examples that I witnessed in the fourth-grade classroom and that I have analyzed above. In fact, Manal's narrative almost immediately incites the beginning of potential *second stories* (Sacks 1992) by Wafiya and Worda, who in subsequent turns, respectively, add "Y también lo hacen en mi clase" **(and they also do it in my class)** and "A nosotros también" **(They do it to us, too)**.[12] In reproducing the grammatical aggravation, "dicen CALLAROS" **(they say SHUT UP)**, the phonological salience, "así gritándonos" **(like that, yelling at us)**, and the negative embodied affect (see framegrab above), of Spanish children's actions, Manal offers a quotation that is not only a representation, but also a commentary about these actions. In this way, she also communicates her own negative affective stance towards them. As Besnier (1993) has shown in his analysis of the affective meaning of reported speech, there are many linguistic strategies that narrators can use as keying devices to express their affective point of view and pass judgment on what they are reporting. By emphasizing in her quotations prosodic and embodied elements whose main function is to communicate affect, in this case Spanish children's negative and critical affect, Manal is also able to convey how these practices make her feel wronged and not accepted by her Spanish peers. Narratives like Manal's give us some indication of how Moroccan immigrant children perceive and emotionally react to these types of interactions with their Spanish peers.

5.5 Moroccan Immigrant Children's Reactions to Practices of Exclusion

The analysis has, thus far, mostly focused on how Spanish children construct marginal, negative social identities for their Moroccan immigrant peers in everyday practices of social exclusion at school, and how, in the context of these interactions, these identities are consistently ratified by other peers and even by teachers. The investigation of how Moroccan immigrant children are treated and positioned by others in routine activities is pivotal to this ethnographic account of the micropolitics of inclusion and belonging. It is also important to analyze how Moroccan immigrant children react to these practices and attempt to position themselves in these interactions. Given the cumulative effect that the repeated ascription of negative social identities may have for children's sense of who they are, it is significant, whether Moroccan immigrant children accept, resist, challenge, or try to subvert these negative social identities, as well as the marginal positions, they are frequently delegated to. Investigating Moroccan immigrant children's reactions is important, since peer harassment based on ethnic characteristics has stronger negative effects on children's momentary self-feelings than victimization based on personal characteristics (Verkuyten and Thijs 2001, 2006).

Examining individuals' emotions at the linguistic and interactional levels can often be fraught with difficulties, because participants may have social, cultural, or personal reasons not to display certain emotional states publicly (Abu-Lughod 1985; Brison 1998; Wikan 1989; Wilce 1995). Nonetheless, it is possible to analyze, and in this case I would also argue that it is even important to consider, how Moroccan immigrant children may experience the negative emotion directed towards them, focusing on their reactions to their teachers' and peers' practices of exclusion. While there was a certain degree of individual variation in the reactions of Moroccan immigrant children to their Spanish peers' practices of exclusion, there was also a typology of observed reactions. This typology ranged from compliance and silence to denial to more confrontational reactions, akin to those that have already been discussed in previous examples, such as Kamal calling Spanish children *payo rojo* (red payo) in response to their insults, or Mimon's public and unmitigated negative alignment against tattling, "No te importa" **(It's none of your business)** (Example 5.1, line 7).

5.6   Compliance and Silence

Perhaps because most of these practices occur in the space of the classroom, one of the most pervasive reactions was compliance and cessation of the problematic behavior. In many cases, Moroccan immigrant children remained silent during these exchanges. In light of both interactional and interview data, I would suggest that Moroccan children's silence has a polysemic value. First, it is important to contextualize children's acquiescence and silence in relation to the strong alignments among Spanish classmates and teachers that were common in the enactment of the practices analyzed above. As discussed, the participation frameworks in these interactions often left Moroccan immigrant children in a defenseless and socially precarious position. An interesting observation is that the higher the number of Spanish peers that joined in these actions and the clearer the positive alignment of the teacher towards the practices of *acusar* (tattling), *mandatos* (peer directives), and *echar leña al fuego* (fueling the fire), the more likely Moroccan immigrant children were to comply silently. It would be a mistake, however, to portray Moroccan children as either unaffected by these practices of exclusion or as passive victims. Given that the children were more likely to remain silent the stronger the positive alignment of their teachers to their peers' practices of exclusion, Moroccan immigrant children's silence should be interpreted in relation to an ethos of displaying appropriate intergenerational respect common among families of the Moroccan immigrant community in Vallenuevo. In households of the Moroccan immigrant community, as well as in other diasporic settings, such as the Arabic-language classes that will be discussed in the next chapter, Moroccan children were shamed as disrespectful if they answered back when reprimanded by an adult. Such norms and meanings of respect have been documented cross-culturally in children's socialization (see e.g., Lo and Howard 2009).

In addition to these cultural norms, however, children's silences carry concurrently other crucial meanings. An important one can be found in the indexes of resistance and opposition that can be seen in the ways in which Moroccan immigrant children often enacted these silences. For instance, in Example 5.4 discussed above, Miriam stopped chewing gum and got up to throw it away in the trash can after two peer directives and the teacher's reprimand. Nevertheless, Miriam did not do so immediately and waited until she had fully completed the music task that she was supposed to perform. Moreover, when Miriam's delay in action after the first peer directive and the teacher's reproof prompted a second peer directive, she turned to her peers, saying "Vale:::" **(OK/Enough)** (line 4) with a marked, elongated vowel length and a tinge of frustration in her voice. Phonological features such as exaggerated vowel length, marked intonation contours, and voice quality are prime resources in the expression of emotion (Goodwin and Goodwin 2000; Ochs and Schieffelin 1989). While complying with peers and teacher's directives, the prosodic features of Miriam's turn also denote a negative affective reaction, conveying simultaneously her exasperation and oppositional stance to the treatment she has just received.

Other instances in which Moroccan immigrant children remain silent for many turns in these sequences can also be analyzed as having this double value of respectful compliance coupled with a negative affective key. Indeed, children's silence in other contexts has sometimes been analyzed as an interactional form of resistance, non-compliance, and even opposition, particularly in social situations when they feel threatened by adult authority figures. In parent-teacher conferences or medical interactions, for instance, children often resort to silence as a deliberate strategy of defense or to express disagreement when they feel the heavy scrutiny and complicity of their parents, teachers, and doctors.[13]

Although the examples discussed here are different from parent-teacher meetings or medical interactions, they are also characterized by the intense policing and surveillance of Moroccan immigrant children's behavior, as well as by the strong alignment of peers, and often also of teachers, against the targeted Moroccan child. It is, therefore, not surprising that Moroccan children show their resistance by staying silent and refusing to participate in interactions in which they may feel harassed, vulnerable, and helpless. The more aggravated the actions and the more intense the complicity of peers and teachers, the more likely Moroccan immigrant children are to adopt silence as their interactional response. This is the case, for instance, in Example 5.6. Although this is one of the longest sequences analyzed, Mimon, after announcing that he has forgotten his homework at home, is virtually silent throughout the rest of the turns, minimally responding with nods to the stern scolding of the teacher or sometimes not even responding at all, as the repeated questions and long interactional silences in these two turns of the teacher evidence:

4.   TEACHER: ¿Qué hacemos, Mimon?(1.0) ¿Te mando a
               tu casa?
               **What do we do, Mimon?(1.0) Do I send
               you home?**
9.   TEACHER: Mimon, ¿qué hacemos? (3.5) No,
               explícame (2.0)
               ¿Cuándo va a venir tu padre o tu
               madre a hablar conmigo?
               **Mimon, what do we do? (3.5) No,
               explain it to me (2.0)
               When is your father or your mother
               going to come to talk to me?**

It is crucial to remember that, in this particular example, the increasingly serious scolding of the teacher is additionally punctuated by the inflammatory comments of at least five of Mimon's peers.

Another important dimension of these silences is the gestures and kinesic behavior of the children during these interactions. Children's embodied dispositions can also hold important clues to the polysemic value of their

Figure 5.4   Mimon and Karim's embodied reactions.

silences. In particular, it is in their embodied displays Moroccan children's own negative emotions regarding these practices of exclusion become most obvious. Children's kinesic behavior is usually characterized by grave and serious facial expressions, by lowered heads, which are sometimes half-covered with their hands, and averted gaze, which often remain fixed on some item on the desk. The two framegrabs in Figure 5.4 illustrate these embodied reactions. The first one is precisely from Example 5.6 when Mimon is being severely reprimanded by the teacher in the midst of peers' inflammatory comments. The second framegrab is extracted from Example 5.2, when, after having been the target of a tattle, Karim's behavior is being censured by the teacher and negatively evaluated by one of his peers.

These embodied displays, which are congruent with reactions typically associated with shame, embarrassment, and humiliation, are good indicators of children's momentary vexation, as well as the potential longer-term impact that their peers and teachers' negative assessments of them may have on Moroccan immigrant children's feelings about themselves. Apart from these embodied dispositions, in interviews where children shared narratives of microaggressions, like the one discussed above, children overtly reported an array of negative feelings similar to those that can be gleaned from children's corporeal reactions throughout these sequences. These feelings ranged on a continuum from anger to distress, with some children, such as Kamal and Wafiya, expressing higher levels of exasperation and readily sharing stories of how they have often fought back, particularly outside the classroom; and some other children, such as Worda and Manal, leaning more towards dejection, expressing how badly not being accepted by their peers made them feel.

5.7   Denial and Confrontation

Sometimes, even in classroom settings, Moroccan immigrant children displayed overt, verbal reactions to counter their peers' allegations and defend themselves. One of the most common responses of this sort found in the examples is the denial of the accusations. An instance of denial can be found, for instance, in Example 5.2, when, after one of Karim's peers reports that he is painting his zipper with markers, he defies the accusation by saying "¿En qué cremallera?" **(On what zipper?)** (line 4), while looking at his jacket zipper with a surprised expression (see Figure 5.5 below).

Figure 5.5   Karim acting surprised.

More commonly, however, children would oppose their classmates' comments and accusations by producing the negative response cry "No:::" in the immediate next turn in a phonologically salient way. This response occurs in Example 5.7 after Cristina informs the teacher that Mimon has taken his chewing gum out of his mouth and put it in his pocket (lines 2 and 4):

Example 5.7
Participants: Cristina, Mimon, and Teacher

```
1.  CRISTINA: Maestra (.) Mimon se ha sacao el
             chicle=
             Teacher (.) Mimon has removed his
             chewing-gum=
             =y se lo ha metio en el bolsillo
             =and has put it in his pocket
```

```
  2.  MIMON:     No:::
                 No:::
  3.  TEACHER:   Mimon (luego) se tiran, ¿eh?
                 Mimon (after) they are thrown away,
                 OK?
  4.  MIMON:     No:: ((To Cristina))
                 No::
  5.  CRISTINA:  ¿No:::? ((Pointing at Mimon's pocket))
                 No:::?
```

Another example of these negative response cries can also be found in Example 5.9, reproduced below, when Susana reports to the teacher that Wafiya is making fun of her (line 2). This type of response cry is commonly used by children in counter-moves when managing conflict and disagreement within their peer groups (e.g., M. H. Goodwin, 1998, 1999a), and can be characterized by indexing a negative affective stance of opposition and defiance toward the action to which they are responding. Yet, Moroccan immigrant children's attempts to oppose the actions of their classmates by emphatically denying their accusations were often not successful in the classroom because peers would respond to these denials with accounts and/ or elaborate demonstrations. These demonstrations often involved the replay of the Moroccan child's infraction for the teacher and for other peers, who would then, much more often than not, positively align with the accusation. These moves are used as proof of the veracity of the accusations that Moroccan children attempt to deny (see, for instance, Example 5.2 above in which Gloria replays how Karim was coloring the zipper in his jacket). In Example 5.7, Cristina also counters Mimon's denial by mimicking his response cry with rising intonation, while pointing at the pocket where Mimon had put his chewing gum.

In a small number of cases, Moroccan immigrant children responded to their peers' actions in an even more oppositional way, verbally confronting their classmates and questioning the appropriateness of their behavior. In Example 5.8, for instance, Wafiya successfully manages to subvert an attempt at tattling by Margarita, one of her Spanish classmates.

Example 5.8
Participants: Margarita, Teacher, Wafiya

```
  1.  MARGARITA:  ¿Qué haces Wafiya?
                  What are you doing Wafiya?
  2.  TEACHER:    Sssssss. Ya: ((proceeds to continue
                  teaching the lesson))
                  Shhhhhh. Enough
```

3.　WAFIYA:　　¿Qué te importa?
　　　　　　　What do you care?

The sequence opens with a loud question by a Spanish girl, Margarita, "¿Qué haces Wafiya?" **(What are you doing Wafiya?)** (line 1). Wafiya at that moment was indeed playing at her desk with a small toy. Wafiya's actions were out of the sight of the teacher, but they were, within the visual range of Margarita, who happened to be sitting next to her. Thus, the question was not deployed to find out about Wafiya's activities at that moment, but, rather, the question can be analyzed as a covert accusation designed to bring the teacher's attention to Wafiya's misbehavior, while avoiding going on record with a tattle. The accusatory nature of the question is underscored by its public nature, since the Spanish student asks the question loud enough for everyone else — including the teacher — to hear it, in spite of her physical proximity to Wafiya. In line 3, Wafiya responds to the Spanish girl's question in a confrontational way by posing another equally *false* question, in that Wafiya's question is another covert accusation and an attempt to shame the Spanish girl for her action. Wafiya's question, "¿Qué te importa?" **(What do you care?)** (line 3), characterizes Margarita's actions as an inappropriate intrusion and effectively questions her right and authority (or lack thereof, in this case) to police her peers' behaviors. In this way, Wafiya deflects the negative identity that Margarita tried to ascribe to her and counter-attacks insinuating another negative social identity for Margarita, that of a tattler or a teacher's pet. In this regard, Wafiya's move is very similar to Mimon's in Example 5.1, in which Mimon attempted to expose the inappropriateness of Rosa's tattling behavior by confronting her with the comment "No te importa" **(It's none of your business)** Example 5.1, line 7).

A crucial common dimension of Wafiya and Mimon's confrontational responses is that they both follow explicit teachers' disalignment with the tattling action performed by their Spanish classmates, Margarita and Rosa, respectively. Unlike in the majority of the examples found in the corpus, in these cases the teacher neither acknowledges nor ratifies the accusations, but rather negatively aligns with them. In Example 5.1, the teacher reprimands, Rosa, the tattler, by telling her "Vamo' a ver, Rosa. ¿Y TÚ por qué me dices que ella no sabe hacerlo?" **(Let's see, Rosa. And why do YOU tell me that she doesn't know how to do it?)**. Similarly, in Example 5.8, after requesting silence, the teacher proceeds with the lesson, "Sssssssss. Ya:" **(Shh-hhhhh. Enough)** (line 2). Earlier I explained that the more intense the scrutiny and the complicity between Spanish peers and teachers, the more likely Moroccan children were to retreat into silence. In this regard, it is significant that, conversely, the few examples in which Moroccan children verbally confront and overtly challenge their classmates, coincide with teachers' scolding of tattlers. These examples reveal the decisive role that teachers can have in the everyday social inclusion/exclusion of Moroccan immigrant children at school. Even a seemingly insignificant action, like disaligning with a tattler, can change the dynamics in participation frameworks so that Moroccan immigrant children are not rendered so socially vulnerable and have more interactional opportunities to defend themselves.

Example 5.9 is another instance of Moroccan immigrant children verbally challenging and confronting their peers' accusations. Susana, a Spanish student, reports to the teacher that Wafiya is making fun of her (line 1). What makes this example interesting and different from the previous instances discussed, is that, apart from Wafiya's denial of the accusation with a phonologically salient response cry (**"No::::"**) (line 2), there is also an effective counter move in the immediate next turn, performed by Mimon.

Example 5.9
Participants: Susana, Wafiya, Mimon

```
1.  SUSANA: Wafiya me está haciendo burla
            Wafiya is making fun of me
2.  WAFIYA: No::::
            No::::
3.  MIMON:  ((To Susana)) Sí tú eres como la seño
            (normal)
            Yes, you are like the (regular) Miss
            (=teacher) ((To Susana))
```

Mimon's reaction in line 3 is reminiscent of Wafiya's confrontational response in Example 5.8, and with his own in Example 5.1, in that it effectively fends off the accusation, while simultaneously shaming the Spanish peer for her tattling behavior. While in those two responses the ascription of a negative social identity for the Spanish tattler is only implied (**"¿Qué te importa?"** – **What do you care?** and **"No te importa"** – **It's none of your business**), in Mimon's response in Example 5.9, this identity is invoked in no unambiguous terms, **"Sí, tú eres como la seño (normal)"** (**Yes, you are like the (regular) Miss**) (line 3). Mimon succeeds in putting an end to the accusation sequence by portraying Susana's monitoring and reporting as inappropriate precisely on the grounds that she is acting like a *teacher* would and not like a *peer* is supposed to act. Like other responses discussed in this section – namely behavioral compliance, silence, embodied displays of emotion, and verbal denials – Moroccan children's overt challenges to their classmates' actions speak to the degree to which they are sensitive to and vexed by these practices of exclusion. Moroccan immigrant children's confrontational responses are also indicative of their awareness of the indexical meanings of their Spanish peers' actions and stances, as well as indicative of their competence to counter them when participation frameworks allow for it, such as when the teacher or peers do not align positively with the tattler.

Overt oppositional responses are crucial in understanding the impact these practices may have on Moroccan immigrant children's sense of not-belonging. The following example is a few turns after the fueling-the-fire sequence analyzed in Example 5.6. After severely admonishing Mimon, the teacher asks him to write a note to his parents in his daily planner about what has happened in class and requests an extraordinary parent-teacher meeting. When a classmate asks the teacher whether she should write the note for Mimon, Mimon turns to his classmate visibly angry and responds "¿Qué te crees- qué te crees que yo soy tonto?" (**What do you think- what do you think, that I am dumb?**) (line 3). Once again, Mimon's strong response comes after the teacher has already responded that he knows how to do it.

Example 5.10
Participants: María, Teacher, Mimon

1.	MARÍA:	Maestra (.) Maestra ¿se lo apunto?
		Teacher (.) Teacher do I write it
		down for him?
2.	TEACHER:	Él sabe
		He knows
3.	MIMON:	¿Qué te crees- [que te crees que
		yo soy tonto?
		What do you think- [what do you
		think, that I am dumb?
4.	TEACHER:	[Él sabe
		[He knows

Responses such as this indicate that Moroccan immigrant children are aware of being regarded as different or, worse, as inferiors, by their own classmates.

5.8 Conclusion

This chapter has analyzed the complex social and linguistic architecture of exclusionary practices that Moroccan immigrant children in Vallenuevo routinely encounter in school. In the last two decades, linguistic anthropology has paid increasingly more attention to the ways in which migrants are stratified, as well as to the ways in which entire immigrant groups are constructed in categories of exclusion in immigration policy.[14] Despite these important developments, there is still much to understand regarding the role of language in the micropolitics of social life in immigrant communities. In considering the origins of the experience of racialized exclusion and alienation as a social-interactional achievement, this chapter has important implications for expanding current understandings of everyday language as an instrument of power and control, and of the power of language to perpetuate social and ethnic inequalities (Alim 2005; Philips 2004; Hill 2001, 2008; Urciuoli 1996). It also provides important insights for other lines of research that examine how language is implicated in the sociocultural and political processes through which symbolic domination and structural exclusion are constructed at macro–social levels (Bourdieu 1991). In trying to understand complex phenomena, such as exclusion, alienation, and discrimination, it is important to consider how language operates at different levels of social processes, from routinized everyday interaction to the hegemonically ideologized discourses of the dominant society. In this chapter, I have shown how much the historically-informed discourses about contemporary Moroccan immigration, discussed in Chapter 2, organize the quotidian social interactions of Moroccan immigrant children in Vallenuevo. Conversely, I have also demonstrated how seemingly banal exchanges reproduce these ideologies and sustain historically-informed discrimination, even in an environment where people are ostensibly promoting alternative discourses, such as interculturality and inclusion.

In terms of the impact that these practices may have on Moroccan immigrant children's sense of not-belonging, it is important to understand how immigrant children are put into positions of being treated differently. Paths to racialized exclusion and alienation involve a complex set of teacher and student social practices. Apart from the differential way in which Moroccan immigrant children are positioned by their Spanish peers in these interactions, it is also critical to take into account that these positionings are sanctioned more or less passively by the teachers. This may become an aggravating factor in immigrant children's feelings of school alienation: it is one thing to be victimized by peers, but, when sanctioned by teachers, even if unwittingly, the practice may acquire an institutional character for immigrant children, who do not find support among school professionals in positions of authority.

In fairness to the teachers at this school, some of these practices of social exclusion are so subtle that they may be difficult to detect by school professionals, who additionally have to tend to many other aspects of pedagogical practice. Fights, insults, and racial slurs are easier to detect and, therefore, to address. Certainly, when violent and abusive behavior occurred (either verbal or physical), it was immediately stopped and addressed by the teachers. The Spanish children in the school were so aware of this fact that they would go to great lengths to avoid displaying openly racist behavior in front of teachers and administrators. Language, however, does not have to be overtly discriminatory or racist to achieve exclusionary goals. One of the main implications of this work, then, is that, beyond insults and fights, there is a need for teachers and administrators to take into account the complexities of children's social worlds and the dynamics of power and social control that exist within them.

Of particular importance is to recognize children's linguistic and communicative behavior as an effective form of social control and exclusion. The conclusions of this chapter challenge assumptions about children's unsophisticated knowledge of, and contributions to, sociopolitical realities concerning ethnic relations. While teachers and other adults may view children's racist behavior as naïve (assuming that they do not understand what they are doing), or as merely mimicking what they hear at home, ethnographic work has begun to show that children have very sophisticated understandings of ethnic marginality (Devine and Kelly 2006; Van Ausdale and Feagin 2001) and are able to perpetuate with their actions larger sociopolitical realities concerning ethnic relations in their immediate environment.

Notes

1   *Seño* is the shortened version of the word *señorita*, "Miss." *Señorita* is the form of address traditionally reserved for females who work as schoolteachers and in clerical jobs, like secretaries or receptionists, regardless of their marital status. As in the United States, many school children in Spain still address their female teachers as *Señorita*, "Miss," particularly in the earlier grades of schooling. Young children often use the shortened form of this title of address, *Seño*.

2   On one occasion towards the end of the study, I recorded a full recess psession in which Worda, Sarah, Wafiya, and Miriam were participating along with some Spanish girls from

fourth grade. Since mixed-ethnic peer play interactions were not very common either in or outside school, I thought it would be important to document one example of these interactions.

3   See also e.g., Alegret and Palaudaries (1995); Ballestín (2011); Carbonell, Simó, and Tort (2002); Carrasco Pons (2003); Franzé (1995); Gibson and Carrasco Pons (2009); Mijares (2004b); Pámies-Rovira (2006).

4   In what Hill (2008) calls the *folk theory of racism*, she traces how individuals of the majority group perpetuate the idea that the racism that persists is just the remnants of bygone times upheld by small fringe and radical groups, rather than a more pervasive and contemporary structural practice upheld by all members of society. This is accomplished through two types of language ideologies, that of personalism and referentialism. *Personalism* is deployed to cast speakers as *intentionally* racist, such as when people use blatantly racist slurs, whereas *referentialism* is invoked to argue that even though speakers may have sounded racist because the words they used have racist connotations, they are not really racist because this was *not intentionally* done, such as in what are commonly called *gaffes* or *slips of the tongue*. In other words, it is the discourse that is racist, and not the speakers themselves, because they did not mean to be racist.

5   In addition to linguistic anthropology, the importance of positive recognition in face-to-face interactions for identity development has been discussed in contemporary philosophy of ethics and identity, e.g. Appiah (2006); Bilgrami (2006); Levinas (1998); Taylor et al. (1994). The relational character of identity development has also been recognized in psychological approaches to the study of immigrant children and youth's development: see, for example, C. Suárez-Orózco's (2004) discussion of lack of social mirroring as racialized symbolic violence.

6   As discussed in Chapters 3 and 4, these 18 hours of videotaped classroom data feature the children of the fourth-grade classroom that I regularly recorded in a number of academic subjects with different teachers, namely in Math, Music, Performing Arts, Social Studies, and Literacy Enhancement classes (Programa de Compensatoria).

7   See, for example, Lytra's (2007) discussion of tattles in a multi-ethnic elementary classroom in Greece.

8   For a more specific breakdown and analysis of the numerical figures in this chart, please, see García-Sánchez (2012).

9   Spanish children relating to these notions of objectivity when policing and tattling their Moroccan immigrant peers is related to one of some of the most common discourse strategies used by speakers of majority groups to advanced racist arguments. As the work of Augoustinos and Every (2007); Blommaert and Verschueren (1998); Martín Rojo (2000); van Dijk (1993); Verkuyten (1998); Woolard (1990) has shown, arguments that are inherently discriminatory are organized and justified around democratic and liberal principles, such as freedom, equality, national legal codes, and individual rights.

10 The tattles "*Teresa no tiene hecho el cinco*" (Teresa doesn't have number five done/complete) and "*Seño, ella tiene el abrigo*" (Miss, she's wearing the coat/she has the coat on) are very similar at the syntactic level. The syntactic similarity between these two tattles comes from the fact that they both share the morpho-syntactic structure *tener + past participle*. This is not readily obvious in the second tattle because the past participle "*puesto*" in "*tener puesto*" (to wear, to have on) is omitted. The context, however, tells us that in "*Seño, ella tiene el abrigo*," the speaker means, that it is against class rules to wear coats in the Performing Arts classroom, and not that she just possesses or has a coat. In spite of this morpho-syntactic

similarity, there are still, however, grammatical grounds to argue that linguistic encoding of agency is much more mitigated in the first example (where the target of the tattle is a Spanish child) than in the second (where the target of is a Moroccan child).

Part of the analytical difficulty of making this argument is that sentences with *tener +* *past participle* in Spanish belong to a group of liminal grammatical constructions that some-times function as passive voice constructions and at other times function as active construc-tions containing a complex, periphrastic verb form. It is often hard to establish the syntactic relationships in these constructions. In *El Español Moderno y Contemporáneo: Estudios Lingüís-ticos* (1996) and in *Estudios de Morfosintaxis Histórica del Español* (2000), noted philologist and linguist Rafael Lapesa Melgar maintains that in most cases, the syntactic valences (passive or active) of these liminal constructions can only be determined by the semantic value of the sentence and the context in which it occurred. While recognizing that there is ample room for ambiguity in these types of grammatical constructions, I argue that "*Teresa no tiene hecho el cinco*" (Teresa doesn't have number five done/complete) is a grammatical construc-tion of the passive analytic kind that emphasizes processual aspects (*pasiva analítica de proceso*). In Spanish, the most semantically direct and unmitigated way of communicating the same information would have been to say simply "*Teresa no ha hecho el cinco*" (Teresa hasn't done number five). By phrasing the tattle, "*Teresa no tiene hecho el cinco*" (Teresa doesn't have number five done/complete), the semantic focus is not only on the fact that Teresa had not done that particular exercise, but also on processual information about the completion of a larger assignment that mitigates the encoding of Teresa's responsibility.

This mitigation is even more evident when we compare the tattle "*Teresa no tiene hecho el cinco*" (Teresa doesn't have number five done/complete) to other tattles that are semantically closer to this one, but directed at Moroccan immigrant children, such as "*Sí no lo ha hecho, seño*" (He hasn't even done it, Miss). Conversely, I analyze "*Seño, ella tiene el abrigo*" (Miss, she's wearing the coat/she has the coat on) as an active construction, where, therefore, "*ella*" (she) occupies an agent-actor subject position, and agency is not grammati-cally mitigated. I consider "*ella tiene el abrigo (puesto)*" (she's wearing the coat) an active form of the complex verbal form "*tener puesto*" (to wear/to have on). This complex verbal form is the more direct way of expressing "to wear" or "to have something on" in Spanish. Most of the semantic value is indeed carried by the omitted past participle, as it is usually the case with complex periphrastic verbal forms. Indeed, even though the past participle is omitted, everyone understands "*Seño, ella tiene el abrigo*" as meaning that she is wearing the coat. In addition, the context in which this tattle was deployed was a class (Performing Arts) in which children were not allowed to wear coats. The tattler is attracting the teacher's attention in an unmitigated way to the fact that one of her Moroccan classmates is wearing a coat.

11   It is interesting to note that this is an example of a directive aimed at a Moroccan student, containing a justification ("you already have your instrument"). Unlike in Example 5.3, where the directive was aimed at another Spanish child we see that in this case the justi-fication follows rather than precedes the directive proper. Therefore, in this case, while the Spanish student who issued the directive does provide a reason for doing so, the justification itself does little to delay the directive proper within the boundaries of the turn, and thus it is not as effective in mitigating the illocutionary force of the directive. The conversational turn starts with a slight on-record ("Shut up") following the name of the Moroccan-girl target of the directive. Moreover, the directive itself is preceded by the emphatic particle *Qué*, which makes the aggravation more pronounced ("Do shut up").

12 Indeed, Wafiya's second story is aborted by my own intervention at that point in the inter-action, aligning with Wafiya and claiming to have witnessed such exchanges in her classroom. Worda would go on to produce her second story and also report how these practices are also done in her class.

13 For example, Clemente, Lee, and Heritage (2008); Silverman et al. (1998); Stivers (2001); Tates and Meeuwesen (2001); Pillet-Shore (2001); van Dulmen (1998).

14 See Dick (2011) for review of this literature.

6

Learning How to Be Moroccans in Vallenuevo: Arabic and the Politics of Identity

Yo, a mi me encanta ir a la mezquita –
me gusta muchísimo escribir en árabe.

I, I love going to the mosque –
I like writing in Arabic very much.

(Wafiya, age 10, Interview Fragment)

6.1 A Tale of Two Teachers

On Tuesdays, Rashid, the new Arabic-language teacher of the LACM Program (*Programa de Enseñanza de Lengua Árabe y Cultura Marroquí* – "Arabic Language and Moroccan Culture Teaching Program"),[1] had a partial day of teaching. When I had finished my recordings and observations, I used to go up to the second floor of the school, where I would find him either in the library or in the computer laboratory, grading students' writing and working on his classes. If he had completed his class preparation, we would often walk back together from the school to the center of town. Sometimes, especially if I had not seen his wife Amina for a few days, he would invite me to walk back with him to the small house they had rented, and spend some time with him and Amina. He usually did not have to twist my arm very much because I greatly enjoyed my conversations with Amina and looked forward to our mutual visits; she had a great sense of humor, and was smart, easy-going, and a good cook. Rashid and Amina bonded with me in interesting ways. They felt that they were outsiders from the rest of

Language and Muslim Immigrant Childhoods: The Politics of Belonging, First Edition.
Inmaculada Mª García-Sánchez.

the Moroccan community in Vallenuevo. They saw themselves as different
from those who, according to nationality, religion, ethnicity, language, and
culture, were considered their "own" people. From the perspective of Spanish
people in the town, however, Rashid and Amina were just like the rest of
the Moroccans. I think that, just like they saw themselves, they also saw me
as an outsider and different from the rest of Spanish people in Vallenuevo.
This was true in many respects, as I was not from that town and I had
moved there just a little over a month after they did. Also, Rashid and I
were both university educated and with similar academic interests. He liked
to talk to me about all aspects of life in Morocco, and discuss with me his
favorite contemporary authors in his exquisitely articulate Spanish, a language he spoke with a barely audible foreign accent. Because of all this,
they felt I could understand better the alienation they both often complained of experiencing since they moved to Vallenuevo.

Rashid also liked to talk to me about Arabic-language pedagogy, especially after I started recording the lessons of the fourth-grade group.[2] From
these conversations, I knew, long before I also started recording after-school
Arabic lessons in the small town oratory-mosque, that Rashid always felt
a little uncomfortable with the idea of his Moroccan students also attending these after-school lessons. He wondered about the quality of the education that children were receiving in what he considered to be a
pseudo-educational setting. It was not until I later started recording the
Arabic lessons in the town's oratory-mosque, however, that I learned that
Bilal, the *fqih* (traditional Islamic teacher) in charge of these classes, did not
think very highly of Rashid's classes at the school either. In numerous
occasions, both Rashid and Bilal, who never developed a personal relationship or visited each other's classrooms, expressed some reservations and
concerns about what they assumed the other one was teaching the children.
Bilal for example, conveyed doubt at what he assumed was a lack of appropriate exposure to Islamic genres, religious literacy, and Muslim cultural
values in the Arabic classes of the teacher at the school. Rashid was skepti-
cal of the quality of language and religious lessons imparted by Bilal, a
man whom he considered not very well educated. Rashid expressed that,
in his view, the *fqih*'s teachings would only reinforce what he considered
to be the "backward" ways of the community. Once during our conversations, he asked me directly about the content of the classes at the town
oratory-mosque, since he learned that I had started doing observations and
recording there. When I responded very generically that the *fqih* was teaching Arabic and Islam, Rashid, visibly losing his composure, said to me: "lo
que ese hombre enseña a los niños no es Árabe, ni es Islam, ni es nada"
("What that man teaches the children is neither Arabic, nor Islam, nor
anything").

This chapter is primarily concerned with an aspect of language education and identity politics that has received relatively little attention in the Spanish context, namely issues of reproduction and the manufacturing of national, ethnic, and religious identifications in the deterritorialized space of the Moroccan immigrant diaspora. More specifically, this chapter examines the politics of authenticity in relation to *Moroccan-ness* and Islamic identifications. Thus, it considers how notions of what it means to be a Moroccan are played out in the teaching of the Arabic language to younger generations of Moroccans, who were either born in Spain, or who immigrated to Spain with their parents when they were toddlers.

Across time and place, immigrant and minority language communities have often shown a strong commitment to maintain the languages of their countries of origin, as both cultural and personal resources, even in the face of strong competition by the hegemonic language(s) of the dominant societies. The tensions "between cultural homogenization and cultural heterogenization," in relation to minority polities' fears of cultural absorption by the dominant and larger polities with which they interact (Appadurai 2002) have, however, taken center stage in recent years. This is especially so given that nation-states are increasingly characterized by linguistic, cultural, and religious diversity. Often, the anxieties generated by these tensions have translated into adults from minority communities becoming hyper-vigilant of their youth. Adults, fearing that their youth are becoming too "Westernized/Europeanized" (Cesari 2007; Pêdziwiatr 2007), too "Americanized" (S. Lee 2005), and so on, may attempt to re-enculturate them to prevent them from becoming too alienated from their local communities and social networks (Samad 2007). The transmission of cultural and religious knowledge and values to the first generation of children born and educated in minority contexts has thus become both an issue of key importance in scholarly circles, as well as an issue of considerable concern for Moroccan immigrant parents and community leaders. In spite of this, the crucial role of linguistic and literacy practices in the context of Arabic-language education, has remained marginal in discussions of these tensions.

In addition, discussions of cultural and linguistic reproduction have often been addressed under the dichotomizing framework of *host*/dominant society and heritage,[3] – or immigrant-origin, community. For example, many of these debates have been framed around whether heritage practices can be integrated within dominant societies or not. Certainly, this perspective is critical in understanding evolving notions of belonging and membership in relation to minority groups and the politics of representation. Equally central to these discussions, however, is the internal dynamism of Moroccan immigrant communities, since, far from being monolithic entities, contemporary immigrant communities are fluid diasporas influenced by strong networks spanning various conventional nation-states. These transnational influences and contacts in the country of origin, in other European countries, and also throughout North Africa and the Middle East has led to rich and diverse *ideoscapes* (Appadurai 2002) within the Moroccan immigrant community itself. When studying issues of reproduction in deterritorialized cultural spaces, then, it is essential to consider how these diverse ideoscapes interact, and sometimes clash, in local understandings of the types of knowledge and identifications that are deemed suitable and authentic for the younger generations to appropriate. Exploring these diverse ideoscapes among different Muslim diaspora communities, like the Moroccan community in Spain, may perhaps be even more critical given Muslim communities' heated debates about ethnoreligious authenticity and continuity in relation to tradition and modernity.[4]

Moroccan immigrant children in Vallenuevo attend Arabic-language classes once a week at the local public school, and after-school religious classes offered three times a week in the makeshift oratory run by the local Islamic cultural association, Assalam. In this chapter, I address similarities and differences in linguistic and literacy practices between these two contexts Moroccan youth's developing national, ethnic, and religious identifications. The figures of the two teachers, Rashid and Bilal, more specifically, are critical in understanding how some of these general trends and debates about authentic ethnoreligious identities play out in the context of the Moroccan community in Vallenuevo. Of particular interest are the different ways in which these teachers embody some of the tensions regarding the role of Arabic-language education in the socialization of younger generations. Related to this, I discuss ideas of what it means to be a Moroccan, many aspects of which often go hand in hand with what it means to be a Moroccan Muslim in Western, minority contexts.

6.2 The Arabic–Language Teacher at the Public School

The Arabic-language teacher at the public school, Rashid, can be considered an *official* leader in that his authority emanates directly from the Moroccan educational authorities that sent him to this Spanish community to impart the Moroccan government-sanctioned curriculum of the "Arabic Language and Moroccan Culture Teaching Program" (LACM). This program is additionally legitimized by Spanish educational authorities in that LACM has been adopted by those elementary schools across the country that requested its implementation, and in that it is part of the required school curriculum for Moroccan immigrant children up to fifth grade. In this light, Rashid can be considered an agent of doxa (Bourdieu 1977), since he is in a position to uphold (and, in many ways, in charge of upholding) the taken-for-granted representations of Moroccan culture and the doxic ideologies regarding the symbolic value of the Arabic language in Morocco). A cosmopolitan man in his early thirties and from the college-educated elite, he tended to separate himself from most of his fellow Moroccan nationals in the town, and barely socialized with them outside his role as the teacher of their children. Certainly, his *official*, bureaucratic position set him apart from the rest of the community. In addition to that, however, he held ambivalent attitudes towards the rest of the Moroccan community in Vallenuevo, whom, as I described in Chapter 2, were mostly from rural areas of the Moroccan Northeast, and whom Rashid often referred in pejorative terms, such as *atrasados* (backward). The political economy of language (Irvine 1989) in Moroccan communities, as well as the ideological value of dialectal varieties of Arabic was a contributing factor to the literal and symbolic distance separating Rashid from the rest of the Moroccan community. For instance, Rashid explained to me in one of the interviews, when we were discussing problems he was facing in Arabic-language classes, he explained that the fact that Moroccan immigrant children in Vallenuevo came from rural areas of Morocco was a problem:

```
1.  T: Y sobre todo el tipo de gente que se
       encuentra aquí en este pueblo (.)
       And above all the type of people found
       here in this town (.)
       son gente procedente del campo.
       They are people ((who come)) from the
       countryside ((i.e., rural areas))
2.  T: No son gente procedente de la ciudad.
       They aren't people ((who come)) from the
       city.
3.  T: Hay una cierta diferencia (.) entre el
       alumno del campo=
       There is a certain difference (.) between
       students from rural areas=
       =y el alumno de la ciudad.
       and students from the city.
4.  T: El dialecto de la cuidad marroquí es un
       dialecto avanzado=
       The dialect of the Moroccan city is an
       advanced dialect=
```

```
        =el dialecto del campo es- muy bajo.
        =The dialect of the countryside ((i.e.,
        rural areas))is- very low.
  5.  T: Es el dialecto que no tiene relación con
        la lengua fusHa.
        It's the dialect that does not have any
        relationship with the fusHa language((i.e.,
        Modern Standard Arabic)).
  6.  T: En las ciudades la gente utiliza las
        palabras de fusHa en su charla=
        In cities, people use words from fusHa in
        their talk=
  7.     =y cuando hablan (.)
        =and when they speak (.)
  8.     en el campo no.
        in the countryside ((i.e., rural areas)),
        they don't.
```

It is important to note that the language variety that Rashid character-izes as "low" is not Moroccan Arabic per se,[5] but the dialectal variety spoken in rural areas where most of his students are from. Rashid considers this dialect as inferior not necessarily in direct comparison with Classical/Standard Arabic, but with the dialectal variety spoken in urban areas by people more like himself in terms of educational and social background. This urban variety, that has been alternatively referred to as the "Middle Variety," "Educated Spoken Arabic," or "Modern Moroccan Arabic" (see Ennaji, 2005), is a form of dialectal Moroccan Arabic heavily permeated by vocabulary and expressions of Classical/Standard Arabic used by edu-cated, urban elites in their everyday interactions in the public space. It is perhaps not surprising that Rashid uses this *educated, modern* dialect as the measure by which he evaluates children's varieties of Moroccan Arabic. After over half a century of partial and not completely successful educa-tional policies of *Arabization* in Morocco, this Middle Variety has been the object of increased *legitimization* in Bourdieu's sense (1991). An index of this increased legitimization is some of the academic nomenclatures used to refer to this variety, namely *Modern* Moroccan Arabic or *Educated* Spoken Arabic.

A crucial aspect of the teacher's evaluation is the naturalness with which it masks the ideological underpinnings of the *Arabization* policies through which Moroccan elites and nationalist intelligentsia used Classical/Standard Arabic to define national and ethnic identity, and cultural authenticity.[6] Indeed, the value of Classical/Standard Arabic as an ethnic and national identity marker for Moroccan immigrant children was pervasive in my conversations with adults in the community, including parents and the *fqih*, in spite of the fact that Classical/Standard Arabic was rarely used in everyday communicative practices, an issue that I discuss in the following section. This authoritatively sanctioned ideology that knowing Classical/Standard Arabic is part of what being a Moroccan means, however, was perhaps most explicitly articulated on record by the Arabic-language teacher in the school. When I asked him about the most important thing he hoped students would learn in his class, he responded:

> "Aprender el árabe es- (0.2) Por lo menos yo **puedo garantizar** para ellos la **identidad espiritual y cultural** de su país en la medida- (.) bueno, asegurar su identidad."
>
> (**Learning Arabic is-** (0.2) **At least I can guarantee for them the spiritual and cultural identity of their country in that-** (.) **well, ensuring their identity**).

Particularly relevant, for the purposes of this chapter, is how this view of Classical/Standard Arabic as embodying a sense of Moroccan national identity and cultural authenticity continues to be reproduced in the social fields of Arabic-language education for younger generations of Moroccan children in migration contexts. This view was apparent not only in the expressed beliefs of adults, but also in classroom language practices, a point to which I will return in the analysis below.

6.3   The *Fqih*

Like the Arabic teacher at the school, Bilal, the Arabic and Islamic religious–education teacher (*fqih*) at the town oratory was also a Moroccan man in his early thirties, recently married, and with a very young child. In spite of these similarities between the two teachers, there were also important differences between them. The *fqih*'s authority did not derive from any official religious role, in that he was not appointed by any Moroccan religious and/or educational authority in the same way the teacher at the school was. Rather, his authority emanated from the grassroots Muslim organization, Assalam, a local association with transnational ties, that had nominated him to teach Classical Arabic and the Qur'an to the town children in the afternoons after school. Also, unlike Rashid, Bilal did not have a college degree. His background was more similar to that of many Moroccan nationals in the town, in that he was from the same region as many of the other families and also regularly worked as a manual laborer to support his family. Bilal was well-known, liked, and respected by the Moroccan parents I had the opportunity to talk to and by other Moroccan adults in the community, who considered him a good man, very patient with the children. In my observations, Bilal also had a good rapport with the children. The focal children who attended his classes always spoke well of him, and, Wafiya and Mimon, in particular, attended his classes with enthusiasm.

Ironically, this positioning of the *fqih* and the public school teacher in relation to each other in Vallenuevo closely replicates some dimensions of what the figure of the *fqih* has come to represent in contemporary Morocco, namely, a somewhat independent figure of religious knowledge who even today, and unlike government school teachers, still enjoys certain freedom from official oversight. He is also a figure who has only retained most of his prestige in rural areas and among the lower socio-economic strata of Moroccan society, who usually go to the *fqih* for a variety of religious and medical needs (Spratt and Wagner 1986/2011). At the same time, however, the figure of the *fqih* in Vallenuevo can also be compared to what has been called in other Moroccan diaspora contexts, such as the Netherlands, *parish* leaders who have influence over Muslim communities at the neighborhood level (Cesari 2007). In comparing these "parish" leaders with cosmopolitan, educated elites of those same Muslim countries, Cesari (2007) has characterized them as seeking "to give new life within a European context to cultural models that originate from Islamic home countries . . . [having] greater tendency to reproduce tradition" (pp. 115 and 117).

The religious and cultural symbolic value of Classical/Standard Arabic for Moroccan immigrant children's sense of self was also prominent in the expressed beliefs of the *fqih* at the town oratory. In informal conversations with me, he told me that learning Classical Arabic was critical not only to building a strong ethnic and religious identity, but also to protecting children from pernicious influences that may lead them down "the wrong path." According to the *fqih*, knowing Classical Arabic was the foundation for being a good Muslim, insofar as it is the path to Qur'anic literacy. In his opinion, without that foundation the children would not know "who they are," and so become more vulnerable to bad influences and behaviors, such as modern music, and clothing, drugs and alcohol, disrespect of parents and authority figures.

A few Moroccan children in Vallenuevo, like Kamal, did not attend either Arabic-language class. As a sixth grader, he was too old for the Arabic-language classes offered at the public school and he preferred to use his after-school time to practice sports. A few other children, like Abdelkarim and his siblings, only attended Rashid's Arabic classes at the public school, and in the afternoons went instead to the after-school study skills and enrichment program. Although this was not surprising given that Abdelkarim's father, Mustafa, was a secular man and a strong believer in the upward mobility effects of education, most Moroccan parents did not send their children to the after-school enrichment program. Most parents preferred that their children attend the after-school Qur'anic lessons at the oratory-mosque.[7] In fact, most of the focal children, and many other children I knew as well, attended both Rashid's classes at the public school and Bilal's after-school classes.

6.4 The Role of Classical/Standard Arabic in Everyday Life in the Community

Like in other European countries (namely France and the Netherlands) that established so-called *first language maintenance* programs for North African immigrant children in the 1980s (Holt 1994), Classical/Standard Arabic (Al-'arabiya Al-fusHa) is also the language of choice in both the town oratory, and in the public school in Vallenuevo.

Classical and Standard Arabic, however, are very rarely spoken in Moroccan immigrant households in Spain. Rather, the mother tongues and languages of everyday interactions with family, neighbors, and friends for Moroccan immigrant children are either Moroccan Arabic and/or one of the three dialectal varieties of Amazigh. In fact, the Classical and Standard varieties of Arabic are not mother tongues for Moroccan immigrant children in Spain, nor for any Moroccan, in general. These varieties are never *acquired* in the home, but are *learned* at school and other formal settings, since the classical/standard and colloquial varieties are fairly distinct. For this reason, in recent years some researchers have problematized the teaching of Classical Arabic in *first language maintenance programs* to immigrant children of North African descent in Europe for being at odds with children's sociolinguistic backgrounds.[8]

Moroccan parents, Moroccan educators, as well as community and religious leaders, however, consider it important for children to attend Classical/

Standard Arabic classes in order to preserve children's linguistic, cultural, and religious heritage.[9] Most parents of the focal children, and other Moroccan parents I had the opportunity to talk to throughout the study, emphasized the sacred nature of this language variety and joined in asserting that it was important for their children to learn it because it was "the language of the Qur'an." Some parents, and certainly the Arabic teacher at the school, also highlighted the political importance and the global communicative value of this language variety as the lingua franca of the Arab and, more generally, the Muslim world.

In addition to not being the language of everyday interactions, knowledge of Classical/Standard Arabic among the Moroccan immigrant adults in this community varied considerably depending on the levels of formal education they had attained and their exposure to the language through mass media and global means of communication, such as the Internet or satellite television. Yet Classical/Standard Arabic plays a significant role in the linguistic repertoires of Moroccan households for religious purposes, and also as a means of keeping up with news and current events from their home country and other areas of the Arab world. For instance, it is extremely common to find Moroccan immigrant families in this community listening to Al-Jazeera newscasts and other popular stations in the Arabic-speaking world during family meals and gatherings. In addition, the sacred value of Classical Arabic is underscored by the contexts in which Moroccan immigrant children come into contact with this language: in family prayers, and in the town oratory, in televised religious speeches that are listened to in Moroccan households during Islamic celebrations, and through the prominent display of Qur'anic suwar (سور)[10] on walls and in common spaces of the households, such as the living-room.

6.5 The Politics of Moroccan-ness in Arabic-Language Classes

The investigation of the sociocultural and institutional milieu in which literacy practices are embedded[11] has emphasized the study of literacy as a set of social practices and cultural ideologies invaluable for children's socialization into values, belief systems, social identities, ways of knowing, and notions of morality and personhood.[12] The ways in which literacy practices are implicated in the formation of identifications and in the (re)production of in-group boundary-maintenance mechanisms have been further developed by Street (1993). Paying attention to the structure of literacy practices themselves is crucial, since literacy practices within a given cultural group have been shown to be organized around the same system of beliefs and values as other group practices associated with the larger social order and with ratified membership in the social, economic, or political life of the community.[13]

Previous research has provided critical insights on the multifaceted interplay among languages, educational practices, identity, and socialization in bilingual and/or immigrant communities. Most findings have been framed either in relation to host-heritage or dominant-minority communities and languages.[14] Interrelated phenomena that deserve particular attention include: (1) the internal variability and paradoxes regarding language use, as well as the cultural and political indexical meanings of language varieties, among different members of multilingual immigrant communities; and (2) how this internal dynamism organizes, adults' socializing efforts in relation to language education, especially where there may be some conflicting interests in achieving literacy by religious and secular elements of the children's communities of origin (Schieffelin 1999; Woolard and Schieffelin 1994). These are particularly important to understand in a contested multilingual, multicultural community where immigrant children have to negotiate *commonality of belonging* (Brubaker and Cooper 2000) in relation to multiple levels of heightened surveillance and in-group/out-group boundary-keeping mechanisms by both members of the Spanish society, and sometimes, by adults of the Moroccan diaspora.

This section examines how the complex paradoxes regarding both everyday use and symbolic value of varieties of Arabic in this community come to life in the discursive resources through which teachers construct what they considered to be appropriate Moroccan-ness and authentic ethnoreligious identities for the children. Comparing language and literacy practices in the *fields* of Arabic-language classes at the public school (Rashid's classes) and in the town oratory-mosque (Bilal's lessons) is productive because it allows us to trace homologies, or similarity of organization in linguistic and cultural (re)production, across these two settings (Bourdieu 1993). At the same time, it also allows us to uncover different kinds of strategies, teachers use in the classroom. Outlining both processes of homology and heterogeneity is particularly important to understand the degree of redundancy in language socialization practices, as well as the possible areas of disjuncture that may impinge upon children's ability to negotiate *commonality of belonging* in their multiple communities. These processes are explored through an examination of the (1) literacy practices and instructional organization of the classrooms; (2) teachers' categorization of students in classroom discourse; and (3) treatment of children's *mistakes* in error-correction practices. These three areas emerged as productive topics for analysis after recursive examination and comparison of 10 videotaped Arabic-language classes at the public school and 12 videotaped lessons at the oratory-mosque. What follows is a limited but representative sampling of teachers' discourses and practices in these three areas of analysis, and the similarities and differences among them.

6.5.1   *Literacy Practices and Instructional Organization*

Literacy practices in Arabic-language classes in the public school and in the town oratory are remarkably similar, although there are also differences in the foci of the lessons, as illustrated in Table 6.3 below. A typical Qur'anic lesson at the town oratory usually starts with children's choral and individual repetition and recitation of Qur'anic suwar, followed by children's recitation of the five pillars of Islam, recitation of the Arabic alphabet and drilling of individual letters, recitation of the months of the Arabic calendar, and a final chanting of a prayer or a song in praise of Prophet Mohammed. In Arabic-language classes at the school, instruction usually opens with an oral discussion about Moroccan traditions and/or religious and national holidays. These discussions about the meaning of secular and religious traditions are always carried out in Moroccan Arabic, and sometimes preceded or followed by children being exhorted to repeat the national motto of Morocco, namely **"Allāh, al WaTan, al Malik" (God, Homeland, King)**.

These oral discussions are then followed by the presentation and drilling of individual letters of the Arabic alphabet. Very much in keeping with the literacy practices that have been described as traditional in Moroccan schooling, the target letter is written on the board in each of its positional configurations (initial, medial, final, and alone), with all the possible short and long-vowel combinations, and as it appears in a few words and one or two short sentences.[15] The drilling of individual letters consists of series of choral and individual repetitions of the target letter, words, and sentences. Depending on how much time is devoted to the drilling on letters, the teacher proceeds with reading of tales and stories in Modern Standard Arabic, usually abridged versions of tales from traditional collections, such as *One Thousand and One Arabian Nights*. The inclusion of these traditional stories – that in the past used to be performed orally in families, coffeeshops, and neighborhood gatherings – is a practice that permeates school curricula and textbooks not only in Morocco, but also throughout the Arab world, where the transmission of cultural values via traditional stories is seen as crucial for children's moral, social, and emotional development.[16] This instructional practice also underscores the symbolic position of Classical/Standard Arabic as the vehicle of the *Great Tradition* of Arabic thought and literature; and promotes a linkeage between Classical/Standard Arabic and Moroccan cultural authenticity (Ennaji 2005). The teacher's reading of traditional tales is followed by a series of oral questions and answers about the story. The final minutes of a lesson are invariably devoted to students copying down in their notebooks the letters, words, and short sentences that have been the object of study.

In terms of the similarities between these two contexts, a crucial common feature is the heavy reliance on rote memorization and recitation as a pedagogical approach to the acquisition of literacy in both classes. Memorization and recitation has been described as a foundational approach to literacy instruction not only in Morocco, but also in other areas of Africa and the Middle East where Islam is an integral part of a community's cultural and religious life.[17] *Guided-repetition* (Moore 2006), a practice that involves modeling by the expert and imitation of the model by a novice, followed by rehearsal and performance by the novice, was the core literacy practice in both settings and also the method that both teachers associated with effective learning. In both Arabic-language classes, modeling was consistently prefaced by bold directives commanding children to be silent, to listen, and to repeat so that they could learn, as can be seen in the two following examples. The first example is extracted from an Arabic-language lesson at the town oratory (Example 6.1) and the other from an Arabic-language lesson at the school (Example 6.2):

Example 6.1
F = Fqih

1.　F: Sst šufu sst. ġadi ngul ana o gulu moraya.
　　　Askat
　　　Shh look Shh. I'm going to say and you
　　　repeat after me. Be silent

Example 6.2
T = Teacher

1.　T: Saktu, khaliwani ana ngul baš ya'araf
　　　Be quiet, let me say it so that you learn

Tables 6.1 and 6.2 illustrate respectively the various ways in which guided-repetition is enacted in the teaching of Arabic to Moroccan immigrant

Table 6.1 Guided repetition in Arabic classes at the town oratory.
Participants: Fqih and Students
Sūrat Al-Kāfirūn[32] (سورة الكافرون The Disbelievers)

Guided-Repetition in Arabic Classes at the Town Oratory

```
 1.  FQIH:      qul ya ayyoha alkāfirūn
 2.  STUDENTS:  qul ya ayyoha alkāfirūn
 3.  FQIH:      la a'budu ma ta'budūn
 4.  STUDENTS:  la a'budu ma ta'budūn
 5.  FQIH:      wa la antum 'abidūn ma a'bud
 6.  STUDENTS:  wa la antum 'abidūn ma a'bud
 7.  FQIH:      wa la ana 'abidun ma 'abadtum
 8.  STUDENTS:  wa la ana 'abidun ma 'abadtum
 9.  FQIH:      wa la antum 'abidūn ma a'bud
10.  STUDENTS:  wa la antum 'abidūn ma a'bud
11.  FQIH:      lakum dīnokum wa liya dīn.
12.  STUDENTS:  lakum dīnokum wa liya dīn.
13.  FQIH:      antuma
                You - second-person plural (= now you
                recite it)
```

---

children in both the town oratory and the public school. In Table 6.1, the *fqih* models a sūrah from the Qur'an sentence by sentence. Each sentence is repeated chorally by all the children in the class. When the sūrah is complete, the *fqih* turns to the children and says "antuma" (**you** – plural) in line 13, prompting the children to rehearse the full sūrah on their own. After a choral rehearsal, individual children are usually called to the front of the class to publicly perform the target sūrah for the *fqih* and for the rest of their classmates.

In Table 6.2, after the teacher has modeled the target letter, syllables, words, and sentences that are written on the board, one of the students in the class, Jalal, is selected to perform the linguistic forms that have just been modeled by the teacher. Jalal starts reading line 1 from the board. After the student completes the first sentence, the teacher scaffolds the student's reading-performance with a prompting question (line 2) whose "right" answer is the next fragment that the student is supposed to read from the board. The teacher continues to prompt Jalal and scaffold his reading-performance with a similar question in line 4. When the teacher is satisfied with the performance of Jalal, a second student, Mimon, is selected (line 8), with whom the teacher engages in a similar format of questions and answers. These exchanges were repeated until all the students in the class

Table 6.2 Guided repetition in Arabic classes at the school.
Participants: Teacher, Jalal, Mimon, and Students in the Class.

Guided-Repetition in Arabic Classes at the School

1.	JALAL:	kharaža ra ra ra kharaža
		he left ra ra ra he left
		almudiru ru ru ru almudiru
		the principal ru ru ru the principal
2.	TEACHER:	min ayina kharaža almudiru?
		From where did the principal leave?
3.	JALAL:	min darihi ri ri ri min darihi
		From his house ri ri ri from his house
4.	TEACHER:	man ladhi kharaž?
		Who left?
5.	JALAL:	almudiru
		The principal
6.	TEACHER:	žumla
		Sentence
		(= put it in a sentence or give me a sentence)
7.	JALAL:	kharaža almudiru
		The principal left
8.	TEACHER:	min ayina kharaža almudiru?
		From where did the principal leave? ((addressing a different student = Mimon))
9.	MIMON:	min darihi
		From his house
10.	TEACHER:	min darihi
		From his house

had an opportunity to practice the target linguistic forms that were written on the board.

A difference to notice between these two examples of guided-repetition is that in Arabic classes at the school, greater attention was placed on students' understandings of the lexico-semantic meanings of the linguistic forms they were learning, whereas at the oratory-mosque the emphasis was on students' exact phonological reproduction of the Qur'anic text, regardless of the children's understandings of the lexico-semantic meaning. It is perhaps not surprising that the transmission of knowledge is more authoritative in the religious context.

This pervasive literacy approach based on guided-repetition in the two classes can be seen as an essential resource for initiating Moroccan immigrant children into the ideologies and identities valued by adults in their communities of origin, namely for these children's socialization into cultural values that are associated with a Moroccan-Islamic identity. The acts of repetition, memorization, and recitation are an integral part of socialization in that other cultural values are enacted in this practice, those of respect and obedience to authority, on the one hand, and of submission to the word of God as embodied in the Qur'an, on the other. Therefore, through participation in guided-repetition practices with their teachers and peers in both Arabic classes, Moroccan immigrant children are learning the Arabic language and the indexical meanings associated with it, as well as learning that the sole source of authority and knowledge is the teacher, whom they must respect and obey. Respect and obedience to authority, particularly to the authority of the father (or in his absence to the authority of the male relative closest in kin), is one of the most salient features of family structure and social organization in Morocco.[18] Respect and obedience to adult authority figures was also a pervasive object of socialization routines in the immigrant Moroccan households that I observed. Children's answering back to parents or refusing to do something they were asked to do was considered disrespectful, and adults often responded to these transgressions with "Hašuma" (**shame** or **shameful**). This ethos of respect for authority figures is also important in relation to Moroccan children's behaviors towards their Spanish teachers analyzed in the previous chapter. While children experienced distress, as expressed in interviews and in their embodied reactions, at being scolded as a result of peers' tattles and fueling-the-fire practices, they nevertheless usually took teachers' reprimands connected to these practices in silent consternation. They rarely attempted to offer excuses or to expose their accusers, or to display any other behavior that could be constructed as answering back to adults.

In addition, in the context of Qur'anic lessons specifically, children's involvement in the act of memorization and recitation is also important for their identities as Muslims. For Muslims, the act of memorization and recitation is considered a form of worship in its own right. In fact, a decline in memorization in contemporary times has been commonly interpreted as an indication of the deterioration of the faith and of the weakening of belief.[19] In the verbatim recitation of Qur'anic suwar (plural form of sūrah), Moroccan immigrant children learn that the only valid source of all truth is God and God's revelation through the Qur'an. Thus, they are taught to accept the authority of the Book (which is understood to be the actual word of God) and of the *fqih*, even when they do not understand (or perhaps because they do not understand) what they are saying. This authoritative stance towards the act of recitation is also underscored by both Rashid and Bilal's emphasis on the exact phonological reproduction of texts and their insistence that children must learn to pronounce words and sounds in Arabic "perfectamente desde el principio" **(perfectly from the beginning)**.

Another crucial similarity in Arabic-language classes at both the town oratory and in the school is how Moroccan Arabic is used in the instructional process. This is mainly due to the fact that Moroccan immigrant children in these classrooms, whose mother tongue is Moroccan Arabic, have not yet developed the necessary linguistic competence for the classes to be conducted entirely in Classical/Standard Arabic. Thus, Moroccan Arabic is positioned in both classrooms as a language to teach *in*, but not as a language worth *teaching*; as the language to teach Moroccan immigrant children about *their* culture, but not as a language that is associated with an appropriate linguistic identity for the children. This is underscored by the fact that Classical/Standard Arabic is centrally positioned in the pedagogical practices of the classrooms as the language that is important to study and learn well, since it is conflated with Islam and the Qur'an, and with the great Arabic literary tradition. In this regard, the teacher and the *fqih* reproduce doxic representations of Classical/Standard Arabic, common in both Morocco and Moroccan transnational networks,[20] as the sanctioned and legitimate source of linguistic and cultural authenticity for Moroccan immigrant children.

However, as illustrated in Table 6.3, there are also crucial differences in content between Arabic-language classes in the town oratory and in the

Table 6.3   Instructional organization of Arabic classes across contexts.

Instructional Organization of Arabic Classes at the Town Oratory	Instructional Organization of Arabic Classes at School
Recitation of sūrahs from the Qur'an	Oral discussions about Moroccan traditions and/or religious and national holidays
Recitation of the Arabic alphabet and drilling of individual letters	Presentation and drilling of individual letters
Recitation of the five Pillars of Islam	Reading of traditional tales and stories
Recitation of the months of the Arabic calendar	Students copy on their notebooks the letters, words, and short sentences
Final prayer or final song in praise of Prophet Mohammed	

school, for example, the higher emphasis on secular literature and civil traditions in Arabic-language classes at the school. Another important difference is the variable treatment that certain linguistic forms are given in both classes. In Arabic classes at the town oratory, in particular, preeminence is given to those linguistic forms that are imbued with cultural meanings associated with Islam to the detriment of other linguistic forms that are considered as emanating from Western and colonial influences in the Arabic language. In both of these settings, for instance, in every lesson children were asked to repeat the day's date in Arabic. The linguistic forms used to teach children how to say and write the date in Arabic appropriately was different, however. In the town oratory, after a period of time of learning and repetition of the months of the Islamic Hijri calendar, children were emphatically taught to say the month and the year for any given date according to the Islamic calendar. The following example is an excerpt from one of the first days in which children were introduced to this calendar:

Example 6.3
F: Fqih   Ss: Students

1.   FQIH: sam'o had aššohur
                 Listen to these months
2.   yanayar, fobrayar, maras, abril, may,
                 yunyu
                 January, February, March, April, May,
                 June
3.   ġadi n'awdolhom žama'atan
                 We are going to repeat them together
4.   →   had aššohur hiys baš kan'arfu aššohur
                 alfaransiya
                 It's with these months that we know
                 the French months
5.   ((Fqih and Students repeat together
                 the first six months of the Gregorian
                 calendar))
6.   →   FQIH: aššohur al'arabiya alHižriya:
                 The Arabic Months are ((literally the
                 Arabic Hijri[33] months))
7.   muHarram, Safar, rabī' alawwal, rabī'
                 azzani, žomoda
                 alawla, žomoda azzaniya.
                 ((Literal translation: Forbidden,
                 Empty, First Spring, Second Spring,
                 First Dry Month or Freeze, Second Dry
                 Month or Freeze))

What is interesting about this excerpt is how the months of the Gregorian calendar are presented as being *French* (in reference to the colonial
legacy of Morocco), in spite of the fact that this is the official calendar that
has been used for decades throughout Morocco for all civil purposes, as
well as for everyday purposes. The months of the Gregorian calendar, which
can be said to have originated from Western influences on the Arabic language, are introduced as foreign to children's primary identification, particularly in contrast to the months of the Islamic Hijri calendar, which are
presented as *Arabic*. The conflation of the ethnic/national adjective with the
religious calendar marks the latter as somehow more *authentic* in relation to
children's identifications. This is underscored by the *fqih's* emphasis on children being able to say the date according to the lunar Hijri calendar in the
lessons following this exchange.

In contrast, in the Arabic classes at school, children learned the Arabic
forms of the months and the year according to the Gregorian calendar. In
every class, before beginning the lesson, the teacher would write the date
on the board and ask individual children to repeat it:

Example 6.4
Participants: Teacher and Yimad

```
1.  →  TEACHER: šanu lyum?
                What's today? ((What is today's
                date?))
2.  YIMAD:      latnin
                Monday ((In Moroccan Arabic))
3.  TEACHER:    aliznaīn
                Monday ((Correcting student in
                Standard Arabic))
4.  →  YIMAD:   aliznaīn sata maris alfaīn wa sata
                Monday, March 6 2006
```

As the previous example illustrates, the schoolteacher's emphasis in these
exchanges was not different calendars, but rather making sure that children
knew the Standard Arabic form and were able to differentiate these forms
from the colloquial variants, which were objects of routine correction in
the *official* space of the class, a point to which I will return later in the
analysis.

While the similarities in practices described above position Classical/
Standard Arabic as the primary source of linguistic and cultural authenticity
for the children, the instructional differences between the teacher and the
fqih can be seen as embodying divergent discourses among Moroccan speech

communities and transnational networks regarding the value and the functions of Classical/Standard Arabic. On the one hand, there is a civil discourse that sees Classical/Standard Arabic as a language that can facilitate Moroccans access to modernity, while safeguarding their cultural identity. On the other hand, there is a religious discourse that considers Classical/Standard Arabic as a means to the reproduction and revival of Islamic values.[21] These larger competing cultural discourses also interact in interesting ways with the desired outcomes expressed by the teachers in this community, since, for the teacher at the school, children's learning of the Standard language was viewed as a remedy to what he considered children's "backward" ways (including ways of speaking), whereas, for the *fqih*, learning Classical/Standard Arabic was a way of instilling in children a sense of who they are in relation to Muslim subjectivities.

6.5.2 *Teachers' Treatment of Mistakes in Error-Correction Practices*

The analysis of teachers' treatment of mistakes in relation to the instructional organization of their lessons, provides further insights into the similarities and differences described above.[22] The organization of mistakes in Arabic-language classes in both the town oratory and the school are characterized by its public and unmitigated nature. As discussed in earlier sections, one of the most common pedagogical features of these two classes is children's public performance in front of the whole class. In this context, when a mistake occurs, it becomes the focus of collective attention and discussion. Therefore, teachers' treatment of mistakes becomes an important tool not only for the socialization of the child who has made the mistake, but also for the socialization of the rest of his/her peers.

This direct approach to the correction of individual's mistakes is reminiscent of some of the ways in which Moroccan immigrant children are also publicly and individually exposed to the censure of the group through the practices of exclusion analyzed in the previous chapter. Unlike *acusar*, *mandatos*, and *echar leña al fuego*, however, mistakes in Arabic-language classes are not treated as individual transgressions that bear negative consequences. Rather, the potentially damaging aspects of the corrective action are usually greatly mitigated by treating the mistake as an error anyone in the class could have made or as a puzzle to be solved by everyone in the class.[23]

When analyzing teacher and *fqih*'s treatments of mistakes, I have looked at the *repair trajectory*, or the unfolding of the sequences involving teachers' corrections, and at the different types of *trouble sources* (Schegloff et al. 1977). Trouble sources refer to children's linguistic acts that prompt corrective action on the part of the teachers. There were two different kinds of trouble sources found in the data: children's use of Moroccan Arabic dialect in the official space of the class[24] and children's misuse of Classical/Standard Arabic linguistic forms. In both settings, public school and local oratory, the teachers are most often the initiators of the repair sequence.

6.5.3   Children's Use of Moroccan Arabic

Very often, particularly in the Arabic classes at the public school, children's responses in Moroccan Arabic were treated as inappropriate and as incorrect, even when children's responses were neither incorrect from a linguistic nor from a communicative point of view. An instance of this practice was already introduced earlier in the chapter in Example 6.4 above, reproduced again here:

1.   TEACHER: šanu lyum?
              What's today? ((What is today's date?
              In Moroccan Arabic))
2.   YIMAD: latnin
              Monday ((In Moroccan Arabic))
3.   TEACHER: aliznaīn
              Monday ((Correcting student in
              Standard Arabic))

Given that the teacher asks in line 1 "šanu lyum?" **(What's today?)** in Moroccan Arabic, the child's response of the day of the week in Moroccan Arabic is not only correct, but also appropriate. The colloquial form is, however, treated as invalid and corrected by the teacher in line 3, who provides the Standard Arabic form for Yimad to repeat. A pattern of not validating children's responses in Moroccan Arabic as appropriate answers to the teacher's questions was pervasive in Arabic-language classes at the school. This pattern can also be seen in the following example:

Example 6.5
Participants: Teacher, Wafiya, Yimad, and Sarah

1.   TEACHER: ra Haraf ra škun ya'aTini kalmat fīha
              Haraf ra'?
              **"Ra" letter "r" who gives me words
              with the letter "r"?**
2.   WAFIYA: gerḍun
              Monkey

3. TEACHER: qiṛdun gbila gultī geṛdun wa
             SahaHtahalak
             Monkey, before you said "monkey" and
             I corrected it for you
4. YIMAD: alfeṛan- feṛan
             The oven, oven
5. TEACHER: furnun
             Oven
6. SARAH: ṛmalun
             sand
7. TEACHER: ṛmalun
             sand

In this example, the teacher asks students to give him words that contained the letter "R" (line 1). In spite of asking the question in Moroccan Arabic, when Wafiya provides "geṛdun" (**monkey** in Moroccan Arabic), the teacher again treats Wafiya's answer as incorrect by providing the Standard Arabic word for monkey in line 3, "qiṛdun." He also adds **"before you said monkey (geṛdun) and I corrected it for you."** The same occurs in lines 4 and 5 when Yimad offers the word "feṛan" (**oven** in Moroccan Arabic) as an alternative example. The teacher only accepts words offered in Standard Arabic as correct. This is what Sarah, the most advanced student in the class, does in line 6 by offering the Standard word for sand "ṛmalun." Sometimes the school teacher enlisted other students in providing the *correct* linguistic form,[25] as in the next example:

Example 6.6
Participants: Teacher, Yimad, Sarah, Mimon, Karim

1. TEACHER: TalHa Yimad
             TalHa Yimad
2. YIMAD: HaDer
             Present
3. TEACHER: Sād Amina
             Sād Amina
4. STUDENTS: [maši hadera
             not present
    STUDENTS: [makainaš
             Not here
    SARAH: [ġā'iba
             absent

```
5.  TEACHER:  aš kangulu?
              What do we say?
6.  SARAH:    ǧā'iba
              Absent
7.  TEACHER:  ǧā'iba (.)'īTat Mimon
              Absent (.)'īTat Mimon
8.  MIMON:    HaDer
              Present
9.  TEACHER:  HaDer (.)Mezyan Karim
              Present (.)Mezyan Karim
```

The practice of taking roll is an important framing activity in that it marks that the serious business of the class has begun. If short informal jokes and games between teachers and students are usually allowed before the teacher starts taking roll, once the teacher has taken roll, these playful activities are reprimanded. Thus, taking roll can also be seen as an activity that frames two symbolic spaces in the class: the *official* space where only the Classical/Standard variety of the language is allowed and the *unofficial* space where children's use of the dialectal variety is not an object of evaluation (see Note 26). While taking roll call, in line 3 of the transcript, the teacher mentions the name of a student who happens to be absent that day. In response, the students offer three different possibilities (line 4): (1) Maši hadera, which is a mixture of the dialectal form ***maši*** (not) and the Standard Arabic form ***hadera***, which means "present"; (2) the second response makainaš is a dialectal form to indicate non-possession or absence of something or, as in this case, of somebody; (3) the third response ǧā'iba is the Standard Arabic form for "absent".

The teacher, picking up on the first two problematic responses given by students, responds by addressing the whole class with the question aš kangulu? **(What do we say?)** in line 5. Like the two previous examples, this is in effect, a next-turn other initiation of repair. This type of repair has been described as indexing a stance of disaffiliation with what has been said in the previous turn (Schegloff et al. 1977), in this case the students' use of the dialectal forms. In spite of this dissafiliative stance, the teacher's question, aš kangulu? **(What do we say?)**, is posed by the teacher to the whole class and in the first-person plural *we*. This feature downplays the harshness of the correction, and the mistake becomes everybody's mistake to remedy. In line 6, Sarah, whose knowledge of Standard Arabic is superior to that of the rest of the students because of the many years of schooling she had in Morocco, again provides the Standard Arabic form of "absent," ǧā'iba. This response is ratified as correct and appropriate by the teacher's repetition of ġā'iba in line 7. This repetition validates students' answers by incorporating them into the official discourse of the classroom.[26]

Although children's use of Moroccan Arabic was also a target of correction in Arabic-language classes in the town oratory, there are some crucial differences between this error-correction practice in the school and the town oratory. While this practice was pervasive in the Arabic classes at the school, in the town oratory data, I only found a handful of examples that focused on Moroccan Arabic as the source of error. Apart from the numerical difference, there was also a difference in the correction strategies used. If in Arabic-language classes in the school, we find mostly *other-initiated repair* correction sequences, in the town oratory, the *fqih* engaged in *preemptive strategies* (Friedman 2006), when drawing attention to Moroccan Arabic as a source of error. Example 6.7 is taken from one of the Arabic lessons at the town oratory. In this segment, students are learning the days of the week. One of the students has just recited successfully the days of the week in Standard Arabic and is proceeding to write "Wednesday" on the board. The *fqih* stops him and, before the student can write anything at all, he asks the class:

Example 6.7
Participants: Fqih and Students

    1. FQIH: mašnū ġadi ndiru azzulatha'a walla
                          attulata?
                          What do we put (meaning=What do we
                          write on the board)
                          azzulatha'a ((Classical/Standard
                          Arabic for Wednesday)) or attulata
                          ((Moroccan Arabic for Wednesday))
    2. STUDENTS: Azzulatha'a
                          Wednesday ((Classical/Standard Arabic
                          for Wednesday))
    3. FQIH: Azzulatha'a
                          Wednesday

"Wednesday" might be a potential source of error for Moroccan children, since the dialectal form **(attulata)** is fairly linguistically close to the Classical/Standard form **(azzulatha'a)**. As the student begins to write the word on the board, the *fqih* intervenes, explicitly drawing attention to features of Moroccan and Classical/Standard Arabic that could be confused more easily. In line 1, he asks the whole class **"What do we put"** (meaning=**What do we write on the board?**) **azzulatha'a (Classical Arabic for Wednesday) or attulata (Moroccan Arabic for Wednesday)?).** The class responds unanimously "azzulatha'a," in the Standard variety. This response is accepted and validated as correct by the *fqih's* repetition of the response in line 3.

In comparison to the *other-initiated repair* sequences used by the Arabic teacher in the school, the *preemptive strategies* used by the *fqih* are less aggravated and do not index such a strong stance of disaffiliation with children's use of the colloquial variety. In addition, the large number of corrections involving Moroccan Arabic in the school data, in contrast with the paucity of this type of correction in the town oratory data, speaks of a heightened supervision of children's use of Moroccan Arabic by the school Arabic teacher. This keen monitoring is very much in keeping this teacher's expressed condescending attitude towards the colloquial variety spoken in the children's homes as "rural" and "backward." While not surprising, it is still important to consider whether a possible disconnect may be engendered in classes which are considered a *first language maintenance program*, but that, in effect, promote heavily children's learning of the Standard to the potential detriment of their home language variety. While the Standard/colloquial concern has been raised in relation to many Arabic programs, including language educational programs in Morocco, this disconnect may be even more significant and consequential in migration contexts where children's heritage languages and identities are already at high risk of being lost in the face of strong acculturation into dominant language and practices.

This disconnect is also underscored by an identical feature of error-correction practices involving Moroccan Arabic in the two settings. In spite of the differences, the correction strategies illustrated in all previous examples, whether from the school or from the oratory, have one thing in common: they are designed to sensitize children to Moroccan Arabic and Classical/Standard Arabic forms that have the same referential meaning, in that they mean the same thing, but have very different indexical meanings in relation to children's cultural and linguistic identity. Namely, Classical/ Standard Arabic is indexically associated with Pan-Arabism, education, literacy, cultural authenticity, and with Islam. Through the devaluing of Moroccan Arabic, particularly the Northeastern rural dialectal variety that many of these children spoke, the only sanctioned and legitimate linguistic identity available for Moroccan immigrant children in these classes is Classical/ Standard Arabic. But this is not the Arabic variety they acquired in their homes as a first language.

6.5.4   Children's Misuse of Classical/Standard Arabic

Another aspect of error-correction practices that is analytically interesting is Moroccan immigrant children's misuse of Classical/Standard Arabic linguistic forms, particularly when comparing Arabic-language classes in school and in the oratory. While children's use of Moroccan Arabic in the official space of the classroom was the focus of heightened surveillance and correction in Arabic-language classes in the school, children's mistakes in Classical/Standard Arabic constituted the core of error-correction practices of Arabic-language classes in the town oratory. In particular, the *fqih's* construction of the nature of the mistakes involving Classical/Standard Arabic deserves separate attention because he often interpreted these errors as emanating from children's participation in Spanish society. In the Arabic-language classes in the town oratory, error correction, thus, becomes a crucial mechanism to mark in-group/out-group boundaries in relation to children's developing identifications with their multiple communities.

In Example 6.8, a student is reading a series of syllables of the Arabic alphabet from the board. This series was designed for children to learn the letter *SāD* (ص). After correctly producing the first three syllables, the child makes a mistake and pronounces the letter *SāD* as the letter *sīn* (س), a letter which corresponds to a different sound in Arabic equivalent to the phoneme /s/.

Example 6.8
Participants: Fqih and Student on the board

```
  1.   STUDENT:  Sa – Si – So – s – ((Reading from the board))
  2.   FQIH:     "S" maši "s" Kayan sīn (س) u Kayan
                 SāD (ص)
                 "S" not "s". There is sīn and there
                 is SāD
  3.   FQIH:     bHal albaraH adrarikolhom katboli
                 Mokhammed
                 Like yesterday all the children wrote
                 Mokhammed
                 farqu ma bin alHā (ح) u lkhā (خ)
                 Distinguish between (ح) and (خ)
  4.   FQIH:     hiya hna fasbanya kayaqraūha Mokhammed
                 Here in Spain they read it Mokhammed
                 Hna 'adna MoHammed
                 We have MoHammed
```

The *fqih* corrects this mistake in line 2 and uses it as a springboard to address a problem he has encountered when correcting children's homework from the previous class. As part of the homework, children were supposed to practice writing the name of Prophet Mohammed. He found that, in doing so, many children had confused the letters *Hā* (ح), the letter with which the name MoHammed should be spelled, and *kha* (خ), a letter that corresponds to a similar, but different sound, and with which many children mistakenly spelled it. The *fqih*'s interpretation of the children's error as having its source in the interference of the Spanish phonological system with the Arabic phonological and writing system is interesting on two counts. First, the multiple letter forms and diacritical marks in Arabic have been described as being particularly susceptible to perceptual error by young children and other novices learning to read and to write in Arabic in Morocco and other Arabophone countries (e.g., Wagner, Messick, and Spratt, 1986).[27] Second, the Moroccan immigrant children in this study live in a rural community in Southern Spain, where the pronuciation of the Spanish phoneme /x/ – to which the letter *kha* corresponds – is strongly aspirated. This aspiration results in an allophonic realization that is closer to the letter *Hā* (ح)– the correct letter in the Arabic spelling of Mohammed – than to the letter *kha*, the mistake that the children had made.

Furthermore, it is important to notice the *fqih*'s use of the pronominal forms **we (Hna** ʹad**na** – **We have-)** and **they** (as encoded in the third-person plural form "kaya- -ū-", of the verb qra, **to read-kaya**qra**ū**ha), line 4. Through the use of these pronominal forms **we** and **they**, the *fqih* identifies himself and the children solely as members of an Arabic-speaking community and as different from the larger Spanish-speaking community. This identification is underscored by the presence of the pronoun *Hna/we*. In pro-drop languages, like Arabic, where pronoun forms are not required (ʹad**na** by itself would have sufficed, since it also means "we have"), the presence of a subject pronoun is always indicative of special emphasis.

Similarly, in Example 6.9, also from the classes in the town oratory, a student is reading a series of syllables of the Arabic alphabet from the board. The syllables involve the letter Tā, both in isolation and with all the possible short- and long-vowel combinations. In Classical Arabic, the suffix -ūn or -wn is usually added to a letter when it is pronounced in isolation. In this example, however, the child encounters the letter Tā with a fatha (ʹ), the diacritic symbol for the short vowel /a/. In this case, the letter Tā is supposed to be read *Ta* and not *Tawn* (or *Taūn*). The *fqih* corrects the student and addresses this differentiation in lines 3 and 4.

Example 6.9
Participants: Fqih, all students, and individual student

1.	STUDENT:	Taūn
		T
2.	FQIH:	ah maši ngul *taūn*,
		Eh we can't say T
3.		mali nalqaū lfatha ngolu Ta
		when we find a fatha (')we say Ta
4.		mali nalqaū hadi wašta nqraūha? ((pointing at the letter on the board))
		When we find this one how do we read it?
5.	ALL STUDENTS:	Ta
		T
6.	FQIH:	Ta mazian (.)
		Ta good
7.		ġadi nšufu had lablad fin rakum wakha
		we'll see with this country you're in, OK.

Although there is no linguistic feature of Spanish that could potentially be the source of the children's error, the *fqih* in line 4 makes a connection between the child's mistake with "this country you're in," meaning Spain. Apart from the disaffiliation stance indexed by the demonstrative *this* (**had lablad** – **this country**), the future tense of the sentence (**ġadi nšufu** – **we'll see**), projects a negative future orientation for the children's development. This negative orientation is suggested by linking children's mistakes in Arabic to their increasing participation as members of the Spanish society. These error-correction examples construct solid in-group/out-group boundaries that may have important consequences for Moroccan immigrant children's socialization and developing sense of membership. Spanish language and Spanish society is positioned as different from the children's primary sources of identification. Moreover, since Moroccan immigrant children's difficulties in the acquisition of Classical/Standard Arabic are sometimes interpreted as originating from their experiences with the Spanish language, children's involvement in Spanish society is constructed as detrimental to the children's Arab-Islamic identities. This involvement is perceived as having negative effects not only on children's linguistic development, but also on children's moral development as good Muslims. This is reinforced by the *fqih's* and other adults' admonitions to stay "off the wrong path." These admonitions often translated into surveillance of children's behavior, particularly of older children and adolescents, regarding their choice of clothing and the type of music they would listen to. Clothing and music were sometimes seen as a potential index of other dangerous and self-destructive behaviors, such as drug or alcohol use.

The error-correction practices in the town oratory, in combination with the preeminence given to linguistic forms that are imbued with cultural meanings associated with Islam, such as the Hijri calendar example above, carry some echoes of religious and national discourses of nativist orientation. Within some Moroccan communities, these nativist discourses advocate for total Arabization to the detriment of Western languages. The latter, particularly those that are seen as colonial, mostly French and Spanish, or neo-colonial languages, such as English, are sometimes constructed in these nativist religious discourses as a threat not only to the purity of the Arabic language, but also as a source of corruption and moral decadence for Moroccan youth. This is accomplished through a double indexical link that associates Western languages with Western culture and the latter with social and moral decadence.[28]

6.5.5   *Categorization of Students in Classroom Discourse*

Following on from the error-correction practices that have just been described, this section is concerned with another pervasive discursive feature found in the town oratory data, namely forms of categorization used to identify students as belonging to an Arab/Islamic community. At the same time, these discursive features position children's lives in Spain as separate from their primary identities as Moroccans and Muslims. The following example is extracted from an extended piece of discourse that the *fqih* delivered on one of the first days of instruction at the town oratory. After an opening statement about the importance of learning the Arabic language well and laying out expectations for children's behavior in the classroom, the *fqih* proceeded to explain what they were going to learn in his class:

Example 6.10
Participants: Fqih and Students

```
1.  FQIH:  ġadi ndīru 'amaliya lhisab,
           We are going to do arithmetic operations
```

2.   =ʾadna ʾibadat, ʾadna tarbayya, ʾadna
      attaqafa alwaTaniyya
      **we have religious practices, we have
      education, we have the national culture**

3.   n'arfu bladna almaġreb, baš nHabbūh o
      kif dayer had almaġreb
      **we (will) know our country Morocco, to
      love it and how is Morocco**

4.   Hasab alwaqt alli ʾadna n'arfu ala'yad
      alwaTaniya wa ala'yad aDDiiniya.
      **Depending on the time we have, we will
      know the national holidays and the
      religious holidays**

5.   n'arfu škun had annabī adyalna MoHammed
      **We (will) know who our Prophet Mohammed
      is**

6.   n'arfu škun howa Allah
      We (will) know who God is

7.   n'arfu kifaš n'išu m'a had lespane
      **we (will) know how to live with these
      Spaniards**

An essential feature of the discursive style that the *fqih* adopts throughout this segment is the *we-voicing* (Friedman 2006), which serves two important functions. First, it allows the *fqih* to identify the students and himself as belonging to the same group membership; second, it is integral for the *fqih's* own authoritative presentation as an animator of the normative view, including the cultural practices, bodies of knowledge and beliefs that are valued in Moroccan immigrant children's communities of origin. These include first and foremost the national culture of Morocco **"attaqafa alwa-Taniyya"** and Islamic religious practices **"'ibadat"** (line 2). These cultural practices and bodies of knowledge are fleshed out in subsequent turns of the *fiqh's* speech (lines 4–6) as encompassing religious and Moroccan national holidays, as well as knowledge of God and of the Prophet Mohammed. It is important to remember that, in this context, the national culture and Islamic religious practices become associated with Classical/Standard Arabic, which is the primary target of instruction in Arabic-language classes.

There are other linguistic features in the we-voicing style of the *fqih* that circumscribe Moroccan immigrant children's identifications exclusively in terms of their heritage communities, including the use of verbal forms in the first-person plural (*we*) and the use of first-person plural possessive pronouns (*our*). Furthermore, the linguistic features of the we-voicing stand in contrast with line 7, in which the *fqih* states that a final thing the children need to learn is "how to live with these Spaniards" **(kifaš n'išu m'a had lespane)**. The distancing effect and the disaffiliation stance indexed by the demonstrative adjective *had/this*, especially in comparison with the profuse use of first-person plural forms that permeates the rest of the discourse, functions as a boundary marker. Spanish people are cast as discrete entities that Moroccan children have to learn to live *with*, and the larger Spanish society as a place that Moroccan immigrant children have to learn how to live *in*, but not as a space that the children are necessarily a part *of*.

In spite of the *fqih's* routine construction of solid in-group/out-group boundaries between the children and Spanish society, and in spite of some nativist aspects of his religious discourse, it would be inaccurate to characterize Bilal unidimensionally in terms of traditional scripturalism, or what has also been called in other European settings *village Islam* (Mandeville 2001, 2007). While he did have a greater tendency to reproduce tradition, other aspects of Bilal's teachings also participated in a more hybridized idiom of Islam in Europe that encourages Muslims living in minority situations to adopt a new pragmatism and to engage in full civic participation with the rest of the society (see Note 4). Bilal telling the children that they were going to learn "how to live with these Spaniards," for example has to be considered along with other instances in which he would regularly remind children that they had to be good students, work hard in school, and respect their Spanish teachers. These are just a few examples of this hybridized and pragmatic discourse that rejects Muslims' ghettoization and isolation from non-Muslims (Tibi 2002), while fostering productive engagement with Spanish institutions and promoting sensible relationships with Spanish people.

A final issue that I would like to address is whether and to what extent the children were picking up on the ideological differences between the two teachers, Rashid and Bilal. I was never completely certain what children made of these differences, or whether they perceived them at all. I tried to find out indirectly by asking which class was their favorite, but even when they clearly preferred one over the other, like in Worda's case, their answers did not address these ideological differences. Worda, for example, preferred Rashid's classes at the public school because she said that the oratory-mosque lessons were too crowded and too noisy, and because she also preferred to pray with her mother and sisters. Sarah also felt this way about the oratory classes. It was clear to me, nevertheless, that children were attuned to the areas of overlap and continuity between these two settings, and that in many ways they saw them as complementary. For the most part, those children who did better and/or seemed to enjoy Rashid's classes at school the most, like Mimon and Wafiya, whose quote opens this chapter, were also among the most enthusiastic and assiduous attendees at the after-school lessons in the oratory. Conversely, those children who struggled most in Arabic-language classes at the school, like Karim, were also those children whose attendance was most sporadic at the after-school Qur'anic classes.

There was, however, one way I observed in which children were more explicitly made aware of these differences. This has to do with Rashid's reactions when the children, perhaps naïvely, would call him **"ya**[29] **fqih"** (literally, **"O fqih"**), addressing him by the title of the religious teacher, Bilal. While sometimes he would let this go for the sake of not interrupting the instructional flow of the class, on a few occasions, he reacted very strongly and negatively and confronted children directly. In reprimanding the children, Rashid would tell them that he was not a *fqih* and that he did not want to be addressed in that manner, but rather as a teacher, **"ya mu'allem."** Sometimes Rashid would go on and talk to the children visibly frustrated about his educational and professional credentials. Other times he would confront the children with rhetorical questions about Bilal, casting doubt about Bilal's knowledge and understanding of Islam and the Qur'an. Rashid's reactions may have been in part related to the differences in social class and educational background between Bilal and him that I already pointed out at the beginning of the chapter. These reactions likely also index, however, deeper tensions about tradition and modernity playing out in Moroccan communities in both Morocco and in the diaspora in Spain. A key aspect of understanding Rashid's reactions to the children is how, particularly with the introduction of universal public schooling in Morocco, the figure of the *fqih* has undergone a progessive loss of status and prestige, as they are not seen as being able to fulfill the types of civic and secular literacy needed for higher education and professional careers (Spratt and Wagner 1986/2011).[30]

6.6   Conclusion

This chapter has explored the complex interactions between language use, literacy practices, and processes of ethnoreligious identification in the context of Arabic-language education among the Moroccan immigrant community in Vallenuevo. I have examined language use in actual teacher-student interactions and in classroom literacy practices in the two settings where the same group of Moroccan immigrant children attend Arabic-language classes. The analysis has focused on the types of identities that are being (re)produced as *appropriate* and *authentic* in teachers' linguistic acts and stances and that, thus, become available for appropriation or negotiation by the younger generations. The previous analyses have shown how the instructional and interactional practices of Arabic language classes in the school seem to be more aligned with civic discourses in the children's communities of origin. These civic discourses see Classical/Standard Arabic as a language that can provide Moroccans access to literacy, education, and modernity, while safeguarding their cultural authenticity and cultural identity. The instructional and interactional practices of Arabic-language classes in the town oratory, however, seem to be aligned with more nativist religious discourses among Moroccan transnational networks that promote a conflation of being Moroccan with Islamic practices and beliefs. These discourses tend to delineate distinct in-group/out-group boundaries between the children and Spanish society at large. While at times they promote Moroccan immigrant children's responsible interactions with Spanish society, at others they also position Moroccan children's involvement in Spanish society as a threat to their primary and *authentic* identifications as Arabic-speaking Muslims.

This chapter underscores the importance of investigating the complex language ideologies that play out in the Arabic-language classes this group of Moroccan immigrant children attend. These language ideologies are an important dimension to understand the contested debates over authenticity in relation to modernity and tradition in Moroccan immigrants in Spain, and in Muslims in Europe, more generally. Another point I emphasize in this chapter is that the different shapes these debates take in different Muslim immigrant communities may be related to the sociocultural and historical particularities of these different groups, as the tensions embodied in the figures of the public school teacher and the *fqih* in Vallenuevo illustrate. Many current debates about the politics of Arabic-language education in Moroccan communities (both in Morocco and in the diaspora) are indeed debates about the search for and preservation of cultural and religious specificity. Yet, they are simultaneously about how to reconcile this with the rapid transformations that many of these communities are undergoing to compete in global markets, particularly when these transformations can be seen as emanating from a Western (neo-)colonial legacy. These debates not only carry over to Moroccan diasporic communities in Europe, but are often accenuated in an immigration context where the Moroccan immigrant community may feel more scrutinized by the dominant community, and where the transmission of their religious and cultural traditions to the younger generations may be, therefore, perceived to be more under threat.

Given the current geopolitical climate surrounding Muslim immigrants in Europe, much recent scholarship has been devoted to how global *ideoscapes* (Appadurai 2002) and transnational influences are reconfiguring migrant populations into transnational and hybrid diasporas who find themselves at the crux of the negotiation between tradition and modernity (e.g., Samad and Kasturi 2007). Much less attention has been devoted, however, to the most immediate, everyday local contexts in which many of these processes are negotiated. Even less consideration has been given to the countervailing influences faced by Muslim immigrant children as they struggle to (re)construct their identities in their daily interactions with members of their heritage communities, as well as with members of the dominant society. In immigrant communities, the complex relationship between individuals and their multiple languages and cultures is deeply intertwined with the multifaceted identities they have to negotiate in different arenas of social interaction. Thus, investigating language socialization practices in Arabic-language classes is crucial in understanding immigrant children's affordances and constraints in developing a strong sense of commonality of belonging in relation to the multiple communities in which they participate.

Research on heritage language education has underscored the fact that these educational practices have the potential to be an important resource for immigrant children's development of a positive sense of social and personal identity in that it can promote feelings of ethnic, cultural, and linguistic pride. Positive connections with the practices and values of their immigrant communities are, therefore, important for Moroccan immigrant children to develop. These positive feelings are crucial in the face of practices of social exclusion and other racist attitudes that these children may encounter in their dealings with the wider Spanish society, (see Chapters 2 and 5 in particular). However, as it has also been described in this chapter, language socialization efforts in Arabic-language classes may engender possible disconnects when children's home language variety is treated condescendingly and not incorporated into classroom practice in a positive way. Future research should investigate if/how children themselves perceive these contradictions, as well as the long-term outcomes in relation to children's processes of identification and of first language maintenance. Another important and productive line for future investigations would be action research devoted to developing programs that build more positively on children's home language variety, while at the same time taking into account adults' (parents and educators) concerns and desires that their children learn Classical/Standard Arabic.

Another trend discussed in this chapter is how language education classes in religious contexts become a means to patrol communal borders and processes of identification that in religious contexts serve as a means to patrol communal borders and identifications that are more strongly rooted in tradition. This type of socialization into strong in-group identity boundaries is not specific to Islamic communities and has indeed been documented as a primary means of identification in many other religious communities (e.g., Fader 2009). In fact, in many immigrant communities, older generations are known to strengthen traditional forms of identifications for the younger generations in response to intense surveillance by the dominant society and also in response to forces of assimilation that they consider a threat to the well-being of their children and their families.[31]

While this may be a widespread phenomenon across immigrant communities, it is still important to consider how older generations attempt to reenculturate children, and how these attempts may impact youth's spaces and opportunities to redefine their identifications. This is significant particularly given the marginalization and exclusion these youth often experience in their dealings with the Spanish society. In this respect, Muslim immigrant children and youth in Spain, as well as in the rest of Europe, often have to negotiate crisscrossing fears from a heritage community who fear that they are becoming too "Spanish" and from a dominant society which attempts to assimilate them in the midst of fears that they are becoming too "Islamic." In the next two chapters, I explore how Moroccan immigrant children in Vallenuevo attempt to manage these countervailing influences and create spaces to generate new and hybrid processes of identifications.

Notes

1 For more information about the LACM program, see Chapter 3.

2 Except for Kamal, all focal children in the study attended Modern Standard Arabic-language classes with Rashid once a week at the public school. See Chapter 3.

3 While there is no official consensus in academic circles on what the label *heritage* in *heritage* languages/cultures/speakers should be applied to, it is routinely used in scholarly work to refer, for instance, to the languages spoken among immigrants, refugees, indigenous, and aboriginal groups. See, for example, the work of Wiley (2001, 2005), for more on definitions of heritage languages and their speakers. In this book, I use *heritage* to refer to the languages and cultural practices rooted in the immigrant children's Moroccan immigrant communities of origin.

4 While the literature on this topic is too extensive for me to do justice to it in an endnote, see, for example, Ramadan (1999, 2004); Lee (1997); Cesari (2004, 2006); Cesari and McLoughlin (2005); Thompson (2003); Bowen (2009, 2011); and Amir-Moazani and Salvatore (2003) for more extended discussions of questions of Islamic authenticity and the debate of tradition and modernity.

5 This stigmatization of vernacular varieties figures prominently in ideologies regarding Classical/Standard Arabic not only in Morocco, but also throughout the Middle East. In

this sense, Eisele (2003) identified three ideological features that are usually ascribed to Classical/Standard Arabic, that is *purity*, *unity*, and *continuity*. In this light, vernaculars are often seen as corrupt versions of the Classical language. Moreover, the closer to Classical/Standard Arabic a dialectal variety is deemed to be, the higher the status of that dialectal variety in relation to other vernaculars is.

6   See, for example, Ennaji (2005); Holt (1994); Suleiman (1994, 2003) for more extended discussions on the role of Classical/Standard Arabic in pro-independence and anti-colonial movements in Morocco, as well as for its role in early nation-building efforts after independence. See also Note 9 below.

7   In addition to the Qur'anic classes for younger children that I recorded, the oratory-mosque also offered classes for older children and adolescents on alternate days.

8   See, for example, Abu-Haidar (1994); Sakkouni (1998); Tilmatine (2002); Van de Wetering (1992).

9   In Morocco, Classical/Standard Arabic is used in town oratories, government administration, the media, literature, and, increasingly, in political and scientific discourse. Furthermore, it is not only the official language of Morocco, but also the language of literacy that, along with French, is sanctioned by educational policies. The push for Arabization and the rise of Classical/Standard Arabic as the official language of the independent Moroccan nation has to be understood in terms of the symbolic position to which Classical/Standard Arabic was elevated during the struggle for independence in the first half of the twentieth century. Like in many other nationalist movements throughout the Middle East, in the Moroccan fight against European colonialism, Classical/Standard Arabic came to be viewed ideologically as a way to access modernity while safeguarding Moroccan national identity and cultural authenticity, (Ennaji 2005; Suleiman, 1994, 2003).

10 The word *suwar* (سور) is the plural form of *sūrah* (سورة), which refers to each of the divisions or chapters of the Qur'ān.

11 Collins (1995); Scribner and Cole (1978, 1981).

12 Baquedano-López (2004a); Duranti and Ochs (1986); Fader (2001, 2009); Moore (2006); Schieffelin (2000).

13 See, for example, Heath (1986); Schieffelin and Gilmore (1986). Also, Fader's (2001, 2009) research on bilingual literacy practices among groups of the Hasidic Jewish diaspora, for example, has shown how boys and girls are socialized to attain differential competence in English and Yiddish. These differences in language use and competence are, in turn, related to sanctioned gender and identities for males and females, as well as to the ways in which communal borders are reinforced in relation to outsiders, such as non-Jews and other Jewish groups.

14 In her study of teachers' language practices in Doctrina and Catechism classes that Mexican-American children attend, Baquedano-López (2000, 2004b) has shown how teachers' differential discursive rendition of the same story promotes alternatively different processes of identifications. In Doctrina classes, the telling of the story promotes affiliative stances that create a unique, positive Latino identity for the children, while in the context of Catechism classes, Mexican ethnicity is treated generically within the US hegemonic model of the *melting-pot*. The complex link between ethnic identity and learning heritage languages has also been explored in heritage language socialization research. He's (2004, 2006) work on Chinese heritage language classes in the United States has demonstrated how teachers pervasively define students in terms of their communities of origin through inference-rich membership categorization devices (Sacks 1992). The deployment of these devices function

to establish similarities between these students and their Chinese heritage communities, and to establish differences between the students and other communities they may regard themselves as members of, such as mainstream US communities. Chinese-American children's resistance towards some of these teachers' discursive practices has led He (2000, 2004, 2006, 2008) to posit whether heritage language development can be said to be contingent upon learners' ability to construct and maintain continuity and coherence between ethnic identity and other aspects of social identity.

15   See Wagner (1993).

16   See Warnock Fernea (1995, pp. 421–422).

17   See Ezakki, Spratt, and Wagner (1999); Moore (2006); Wagner, Messick, and Spratt (1986); Wagner (1993).

18   This family structure and social organization has also been described as common, and as a feature that is the object of socialization routines directed at children throughout the Arab world from an early age. See Belarbi (1995) and Warnock Fernea (1995).

19   See Hefner (2007) and Wagner, Messick, and Spratt (1986).

20   See Ennaji (2005); Gill (1999).

21   See Ennaji (2005) and Mouhssine (1995) for further elaboration of this topic.

22   Error-correction is a very important aspect of teachers' language practices, since corrective feedback in the classroom is consequential for students' learning and performance. Beyond the effect that error-correction strategies have for novices' acquisition of linguistic forms (Chaudron 1988; Van Lier 1988), language socialization research has examined these strategies as culturally mediated practices through which novices are socialized into the socially and ideologically constructed meanings of linguistic forms, as well as initiated into local epistemologies, social roles, and identities (Friedman 2006; Sterponi and Santagata 2000). Error-correction strategies are particularly useful to illuminate how the intersection between language socialization and language ideologies plays out in children's socialization into the use of national and/or vernacular languages (Friedman 2006; Jaffe 1993). In the context of language revitalization programs in Ukrainian classrooms, Friedman's (2006) study of error-correction, in particular, underscores the ideological linkage between teachers' socializing strategies into speaking Ukrainian *correctly*, for example free of Russian influences, and what being a citizen of a distinct Ukrainian nation means.

23   This treatment of mistakes has been described as common in educational systems that use public performance by students, or *the blackboard activity* (Sterponi and Santagata 2000), as a focal pedagogical strategy in classroom practice. See Sterponi and Santagata (2000) for an expanded discussion of public corrective strategies in Italian classrooms.

24   It is important to say that there was a great deal of *by-play* (Goffman 1981b) among the children in Arabic heritage-language classes. This *unofficial* discourse was conducted in Moroccan Arabic, the mother tongue of the children in these classes. Children's by-play in the unofficial space of the classroom was an object of teachers' attention only in terms of maintaining discipline and order in the class; children's choice of language during these interactions was virtually ignored.

25   The use of peers to help correct errors has also been described in other classroom environments where language ideologies of speaking correctly means is also crucial for children's development of ethnic and national linguistic identities (Friedman 2006).

26   See Duff (2000); Cullen's (2002) discussions for other examples of teachers' use of repetition to validate an answer in the official space of the classroom.

27 The pervasiveness of this type of error has also been documented in children's acquisition of literacy in other languages that also use diacritical marks or dots to distinguish between certain letters, such as Hebrew (Feitelson 1980).

28 See, for example, Ennaji (2005); Holt (1994); Mouhssine (1995); Suleiman (1994, 2003).

29 "Ya" is a vocative particle in Arabic that must precede all titles of address, and sometimes even proper names.

30 Spratt and Wagner (1986/2011) have written a detailed account of the transformations experienced by traditional Islamic teachers, starting in the colonial period and continuing after Moroccan independence when the government started opening public schools all over the country.

31 See, for example, Alexander (2007); Engbersen (2007); Lee (2005); Mohammed-Arif (2007); Samad (2007).

32 Because Surat Al-Kāfirūn is part (Chapter 109) of Al-Qur'ān, a sacred text, which Muslims believe to be the word of God, I will not offer my translation here.

33 The Arabic word *Hijrah* means "emigration." The Islamic calendar is a lunar calendar based on the year Prophet Mohammed fled to Medina, in 622 of the Gregorian calendar.

7

Becoming Translators of Culture: Moroccan Immigrant Children's Experiences as Language Brokers

A mi me gusta mucho traducir español y árabe –
siento que me pongo contenta.

I like translating Spanish and Arabic very much –
I feel it makes me happy.

(Worda, age 10, interview fragment)

Aprendo cosas que no sabía y eso –
algunas veces me dicen algo, y no las entiendo,
y vengo y las busco en el diccionario.

I learn things that I didn't know and that –
sometimes they tell me something and I don't understand them,
and I come back [home] and I look them up in the dictionary.

(Abdelkarim, age 10, interview fragment)

7.1 Just a Routine Medical Visit

It was a winter afternoon at the local health center, and Dr. Rocío, the Spanish pediatrician, had already been seeing patients for a couple of hours. The next patient walked in: a small Moroccan boy, ʿAli, accompanied by his mother and a neighbor, a Moroccan girl, Fatima, who often acted as translator between Moroccan mothers and the doctor. It was just a routine medical checkup to monitor the boy's development, a follow-up to a visit that had taken place a few weeks earlier. The mother was complaining that

Language and Muslim Immigrant Childhoods: The Politics of Belonging, First Edition.
Inmaculada Mª García-Sánchez.
© 2014 John Wiley & Sons, Inc. Published 2014 by John Wiley & Sons, Inc.

she had a lot of problems getting her son to take the syrup that the doctor had prescribed during the initial visit, and that the syrup had not been effective in increasing the boy's appetite. Otherwise, both the visit and the Moroccan Arabic-Spanish translation were proceeding smoothly. While the doctor was comparing test results and writing a few notes on the boy's medical chart, the mother turned to the girl-translator and asked her whether she spoke "**tmaziġt,**" one of the dialects of Amazighe: **šam tassawalad tmaziġt?**[1] Fatima answered positively, **am**, adding that she spoke a little. The mother, taking advantage that her little boy did not speak Amazighe, then asked the girl to help her invent a story that would scare the boy into eating. A pregnant pause followed the exposition of the maternal stratagem, as the mother looked hopefully at Fatima, waiting for the girl to say something, and Fatima glanced sideways at the mother, while playing with the fringes of the woolen poncho she was wearing. Perhaps thinking that the girl did not speak Amazighe all that well after all, after a few seconds the mother lowered her voice to almost a whisper and proceeded to speak to Fatima in Moroccan Arabic, while Dr. Rocío continued to pore over ʿAli's most recent medical records.

The mother proposed telling ʿAli that, if he continued to refuse to eat, they would have to come back to the doctor's office for little pieces of his ears and his head to be removed: **šufi kolilha ila mabġaš yakol waš nraṭolhom baš taklaʿlo šwiya man alwadnin warras (look, tell him that if he doesn't want to eat, we'll bring him back to remove a little of his ears and head)**. Fatima looked nervously at the mother and the doctor alternatively, softly biting her lips. The doctor, who by then had finished taking her notes, also looked inquisitively at the family, waiting for a translation of what had just transpired between them. The girl hesitated for a few seconds and, finally, composing herself, said to the doctor that the mother wanted to confirm whether the boy had to take the syrup for the next two months Dice que si tiene que tomar dos meses de esto (**she says whether he has to take two months of this**). The pediatrician responded affirmatively, repeating the instructions she had given earlier in the interaction: a small dose of the syrup every day with or before breakfast: Durante dos meses. Una botellita al día con el desayuno o antes (**For two months. One little bottle a day with breakfast or before**). Fatima turned to the mother and told her in Moroccan Arabic that the doctor had said the same thing about the syrup that she had said before: **kalatlak kimma kalatlak kbila (She told you like she told you before)**. After that, both mother and girl thanked the doctor and left the office.

This vignette illustrates the complex experience, beyond language competence, of being a child interpreter. Even the most cursory inspection of the burgeoning scholarship on community interpreting[2] suggests that these situations involve varied asymmetries between institutional figures and members of subaltern societal groups that always greatly complicate the translation process, beyond encoding and decoding messages into two different languages. This literature also indicates that, as a consequence of these sociocultural, political, economic, and linguistic asymmetries, the supposed invisibility and impartiality of interpreters in these interactions can be seen more as an ideal than an attainable reality. Indeed, there is increasing evidence that it is when interpreters are themselves members of less dominant communities, yet have to act as social agents of institutions, when interpreters' conflicts around issues of neutrality, power, agency, involvement, and advocacy come to the forefront of these interactions more visibly.[3] As a special case of community interpreting, when Moroccan immigrant children in Vallenuevo act as linguistic brokers and sociocultural mediators between their families and members of Spanish institutions, they cannot escape having to negotiate this dual social identity. As interpreters of record in these interactions, they act simultaneously as both agents of the institution and advocates of their immigrant families and communities, often protecting the latter from outside surveillance, even as they may at times open their families up for scrutiny and evaluation.

In the previous interaction, for example, Fatima might not have complied with the mother's request (at least in the doctor's presence) to frighten the boy because in inventing such a story that misrepresented the doctor's words and character, she would be overstepping the boundaries of her role as impartial interpreter and agent of the medical institution. Similarly, she might have "lied" to the doctor in her translation of the exchange with the mother to protect her from an institutional authority figure. Perhaps she worried about how the Spanish doctor would interpret and react to the mother's methods of exercising parental authority. It could even be possible to argue that, in not wanting to convey to the doctor the frightening story the mother wanted to use to scare her child into eating more, the girl was protecting her whole community from negative stereotypes and routine misrepresentations of Moroccan immigrants' cultural practices commonly held by members of Spanish society (see earlier discussions in Chapter 2).

While it is impossible for me to know with certainty what Fatima was thinking during the translation process, it is clear from the vignette that she was making a judgment about what should and should not be passed on to the pediatrician, and also on to the patient, little ʿAli. Moreover, what Fatima chose to say and not say in this encounter demonstrates her awareness of the importance of not misrepresenting therapeutic courses of action and institutional ways of operating. It also demonstrates her awareness of the importance of not conveying information to the doctor that could lead the doctor to misinterpret ʿAli's mother's attempt to encourage her child to eat, and by implication also lead the pediatrician to misjudge Moroccan parental practices more generally. From this perspective, we can see Fatima acting with an orientation to her responsibilities towards the clinic as a translator, but also with an orientation to her role as family/community advocate.

The vignette also illustrates the sociocultural, ethical, and interactional paradoxes that Moroccan immigrant children manage in mediating institutional encounters. Child language brokers, like Fatima, are in a position to exercise discretion; yet, they may also feel constrained by being between two adult authority figures. In the course of translation, they have to make consequential decisions on behalf of both parties; yet, these decisions sometimes entail delicate moral dilemmas. They have to be competent in the multiple languages involved in the interactions; in addition, they also have to be aware of distinct, often incongruous, sociocultural worldviews, ideologies, assumptions, expectations, practices, and ethical universes. They are expected to be *neutral* and *detached* translators; but in practice, they have to assume multiple identities as *institutional interpreters*, *patients*, *immigrants*, *children*, *family advocates*, and *members of both the Spanish and Moroccan communities*. Some of these paradoxical positionalities have already been pointed out by previous research on immigrant children language brokering (N. Hall 2004; García-Sánchez and Orellana 2006; Orellana et al. 2003a, 2003b; Orellana 2009; Reynolds and Orellana 2009). This chapter, however, focuses on how Moroccan immigrant children in Vallenuevo act contextually when translating between their families and doctors in pediatric encounters at the local health center. In particular, I pay attention to how they manage their varied positionalities and identities, becoming important participants themselves, through their own translational practices and filters. This is a topic for which we have very little grounded ethnographic research and evidence of the kind that I report and analyze in this chapter. Indeed, previous scholarship that has presented naturally-occurring interactional data on immigrant children acting as interpreters for adults in medical contexts has been extremely limited, and mostly from US contexts.[4]

In examining how Moroccan immigrant children attend to the contingencies of these positionalities, I want to bring analytic attention to how these children assume responsibility for their own words and for conveying the words of others. More specifically, I focus on what they choose to say and not say and to whom, and what they choose to modify in translation. In so doing, I will emphasize that even though children demonstrate ample competence in asserting authorial responsibility, distinctly marking their own words from those of others, they also exhibit a great deal of sophistication in disavowing authorial responsibility, when they blend their own words and perspectives with the words of others (Voloshinov/Bakhtin 1973). In these cases, their translations end up becoming double-voiced renditions of the original utterances (Bakhtin 1981). In this sense, aspects of what Lambek (2010) has called *ordinary ethics*, as constituted through criteria and commitments that are instantiated in everyday speaking, resonate forcefully in this realm of the children's social lives.

While *ordinary ethics* – that is, ethics as located in everyday practice rather in objective knowledge of rules – can be said to be generally entailed in all speech and action (see Lambek 2010; Rumsey 2010; Sidnell 2010), the contingencies that Moroccan immigrant children face in this arena of their sociocultural experience create moral quandaries that are often inescapable. One aspect of this inescapability is the heightened discursive regimes surrounding individuals' actions as translators, strongly associated with total fidelity and neutral repetition of original texts or utterances. There is indeed a strong tradition in translation/interpretation theory and practice of locating ethics in the possible gap between what is said and what is translated, as well as in how well translators manage to hide the agency they exercise in constructing meaning (Arrojo 2013, 1998; Venutti 1998). Although not professionally trained, Moroccan immigrant children at the local health center can certainly be seen as orienting to these idealized, popular exemplars of translators' codes of ethics.

Another aspect of the inescapability of these ethical dilemmas, however, is small moments in these exchanges when a detached, faithful translation might not be the best course of action to protect the interest or the image of Moroccan families. This is especially the case given the power asymmetries, racialized prejudice, cross-cultural miscommunication, and other social tensions that sometimes characterize interactions between immigrants and institutional officials in public administration and other Spanish social services (Codó Olsino 2008). That Moroccan immigrant children exhibit a discerning ethical sophistication about these small moments, heightened in their case by generational asymmetries, is obvious to me in the vignette presented above and in other examples that I discuss throughout this chapter. These moments, although brief and fleeting, provide a fruitful ethnographic locus to explore the still not well-understood aspects of how ordinary ethical sensibilities are shaped and hardened by broader sociopolitical forces and sociocultural ideologies, especially in children. From this perspective, I am interested in the liminal aspects of ordinary ethics for immigrant children as they display their awareness of the different sociocultural views and expectations that the parties in these interactions may hold, and as they contend with racialized images of their own Moroccan community.

The translation filters that children use, in that they allow certain kinds of self-distancing, may be particularly amenable to this exploration of how Moroccan immigrant children come to understand different points of view, through their dual roles as interpreters and advocates. As Keane (2010) has argued in discussing other semiotic forms that also mediate modalities of objectification involved in people's social relations (namely, storytelling and gift-giving), "if ethics is a function of life with others, those others are neither wholly other to the self . . . nor do they snuggle down comfortably together with it . . . the moment of objectification can turn in any number of directions" (p. 82). Through the analyses below, I examine some of these possible directions. I will argue that Moroccan immigrant children in Vallenuevo, through translating practices, display their awareness of sociocultural practices, generational expectations, and processes by which Moroccans are *marked* as different. I analyze how the children attempt to manage these contingencies and build bridges among their families, healthcare professionals, and themselves, by the way they creatively modify texts, or decide not to translate certain things rather that translating verbatim.

7.2   Research on Immigrant Children as Language Brokers

Over the last three decades, the widespread activities of immigrant children as sociocultural brokers and linguistic mediators between their parents and representatives of social institutions of destination countries have become an increasingly important focus of attention for researchers across different disciplines. This role has been identified, for example, for Latino and Chinese immigrant children in the United States (e.g., Chao 2006; Orellana 2001, 2003; Tse 1995, 1996a; Valenzuela 1999; Valdés 2003); Chinese immigrant children in the United Kingdom (Song 1997); Pakistani immigrant children in the United Kingdom (N. Hall 2004); for Moroccan and Sub-Saharan African immigrant children in Spain (Valero Garcés 2001; García-Sánchez 2009), and for South Asian, as well as North and Sub-Saharan African immigrant children in Italy (Antonini 2011; Cirillo et al., 2010). While the academic focus on this phenomenon is relatively new, it must be said that immigrant children having to speak for adult members of their immigrant communities is not particular to the current sociohistorical context. In fact, we have a number of historical accounts and memoirs of people reminiscing about their experiences as language brokers and translators for their families, mostly in the United States and Canada, as early as the nineteenth century.[5]

The global nature of contemporary migrations, however, has made the need for translators and interpreters increasingly necessary in countries, such as Spain, that have only become a destination for immigrants in recent decades. Issues of linguistic access and bureaucratic gate-keeping in the provision of public services to immigrants in Spain, for example, have indeed begun to resonate forcefully in the scholarly literature in the last few years (Codó Olsino 2008; Valero Garcés 2008; Valero Garcés et al. 2008; Unamuno and Codó Olsino 2007). While there have been some efforts at professionalization of interpreting services to ameliorate the exclusionary effects of bureaucratic language and other forms of linguistic inequalities (Alonso and Baigorri 2008; Collados Aís and Fernández Sánchez 2001), the fact remains that in Spain, like in most of the countries mentioned above, the provision of adequate linguistic services to immigrants is usually a low policy and budget priority, if a priority at all. In addition, the provision of these services is usually highly controversial among the general population. As a consequence, the reliance of institutions and communities on ad hoc, lay interpreters, who often end up being their own children, has made the phenomenon of child language brokering increasingly visible across a larger number of countries and institutions.

Due to the increased academic attention that this phenomenon has received, the terminology to describe it has flourished. Harris and Sherwood (1978) first used the term "natural translation" to refer to bilingual children's spontaneous translations.[6] Orellana (2009), however, has argued that this terminology is problematic, since it misrepresents how difficult and "unnatural" real-time translation can be. Tse (1996: 226) coined the term "language brokers" to refer to immigrant and ethnic minority children who act as translators and mediate interactions between people of different cultural and linguistic backgrounds in both familial and educational contexts. Also, Chu (1999) put forward the term "immigrant children mediators" and Valdés (2003) has used the phrase "family interpreting." Orellana et al. (2003a, 2003b) have criticized these last three designations, arguing that although the terms capture translating and mediating aspects of the work that immigrant children do, they obscure the power imbalance that their position as children of immigrants interacting with members of dominant society institutions entail. They have suggested, instead, the term "para-phrasing." "Paraphrasing" is a pun on the Spanish preposition *para* (for/in order to) and the English verb "paraphrase," to highlight the ways in which Latino immigrant children use their knowledge of both languages and cultures "to speak *for* others and *in order to* accomplish social goals" (Orellana et al. 2003b, p. 508). Alternatively, Wandesjö (1998, 2006) has helped to popularize the notion of "community interpreting" to refer to situations in which untrained volunteers, usually friends and family members of immigrants and refugees, serve as translators in institutional settings, regardless of whether these volunteers are children or adults. While acknowledging there are potential shortcomings involved in different kinds of terminology, in this chapter, I will use the term "language brokers/-ing" (one of the most popular terms in the literature), interchangeably with "child-translators/-ion" and "children as sociocultural and linguistic mediators," to refer to both the children and the practice itself.

While the study of language brokering is still a fairly new research enterprise, its lens has already been used to examine a range of phenomena. Most of this scholarship has focused on determining the educational and psychological outcomes of this practice, very often using questionnaires and interviews as methodological tools.[7] More relevant to my analysis of Moroccan immigrant children as language brokers are a few ethnographic studies that consider the impact of language brokering on the (re)negotiation of children's social identities and relationships. Although, as mentioned above, the ethnographic study of this phenomenon is scant, there are a handful of thick ethnographic accounts that examine how children's contributions and involvement as language brokers impact their daily lives and their ongoing processes of sociocultural development and identification (García-Sánchez and Orellana 2006; N. Hall 2004; Katz 2014; Orellana 2001; Orellana 2003; Orellana 2009; Reynolds and Orellana 2009; Song 1997). From an interactional angle, more specifically, Hall (2004) has investigated how Pakistani immigrant children in the United Kingdom handle cultural and hierarchical contingencies in the context of parent-teacher meetings. These meetings were, however, mock encounters involving a script, as well as actors playing the roles of parents and teachers. From this standpoint, more realistic is the linguistic anthropological perspective offered by García-Sánchez and Orellana (2006), Reynolds and Orellana (2009), and Katz (2014). Focusing on naturally-occurring parent-teacher meetings, García-Sánchez and Orellana (2006) examined how children downgraded teachers' positive assessments and amplified teachers' negative evaluations, when translating teachers' narratives about their academic performance to their parents. In commercial encounters, Reynolds and Orellana (2009) investigated how immigrant children negotiated racialization processes, engaging in active face-work on behalf of their families. Katz's (2014) recent ethnography on Latino immigrant children as language brokers provides new insights of this practice in relation to medical encounters, and most originally, in relation to family use of media. Building on this research, the analysis below addresses an area of children's language brokering that remains understudied, namely how immigrant child language brokers manage their conflicting ethical responsibilities in relation to different sociocultural and generational expectations and asymmetries.

7.3 From "Natural Translation" to Everyday Interpreting as an Interactional Achievement

Interpreting encounters are not just linguistic exchanges, but also sociocultural exchanges in which any meaning is situated within structural asymmetries, as well as within partially overlapping, and often contradictory, networks of histories, ideologies, and world views. From this perspective, language brokering provides us with an excellent window to explore immigrant children's role in building bridges across linguistic and sociocultural boundaries.

In early studies of translation in relation to bilingual children, translating was considered to be a transparent task, an innate skill for bilingual children, as something that came naturally as part of being bilingual, and, particularly, as something that did not have any bearing on these children's developing sociocultural competence. These views on bilingual children's translation abilities were based on how translation and communication, in general, were being theorized at the time; namely, as a cognitive process that only involved the encoding and decoding of messages in a unidirectional process of transfer. The translator was seen as a mere *conduit* of information, or as a decoder of messages in one language that have to be re-encoded in another language (Harris 1977; Nida 1964; Reddy 1979).

This theory of translation was based on two flawed assumptions: (1) the sociocultural and communicative context in which translation/interpretation takes place is relatively unimportant; and (2) there is a shared objective reality for all of the parties in the interaction. In this ideological milieu, it is perhaps not surprising that complete faithfulness to the original message took hold not only as a central principle organizing translators' tasks, but also as an unproblematically attainable goal. The *literal fidelity* premise, underlying this natural theory of translation, has had such a long tradition and has been so highly influential that it can also be seen as having implicitly framed the study of speech events related to simultaneous interpreting. The linguistic study of reported speech, for example, has had a long history of considering quotations as verbatim reproductions (see Clark and Gerrig 1990, for a review and critique of this literature). Limitations of these approaches are that (1) they grant privileged status to the internal linguistic structure of the messages, and (2) ignore the different, often conflicting, pragmatic expectations of interlocutors that immigrant children consider and incorporate in their translations.

Wandesjö (1998, 2006) has discussed how these normative views still have a powerful impact on popular and professional ideologies surrounding what the act of interpreting entails. Some of these cognitive-oriented beliefs also continue to influence ideas of who is bilingual enough to produce reliable translations. In the field of translation/interpretation, for instance, only those individuals who can be said to have attained an idealized native-like mastery over the two languages are considered to be *true* bilinguals. This conceptualization contrasts with current notions of bilingualism in other fields, such as education and sociolinguistics, which no longer take the relationship between bilingualism and translation as natural and transparent. Furthermore, these fields understand bilingualism as a range of linguistic and sociocultural competencies that may vary among the different languages in individuals' linguistic repertoires (Valdés et al. 2000; De Ment et al. 2005; Zentella 1997). In light of ideas associated with natural translation theory, though, immigrant children's failure to produce verbatim or literal translations of original messages can be easily constructed as a sign of linguistic incompetence and incomplete bilingualism. Indeed, some of the controversies associated with immigrant children serving as language brokers in medical contexts are often based on the fear that children could get something wrong in translation and, thereby, jeopardize the health of other patients.[8] Alternatively, from an interactional and pragmatic point of view, however, inexact repetitions may actually reflect the child-translators's competence, if they satisfy communicative obligations and other contextual demands.

The last two decades have witnessed a social and interactional turn in the ways in which translation and interpretation practices are theorized and studied in context, particularly the latter. This departure from earlier cognitive-linguistic models has been heavily influenced on the one hand, by the ideas of Bakhtin (1981) and his circle (Voloshinov 1973) about heteroglossia and polyphony, or the multivoiced and sociohistorical situated nature of speech. On the other hand, it has also been influenced by Goffman's (1981a) notions of footing (participants' stance towards what is being said or done), and participant roles (which address the relationship between the speaker and what is being said, including author, animator, and principal). Communicative, sociolinguistically-, and ethnomethodologically-informed approaches to the study of multiparty, dialogue-interpreting highlight the importance of cultural context, type of activity being enacted (e.g., testimony, interview), social setting (e.g., court, school, hospital), and situational factors (e.g., how the parties know each other) for the co-construction of meaning in these interactions (Angelelli 2004; Berk-Seligson 1990; Hatim 2006; Hatim and Mason 1997; Mason 2006; Wandesjö 1998, 2001, 2006). Wandesjö's work, in particular, has emphasized how asymmetrical distribution of knowledge and power, audience expectations, social and ethnic identities, and even physical arrangement of the parties are all consequential in interpreters' communicative choices, as well as in the interactional shape of encounters involving adult professional and community interpreters.

When the Moroccan immigrant children in Vallenuevo translated for their families, they often found themselves having to bridge not only linguistic boundaries but also the borderlands between different practices, expectations, and social and generational asymmetries. In these cases, *literal* translations can sometimes be relatively easy to render linguistically, but may lead to misattributions and misunderstandings.

7.4 Moroccan Immigrant Children's Experiences as Language Brokers

The examples that follow, as well as the vignette that introduces the chapter, are based on nine videotaped pediatric consultations at the clinic in Vallenuevo, as well as numerous observations and informal conversations with doctors and nurses.[9] As I described in Chapter 4, the health center was not the only context in which Moroccan immigrant children helped their families as language brokers; it was the last institutional context in which they were both still allowed and needed, particularly in the afternoons and evenings when no official interpreter was available. During the visits and recordings in the health center, my first observations suggested that, in spite of the difficulty of the task, Moroccan immigrant children exhibited a great deal of skill. They acted with a strong orientation to their roles as interpreters and attempted verbatim translations most of the time. I also observed that they sometimes modified their translations of what their families said, either by subtly modifying the original utterances, or by leaving them untranslated altogether, like in the vignette above. Perhaps letting the adult in me trump the analyst, I initially thought that this could be due to children's attempts to paraphrase words and sentences that were difficult for them to translate. As the recordings and observations continued, I realized that these *modifications*, however, displayed a different interactional shape than when the children were clearly experiencing problems with the translation task. Looking at the nine consultations more systematically and comparing instances of modifications with moments in these exchanges when children were having linguistic difficulties and problems understanding convinced me that these two types of interactional sequences were indeed different. Given these differences, and the level of skill that children were for the most part otherwise able to display, I came to understand the potential of these modifications to provide glimpses into how Moroccan immigrant children managed their conflicting roles as language brokers, negotiated social and familial relations, and made sense of the broader social forces that impinge on these interactions.

Before delving into these different sequences in relation to Moroccan immigrant children's sociocultural experiences, it is important to say that a careful analytic parsing of the video data yielded three possible interactional directions that Moroccan immigrant children's translation practices could take:

(1) *Verbatim* translations, which comprise the largest number of translating interactions that I recorded and observed.

(2) Selective *modifications* of some part (or all) of the talk they had to translate. Children deployed these modifications both when translating for the doctor, but also when translating for their families.

(3) Linguistic and interpreting problems. These difficulties included moments when children plainly indicated that they did not understand something or did not know how to translate it, as well as instances of obvious mistranslation. These mistranslations entailed grammatical or lexical *mistakes* and were often accompanied either by hesitations and other embodied displays. These verbal and gestural displays indicated that, even though the children were attempting to carry out the translation task, they were having problems expressing themselves.

7.4.1 *Verbatim Translations vs. Selective Modification*

There is little doubt that the vast majority of the Moroccan immigrant children observed and recorded at the health center in Vallenuevo were able to produce accurate translations for the doctor and their relatives, often without major linguistic problems or difficulties. Most of the utterances in my recorded data belong to this kind of *literal* translating practice. Before discussing the selective modifications that Moroccan children sometimes interjected in their translations, let me give an example in which a child makes an obvious attempt to provide a direct, or literal translation. In the excerpt below, there are four participants: Dr. Rocío, Fatima, the nine-year-old Moroccan girl who was introduced in the initial vignette, a Moroccan woman who is a relative of Fatima's, and her son, ʿAli, who is the patient. As alluded to in the vignette above, ʿAli had been consistently losing weight over the previous months and not eating well. This was the second medical

Figure 7.1 Participants in translation encounters, Examples 7.1, 7.2, 7.5, and 7.7.

visit regarding ʿAliʾs weight loss and nutritional problems. In this visit, a delicate interaction between the doctor and the mother is being played out in terms of determining who is responsible for ʿAliʾs lack of progress. Each wants to be viewed respectively as a good doctor and as a good mother, as having taken the appropriate steps in facilitating ʿAliʾs recovery. An example of a fairly *literal* translation takes place right at the beginning of the visit.

Example 7.1
Key: Spanish (regular font) – Moroccan Arabic (***bolded and italicized***)
Participants: Doctor, Fatima, Mother

```
1  DOCTOR: A ver (.) Fatima, ¿qué le pasa a ʿAli?
           Let's see (.) Fatima, what's wrong with
           ʿAli?
2  FATIMA: Maleh?
           What's wrong?
3  MOTHER: Ma ta yakolš,
           He doesn't eat
4  FATIMA: Que no come
           That he doesn't eat
5  DOCTOR: ¿No come?=
           He doesn't eat?=
```

There are two examples of relatively *verbatim* translation[10] in this brief initial segment. In producing these *literal* translations in line 2 (***"Maleh?"*** – **what's wrong**) for ʿAliʾs mother and line 4 ("Que no come" – **that**

he doesn't eat) for the doctor, Fatima acts as an *animator* (Goffman 1981a) or as a sounding box for the doctor and 'Ali's mother's words. As animators, child-translators deliver someone else's thoughts and words. Translators are never officially the *authors* of the words they utter, because of the ethos of detachment that translators and interpreters are expected to maintain. In community interpreting, in particular, this neutrality has been problematized *in practice* on the grounds that what constitutes *neutrality* varies in relation to the parties involved in translator-mediated, multiparty, face-to-face exchanges (Wandesjö 1998: 240). Moreover, in these contexts very often the interpreter has an important advocacy role to fulfill.[11] Bakhtin's (1973) notions of polyphony would also seem to support a more agentive role for interpreters in that his theory argues that reported speech and quotations always depict referents from a vantage point. Narrators' perspectives are likely to intrude in the original utterance in many reporting speech situations, leading the voices of the *author*, the original source of the words, and of the *animator*, the person who delivers the words, to become fused. This double-voicing is precisely what I claim transpires in these interactions when immigrant child-translators engage in creative modification and "selective depiction" (Clark and Gerrig 1990) of adults' chunks of talk.

These selective modifications are neither random nor due to children's linguistic incompetence but rather due to immigrant children's growing awareness of the sociopolitics of language and identity. This awareness includes sophistication about their conflicting roles as agents of the institution and as representatives of Moroccan families, as well as their knowledge of distinct worldviews and expectations. Moroccan immigrant children strategically deploy these modifications in their translations when they are confronted with conflicting moral universes, beliefs, and practices concerning child-rearing and health issues.

The following example is from the same medical consultation discussed in Example 7.1. Before the segment begins, the doctor and the mother have just established that one of the problems affecting 'Ali's recovery may be that he is eating too much candy between his regular meals. The doctor and the mother begin to discuss ways to improve 'Ali's eating habits. Unlike in the previous example, however, Fatima does not render the message literally, rather she selectively translates and modifies the scenario that 'Ali's mother describes for the doctor.

Example 7.2
Key: Spanish (regular font) – Moroccan Arabic (***bolded and italicized***)
Participants: Doctor, Fatima, Mother

1. DOCTOR: Tiene que intentar que no coma tantas
    golosinas
    **She has to try to stop him from eating
    so much candy**
2. FATIMA: *Khassak addiri baš mayakolš bezzaf
    delHalwa*
    **There's a need for you to do
    (something)
    so that he doesn't eat a lot of candy**
3. MOTHER: *Ki ndir? Ka yabqa izagui (faddar)*
    What can I do? He starts screaming
    (1.8)
4.   *ka yabqa yabkili, o yaqder iġdab ʿla
        el makla=*
        **he starts crying, he gets angry with
        the food=**
5. MOTHER: =*Kaʿ mayabġish yakolli, Kay ʿassabni,
        kanḍarbu*
        **=He never wants to eat, he makes me
        nervous, I hit him**
6. FATIMA: Te dice que no, que cuándo le riñe o
    algo
    **She says to you that no, that when
    she tells him off or something=**
    =empieza a llorar y:::-
    =he starts crying a:::nd-
    (0.7)
7. DOCTOR: Y se lo tiene que dar, ¿no?
    And she has to give it to him, right?
8. FATIMA: Y se lo tiene que dar
    And she has to give it to him

In line 2, Fatima produces an almost *literal* translation of the doctor's recommendation **(There's a need for you to do something so that he doesn't eat so much candy)**. Once again, Fatima is primarily acting as an *animator* of the words of the doctor. Even in this fairly verbatim translation, however, it is possible to find evidence of modification in that Fatima's translation mitigates the stronger sense of obligation conveyed by the doctor's use of the modal verb "tiene que" **(She has to/she must)** in Spanish with an impersonal construction in Moroccan Arabic "*Khassak addiri*" **(There is a need for you to do - something)**. This mitigation may indicate both Fatima's awareness of her position as a child talking to an adult, as well as her adherence to culturally-appropriate notions of respect that a child owes to older neighbors and relatives.

In reaction to the doctor's recommendation, 'Ali's mother goes on to produce a narrative loaded with negative affect and emotional stress surrounding Ali's eating habits (lines 3–5). The mother's opening rhetorical question "***Ki ndir?***" **(What can I do?)** indicates her sense of powerlessness in managing 'Ali's eating problems. Her description of 'Ali's behavior consists of four syntactic parallelistic utterances: "***Ka yabqa izagui; ka yabqa yabkili; o yaqder iġdab 'la el makla; ka' mayabġish yakolli***" **(He starts screaming; he starts crying; he gets angry with the food; he never wants to eat)**. Also, in many of these constructions, the verbs (i.e., ***yabki*** – **he cries**; ***yakol*** – **he eats**) are upgraded affectively by the final addition of dative-case marking prepositional phrase, ***li*** **(to me/for me)**.[12] As Ochs and Scheiffelin (1989, p. 12) have pointed out, dative-case marking denotes an intensification of the speaker's affective stance and emotional involvement towards what is being said. Furthermore, the mother uses the auxiliary verb "***abqa,***" which in Moroccan Arabic denotes continuous aspect. These four linguistic features in the mother's narration (i.e., rhetorical question, syntactic parallelism, dative-case marking, and continuous verbal aspect) underscore the habitual nature and the recursivity of the stressful, and highly emotional, mealtime interactions between her and her son. The upshot of her dramatic narrative is that she gets upset and nervous and hits the boy: "***kanḍarbu***" **(I hit him)**. This last detail is important because, in addition to being an emotionally-heightened narrative, it is also a narrative that might potentially get 'Ali's mother into legal problems with Spanish child welfare services.

Fatima's translation of this emotional narrative (lines 6 and 8) is reduced and modified linguistically in two counts: first, she significantly downgrades the negative affect expressed by the mother and, second, Fatima replaces physical punishment with a verbal form of discipline, a telling-off or reprimand. The dramatic scene of the mother's feelings of helplessness and the boy's screams, cries, and anger get reduced to a more emotionally contained: "Te dice que no, que cuándo le riñe o algo empieza a llorar y::" **("She says to you that no, that when she tells him off or something, he starts crying a::nd-")**. Second, in this more neutral version of the mother's narrative, instead of saying that the mother hits the boy, Fatima translates that the mother reprimands the boy. There is nothing in the semantic structure of the verb *reñir* (to tell off; to reprimand verbally) in Spanish that could remotely denote physical punishment. More specifically, Fatima says: "cuándo le riñe o algo" **(when she tells him off or something)**. This is important because by adding "o algo" **(or something)**, Fatima is suggesting in the translation that there are other strategies or forms of discipline that the mother may use to stop ʿAli from eating candy and to get him to eat more nutritious food. However, she is leaving those other maternal strategies unspecified.

In addition, whereas in her other translations, such as in Example 7.1 discussed above, Fatima has not been using any explicit reporting device such as "she says," in this instance, however, where Fatima departs so significantly from the original material, she introduces her modified translation with the reporting device "Te dice"– **(She says to you)**. This is an interesting choice in that usually people tend to use this kind of explicit reporting device when they want to distance or detach themselves from the assertions of the original source (Celce-Murcia and Larsen-Freeman 1999b), or in other words, when they want to present themselves as mere animators, not authors, of the words they are uttering.

The ambiguity introduced by the addition of **"or something"** continues when, after downgrading the mother's narrative, Fatima trails off instead of offering a definite completion to the story. In reviewing the functions of trailing-off in conversation, Lerner (2013) has discussed how such interactional moves are deployed around delicate subject matters that the speaker would rather avoid voicing. When the trailing-off is followed by a long inter-turn pause, as in this case, it also constitutes an invitation for other-completion of the matter that is being discussed. This is precisely what happens in this example, when after Fatima trails off and does not continue to elaborate on the story, the doctor comes in with a candid completion of the mother's narrative in line 7: "Y se lo tiene que dar, ¿no?" (And she has to give it to him, right?), with a confirmation request at the end of her turn. In line 8, Fatima accepts the doctor's candid ending, which to a certain extent capture's the mother's inability to stop her son from eating too much candy, while at the same time avoiding having to go on record with more details about the stressful mealtime interactions.

Selective modification does not only occur when children are translating what their families say to representatives of Spanish institutions, such as nurses or doctors; similar selective modifications can also be found when children translate what doctors say to their families. In the following example, there are also four participants in the interaction: the Spanish pediatrician; Laila, a 14-year-old Moroccan girl who is both the language broker and the patient, Laila's mother, and Laila's younger brother. Laila and her mother have come to the doctor to get the results of some medical tests that were performed in earlier visits after Laila complained of strong stomach pains and headaches. Because Laila is both the patient and the

Figure 7.2 Participants in translation encounter, Example 7.3.

translator, Laila and the doctor address each other throughout most of the interaction. At intervals, Laila's mother intervenes to request a translation, make comments to her daughter, or ask clarification questions.

Immediately before the segment below, the doctor has just informed Laila of the results of the tests, and she proceeds to ask Laila a few questions to monitor the status of the symptoms.

Example 7.3
Key: Spanish (regular Font) – Moroccan Arabic (***bolded and italicized***)
Participants: Doctor, Laila, Mother

```
1.  DOCTOR:  ¿Y el dolor te ha vuelto a pasar?=
             And the pain has it happened to you
             again?=
             =Ese dolor que dices- ¿suele pasar?
             =That pain that you say- does it
             usually happen?
2.           ((Laila nods))
3.  DOCTOR:  ¿Tienes regla tú?
             Do you have your period?
4.  LAILA:   Sí
             Yes
5.  DOCTOR:  [¿Desde cuándo?
             [Since when?
6.  LAILA:   [(xxx)
             [(xxx)
```

```
 7.  DOCTOR:  ¿Cuánto tiempo?
              For how long?
 8.  LAILA:   Desde dos o tres años
              For two or three years
 9.  DOCTOR:  ¿Desde hace dos o tres años, no?
              Since two or three years ago, right?
10.  DOCTOR:  ¿No coincide el dolor cuando tienes
              la regla?
              Doesn't the pain coincide when you
              have your period?
11.  LAILA:   No ((Shaking her head))
              No
12.  MOTHER:  madam tanna? ((In Amazighe. to Laila))
              What does she say?
              (3.0)
13.  LAILA:   galatli mnin tžik makatwaž'ak
              She's said to me if it hurts when it
              comes
14.  MOTHER:  am
              OK
15.  MOTHER:  ((To the young boy)) rayyaH matakhrabš
              Ndarbak
              Sit down. Don't touch. I'm going to
              hit you
```

After a several-turn discussion between the doctor and Laila about the possible relationship between Laila's stomachaches and her menstruation, Laila's mother asks her daughter to translate for her what the doctor has been saying in line 12: **"madam tanna?"** (What does she say). It is important to notice first that there is an almost three-second delay between the mother's question and Laila's translation in line 13. When finally Laila does offer a translation, the translation is not only greatly reduced linguistically in comparison to the length of the interaction and the number of questions that have transpired between Laila and the doctor, but it is also obscure in terms of linguistic reference: **"galatli mnin tžik makatwaž'ak (She's said to me if it hurts when it comes)**. Central to the obscure referentiality of the translation is the deictic nature of the impersonal pronoun *it*. While the meaning of deictic elements is highly dependent on the discursive and sociocultural context within which they are embedded (Hanks 2005), it is important to remember that the mother does not speak Spanish, therefore, having only very little access to the previous discursive reference of what this pronoun might stand for or refer to. In spite of the apparent difficulty of establishing the semantic referent of the pronoun *it* in **"it hurts"** and **"it comes,"** Laila's mother accepts the information with the minimal uptake token **"am"** **(OK)**. Unlike in other parts of the interaction, where she follows up on some of her daughter's translations, she closes the sequence and turns to monitor the behavior of her younger son, without asking any clarification questions. Laila precedes her translation with the reporting device **"she says to me"** (*galatli*) which, as I explained earlier, may be a way to distance herself from the questions about her menstruation that the doctor has been asking her.

An important question to consider is, of course, why Fatima and Laila would engage in these subtle modifications of the source material they translate. In the first example, the issue of physical punishment to discipline children is at stake. Corporal punishment as a form of discipline has become increasingly frowned upon in Spain over the last few decades and is now subject to severe legal penalties. In addition, as part of the commonplace problematization of Moroccan immigrants, mass-media discourses in Spain routinely associate Moroccans with higher incidence of domestic violence and child abuse. Children like Fatima are exposed to these negative depictions towards their heritage community through daily experiences at school. Many times, I was able to document Spanish teachers' hypervigilance to what they perceive as higher rates of child abuse and violence in Moroccan households. I saw how Moroccan children were often interrogated, far more than Spanish children, by teachers about how they got certain wounds and bruises. Sometimes the teachers directly asked the children whether their parents inflicted these injuries on them. While it was obvious that teachers were concerned that Moroccan immigrant children may be suffering higher rates of corporal punishment at home, reliable statistics about actual rates of physical punishment are limited, as far as I know, and difficult to interpret because they often get conflated with many other forms of domestic violence. I can say, however, from my own observations in Moroccan households, that while mothers, in particular, would often use verbal threats of physical punishment quite liberally, I never witnessed any mother actually follow up on these threats. It was clear to me, both from the almost casual way in which these threats were delivered and from children's placid reactions to them, that they were more of a rhetorical strategy for mothers to control their young children's behavior than a prelude to actual hitting.

Perhaps due to the scrutiny immigrant children experience at school, the second immigrant generation displays greater awareness than adults of the surveillance and problematization to which they and their families are routinely subjected. The active face-work that children, like Fatima, deploy to achieve a certain social presentation of self on behalf of their families illuminates their awareness of how their families and communities are racialized and ascribed negative characteristics.

In Example 7.3, women's health issues, especially sexual maturity or behavior, is another area where the practices of the Spanish and Moroccan communities of the children may potentially enter in conflict. Discussing openly and publicly menstruation is still largely associated with shame in many areas and social sectors of Morocco. These attitudes are particularly pronounced in rural areas, such as those of Northeastern Morocco where most of the immigrant families in this study come from. In these areas, girls are encouraged to treat topics such as menstruation with utter discretion, and speaking about these issues in the social, and even the familial realm, can be considered inappropriate behavior. Perhaps because of this, it is not surprising to find that there are a plethora of expressions in Moroccan Arabic to refer to menstruation, most of them either highly euphemistic and opaque in meaning, or with decidedly negative connotations.[13]

Although I did not investigate directly how Moroccan women and girls in Vallenuevo conceptualize menstruation, being a woman myself, the topic unavoidably came up a few times in my own interactions with Moroccan women and girls. When I hung out a few times socially with Moroccan young women, such as Worda's eldest sister, Nada, and her friends, the adolescents would refer to theirs and other women's menstruation in a matter-of-fact way in Spanish as *la regla*. *La regla*, literally "the rule," is the most common colloquial euphemistic expression to refer to menstruation in Spanish; not surprisingly, this is also the doctor's choice with Laila in the medical interaction above. In addition to being the most common expression in Spain, *la regla* may be made more familiar to the young women by the fact that the exact equivalent euphemistic expression in French, *la règle*, is also the expression of choice among young women from urban areas in Morocco. Indeed, this is an expression I often heard my Moroccan friends use when I was myself a student in Morocco.

When young women were with their mothers, however, my sense was that they were much more self-conscious and reserved around the issue of menstruation. As a point of comparison, I remember one weekend afternoon that I was having tea with Worda's mother and grandmother., Nada and her best friend were also present, as were the rest of the girls in the family, Worda, Salma, and little Dunia. At some point, Nada had to make reference to her own menstruation and, addressing her mother, she used the deictic demonstrative pronoun *hadik*, literally "that" or "that one".. The reference to *hadik* would have completely escaped me if it had not been for Nada's best friend, who turned to me and whispered in my ear" *tiene la regla*, (she's on her period), or more (literally, "she has the rule"). It is interesting to ponder whether older girls like Laila modify their translation

of questions about menstruation to protect themselves from the moral disapproval of their parents or to adhere to ideals of discretion when dealing
with such a delicate subject. Alternatively, and beyond culturalist interpretations of this encounter, it is also important to consider generational issues,
since public talk about menstruation in the presence of their families could
be embarrassing for many teens, not just Moroccan immigrant girls in Spain.

As discussed above, Moroccan immigrant children may indirectly become
aware of the sensitivity of some issues and their potential for misunderstanding in other arenas of their social lives, such as schools or family contexts.
Being a language broker itself, however, is itself an experience where children learn over time the importance of not opening up Moroccan families
to the kind of institutional scrutiny (or themselves to parental scrutiny) that
may lead doctors or parents to possible misinterpretation. Some Moroccan
immigrant families felt a sense of vulnerability when having to interact with
representatives of Spanish institutions. Familial misgivings and anxieties
about these interactions were sometimes communicated to the children, in
the form of instructions about things they should not reveal directly to
doctors.

For instance, when Karim's younger sister was born, I had the opportunity to videotape a couple of Karim's mother's visits to the pediatrician. In
the first visit, Karim's mother was accompanied by a friend of hers who
was able to speak and understand some Spanish, and by Houda. Houda, a
young child translator whom I introduce later in this chapter, was the
daughter of another neighbor of Karim's family. In this first visit, Karim's
mother, her friend, and Houda formed a successful team to negotiate the
interaction with the pediatric nurse. A few weeks later Karim's mother had
to bring her baby back, but this time only Houda was able to come with
her. While they were waiting to be seen by the doctor, Karim's mother told
Houda **"wakhkha makanaʿrafš Asbalyuniya makuliš makanfhamš"**
(Although I don't know Spanish, don't say I don't
understand). Thus, children who are often called on to act as language
brokers on behalf of adults, like Fatima, Manal, or Abdelkarim, learn through
these kinds of instructions the importance of saying just enough about
certain areas and the advantages of leaving some room for ambiguity. Not
surprisingly, older children or children with a lot of experience as language
brokers were quicker at making subtle modifications and more likely to
interject themselves as participants through their translation filters than the
youngest or most inexperienced child-translators I was able to observe.

Before showing how the interactional contours of this subtle practice are
different from moments when children encounter linguistic difficulties, I
discuss one more example of modification. While in the three instances
described so far, it was fairly transparent to me where the ethical and inter-

Figure 7.3 Participants in translation encounter, Example 7.4.

actional conflict might have lain for the children, there were other instances in which children's translation filters were observable, but more ambiguous. Example 7.4 below is one of those instances. In this example, we find Asmaa, an adolescent girl of 16, translating for a relative who has come to the doctor with her two children, a boy and a girl. The main object of the visit was for the doctor to examine a rash that had broken out on the girl's lower body. After examining the young girl and prescribing some cream for the rash, however, the mother also had some general questions about the boy's health that she wanted to ask the doctor before leaving. The mother's main concern was that her son's bad breath could be caused by a more serious underlying disease.

Example 7.4
Key: Spanish (regular font) – Moroccan Arabic (***bolded and italicized***)
Participants: Doctor, Asmaa, Mother

```
   1.   MOTHER:  Daba kolilha Hatta annafs adyalo
                 khanaz=
                 Now tell her that his breath also
                 smells bad
   2.            =yamkan ʿando ši wlases ahnaya=
                 It can be that he has something here
                 ((pointing at her throat))
   3.            =mnin kaySuT aʿliya, annafs antaʿo khanaz=
                 when he breathes, his breath smells bad
   4.   ASMAA:   haduk ġir man assannin (.) Hatta anaya-
                 Those only from the teeth (.) I also-
   5.   MOTHER:  o Hatta ʿando ši Haža ahnaya
                 And also he has something here
                 ((pointing at her throat))
```

```
6.  ASMAA:  alla, alla ġir man assannin=
            no no only from the teeth
7.          =Hatta ana kanat taSrali=
            It also happened to me ((literally= It
            also arrived/came for me))
8.          =ġir naġsalhom safi
            I only clean them and that's it
```

In this exchange, as it is obvious in line 4 and lines 6 through 8, Asmaa refuses to pass on the mother's fears about the boy's bad breath to the doctor, asserting instead that in her own experience the boy's bad breath is linked to his lack of dental hygiene. This is definitely the most forceful intervention in my recorded samples of language brokering. Like Fatima in the vignette that opens this chapter, Asmaa does not translate the mother's concerns. Unlike Fatima, however, Asmaa plainly expresses to the mother that she is not going to translate what she said, in spite of the mother's insistence in line 5. Nevertheless, what is ambiguous here, particularly considering that Asmaa is the oldest language broker I videotaped, is whether her refusal to translate the mother's questions is related to her own disagreement with their mother about the cause of the boy's bad breath (based on her own experience with bad breath), or to potential embarrassment related to her awareness of racist discourses about Moroccans' supposed dirtiness and lack of hygiene. Given the focal girls' multiple narratives about their own experience with this stereotype and the insults they often received from their Spanish peers telling them to shower, I have direct evidence that Moroccan immigrant children much younger than Asmaa are very well aware of this form of racialization. From this perspective, Asmaa may be trying not to reinforce the stereotype that, as Wafiya and Manal put in one of these narratives I already shared in Chapter 4, "they think we're are all dirty." In any case, unlike my previous examples of modification-in-translation, the roots of Asmaa's intervention remain ambiguous to me.

7.4.2   *Selective Modification vs. Linguistic Problems and Mistranslations*

Because of the specialized knowledge and high linguistic demands of medical interactions, there were times when Moroccan immigrant children did encounter problems executing translating tasks. Indeed, other interactionally-based studies of how untrained (adult) interpreters handle technical medical terms have emphasized the problems surrounding lack of knowledge of the correct term in the other language and the need to render such terms in familiar language (Meyer 2001). Translation problems children encountered were often due to the still developing linguistic competence of the child, or more general problems of understanding medical procedures, terminology, and health practices. This section describes the interactional structure and trajectory of children's linguistic mistranslations as different from *selective modifications*. The most obvious difference between *modifications-in-translation* and moments of linguistic and interpreting problems was that in the latter the presence of a problem was almost always acknowledged either by the children themselves or by correction sequences initiated by the adults, both mothers and doctors.

Children acknowledge having problems with the translation task In most cases, when children found themselves at odds with the task of translating, they admitted openly that they did not know how to translate something and actively recruited help from the adults in the interaction. The following example is also extracted from the medical visit that I discussed in Examples 7.1 and 7.2 above. In Example 7.5, when the doctor is trying to determine the reasons for the lack of effectiveness of the boy's treatment, she asks the mother how long ʿAli has been taking one of the medicines she had prescribed. When Fatima attempts to translate the mother's answer in line 4, she interrupts herself and, after acknowledging that she does not know how to translate it **"Tres- ¿como se llama?"** **(Three- how is it called?)**, she mistranslates the word **"boxes"** (cajas) and instead says **"bottles"** (botellas). The doctor corrects her in line 5 by repeating emphatically **"three boxes"** (tres cajas), while ʿAli's mother nods and makes the shape of a box with her hands:

Example 7.5
Key: Spanish (regular font) – Moroccan Arabic (***bolded and italicized***)
Participants: Doctor, Fatima, Mother

1. DOCTOR: ¿Cuánto tiempo tomó?
    For how long did he take them?
2. FATIMA: ***šHal min- šHal howwa išrab fhadik?***
    For how long- how long did he take that?
3. MOTHER: ***šrab tlata delakraTan, tlata del paket***
    He drank three boxes, three packages
4. FATIMA: Tres- ¿cómo se llama?
    Three- how is it called?

```
        tres botellas que se había comprao
        Three bottles that had been bought
5.  DOCTOR: Tres cajas
        Three boxes
6.  MOTHER: Huhm Huhm ((making a rectangular shape
        with her hands and nodding))
7.  FATIMA: Sí
        Yes
```

Apart from explicitly stating that they did not know how to translate something, children also had other ways of communicating that they were having a problem with the task. These included hesitations, false starts, and sudden cut-offs, accompanied by alternate looks at the doctor and their families, who usually immediately realized that the child needed help. Gestures and body language were an extremely important semiotic indication that the children were struggling with something. As illustrated in the framegrab above, when Fatima cannot find the right translation for "boxes," and cuts off her turn in progress, she is looking up trying to perform a wordsearch (Goodwin and Goodwin 1986; Lerner 1995; Schegloff, Jefferson, and Sacks 1977). As she performs the wordsearch, Fatima is drawing with her hands the box shape of the medication container, even though she subsequently comes up with the word "bottles." The doctor, however, knows that the kind of medication she prescribed to ʿAli does not come in bottles, but in boxes, and in line 5 offers the correction "Tres cajas" **(Three boxes)**. ʿAli's mother who has been monitoring the interaction ratifies the doctor's correction in line 6 and also starts drawing with her hands the rectangular shape of a box, with Fatima also acknowledging the correction in line 7.

A similar sequence can be found in the following interaction between Houda, Karim's mother, Karim's mother's friend, and the doctor's pediatric nurse. At seven years old, Houda was the youngest language broker I recorded. The object of the visit was Karim's newborn baby sister, who, as already mentioned in previous chapters, was born during the course of the study.

Example 7.6
Key: Spanish (regular font) – Moroccan Arabic (***bolded and italicized***)
Participants: Pediatric Nurse, Houda, Neighbor, Karim's Mother

```
1.  NURSE:   ¿Cuánto tiempo le ha estao dando dos
        veces al día? (.)
        How long has she been giving her
        twice a day?
```

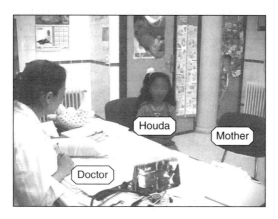

Figure 7.4   Main participants in translation encounters, Examples 7.6 and 7.8.

```
2.                 ¿Cuánto?
                   How long?
                   (0.6)
3.    HOUDA:       ¿E::h?
                   Hu::h?
4.    NURSE:       ¿Cuántas veces le ha dado dos veces
                   al día?
                   How many times has she given her
                   twice a day?
5.    HOUDA:       foqaš aʿTitiha waHad anhar [(xxx)?
                   When has she given her one day[(xxx)?
6.    NEIGHBOR:    [foqaš aʿTitiha žouž khaTrat fanhar?
                   [When has she given her twice a day?
```

Just prior to this exchange, Dr. Rocío's nurse has found out that Karim's mother has been giving the baby some vitamins twice a day that she was only supposed to give her once a day, and is trying to ascertain how long this situation has been going on. After asking Houda to translate **"How long has she been giving her twice a day,"** however, Houda pauses, and in line 3, finally indicates that she either has not heard or not understood what the nurse said, **"Hu::h?"** The nurse, then, provides an alternative phrasing of the same question that Houda tries to translate. Karim's mother's friend and neighbor, who was also present at this interaction and who spoke a little Spanish, cuts Houda off when she realizes that Houda is about to mistranslate what the nurse is asking, and provides a more direct translation building on the work that the girl has already done.

Although in these examples the problems were solved fairly quickly, overt and/or implicit requests for help sometimes ensued in more lengthy sequences of back and forth questions among medical personnel, children, and family members who continued to check each other's understanding of the situation until the problem of understanding and translation had finally been resolved. Regardless of the sequence length and the complexity of the misunderstanding, an encouraging common denominator in all these interactions were the ways in which families, children, and medical staff brought their different kinds of knowledge and skills together to ensure an acceptable outcome in every translation encounter. This collaboration greatly helped children manage the difficulties of their tasks as language brokers, as well as providing a comfortable space for children to recruit adults' help when they felt they needed it.

Admitting openly that they had problems performing an interpreting task was not only a frequent response by children in the medical encounters that I videotaped, but also a common way in which children narrated their difficulties as language brokers in interviews. The following interview fragment is an excerpt from an interview with Manal. Just before the fragment, she has been telling me how much she enjoys acting as a language broker for her family, much in the way Worda and Abdelkarim do in the interview quotes that opens the chapter: "siento como que estoy trabajando- como- como- a ver- me gusta (.) siento como relajada" **(I feel like I am working- like- like- let's see- I like it (.) I feel relaxed)**. I asked her if there were aspects to interpreting that she found more difficult, and she replied that translating specialized medical terminology was the most difficult for her. I followed up by asking her what she usually did in those situations, and this is how she replied:

Manal: Un día he ido con una mujer porque estaba mala de los ojos-
One day I went with a woman because she was sick in her eyes-
no sé qué le pasaba en el ojo-
I don't know what was wrong with her eye-
estuvimos en el parque y luego me dijo mi madre=
We were in the park and then my mother told me=
="vete con ella," porque ella también no oía un poco=
="go with her," because she didn't hear well either=

```
=y claro, he ido con ella al médico y
le- y le dijieron-=
```
**=and of course, I went with her to the
doctor's and her- and they told her=**
```
=a ver no me acuerdo lo que le dijieron
pero yo le expliqué todo=
```
**=let's see I don't remember what they told
her but I explained everything to her=**
```
=menos una cosa que ahí me lo explicaron y-
```
**=except for one thing that they explained
to me there and-**
```
me lo explicaron y yo ya se lo expliqué.
```
**they explained it to me and I then
explained it to her.**

Underlying Manal's narrative is the girl's confidence that, even when she finds certain aspects of language brokering difficult and there are things she does not know or understand, she can always express openly her lack of understanding and count on the adults in these interactions to help her out.

Adults address a problem with the translation children have rendered   There were other cases of problems with the translation task in which, even though children did not display any hesitation or confusion, the adults in the interaction (both mothers and doctor) disrupted the flow of the translation and engaged the children in correction and clarification sequences. These situations happened when children made grammatical mistakes in their translations, usually involving a problem with syntactic or morphological features of the language, such as grammatical agreement or pronouns, and less commonly problems with vocabulary. While children most probably did not realize that they were making mistakes, these errors did not pass unremarked. There was often a reaction on the part of the adults that usually took the form of gentle correction or amused teasing. Dr. Rocío was especially likely to engage in this process of clarification and correction of the children. Example 7.7 also features 'Ali's visit. Dr. Rocío wants to know whether the last medication she prescribed for the boy had any effect on his appetite.

Example 7.7
Key: Spanish (regular font) – Moroccan Arabic (**bolded and italicized**)
Participants: Doctor, Fatima, Mother

```
1.  FATIMA: Pero:::: cuando le has mandao ese
            jarabe no come también bien
```
**Bu:::t when you prescribed him that
syrup he didn't also eat well**

```
2.  DOCTOR: Tampoco comía bien
            He didn't eat well either
            (2.1) ((Fatima nods))
3.  DOCTOR: (°A~ver~espera) Es que tiene un
            poquito bajo el hierro
            (°Let's~see~wait)It's that he's a
            little low in iron
```

Fatima proceeds to translate what the mother has just told her, namely that, in spite of the syrup prescribed by the doctor, the boy did not eat well either. Instead of saying "tampoco" (which means "either/neither" and is used in negative statements), Fatima says "también" (which means "too/also" and is used in affirmative statements): "Pero:::: cuando le has mandao ese jarabe no come también bien" **(Bu:::t when you prescribed him that syrup he didn't also eat well)**. The doctor rephrases Fatima's response in line 2 as "Tampoco comía bien" **(He didn't eat well either)**, which Fatima acknowledges by nodding her head. Since the use of "también" can render Fatima's response slightly ambiguous, we can understand Dr. Rocío's reaction as both an attempt to correct Fatima's grammar and a check for understanding to make sure she was recording the right information about the boy. In this sense, it is not surprising that the pediatrician engaged in these sequences much more systematically and consistently than mothers did, since research in other cross-linguistic service encounters has also documented this type of information confirmation repetitions (Kuroshima 2010).

While mothers were not as assiduous as the pediatrician in correcting children's errors-in-translation, they also often marked children's mistakes by their reactions. Example 7.8 is extracted from the second medical visit of Karim's mother to the pediatrician, when Houda was translating by herself without the assistance of Karim's mother's friend.

Example 7.8
Key: Spanish (regular font) – Moroccan Arabic (**bolded and italicized**)
Participants: Doctor, Houda, Mother

```
1.  DOCTOR: Ya cuando venga a la revisión de los
            cinco meses entonces=
            When she comes to the five-month
            checkup, then=
            =ya le dirá Ana que le puede dar a:h
            potitos o purés
```

```
               =Ana will tell her that she can give
               her baby food or purées
2.   HOUDA:    Vale
               OK
3.   DOCTOR:   De momento sólo leche
               For the time being only milk
4.   HOUDA:    galatlak safi
               She's said to you that that's it
5.             mnin tkun ʿandha khamsa yyam, tqadri
               taʿTiha bHal almakla u dak ašši
               when she is five days old, you'll be
               able to give her food or something
               like that
6.   MOTHER:   safi ((laughs)) (2.8) khamsa yyam walla
               khamsa šhur?
               Ok ((laughs)) (2.8) five days or five
               months?
7.             galatlak mnin tkun ʿandha khamsa yyam?
               maši khamsa šhour?
               ((laughing))
               Did she say to you when she is five
               days old? not five months old?
```

When Houda is translating the doctor's recommendations for the baby's nutrition, she translates **"when the baby is five days old"** instead of "five months old": "*mnin tkun ʿandha khamsa yyam, tqadri taʿTiha bHal almakla u dak ašši*" (when she is five days old, you'll be able to give her food or something like that) (line 5). Since the baby was already three months old at the time of this visit, the mother immediately realized the mistake and, after acknowledging the information Houda has just translated for her, she proceeded to tease Houda kindly: "*safi ((laughs)) (2.8) khamsa yyam walla khamsa šhur?*" (OK five days or five months?) line 6) and "*galatlak mnin tkun ʿandha khamsa yyam? maši khamsa šhour?*" (Did she say to you when she is five days old, not five months old?) − (line 7).

Sometimes, however, usually when children's mistakes did not significantly affect the understanding of the content of the message, they often passed unnoticed by family members. Example 7.9 is an instance of this type of mistranslation. In Example 7.9, Naima, an 11-year-old Moroccan girl is translating on behalf of her mother. The object of the visit was her newborn sister.

Figure 7.5   Participants in translation encounter, Example 7.9.

Example 7.9
Key: Spanish (regular font) – Moroccan Arabic (**bolded and italicized**)
Participants: Doctor, Naima, Mother

  1. DOCTOR: Bueno, y:: cuando: su madre e::h-
              cuando su madre le da el pecho=
              OK, and when her mother- when her
              mother breastfeed her=
              =¿ella la mira a ella? ¿La mira?
              =does she look at her? Does she look
              at her?
  2. NAIMA: *galatlak min kata⁽Ti liha albazzula*
              wash katšuf fik?
              She says to you when *she breastfeeds
              you* does she look at you?
              ((*Naima translates when the baby
              breastfeeds the mother))
  3. MOTHER: sí
              yes
  4. DOCTOR: sí
              yes

The pediatrician asked a series of routine questions, such as whether the baby looks at the mother when she is breastfeeding her. Naima, however, made a mistake with the use of pronouns and translated **when the baby breastfeeds the mother** "*galatlak min kata⁽Ti liha albazzula wash katšuf fik?*" (**She says to you when she breastfeeds you does she look at you?**) – (line 2). In spite of the mistake, the mother understood the translated doctor's question and answered affirmatively without remarking on the mistake Naima has just made. These instances of children's mistakes and how they are managed by adults in the interaction, particularly mother's management of children's errors, are reminiscent of how children's mistakes are handled in first language acquisition. Structural grammatical features usually go uncorrected, while vocabulary mistakes are almost always corrected as in Example 7.8, because adults are more concerned with the truth value of a proposition (e.g., Brown and Hanlon 2004).

The interactional organization of the trajectory of the previous examples, particularly how participants themselves treat what is going on at that point in the interaction (i.e., that there is a problem with the translation), indicate that children's *selective modifications* discussed above are strategic deployments on children's part rather than actual mistakes due to linguistic incompetence. These modifications are never treated either by the children or by the adults as constituting a problem of translation or misunderstanding. This is especially obvious when comparing the interactional sequences of Examples 7.2, 7.3, 7.4, as well as the vignette that opens the chapter, with Examples 7.5 and 7.6. 7.7, 7.8, and 7.9.

7.5 Conclusion

In the previous analyses, I have shown how immigrant children as language brokers display a keen awareness of conflicting sociocultural expectations, practices, and value systems, and take interactional steps, involving *selective quotation* and *modification* to create social and moral equilibrium for the doctor, their families, and, ultimately, for themselves. Children's selective modification-in-translation is a powerful example of the knowledge and discretion deployed by immigrant children in traversing the conflicting cultural spaces of the multiple communities they belong to. Any communicative event involving interpreting and reporting another's speech is not only a matter of grammar but also of sophisticated pragmatics and sociocultural knowledge (Celce-Murcia and Larsen-Freeman 1999b). In medical interactions, where immigrant children have to negotiate conflicting social roles as agents of the institution, representatives of Moroccan families, and as children of economic migrants, reporting the words of others also involves delicate ethical considerations heightened by structural asymmetries and racialized politics of immigration. In attempting to manage these contingencies, Moroccan immigrant children's innovations, adaptations, and selective quotations constitute a window into their agency in becoming members of a linguistically and socioculturally complex society, as well as their competence negotiating crucial processes of continuity and change.

In this chapter, I have examined how in their modified translations, children build on their knowledge of sociocultural and situational expectations and on their daily life experiences in both Spanish society (school, health center) and immigrant diaspora community (home, peer group) interactions. Language brokering as a hybrid cultural activity thus offers a privileged vantage point to explore to what extent immigrant children perceive and are able to navigate sociocultural and generational issues across settings. Understanding how Moroccan immigrant children act as language brokers provides an ethnographic locus for theorizing the crucial role of immigrant children as agents of cultural continuity and shift in hybrid immigrant communities that are undergoing rapid change (Garrett and Baquedano-López 2002; Paugh 2012). From this perspective, we can see how Moroccan immigrant children in Vallenuevo deftly manage incipient sociocultural, political, and ethical sensibilities, and are successful agents in building constructive bridges among their families and healthcare professionals. In addition, in their role as language brokers, they provide an important social service to their own immigrant communities and to Spanish institutions by facilitating access to healthcare, which itself may ameliorate many health inequalities that affect migrant populations (Sargent and Larchanché 2011).

Notes

1 While Amazighe and Arabic are two very different languages, for consistency, the few phrases and conversational turns in Amazighe present in the data have been transcribed phonetically using the same transliteration symbols used throughout the book for varieties of Arabic. See Appendix 2. **šam** is a second-person singular subject personal pronoun (you); **tassawalad** is the corresponding second-person singular form of the verb **siwal** (to speak); and **tmaziǧt** refers to one of the three dialectal varieties of Amazighe spoken throughout Morocco.

2 Community interpreting (also known as community-based interpreting, liaison interpreting, cultural interpreting, dialogue interpreting, or public service interpreting in the United Kingdom) is the kind of interpreter-mediated interaction that takes place between individuals of immigrant, indigenous, or minority communities (of which the interpreter is also a member) and professionals/officials of host-country institutions (social, medical, police, or legal services). For two recent reviews of this literature, see Russo (2013) and Pöllabauer (2013) and for seminal work in this area of research, see Wandesjö (1993/2002; 1998).

3 See, for example, Mason (2001); Gentile et al. (1996); Merlini and Favaron (2007).

4 Most ethnographic accounts of child language brokering that present naturally-occurring interactional data tend to feature translation events in children's households (e.g., García-Sánchez 2010; Orellana et al. 2003b), in educational contexts (García-Sánchez and Orellana

2006; García-Sánchez, Orellana, and Hopkins 2011; Orellana 2009. See also Note 5), or in service encounters (Reynolds and Orellana 2009). In the exceptional cases where naturally-occurring data of child-language brokering in medical interactions have been presented (see Orellana 2009, Chapter 4, pp. 74–77; and Valdés 2003), examples have usually been limited to one or two short ones in the context of more extensive work devoted to the phenomenon of child language brokering more generally. A notable exception to this trend is Katz's (2014) very recent work on child language brokering in relation to media and medical encounters.

5   Italian-American educator Leonard Covello (1887–1982) discussed his experiences as child language broker in his autobiographical work, *The Heart is The Teacher* (1957).

6   It must be noted, however, that these researchers did not study immigrant children as translators per se, but, rather, children growing up in relatively privileged bilingual households.

7   Educational researchers, for example, have examined the literacy demands in children's translations of written texts (e.g., Orellana et al. 2003b) and their implications for immigrant children's development of academic skills (e.g., Malakoff and Hakuta 1991; Valdés 2003). The skills that Latino immigrant youth deploy as family translators can facilitate their acquisition and development of academic literacy skills, such as school writing tasks (Orellana and Reynolds 2008; Martínez et al. 2008). Language brokering in home-school communication allows child language brokers to act as facilitators in these intercultural encounters (García-Sánchez, Orellana, and Hopkins 2011; Tse 1996b), helping bridge the often wide gap between immigrant families and educational institutions (Quiroz et al. 1998, 1999; Trumbull et al. 1998; 2001). Also, studies have identified immigrant children's attitudes towards translating and the relationship between children's work as translators, academic achievement, and psychological outcomes such as self-efficacy (e.g., Acoach and Webb 2004; Buriel et al., 1998; Dorner, Orellana, and Li-Grining Forthcoming; Parke and Buriel 1995; Tse 1995, 1996a; Weisskirch and Alva 2002). Additional outcomes investigated are the impact of language brokering on family dynamics, immigrant adolescents' mental health, and processes of settlement in the host society (e.g., Buriel, Love, and De Ment 2006; Chao 2006; Chu 1999; Orellana 2001, 2003; Orellana et al. 2003a; Song 1997; Valenzuela 1999).

8   In her 2009 book, Orellana discusses, for instance, a popular hospital TV drama shown in the United States, in which a child language broker makes a mistake in a tension-filled translation scene that almost results in the death of one of the child's family members.

9   For more details about data sources, access to the clinic, and other details of data collection in this context, see Chapter 3.

10 In Fatima's translation in line 2, the name of the boy ('Ali) is, however, omitted.

11 While the critiques of traditional notions of translators' neutrality have been more pointed in the literature on community or liaison interpreting (see Russo 2013 and Pöllabauer 2013 for a review of these critiques and further bibliography), other scholars studying professional interpreters and even written translation have also strongly criticized the notion of translators' neutrality, emphasizing the influential and agentive work of interpreters/translators in the process of meaning construction, see Angelelli (2004); Arrojo (1998); Venutti (1998).

12 The literal translation of these two utterances is "he starts crying to me/for me" and "he doesn't want to eat to me/for me."

13 While attitudes towards menstruation are rapidly changing, particularly among young urban females, and while many Moroccan women are redefining their relationship to this and

other women's health issues, it is still fair to say that in Moroccan communities, people's reactions to menstruation are still largely shaped by religious beliefs and practices. From this perspective, there is a strong legacy of treating menstruation as something shameful and impure. Hence, there exists a range of purification rituals associated with menstruation, as well as a rich variety of euphemistic linguistic expressions to refer to it. For more information about attutides, rituals, and linguistic expressions for menstruation, see Sadiqi (2003) and Mateo Dieste (2012).

8

Heteroglossic Games: Imagining Selves and Voicing Possible Futures

A ver, en los juegos, yo hago nombre español,
que me gusta el nombre Carolina y juego como española-
pero yo siento las dos cosas, marroquina y española [. . .]
Me gusta ser española porque- para tener amigas españolas.

Let's see, in games I use a Spanish name,
that I like the name Carolina, and I play like [as if I were] Spanish-
but I feel both things, Moroccan and Spanish [. . .]
I like being Spanish because- of having Spanish friends.

(Manal, age 11, interview fragment)

Carnival was a popular holiday with the children, and with good reason, too. Celebrated in the last week of February, it brought rambunctious color and joy to cold, gray winter school days, while foreshadowing that spring was almost around the corner. Teachers and students worked hand-in-hand to put together an annual Carnival Jamboree that included a costume parade along the main avenue of Vallenuevo. The culminating event of the jamboree was a dance festival at the school, in which all grades, from the little kindergarteners to the older sixth-graders, participated with student-produced choreographies. The dance festival was open to all parents, family members, and neighbors. The day of the jamboree, the children were all giggling as they waited in line for the costume parade to start, holding hands with their partner-buddies. I had volunteered to be one of the adult chaperones of the fourth-grade group during the parade along the streets of Vallenuevo, and my partner-buddy was Karim. The vice-principal, Pepa, rocked the house when she appeared to lead the parade dressed up as a

Language and Muslim Immigrant Childhoods: The Politics of Belonging, First Edition.
Inmaculada Mª García-Sánchez.

hobo-ghost, complete with a patched-up sheet and a ragged hat. Everyone on Vallenuevo's main avenue , shop-owners, customers, some parents, lots of grandparents, and passers-by, came out and stopped to watch the costume parade and applaud the children, as we all chanted and sang on our way back to school. And later at the dance festival, when it was the fourth-grade's turn to do the choreography, teachers, students, and volunteers did not dare to look each other in the eye for fear that we might explode into laughter as we wriggled and wiggled across the stage doing the "chicken dance." The Carnival Jamboree was that kind of day. So, in retrospect, it was no surprise that all the children broke out into a jubilant uproar, when Guadalupe, the fourth-grade classroom teacher, announced that preparations for the Carnival Jamboree had to begin a month before the event.

Since fourth grade would dance to the Chicken-Dance music, it was also decided that they would dress up as birds, since that popular tune is known in Spain as "Los pajaritos" (The Birdie Song). Children were supposed to craft their own costumes during Plastic Arts class helped by the teacher and adult volunteers, like me, and a few mothers that Guadalupe hoped to recruit. During the Plastic Arts class session following this discussion, Guadalupe showed the children a couple of examples of beaked masks and feathery capes that she had made with the other fourth-grade teachers and elicited children's feedback. She also discussed materials and demonstrated different forms of craftsmanship that would achieve the desired shapes and color combinations. Plastic Arts class was always a little more informal than the core academic subjects. On that afternoon, however, the children were particularly raucous and jolly. They were bustling about the classroom already consulting their friends about possible designs for their *papier-mâché* beaked masks, looking at samples of colorful fabrics, comparing crêpe and tissue paper for different feathery effects, and so on.

Although the whole fourth-grade class was dressing up as birds, children had the prerogative to choose how they were going to shape the beaks of their masks, as well as the dominant color of their feathery cape designs. Most of the Spanish girls, who had been moving around the class, found themselves coalescing around a small group of girls, whose mothers had a history of volunteering to help with children's costumes. All the girls, led by Cristina and Estrella, busily started to plan designs, paper arrangements, and different ways of laying out the arrangements so that, even with the same dominant color, they could have a little distinctiveness. As for their dominant color, they soon had a conclusion and they went to the teacher to ask if they could have pink. Guadalupe happily agreed. Throughout all of this, Wafiya, Miriam, and Sarah, the three Moroccan girls in this classroom, had also been talking among themselves near the larger group of Spanish girls. Because of the ways in which they were glancing at the

Spanish girls sporadically, it was obvious that Wafiya, Miriam, and Sarah were overhearing and following the discussion of the bigger group of girls, and, at times, it seemed as if they were trying to gather the courage to approach and join them, although they never did.

After some hesitation, they did eventually go up to the teacher, instead, and asked whether they could also have pink as their dominant color. When Guadalupe granted Wafiya, Miriam, and Sarah's request to have pink, a few of the Spanish girls raised their heads and, with worried looks, tried to argue with the teacher that they had requested pink first. Guadalupe looked at them disapprovingly and retorted: "¿Y qué me queréis decir con eso?" **(And what do you mean by that?)**. When the Spanish girls remained silent, the teacher, then proceeded to add that as far as she was concerned there were no limit to the number of students who could have pink, and she also reminded them that color was a student's individual choice. The Spanish girls acquiesced sullenly, but after a few minutes, Cristina approached the teacher and informed her that they had changed their minds and now wanted blue as the dominant color of their outfit. Guadalupe gave me a dismayed look and shook her head, as she said to the group of Spanish girls: "Suit yourselves."

While this was certainly not the most aggravated way in which I witnessed Spanish children build boundaries of separation and distinction between themselves and their Moroccan immigrant peers, as I have explored in Chapter 5, there was something very moving about how this particular vignette unfolded. This episode haunted me more than others I had witnessed, and I found myself thinking about it often. I know that, at the most immediate experiential level, part of the emotional resonance of this incident for me had to do with the impact of encountering such petty behavior, even in the middle of all the joy, laughter, and excitement that Carnival preparations had precipitated. On further reflection, perhaps the poignancy of this episode also lay in the juxtaposition between Moroccan immigrant girls' desire to be accepted as full-fledged participants of the fun, to belong and not to be seen as different, and the spiteful way in which their opportunities to access regimes of knowledge and taste was denied by their own peers, even in something so seemingly inconsequential.

Something else that this vignette brings to the forefront, and that I found very striking at the time, is Moroccan immigrant girls' deep awareness of the importance of possessing the *right* kind of cultural capital and the *right* kind of insider knowledge (Bourdieu 1991) in negotiating membership successfully and in trying to establish commonality of belonging with their Spanish peers. In this chapter, through an investigation of these children's bilingual linguistic practices in the midst of play, I focus on this awareness and consider how children themselves are making sense of these various aspects of belonging and the barriers they encounter. I examine the situated ways in which this group of Moroccan immigrant girls in Vallenuevo explore possible forms of identification and create imagined, alternative life worlds in which *they get to have pink*; or in other words, imagined life worlds in which they position themselves as insiders with the power to destabilize racialized, gendered, and class-based expectations. In my analysis, I am circumscribing *play* to those ludic activities that Moroccan immigrant children engage in outside adult supervision.[1] The rich verbal and sociocultural environment of Moroccan immigrant children's peer groups provide us with an excellent window to investigate how immigrant children negotiate, transform, and subvert in the midst of play the processes of racialized exclusion and sociocultural constraints that they encounter on a daily basis.

Drawing on Vygotskian approaches to play[2] and on Bakhtin's (1981, 1986) notions of heteroglossia and dialogism, the chapter examines the use of Moroccan Arabic and Spanish in girls' pretend-play, and the resulting heteroglossic polyphony of voices, which imbues these linguistic codes with sociopolitical and moral tensions. In particular, the analysis highlights code-switching practices and clandestine *tactics* (De Certeau 1984) that Moroccan immigrant girls deploy in pretend-play to construct desirable female identities in the context of idealizations of Spanish femininity. These idealizations, however, act as subversive narratives to the socioeconomic subaltern roles to which immigrants and their children are usually relegated. Additionally, they can be seen as transgressional among Moroccan diaspora communities. Neighborhood peer-group play affords Moroccan immigrant girls' transformations and engagement in subversive *tactics*, in that these activities take place outside the scrutiny of parents and other adults. Also relevant to this chapter is Ortner's (2006) discussion of *serious games*. This notion refers to the routine practices and intentionalized actions of culturally variable and subjectively complex social agents through which the latter (re)produce and/or transform the larger forces of social life. Serious games are always embedded in relations of power, inequality, and competition, but also of solidarity. Inherent in serious games is social actors' potential to disrupt the game in a synchronically, ad hoc fashion, and thereby "the very continuity of the game as a social and cultural formation over the long run" (p. 151).

When Ortner introduced this notion, she used *serious games* in a metaphorical way to refer to how social actors engage with each other to negotiate the micropolitics of social life; how the notion could be applied to discuss the significance of actual children's games may not have crossed her mind. Nevertheless, the concept may be doubly apt here to capture the complex dimensions of the subjectivity of these Moroccan immigrant girls, as well as to illuminate how they understand their constraints and affordances in relation to the larger sociocultural forces that impinge upon their lives. Much like other examples of social activity, the doll pretend-play that this group of immigrant girls enacts is deeply immersed in the micropolitics of belonging that immigrant groups have to negotiate. As they are making sense of their social lives and relations, and as they are imagining possible selves and futures, the girls' actions-in-play, particularly in their subversive, tactical nature, involve both the reproduction and change of some of the sociocultural formations they have to contend with on a daily basis.

8.1 Communicative Practices and Play in Children's Peer Groups

Previous research on children's communicative practices in peer networks has shown these contexts to be crucial for processes of language socialization, in that they allow children to construct autonomous arenas for action where they can develop competencies as language users and social actors relatively free from adult censure, disapproval, and scrutiny (e.g., Aronsson and Thorell 1999; Blum-Kulka and Snow 2004; Corsaro 1988a, 1988b, 1994, 2000; M. H. Goodwin 2000, 1998, 1997, 1990a, 1990b; Goodwin and Kyratzis 2007, 2012; Kyratzis 2004; Lloyd 2012). Children use the multiple languages available in their linguistic repertoires to structure games and other activities, as well as to challenge, transform, and reproduce societal ideologies about languages and ethnic relations (Howard 2007; Minks, 2010). Hybrid linguistic practices, in particular, have been shown to socialize peers into alternative notions of morality, and facilitate the negotiation of hierarchies and multiple, fluid identities (e.g., Cekaite and Aronsson 2004, 2005; Evaldsson 2005; García-Sánchez 2005; Jørgenssen 1998; Kyratzis 2010; Rampton 1995, 1998; Reynolds 2010; Zentella 1997, 1998).

More specifically, children have been documented to use codeswitching to differentiate between "negotiation of the play" and "in-character play," as well as the social negotiation of ongoing social interaction – teasing, by-play, displays of power or anger, participants' roles, and topic changes (Cromdal and Aronsson 2000; Cromdal 2004; Ervin-Tripp and Reyes 2005; Gudal 1997). Codeswitching is used to signal different *subregisters* during play, namely "in-character play" and "negotiation of the play," and to enact different *voices*, namely the voice of the child, that of the role-character, and that of the director. In this regard, a number of studies have consistently found that in multi- or bilingual situations, play characters speak and are spoken to in one language, while running metacommentary on the game is usually carried out in a different code (Kwan-Terry 1992; Halmari and Smith 1994). Codeswitching during play has also been shown to be an important resource for children's constructions of their emerging understandings of how contrasting languages index social identities, activities, and language ideologies (Garrett 2007; Minks 2010; Paugh 2005). In Dominica, for instance, where children's use of Patwa is closely monitored and forbidden by adults, Paugh (2012) found that, in peer-group contexts where they are free from this linguistic surveillance, children use Patwa to enact specific adult activities, such as bus-driving or hunting, and English to enact other roles, such as the role of mother or teacher.

A second important line of inquiry for the present analysis is sociolinguistic research on peer groups of immigrant youth of North African descent and other ethnic minorities in Europe. These youth groups also come to be under adult surveillance and are frequently racialized as "young delinquents" and "trouble-makers." Drawing on Corsaro's notion of *interpretive* reproduction,"[3] Poveda and Marcos (2005), for instance, have argued that Spanish Romany minority children use playful transformations of popular songs and rhymes in the safe contexts of their peer groups as a way to assert themselves socially against the larger backdrop of social exclusion and discrimination. These playful interactions provide them with resources to confront racially-marked facets of their daily experiences.

Tetreault (2008, 2009, 2010) investigated the hybrid language practices of adolescent peer groups of Algerian descent in France and the importance of these practices for articulating ties to immigrant origins and emergent adolescent subcultures. In her analysis of parental name calling in ritual insults (2010) and in her recent study of these youths' use of mock-French TV-host register (2009), Tetreault illustrates how communicative practices in the peer group constitute an intricate web of personal and cultural relations in the self-presentation of these adolescents. More importantly, these interactional practices also reveal how French adolescents of North African descent subvert, transgress, and reinforce different forms of identification and gendered expectations in both French dominant discourses and their immigrant communities. For female adolescents of North African descent, in particular, gendered identifications are fraught with anxieties and moral ambivalence. This ambivalence involves a complex processes of simultaneous identification and dis-identification with their choices of self-representation (Tetreault 2008). Similarly, Hall's (1995, 2002) descriptions of how British Sikh youth negotiate – and often subvert – gendered expectations across the cultural worlds of their families, peer groups, and other ethnic communal arrangements, have shown how the process is profoundly conflictual and ambivalent for these youth.

8.2   Interactional Frames and Identity Construction in Pretend–Play

Pretend-play was frequent in the Moroccan immigrant girls' peer group that I was able to follow most closely in Vallenuevo. Out of the 11 videotaped hours of children's games that I collected, seven focus on the peer play of my focal girls' extended network of friends.[4] Even though these recordings were randomly made and without much previous planning, other than trying to find out, if possible, where the girls would be playing on a particular afternoon, games of pretend still account for roughly 40% of the total play time videotaped among these girls. In my observations and recordings, no other type of game occupied so much of the girls' time and energy. In fact, the remaining 60% of the playtime videotaped included a broad rage of sporadic games and pastimes, including jump rope, hopscotch, clapping or hand games, singer imitations, as well as playing on the monkey bars, swings, and other playground equipment.[5] In their pretend-play, girls included enactments related to ordinary routines of their lives, such as school, sports practice, and errands and chores they performed on a regular basis. Pretend-play also involved, however, enactments related to more extraordinary and fantastic aspects; the latter were often rooted in special events, such as town festivals and celebrations, in which the girls participated only peripherally, if at all, but sometimes they were also clearly inspired by mass media and popular culture. In my recordings, I have examples of girls role-playing school, popular movies, TV soap operas, and pretend-play with dolls. Whether enacting everyday or extraordinary situations, what Moroccan immigrant girls consistently bring to pretend-play activities is a double orientation to the cultural and linguistic dispositions of their heritage community and to the larger Spanish community. Linguistic practices in pretend-play, in particular, the high rate of codeswitching between Spanish and Moroccan Arabic, are primarily the means by which this double orientation is accomplished.

In this chapter, I focus on two extended games of pretend-play involving doll figures. I highlight these particular sequences for analysis because they are the longest and most elaborated of all of the pretend-play sequences that I was able to videotape. Coincidentally, I think that these doll games are particularly illuminating of how this group of girls is thinking about issues of difference and belonging, as they simultaneously experiment with social roles and rehearse possible identities. Additionally, pretend-play activity involving dolls is especially interesting because, as the girls construct imaginary life worlds for their dolls, they interweave ordinary routines and settings with the extraordinary, idealized life styles that female characters are likely to lead in TV series. The codeswitching found in these extended sequences not only signals girls' orientation to the multiple communities in which they participate, it also evidences the "double-voicedness" (Bahktin 1981) of this linguistic practice. This is particularly so in those instances of codeswitching that point to girls' ambivalent and clandestine orientation towards the activities they enact in play. The *reflexivity* inherent in these girls' transgressive agency in play frames, and the *addressivity*[6] involved in how they enact the tensions between activities and linguistic varieties can be clearly seen in their keen awareness that they could be "discovered."

These particular extended doll-play games involve two of the focal girls, Worda and Wafiya, and three other girls who participate on and off throughout the sequences: Worda's eldest sister Salma, as well as her youngest sister, Dunia, and Worda's next-door neighbor, Lamia. In both occasions, the girls are playing a few houses down the street from Worda's family's home, where they often met on weekend afternoons. On such afternoons, their mothers were at home either tending to house chores or having tea and visiting with other female neighbors and relatives, and their fathers were in the town square or locally-run Moroccan coffee shops meeting other male friends.

8.3   Patterns of Code Choice and Use: Managing Play and Interactional Frames

This group of girls uses Spanish and Moroccan Arabic in most social situations of their daily lives. As discussed in Chapter 4, they only use Spanish in school in their encounters with teachers and Spanish peers, but they often use Moroccan Arabic to interact among themselves. Similarly, at home while Moroccan Arabic tends to predominate in most interactions between the children and their parents, the children among themselves, particularly those who have spent a long period of time in Spain, frequently use Spanish. In the context of their pretend-play, they overwhelmingly use Spanish – and more specifically a stylized register of Spanish – when ventriloquizing their dolls and for stage-setting and narrative emplotment (Kyratzis and Ervin-Tripp 1999). Conversely, Moroccan Arabic is used (1) to negotiate the specifics of the game; (2) for metacommentary on the play frame; (3) to resolve conflict among the girls (usually conflict springing from the game); (4) to monitor and control the behavior of younger siblings, who are present in the interaction, even if they are not fully ratified participants of the game sequence; and (5) to interact with passers by (usually other Moroccan neighbors, family members, or acquaintances). Thus, codeswitching between Spanish and Moroccan Arabic is essential to create and sustain interactional

Table 8.1 Distribution of code choice and use.

Spanish	Moroccan Arabic
In-character dialogue	Negotiating parameters of the game
Stage-setting	Metacommentary on the play frame
Narrative emplotment	Resolving conflict among participants
	Monitoring the behavior of younger siblings
	Interacting with passers-by

and play frames during doll games. Table 8.1 summarizes the distribution of code use and codeswitching patterns during pretend-play activities. As mentioned above, a similar distribution of code labor has also been observed in children's games in bi/multilingual play in other speech communities.[7]

In the present study, there are also important differences with regards to language choice and use between enacting the voices of the dolls and creating a fantasy play space on the one hand, and interactions among the children to negotiate parameters of the play frame and solve intra-group conflicts on the other (see Table 8.1). Interestingly, the issue of which code to use when speaking *in character* is in itself a matter of metalinguistic awareness among the girls. Indeed, the choice of Spanish to ventriloquize the dolls is one of the parameters of the game that the girls themselves settle early on in their play interaction. The following example takes place towards the beginning of the play sequence. Immediately before the beginning of this excerpt, the girls had been speaking in Moroccan Arabic about the different hairstyles of their dolls and about the array of props and doll accessories that they have brought to play with. This excerpt inaugurates the play frame, in that this is the first time that the girls ventriloquize the voices of the dolls:

Example 8.1
Key: Spanish (regular font) – Moroccan Arabic (**bold italics**)
Participants: Worda, Wafiya, and Salma

((Worda and Wafiya pretend their dolls have met on the street and greet each other))

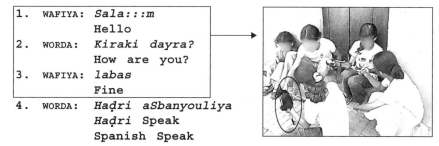

1.	WAFIYA:	*Sala:::m*
		Hello
2.	WORDA:	*Kiraki dayra?*
		How are you?
3.	WAFIYA:	*labas*
		Fine
4.	WORDA:	*Ḥaḍri aSbanyouliya*
		Ḥaḍri Speak
		Spanish Speak

```
 5.  WAFIYA:   Hola
               Hello
 6.  WORDA:    ¿Qué tal?
               How are you?
 7.  SALMA:    Nn::: ((Vocalizes to signal to Wafiya that
               she has dropped her doll's purse))
 8.  WORDA:    ¿Se te ha caído el bolso?
               Did you drop the purse?
 9.  WAFIYA:   y yo también
               and me too
10.  WORDA:    ¿Te vas a la playa?
               Are you going to the beach?
11.  WAFIYA:   Sí vamos
               Yes, let's go
12.  WORDA:    Vale
               OK
```

Worda and Wafiya stage a scenario in which their dolls have run into each other on the street. The sequence opens with an exchange of greetings that is realized both verbally (lines 1–3) and kinetically with a mutual exchange of kisses on the cheek (see framegrab above).[8] It is important to note that, although the girls perform this initial greeting in Moroccan Arabic, Worda explicitly instructs Wafiya to speak Spanish in line 4 with a repeated imperative in Moroccan Arabic: "*Haḍri aSbanyouliya Haḍri*" (**Speak Spanish Speak**). Wafiya orients positively to this command by initiating a second greeting exchange in Spanish in line 5: "Hola" (**Hello**) – that closely mirrors her initial greeting in Moroccan Arabic in line 1 – "*Sala:::m*" (**Hello:::**) –. Similarly, Worda responds to this new greeting in Spanish with a sequentially appropriate: "¿Qué tal?" (**How are you?**) in line 6 that is equivalent to her greeting in line 2 – "*Kiraki dayra?*" (**How are you?**). After this second greeting exchange in Spanish, code alternation between Spanish and Moroccan Arabic is fairly consistent throughout the game, and the girls speak Spanish only when speaking *for the dolls*. In addition, it is important to mention that some of the activities the girls begin to enact in this opening excerpt – in line 10, "Te vas a la playa?" (**Are you going to the beach?**) and line 11, "Sí vamos" (**Yes, let's go**) – could be assessed negatively by adults. Unlike their male siblings, some of the girls participating in this doll-play, in particular Worda and her sisters and Wafiya, were not allowed to go to the municipal swimming pool during the summer.[9]

The pattern of code choice, as established by the girls themselves in the opening sequence of their pretend game, is crucial not only to sustain and signal shifts between *in-play* and *off-play* interactional frames but also to mark children's changes in footing (Goffman 1981) and affective stances towards the game itself and towards each other. For instance, although in their daily lives interactions with siblings often take place in Spanish, *off-play* interactions among siblings throughout the game are carried out in Moroccan Arabic. In particular, negotiating disagreement and controlling the rogue behavior of siblings as well as the mischievous behavior of other girls are two activities that very often trigger switches into Moroccan Arabic. In this sense, codeswitching can also be considered as playing an important interactional role in the construction and enforcement of in-group norms of behavior that regulate interactions among peers. In addition, older siblings' linguistic behavior also has important implications for intergenerational culture and language maintenance.

Example 8.2 illuminates ways in which codeswitching is a crucial linguistic resource not only for signaling shifts between on-play and off-play interactional frames but also for this group of girls' interactional management of sibling conflict and appropriate conduct during the game. The excerpt opens with an exchange in Moroccan Arabic between Worda and her sister Salma. Salma has repeatedly refused to participate with her doll in the pretend-play that her sister and the other girls are enacting, and, furthermore is upset because of the way her doll looks. Worda has been trying to calm her down and to convince her to participate in the game. In line 1, Worda attempts to convince her sister one more time to participate in the game. Immediately before this excerpt, Worda has been dressing and styling Salma's doll.

Example 8.2
Key: Spanish (regular font) – Moroccan Arabic (***bold italics***)
Participants: Worda, Wafiya, Salma, and Lamia

```
  1.  WORDA:  šuf druk raha žayya Hsan man gbila,
              yaki?
              Look now, she's better than before,
              right? ((Referring to Salma's doll))
              ((Wafiya communicates with Salma with
              gestures expressing that the doll
              looks very pretty.))
```

2. SALMA: **Nn::::**
             ((Salma vocalizes,
             unhappy))[10]

3. WORDA: *iwa haki, go'di*
             Listen take it,
             sit down

4. SALMA: **Nn:::: Nn:::**
             ((Salma vocalizes,
             still unhappy))

5. WORDA: *mabġitiš? iwa*
             ruHi barra
             you don't want?,
             OK Go away

6. WORDA: Estamos tardando mucho, ¿eh?
             We're taking a long time, eh?
7. WAFIYA: ¿Y el collar te lo has traído?
             And the necklace did you bring it?
             (. . .)
8. WORDA: Vamos, vamos que hemos tardao mucho
             Come on, come on. It's already taken
             us a long time
9. WORDA: Uy ya hemos llegado. Me voy a dormir
             así la siesta
             We have already arrived. I'm going to
             take a nap.
10. WORDA: Vamos a qued- *matšaddihaš man š'ar*
             tfu (xxx)
             Let's stay- don't grab her by the
             hair (xxx)

Worda responds to Salma's refusals to participate in the game with a series of bold directives in line 3: **"*iwa haki, go'di"* (Listen, take it, sit down)** and line 5: **"*ruHi barra"* (Go away)**. This last directive is particularly aggravated, as it can also be seen in Worda's gesture in the frame grab above, and results in Salma being asked to leave the group. Immediately following this last directive, Worda codeswitches into Spanish in line 6, closing the *off-play* sequence and resuming *in-character dialogue*. Moreover, in ventriloquizing the voice of the doll as saying: **"Estamos tardando mucho, ¿eh?"** **(We are taking a long time, eh?)** (line 6), Worda is not only effectively shifting frames but also constructing the *on-play* interactional frame as the main activity. She treats the preceding exchange with her sister as a parenthetical insertion, clearly separate and distinct from the *on-play* interactional frame. A second interesting instance of codeswitching takes place a few turns later in line 10. Worda and Wafiya are engaged in *in-character dialogue* and are enacting a play scene between their dolls involving a trip to the beach. In the midst of their dialogue, Wafiya grabs Worda's doll by her hair with a forceful movement. Worda then interrupts her turn in mid-sentence and codeswitches into Moroccan Arabic with the bold directive: **"*matšaddihaš man šᶜar tfu"* (Don't grab her by the hair)**, rebuking Wafiya for her careless handling of the doll.

The previous examples demonstrate the interactional importance of codeswitching between Spanish and Moroccan Arabic for the ongoing organization of distinct interactional and play frames, for social control of siblings and other girls, and for management of pretend-play peer norms, preferences, and expectations. The following sections examine how codeswitching also plays a crucial role in girls' construction of gendered identities for their play characters.

8.4 Linguistic Resources for the Construction of Social Identities and Life Worlds

The indexical meanings (or metaphorical meanings, Gumperz 1982) of children's codeswitching practices to create social identities for play characters, as well as of children's own metacommentary on these enactments, is particularly relevant in multilingual immigrant contexts. Because these contexts are not only linguistically complex, but socially, culturally, and politically complicated as well, Bakhtin's (1981) notion of heteroglossia is particularly useful to get at all the socio-ideological layers of children's bilingual and polyvocal voicing. To examine how all these layers co-occur to index class-, ethnicity-, and gender-inflected social identities, it is important to pay attention to three aspects of language-use in girls' codeswitching practices: naming practices, in-character dialogue, and stage-setting narration.

8.4.1   Naming Practices

The power inherent in naming, as both a language and an identity act, has been highlighted cross-culturally in studies on names and naming practices.[11] Far from being arbitrary or a one-time fixed label, a name can be constitutive of personal and social identity, in that naming is thoroughly embedded in the way people constitute relationships with themselves, with one another, and with the world that surrounds them (Blum 1997; Rymes 1996). Choosing *appropriate* names for their dolls and for other imaginary play characters is an important activity in Moroccan immigrant girls' pretend-play. The social and indexical meanings of this group of girls' naming practices become even more relevant against the backdrop of sociocultural and linguistic subversion that characterize their peer-group codeswitching practices and interactions. Example 8.3 is excerpted from one of the negotiation sequences involving the assignation of names for play characters. As part of this negotiation, different names of Spanish and Arabic origins are proposed; the first are accepted and ratified, while the latter are invariably rejected. In this sense, the excerpt illustrates the indexical value of codes for the construction of the social identities of the play characters. The segment starts in Spanish, since the girls have been ventriloquizing their dolls in the previous turns. In line 3, Worda codeswitches into Moroccan Arabic, shifting frames as the girls begin a negotiation sequence to decide the names of their dolls. This negotiation ends in line 14 when all the girls have chosen *appropriate* names for their dolls, and Worda codeswitches again into Spanish, resuming *in-character play*. In addition to codeswitching, this shift in frame is also achieved by the Spanish discourse marker[12] *vale*, which is often used as a closing sequence device to signal that agreement has been reached by all parties in an interaction about a particular topic.

Example 8.3
Key: Spanish (regular font) − Moroccan Arabic (**bold italics**)
Participants: Worda, Wafiya, Dunia, Lamia

| 1. | WORDA: | ¿Cómo te llamas? Yo Carolina
What's your name? I am
Carolina | Worda claims *CAROLINA* as the name for her doll |

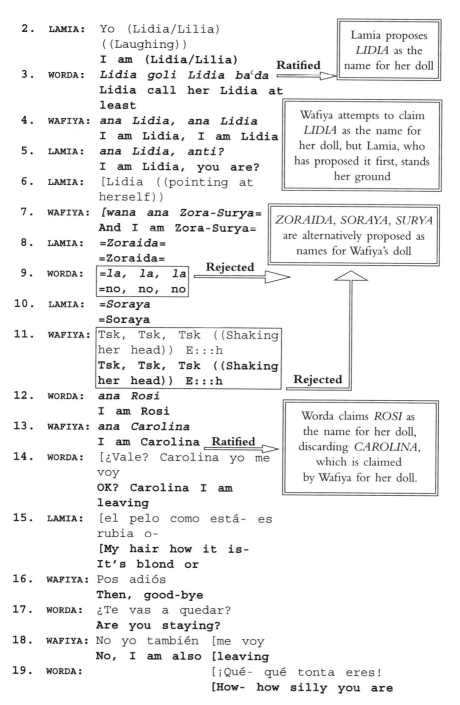

The act of naming that these girls perform during role-play is crucial for imparting an identity for their play characters. In negotiating what names are acceptable for their dolls, the girls construct specific ethnic and gendered social identities, while simultaneously rejecting other identities associated with first generation Moroccan immigrants. Only Spanish names are ratified and accepted (Lidia, Rosi, and Carolina, respectively), while names of Arabic origin, such as Zoraida and other phonetically-similar non-European names (Soraya and Surya[13]), are repeatedly rejected (in lines 9 and 11). This ratification of Spanish names parallels the girls' choice of Spanish to *ventriloquate* (Bakhtin 1981) the dolls with the voices of their imaginary characters. Through Spanish naming practices, girls attempt to access *technologies of power* (Foucault 1982) by appropriating for their dolls the names and code of the dominant society, or the *codes of power* (Delpit 2006; Morrell 2008). Thus, in the play frame, they become full-fledged *insiders* of the dominant society, able to exert power and agency, and with the ability to realize social and economic advancement. These links between names and linguistic codes, on the one hand, and with socioeconomic status, on the other, becomes more obvious as the pretend-play sequences unfold. The naming practices in this excerpt are also reinforced in a later iteration of this game, when the dolls turn out to be married to Spanish men; the choice of Spanish names for the dolls' *husbands* (Eduardo, Miguel, and Alfredo, respectively) is also crucial in establishing identifications for these other imaginary characters.

Beyond play contexts, the meaning of these naming practices for the girls reverberates strongly in the interview quote by Manal, which opens this chapter. While she was not present during the two play events analyzed in depth here, due to the spontaneous character of children's games and to the random nature of my videotaping, Manal also enjoyed games of pretend, especially those involving dolls, of which she was particularly fond. In the opening quote, Manal explained that during games, she liked to create a Spanish persona, whom she named Carolina, and to play "como española" (as [if she were] Spanish). Manal's quote is particularly powerful because, in the specific interview from which this quote is extracted, Manal and I were not talking about her favorite games, or about what she liked to do during her free time, but rather I was exploring with Manal how she felt in terms of community identification. I was trying to ascertain whether she identified more strongly with being Moroccan or with being Spanish, if either at all, and how she liked to be identified. Although Manal felt that she herself identified with being both Spanish and Moroccan, she was aware that others saw her only in terms of a Moroccan identity and did not recognize a Spanish identification for her. Manal did not wish to be treated as different, but rather she wanted to be accepted by her peers as a full-fledged member of the group, just as Sarah, Wafiya, and Miriam wanted to have pink as the color of their outfit along with the Spanish girls in fourth grade. When Manal found it difficult to explain to me how she wanted to be recognized also as Spaniard and to have Spanish friends, she resorted to describe what she usually did in her games as a way of conveying what she meant to say. This is further evidence of how, through games of pretend, this group of girls is trying to work out the constraints they often encounter on a daily basis, exploring some of the meanings and implications of these barriers in their present life and in their potential futures.

These girls' naming practices in imaginary play also raise the very serious issue of the significance of names in contemporary Europe, particularly among Muslim immigrant communities. One of the most productive lines of research for social scientists studying Muslim immigrants' social integration in countries such as France, where they have a longer history of settlement, has indeed been the effect of economic incentives in naming decisions for the second generation. What is now known in scholarly circles as "the Muslim effect," consists precisely of a series of well-documented and severe economic penalties, from higher unemployment rates to rampant housing discrimination, associated with having an Arabic name (e.g., Adida, Laitin, and Valfort 2010). Because of this, immigrant parents have been known to factor an expected future economic cost in their decision to transmit Arabic versus non-Arabic names to their children already born in European countries (e.g., Algan, Mayer and Thoenig 2013). What the girls are doing in this game can be seen as slightly reminiscent of immigrant parents taking into account the impact that choosing a culturally-distinctive name may have in the future of their children. The ways in which this group of girls go on to construct lifestyles for their Spanish-named and Spanish-speaking play characters – lifestyles full of social, professional, and economic success – is extremely suggestive of these girls' sophistication about what is involved in belonging-difference, integration-marginalization, and inclusion-exclusion.

The girls' local versions of Spanish femininity (or what being a Spanish female means to them), become even more subtle and complex as the interaction unfolds. First, the girls shift to a highly stylized feminine register of Spanish during *in-character dialogue*. In addition, they also start constructing idealized life worlds for the dolls, an idealization that is accomplished through the combination of *in-character dialogue* and *stage-setting narration*. These discursive practices, described below, which the girls bring to bear in *the voices* they enact *for the dolls*, are crucial in unpacking how social identities encapsulated in these names are related to the girls' perceptions of the links between language, social roles, status, and expectations.

8.4.2   Register Shifts in "In-Character Dialogue"

Many times when voicing the play characters, the girls shift to a stylized register of Spanish that is highly distinct from the Spanish variety that the girls use in most contexts of their daily lives. The ways in which the voices of the play characters are enregistered (Agha 2005) are crucial for girls' construction of idealized versions of Spanish femininity, in that the indexical value of this register is rooted in its recognizable association with upper-class, *fashionable* women. The *in-character dialogue* register that the girls use to *ventriloquize* the dolls is characterized by exaggerated affectation of manners and stance. This heightened affective orientation and artificial posturing operates concurrently at several levels of linguistic structure: phonological, morphological, and discursive (Ochs and Schieffelin 1989). At the phonological level, the register is characterized by the use of exaggerated intonation contours, amplified pitch, and vowel elongation, such as in:

    (a) WORDA: ↑Eduardo::: (.) ya ha venido mi marido
               Eduardo
               **↑Eduardo::: (.) my husband Eduardo has
               already arrived**

And, also, by the hyper-pronunciation of final sounds (i.e. /s/), as in

    (b) WAFIYA: yo- lo que pida**S**, pídelo
                 **I- what you order, order it
                 (=meaning whatever you order, order
                 it for me as well)**

This hyper-pronunciation of final /s/ is particularly salient in the sociolinguistic environment of southwestern Spain, where one of the most widespread dialectal features is the systematic aspiration or dropping of all final sounds. In addition, the affectation indexed by this kind of hyperpronunciation is rendered more powerful by its co-occurrence with equally affected gestures and other non-verbal behavior. Although it is difficult to convey the full range of a hand gesture in a single image, the framegrab below captures the endpoint of a continuous hand gesture, whose upward and outward trajectory is rendered by the curved arrow. This gesture is frequently used to express one of the affectations of higher-class women. Girls' linguistic and corporeal behavior, in this regard, is reminiscent of hypercorrection phenomena documented as common among socially insecure groups of low socioeconomic status (Labov 1964, 1966), who appropriate linguistic features of socioeconomic dominant groups in an attempt to gain social and cultural capital (Bourdieu 1991).

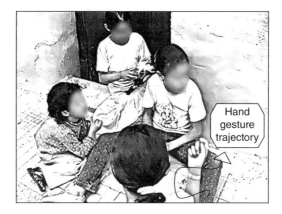

Figure 8.1 Wafiya's gesture and affectation.

At the morphological level, this stylized register is characterized by a conspicuous use of affect-loaded suffixes, such as *-ito*, as in:

(c) WORDA: = ↑**UY** ¡qué cafeci:to me voy a tomar!
       = ↑**UY** **what a good little coffee I am
       going to have!**

Finally, at the discourse level, the affected quality of this register is accomplished by the deployment of stereotypical speech genres of girl talk, such as the *demure* or *fake-embarrassment* genre. In Example 8.4, one of the girls enacts this appearance-conscious genre when voicing her doll's repeated requests for attention to the way in which she is wearing her imaginary bikini.

Example 8.4
Key: Spanish (regular font)
Participants: Worda, Wafiya, Dunia, and Lamia

1. WORDA: ↑**O:::H,** Me lo he puesto al revés. ¿Me
       lo he puesto al revés o no? (1.5)
       ¡Di:::!
       ↑**O:::H, I have put it on inside out.
       Have I put it on inside out or not?
       (1.5) Te:::ll me!**
2. WAFIYA: ¿Qué?
       What?
3. WORDA: ¿Qué si me lo he puesto al revés?
       Whether I have put it inside out?

```
4.  WAFIYA:  ¿Qué es?
             What is it?
5.  LAMIA:   ¿Qué?
             What?
6.  WORDA:   El bikini
             My bikini
             ((Girls laugh))
7.  WAFIYA:  °No:
             No
8.  WORDA:   Vaya
             Oh, well.
```

As noted above, many of these girls, including Worda and Wafiya, are not allowed to wear swimwear in public. In this respect, what is also striking about this excerpt is that the doll is actually not wearing a bikini. Yet, Worda performs this genre in an affected and emphatic manner as evidenced by the initial, phonologically salient: "O:::H" in line 1 and by her repeated requests for other girls' attention in line 1: "¡Di:::!" **(Te:::ll me!)** and in line 3: "Qué si me lo he puesto al revés?" **(Whether I have put it inside out?)**. Once she has secured other participants' undivided attention, Worda delivers the punch line with maximum effect in line 6: "El bikini" **(My bikini)**. The subsequent eruption of laughter indexes girls' embarrassment and their awareness of the transgressional possibilities of their game.

8.4.3   *Emplotment through Stage-Setting Narration and In-Character Dialogue*

Although some facets of emplotment of play dramas are accomplished in Moroccan Arabic, much stage-setting of the activities the dolls are to perform is carried out in Spanish. Narratives enacted through the voices of the play characters create an idealized Spanish high-society lifestyle, with independence, access to financial resources, professional success, and a lively social agenda of activities that take place outside home domains.

The doll characters, as performed by the girls, spend much of their time socializing with their *friends* (i.e., the other dolls): They go to the beach and the swimming pool; they go out to have coffee, dine in restaurants, and they go to nighttime parties, where they dance the batuka, a Latin-fusion dance that was extremely popular in Spain at the time of the study. The dolls are portrayed as financially well off and go on several shopping trips for cell phones and clothes. In addition, they make plans to go to a nearby town to look for an apartment to rent, since they have just gotten jobs as *directora* (manager) and *profesora* (professor). Example 7.5 is part of a larger sequence in which the girls enact a social outing to have coffee and dinner with friends.

Example 8.5
Key: Spanish (regular font) – Moroccan Arabic (**bold italics**)
Participants: Worda, Wafiya, Lamia, and Dunia

```
 1.  WORDA:   Estamos  en  la  cafetería=
              We're  in  the  cafeteria
 2.  WAFIYA:  =VaMOS  ((inaudible))
              =Let's  go  ((inaudible))
              ((Worda  and  Wafiya  sit  their  dolls  in
              a  circle  they  have  created  with  their
              legs))
 3.  WORDA:   alla alkašni dyal hadi a Wafiya
              No,  no,  Wafiya,  that's  the  shawl  of
              this  one
              ((Worda  rebukes  Wafiya  for  taking  a
              piece  of  clothing  that  belongs  to
              Lamia's  doll  and  returns  the  shawl  to
              Lamia))
 4.  WAFIYA:  He  he  he  ((laughing))
 5.  WORDA:   A Wafiya ((inaudible))
              Wafiya  ((inaudible))
 6.  WAFIYA:  ¿Qué  tal?
              How  are  you?
 7.  WORDA:   Bien
              Fine
 8.  WAFIYA:  Estamos  aquí
              We  are  here
 9.  WAFIYA:  ¿Te  lo  pongo?
              Do  I  put  it  on  for  you?=  ((Referring
              to  Lamia's  doll's  shawl))
10.  WORDA:   =  ↑UY  ¡qué  cafeci:to  me  voy  a  tomar!
              =  ↑UY  what  a  good  little  coffee  I  am
              going  to  have!
11.  WAFIYA:  Y  yo  también
              And  me  too
12.  DUNIA:   Toma,  toma  ((Giving  a  toy  purse  to
              Lamia))
              Take  it,  take  it
13.  DUNIA:   Se  te  [cayó  ((Still  speaking  to  Lamia))
              It  [fell
14.  WORDA:   [Qué  guay
              How  cool
```

(. . .)

15. WORDA: No. Yo he pedido na más ketchup con
             pollo y::: pescado
             **No. I have only ordered ketchup with
             chicken and fish**

16. WAFIYA: Pollo, pescado [patatas fritas
              Chicken, fish, [French fries

17. WORDA: [y, y
                                    [and, and

18. WORDA: y whisky
             And whisky

19. WAFIYA: Yo whisky y patatas fritas con
              ketchup y pollo y pescado
              **I want whisky and French fries with
              ketchup and chicken and fish**

This excerpt illustrates how these idealized life worlds are created in both *in-character dialogue* (lines 6–11, and line 14; see also, lines 15–19) and *stage-setting narration* (line 1 and line 8).[14] As they dramatize this cafeteria outing and, through the voices of the dolls, engage in transgressional behaviors, such as drinking alcohol and going to nightclubs, the girls are also exploring imagined possibilities that are part of their repertoires of selves, identities, and moral worlds. The imagined possibilities that the pretend-play and the dolls, as part of the girls' material culture, afford are constrained in the real world: some are constrained by family expectations and control over girls' behavior; other possibilities are constrained by unequal structures of Spanish society which considers them outsiders, and by the socioeconomic positions of their families within these structures. Yet, as the girls construct through the voices of the dolls alternative social realities and life worlds in which they hold decision-making authority, they momentarily challenge, subvert, and transform restrictions and conflicts they experience in other everyday environments. In this sense, *in-character dialogue* and *stage-setting* function as powerful counter-narratives to subject and economic subaltern positions assigned to them by the dominant society and to other cultural narratives about female behavior in their diasporic communities.

The role of the peer group as a relatively autonomous arena for action with limited, if any, adult supervision is critical for these immigrant girls' explorations of ways of being in the world that their families could consider transgressional, such as drinking alcohol, attending night-time parties, or exposing their bodies in swimwear. Furthermore, the extraordinarily dreamy life worlds that the girls construct for their play characters, along with the highly stylized register of Spanish with which they enact the social voices

(Agha 2005; Bakhtin 1981, 1986) of the dolls, also suggests an idealization of Spanish femininity as desirable. Desire often reverberates interactionally when the girls, *through the voices of the dolls*, make enthusiastic evaluations of the activities they are enacting, as in Example 8.5: "¡Qué guay!" **(How cool!)** (line 14).

8.5   Ambivalent Stances and the Moral Inflection of Codes

Although a positive stance of playfulness and desire dominates pretend-play, a closer analysis of girls' codeswitching practices reveals a more ambivalent stance towards the actions and gendered identifications that they are performing in their games. The ambivalent stances that permeate Moroccan immigrant girls' doll-play are reminiscent of other ethnographically situated accounts of identity formation among immigrant youth in other communities across Europe (Hall 1995, 2002; Tetreault 2008). These accounts often highlight the deeply conflictual nature of youths' enactments of values and identities, regardless of whether the latter emanate from the dominant society or from their immigrant communities. Example 8.4, discussed above –where all the girls broke into embarrassed laughter when Worda pretended that her doll was wearing a bikini— already offered a glimpse into girls' ambivalent stances towards the values and gendered identities that they are role-playing in these pretend-play sequences. Laughing constitutes a powerful form of metacommentary in that, through laugh tokens, participants can communicate their *footing* (Goffman 1981a) towards what is being said or done in ongoing interactions (e.g., C. Goodwin 2007). Throughout the two extended game sequences, laugh tokens mediate semiotically the conflicting affective stances that girls seem to have towards the actions they themselves are enacting through their imaginary play characters. It was the presence of these laugh tokens that first alerted me analytically that the identities this group of girls are performing in play are not necessarily gendered identifications that they aspire to or desire whole-heartedly. Rather, these are values and identities that, on the one hand, the girls may find appealing and alluring, but that, on the other hand, they may not find entirely advisable or beneficial. From this perspective, because play frees children from the situational constraints of everyday life (Vygotsky 1967) and also from close adult supervision, play contexts become a natural setting for girls to act out these conflicts and explore these transgressional possibilities.

   In these game sequences, in addition to laugh tokens, girls also use codeswitching practices to express their ambivalent stances. In particular, codeswitching into Moroccan Arabic to make metacommentaries about girls' own behavior, the behavior of the other girls, and the actions enacted in imaginary play serve as an important function for the interactional management of girls' conflicting affective stances towards their idealized *Spanish* gendered identifications. Instances of metacommentaries interspersed throughout the game indicate a high level of *reflexivity* (Bakhtin 1981) in that girls are aware that they are acting transgressionally. Example 8.6 opens with the girls ventriloquizing the voices of the dolls as they are getting ready to leave for the beach. When Salma refuses to join in the pretend-play, an explosion of laughter follows. Lamia happens to laugh particularly boisterously. Worda then codeswitches into Moroccan Arabic to reprimand Lamia's noisy behavior, because it has the potential *to give them away*:

Example 8.6
Key: Spanish (regular font) – Moroccan Arabic (***bold italics***)
Participants: Worda, Wafiya, Salma, Lamia, and Dunia

```
1.  WORDA:   Yo me voy, ¿eh? Vamo:s
             I'm leaving, ah? Let's go
2.  WAFIYA:  Vamo:::s
             Let's go!
3.  WORDA:   ((inaudible)) yalla ((To Salma))
             ((inaudible)) let's go
4.  SALMA:   Nn::: Nn:::: ((Shaking her head))

    ((Wafiya starts laughing and
    Lamia laughs extremely loudly))
```

```
5.  WORDA:   a Lamia ġadi tfaḍHina
             Lamia is going to give us away
             ((To Lamia))ruHi galsi alhiha falbab
             adyalna
                  go sit down by our door
```

The metacommentary in line 5 marks the pretend-play they are engaged in as a *clandestine interaction* (De Certeau 1984; Sterponi 2004, pp. 96–97) meant to take place surreptitiously away from the gaze and the ears of adult authority figures. Central to the construction of the doll-play as *clandestine* is the semantics of the verb *fḍeH*, (to give away), used when one has a secret to protect or is doing something stealthily. Making too much noise by laughing too loudly is in this context dangerous, because it may attract the attention of parents and others to the activities of the girls in the peer group. Girls' own construction of their pretend-play as a clandestine activity and the ambivalence this reveals towards the actions they perform as part of the game infuses the social meanings of codes in this peer group. Use of Moroccan Arabic and Spanish in this pretend-play results in a heteroglossic polyphony of voices imbued with moral tensions (Bahktin 1981, 1986). The dialogic *addressivity* (in Bakhtin's sense) between the Moroccan voices of the girls in their metacommentaries and the Spanish voices they enact for their play characters inflects the codes with ethical valences. Moroccan Arabic is the code in which the girls voice their moral ambiguity, and Spanish is the furtive language that they bring to bear in their clandestine explorations of imagined transgressional possibilities, repertoires of selves, and ways of being in the world. The hybrid linguistic practices allow the voices of the *characters*, the voice of the *narrator*, and the voice of the *director* to represent distinct points of view on the world.

8.6 The Peer Group as a Context for Language Socialization into Communicative Practices and Gendered Identities

The examples discussed in this chapter illustrate immigrant children's acute sensitivity to the power of contrasting languages and registers to index and construct stances, acts, activities, and social identities (Ochs 1992, 1993, 2002). How do children learn the complex linguistic and sociocultural knowledge that they deploy in ludic interactions among peers? As noted above, in pretend-play girls interweave ordinary aspects of their lives with idealized high society and glamorous behaviors, actions, and even ways of speaking. Some of the behaviors that the girls make relevant in their pretend-play can be traced to girls' everyday activities, such as training for and running in public stadium races, watching TV, going to the store and so on. Codeswitching as a practice is itself part of the girls' repertoire of everyday ways of speaking. At the same time, the girls' role enactments include a range of behaviors (including ways of speaking, such as the highly stylized register of Spanish that they use when ventriloquizing the dolls) that are far removed from their daily lives. They are, after all, enacting *being adult women* many of whose behaviors are barred for them, because of age constraints, socioeconomic barriers, or moral expectations. I would like to consider further these more extraordinary enactments.

Some enactments in pretend-play were remote for the girls due to the difficult socioeconomic situation of many of these immigrant families (e.g., expensive shopping trips for clothes and gadgets), or to family prohibitions (e.g., going to the local swimming pool in the summer or participating in some of the festivities that take place annually in the town, such as the Spring Fair). Parental sanctions are particularly relevant because, as Kulick and Schieffelin (2004, p. 335) have discussed in their account of language socialization in relation to culturally-discouraged subject positions or "bad subjects," prohibitions may act as an instigator of desire: "verbal admonitions which are intended to discourage particular desires, in fact often sustain them," (2004, p. 357). This dynamic may partially account for the idealization and stance of desire that permeates the Spanish-dominant doll pretend-play interactions analyzed in this chapter. Alternatively, although their mothers or elder sisters would very rarely go out to coffee shops or engage in the kind of social outings that the girls perform in the course of the doll-play, the girls would observe many other groups of women going to bars, restaurants, and coffee shops on weekend afternoons and early evenings. They were also exposed to their female teachers' conversations in informal school settings, including my own as a Spanish female researcher, where plans and weekend activities were often discussed. In addition, they would also frequently overhear exchanges among the most socially popular female peers in their classes about shopping trips to nearby, larger cities, where many of them often went to purchase clothes and school materials.

Another crucial aspect to consider in the girls' constructions and idealizations of the dolls' femininity is the influence of TV sitcoms and soap operas on these girls' imaginative play. Many of the girls that I studied were avid consumers of these types of programs. As mentioned earlier in the chapter, characters and plots from these television programs were some of the most common themes of pretend-play in these girls' peer groups. Discussion about the "previous day's episode" was common in school during class breaks and other social venues not only among Moroccan immigrant girls but also among their Spanish female peers. These mass media portrayals no doubt also interact powerfully with the highly stylized, Barbie-like appearance of the dolls that the girls were manipulating as part of the games analyzed here. Toys, as semiotically-meaningful artifacts of material culture, provide certain affordances in the lives of children and in how children organize their play interactions (Schwartzman 2006). Beyond games, children have also been documented to exploit the affordances offered by material culture as they learn to navigate their own ways through societal structures and hierarchies (Thorne 2008). Girls' socialization into gendered identities and socioeconomic hierarchies of the dominant society, including indexical associations for different codes and language practices, is afforded by their familiarity with varied ways of speaking and possible ways of being in the world as females. This process is modulated by their exposure to mass media, by dolls as an expression of material culture, as well as by observation and vicarious participation in adult and classmate-organized activities.

An important dimension that I would like to highlight is how the peer group itself is a crucial context for children's socialization into communicative practices and processes of identification (Blum-Kulka and Snow 2004; Goodwin and Kyratzis 2007, 2012; Kyratzis, 2004; Paugh 2012). As noted in Chapter 4, Moroccan immigrant peer groups are composed of children of different ages and with different levels of expertise in and experience with Moroccan and Spanish linguistic and sociocultural practices. In pretend-play, older girls, or girls with longer migratory histories, also expose and socialize younger children and children with shorter lengths of stay in the country into hybrid uses of language varieties available to them and into ways of (re)fashioning alternative social identities.

The significance of play for children's sociocultural learning has been highlighted in a number of fields. Play, for instance, was thought by Vygotsky (1966/1967) to create its own zone of proximal development for children.[15] Vygotsky noted that play allowed children not just to explore the meanings and constraints of serious life, but also to place these meanings at the center of attention and experiment with them (p. 552). Pretend-play is especially productive context in this regard because of the ways in which sociocultural and developmental aspects come together (Vygotsky 1966/1967). In a neo-Vygotskian fashion, Goodwin (1985, pp. 316–317) has also argued that a continuity exists between hierarchical forms of interaction within games and non-game domains of experience. Moroccan girls' play allows them to experiment with the meaning of sociocultural processes in game domains and with the meaning of those processes in other domains of their daily lives. Rogoff (1998), in particular, has acutely examined how in play children contribute to each other's learning as well as to their own sociocultural development. Play encourages these powerful and effective ways of learning because social organization during children's games very often involves a form of participation that Rogoff et al. (2003) have called "intent participation." Intent participation involves collaboration between children experts and novices in a shared endeavor. It also entails the keen observation of an ongoing activity in which the novice is already participating, usually peripherally, but in which the novice will be expected to participate gradually over time.

In the pretend-play sequences under analysis, intent participation organizes the learning process of child novices in powerful ways. Throughout the games, child novices, such as Dunia, Worda's youngest sister, can be seen keenly observing the actions of her older peers, often in anticipation of participation (see Figure 8.2 below). Many times in these pretend-play sequences, Dunia picks up her sister's and other girls' dolls, while the rest argued and negotiated different parameters of the game, to practice and rehearse the actions that she had seen the other girls previously enact, often carrying out quasi-whispering self-dialogues with the dolls. Dunia always ran after her peers whenever they went to their houses or to the nearby construction site to pick up further props for their games. In addition, Dunia's emerging participation and understanding of the practices enacted in this doll-play interaction can be observed in her self-appointed role as a "look-out," collecting doll props, such as toy purses or glasses that fell off the dolls in the midst of play (see for example, lines 12 and 13 of Example 8.5 discussed above). Most importantly, in her role as a "look-out," she also warned her sister and the other girls whenever any adult or adolescent boys approached the peer group, such as, for instance, when Worda's elder brother appeared with another boy from down the street and approached them unexpectedly.

The peer group is a primary locus for immigrant children's language socialization as well when they share stories with each other about some of the social outings in which they were allowed to participate. They would often incorporate events of these outings in their games. Not all Moroccan girls in this study experience the same levels of restriction and monitoring. While some parents would not permit the daughters' participation in extra-

Figure 8.2 Dunia's observation and intent participation.

curricular school trips, other parents did not object to such activities. One of the trips that took place during my fieldwork was an outing to a movie theater in a nearby, larger city to see the popular movie *The Chronicles of Narnia*. A day after this excursion took place, a large number of Moroccan girls gathered in the park after school. Among them were three of the participants in the doll pretend-play (Worda, Wafiya, and Dunia). Those girls who had been allowed to go to the movies started telling the other girls their experiences in the theater and described the plot of the movie. Eventually, all the girls decided that they were going to pretend-play *The Chronicles of Narnia*, which I had the opportunity to record. In these ways, pretend-play with peers offers a prime context for immigrant children's sociocultural and linguistic learning, and socialization into dominant cultural dispositions and practices otherwise out of reach for many of the girls in this study.

8.7   Conclusion

The minimal adult supervision of peer-group activities makes pretend-play a crucial context for immigrant children to become active agents in their own and other children's socialization into communicative practices, sociocultural norms, and ways of being in the world. The rich verbal and sociocultural environments of peer groups provide an excellent window to investigate how, through play, Moroccan immigrant children in Vallenuevo negotiate their own understandings of difference and belonging, as well as subvert the constraints and processes of racialized exclusion that they encounter on a daily basis. This research underscores the importance of children's language-use and choice in play for larger processes of cultural continuity and transformation in transnational, diasporic communities undergoing rapid change (see also Paugh 2012). Codeswitching between Spanish and Moroccan Arabic play a critical role in how this group of girls explores various aspects of the micropolitics of belonging in relation to the larger sociocultural and economic forces that impinge upon their lives.

This analysis has highlighted the importance of these kinds of bilingual linguistic practices in immigrant girls' explorations of alternative processes of gendered identification and potential life paths. Examining the role of language in these imagined explorations may be even more crucial in multilingual, culturally-syncretic environments where, not only languages, but also ways of being in the world may be a source of tension in immigrant children's lives. As Hall (1995, p. 244) noted in her discussion of how young British Sikhs imagine their futures in relation to numerous possible identities, and as they contend with the contrasting ideologies of their families and the dominant society: "Identity formation is not simply a matter of preserving a cultural tradition handed down by one's parents. For ethnic minorities marginalized by the forces of racism and nationalism as well as forms of class and gender inequality, cultural-identity formation, I will argue, is an inherently political process." In this fashion, I argue that how Moroccan immigrant children in Vallenuevo are making sense of the micropolitics of social life in relation to gender, class, and ethnic aspects of difference and belonging, is inextricably linked to how they understand and experience their own processes of identification as well. Language-use within play interactions, and in contexts where children have more agency and freedom for social action, provide a crucial ethnographic locus to explore these political processes.

While language-in-play has most often been studied to understand children's learning and other important issues of psychosocial development, such as how children learn to take the perspective of others or to deal with disagreement and conflict, the political dimensions of play have not figured as prominently in scholarly literature (see, however, Urla and Swedlund 1995, and Paugh 2005). This chapter emphasizes the political aspects of play, and of language-use within play, more specifically, in relation to belonging and identity. The indexically-complex linguistic practices in this immigrant girls' peer group, for example, illuminate important aspects of the relation between codeswitching and social identity. Many instances of codeswitching, particularly those involving shifts to a register highly distinct from the Spanish that the girls use in their daily lives, are more related to the dynamic aspects of translingual phenomena, such as Rampton's (1995, 1998) description of *crossing*,[16] than the one-to-one mapping between codeswitching and social identity, such as solidarity-distance and in-group/out-group dichotomies, that characterized some of the earlier research on codeswitching (see Woolard 2004 and Auer 1998 for a review of this literature). In addition, narrative emplotment, in-character dialogue, and running met-acommentary inflect the codes with sociopolitical and moral values. The girls' own ideological interpretations of and stances towards these values, mobilized in the course of their play and codeswtiching practices, offer a vantage point into their developing gendered and ethnic subjectivities and sociocultural consciousness (Hill 1985; Gal 1987), as well as into their incipient political consciousness. The investigation of children's development of gender, sociocultural, and political consciousness, particularly the role that everyday linguistic and social practices play in them, may be particularly important for immigrant girls' complex and ambiguous processes of identification.

Notes

1   Lytra (2007) has analyzed play as encompassing a range of non-serious activities for the purpose of entertainment, even in contexts, such as schools and classrooms, where they are under direct adult supervision. These forms of play are also very important. In this chapter, however, because I want to explore children's activities in arenas where they have more room for independent action, I am limiting my analytic gaze to forms of play that occur in peer groups with little or no adult presence.

2   In this, I include not only Vygotsky's (1966/1967) seminal work on play, but also more contemporary work that takes a sociocultural, neo-Vygotskian approach to development and learning, e.g., Rogoff (2003).

3   Corsaro's (1994, 1997) notion of "interpretive reproduction" suggests that in the peer cultures in which children participate and create, children do not just merely reproduce aspects of the adult social world. Rather, by creatively appropriating information and knowledge about the larger social world, they are able to extend it and transform it, as well as reproduce it.

4   The other four hours focus mainly on recordings of boys' peer group activities, particularly those of Kamal's extended network of friends. Boys' activities were harder for me to record because often times they would play games like soccer that involved running around over large open spaces. I often watched them play these games as I walked about town. The boys' peer games that I did manage to record were those involving marbles and some forms of tag that were more spatially contained. Also, in these four hours, I have a couple of examples of boys and girls playing circle-singing games together in the park.

5   As I also mentioned in Chapter 4, and in previous work and analysis(García-Sánchez 2010c), I have examined games of hopscotch and jump-rope among this female peer network to discuss how participation arrangements and certain forms of sociocultural learning are facilitated by the flexibility with which these girls inhabit the roles of novice and experts in their interactions.

6   Reflexivity and addressivity are also Bakhtian notions that make reference to the dialogic quality of human language. Utterances are dialogic in that, while expressing the point of view, or the *voice* of an individual, they also take into account previous discourse or other *voices* being addressed. In the analysis above, I mean to emphasize that certain linguistic practices, i.e., codeswitching, and certain interactional frames, i.e., play frames, maximize this inherent polivocality of language.

7   Cromdal (2004); Gudal (1997); Halmari and Smith (1994); Kwan-Terry (1992); Paugh (2005, 2012).

8   Kissing on both cheeks is a pervasive, ritualistic feature of greetings among friends and acquaintances in both Moroccan and Spanish communities.

9   In conversations with the girls and their mothers, I learned that this prohibition was related to parents' concern about their daughters exposing their bodies publicly in swimwear. Interestingly, the issue of swimwear is also made relevant by the girls later in the game (see Example 8.4).

10   As described in Chapter 4, Salma suffered a serious ear infection as a baby. As a consequence, she lost most of her hearing and cannot speak.

11   See for example, Alford (1988); Blum (1997); Eid (1995); Markstrom and Iborra (2003); Rymes (1996). The importance of names has been particularly emphasized in research on

naming in relation to gender and identity (Alford 1988; Eid 1995). For example, in their study of Navajo female rites of passage, Markstrom and Iborra (2003) have discussed how the new names adopted in these ceremonies defined adolescent girls' changing identities, as well as new social roles and expectations.

12   Discourse markers have also been described as an important interactional resource by which children in monolingual contexts manage different interactional and play frames in peer interaction (see Kyratzis and Ervin-Tripp 1999).

13   Soraya is a name of Persian origin and Surya is a Hindi name of Sanskrit origin.

14   Lines 3–5 involve negotiation of conflict over a garment for the doll. As mentioned earlier when discussing play and interactional frames, negotiations interspersed in the emplotment of the pretend-play are carried out in Moroccan Arabic. Lines 12–13 are part of a concurrent interaction between Dunia and Lamia. Lamia is dressing up her doll to meet the other dolls in the cafeteria, and Dunia gives her a toy purse that Lamia had dropped.

15   Zone of proximal development can be defined as the distance between the actual developmental level of the child as determined by independent problem-solving and the level of potential development as determined through problem-solving in collaboration with more capable peers.

16   Rampton's (1995) notion of crossing refers to the act of codeswitching into a code or linguistic variety (usually a minority language) that is not "owned" by the speaker, but rather belongs to a group which they cannot legitimately claim to be part of.

9

Conclusion

Yo me siento las dos cosas porque
si hablo marroquí y español, soy las dos cosas.

I feel that I am both because if I speak
Moroccan [Arabic] and Spanish, I am both.

(Kamal, age 11, interview fragment)

This book has underscored the importance of studying immigrant children's everyday lives and discursive practices to trace how the countervailing forces at play in transnational settings affect these children's sense of belonging and emerging processes of identification in the most immediate contexts of their daily existence. In particular, this study has focused on how Moroccan immigrant children in Vallenuevo are able to navigate (and are affected by) both local and larger politics of inclusion/exclusion against the backdrop of increased levels of problematization and surveillance directed towards Muslim and North African immigrants in Europe. Moroccan immigrant children walk a tightrope between difference and belonging as they simultaneously participate in their own immigrant community and a Spanish society deeply ambivalent towards the prospect of cultural change and the multicultural politics of belonging provoked by recent migratory trends.[1]

In contemporary Spain, this ambivalence resonates forcefully in the current geopolitical climate of suspicion surrounding Muslim and North African immigrants as the enduring historical actualizations of the *Moorish* invaders of centuries past. In Chapter 2, I focused on some of the semiotic mechanisms of entextualization and interdiscursivity (Bauman and Briggs 1990; Silverstein and Urban 1996) through which the models of

Language and Muslim Immigrant Childhoods: The Politics of Belonging, First Edition.
Inmaculada Mª García-Sánchez.

personhood indexed by the sociohistorical, cultural, and linguistic form *los moros* have *congealed* (M. A. Silverstein 1992) at the semantic level, and become consistently associated with contemporary Moroccan immigrants. Fueled by the ideology of *frontier orientalism* (Gingrich 2010), which brings to bear a mytho-historical Spanish past as the organizing logic to explain contemporary Muslim and North African immigration, *los moros* work as a powerfully palimpsestic, chronotopic representation (Bahktin 1981, Agha 2007b). Contemporary social actors use this condensation of personhood-in-time-and-place to make sense of present-day Moroccan immigrants. These figures of personhood emerge at the axis of cross-chronotope alignments between historical figures of the Moor and contemporary Moroccan immigrants. In these cross-alignments, historical chronotopic anxieties are displaced into the here-and-now and transformed into a contemporary chronotope, which conflates these historical fears with present fears of religious fanaticism, terrorism, and security. In Chapter 2, I unpacked how the sociohistorical category *los moros*, as a chronotopic figure, became an extractable text that subsequently moved through historical space-time, being decontextualized and recontextualized across narratives and discourses. As instances of such processes, I gave examples of both traditional mytho-historical literary narratives, as well as contemporary political speeches. In addition to these discourses that circulate in the national imagination, I also explored the more local phenomenal textuality of everyday and political discourses about *los moros* in the small rural community of Vallenuevo more specifically. I paid particular attention to how these local discourses are produced at the complex intersection among anti-immigrant sentiment, historical anxieties, and contemporary fears about security and identity. This conflation is particularly visible in discourses surrounding the construction of a mosque and Islamic cultural center, and the ways in which this event was regarded as a threat in Vallenuevo.

Recognizing these ideologies and unraveling the various types of discourse that sustain them is critical to understand Moroccan immigrant children's everyday lives. The forms of social categorization and racialized stereotyping implicated in these ideologies intrude at varying degrees of relevance throughout different social spheres of children's experiences and interpersonal relations. The rest of the chapters in the book, specifically Chapters 4 through 8, examine children's daily social engagements and face-to-face interactions in dialectic relation with broader cultural logics and sociopolitical discourses implicated in conceptualizations of inclusion/exclusion, precisely in the light of this ideologically and historically-saturated problematization of Moroccan immigrants. One of the issues that I have tried to underscore in this book is precisely how language, because of its symbolic, indexical, performative, and phenomenological capacities (cf. Ochs

2012), is deeply involved in the politics of belonging at what Agha (2007b) discusses as different "scales of relevance" and "modes of semiosis." These range from smaller-scale (e.g., face-to-face interactions between people, everyday discourses) to larger-scale (e.g., political and mass-mediated discourses) participation frameworks. While language scholars have tended to focus on specific modes of semiosis or analytic levels of granularity, in my analysis throughout this book I have emphasized the importance of looking at the interplay of different scales of relevance for developing a holistic understandings of both constraints and affordances that Moroccan immigrant children encounter in negotiating "difference" or "commonality of belonging" (Brubaker and Cooper 2000).

9.1 Racialized Exclusion in Moroccan Immigrant Children's Lives

In exploring some of these constraints, I have traced how racialization, historically informed prejudice, and discrimination are instantiated in children's daily lives through discourse and interactional practices. Chapter 2 analyzed some of the semiotic mechanisms by which Moroccan immigrants and their children come to be viewed as unassimilable, as well as the historical, political, and cultural logics that underlie these classificatory systems and racialized models of personhood. Subsequent chapters examined, on the one hand, how these classificatory systems affect the daily living conditions of Moroccan immigrant children in Vallenuevo and, on the other hand, how these racialized models of personhood constitute what Heidegger (1927/1962) called "ready-at-hand technologies"[2] that are (re)produced in social practice. At school, for instance, as was outlined in Chapter 5, these ready-at-hand logics underlie linguistically-mediated regimes of surveillance that Spanish peers enact towards Moroccan immigrant children in the form of tattle-tales, peer directives, and fueling the fire. These practices function as *processes of distinction* (Bucholtz and Hall 2004), produce salient social difference. Through these regimes of linguistically-mediated surveillance, Moroccan immigrant children are depicted as troublemakers, irresponsible, dirty, and uncouth, thus unworthy of full-fledged membership in the social group of the Spanish classroom. In marking the behavior of their Moroccan immigrant peers as deviant, Spanish children establish the boundaries of unmarked ideological fields of naturalized social norms and behaviors. These normative fields are then used as the background against which Moroccan immigrant children are *marked* and positioned into the new *savage slot* (Trouillot 1991). They also become the ethical standard that allows Spanish children to reject and police the behavior of the *Other*.

Racialized exclusion reverberates beyond the walls of the classroom, as evidenced by the lack of mixed-ethnic peer groups in the school playgrounds and in the town (Chapters 4 and 8). Other powerful examples of this racialized exclusion include the systematic avoidance that characterized the behavior of Spanish children towards their Moroccan peers during school trips, sports competitions, and other informal activities in which both groups of children participated *together*, but separately (see Chapters 4 and 5). In examining how racialized exclusion is a product of everyday practice and of interpersonal relations, this book highlights the role of everyday talk and face-to-face interactions in how processes of racialization establish inclusion/exclusion boundaries and reinforce social inequalities.

This attention to everyday face-to-face talk-in-interaction is important both theoretically and analytically to complement the rich body of scholarship on language and racialization that has so far focused more intently on the political and institutional discursive construction of social difference and racialized categories for immigrants and minorities. The analysis in this book illuminates an aspect of racialization through language that has been less thoroughly examined: how everyday face-to-face talk can also affect social power and *markedness*. Daily interactions indeed (re)produce the boundaries of social structures and racialized categories for immigrants, as they go about the routine business of their lives and interact with members of the wider community in different social contexts. Understanding the interactional architecture of everyday racialized exclusion is critical for two reasons. The first reason is that these interactional processes can constitute, in and of themselves, linguistically-mediated forms of racism and discrimination. The second reason is that these interactional processes may dangerously help normalize discrimination precisely because of their subtlety. On the one hand, the racism driving these interactional forms of discrimination is implicit and not overtly acknowledged, and, on the other hand, the effects of exclusion are cumulative over time, but not immediately visible. In other words, the racialization indexed by blamings, accusations, or directives is masked and indirect but it, nonetheless, represents Moroccan immigrant children as troublemakers, dirty, and uncouth (e.g., `Karim is painting on his zipper with makers`; `Mimon has removed his chewing-gum and put it in his pocket`; or `Wafiya is making fun of me`). These are all stereotypes ideologically relatable to problematic models of personhood about Moroccan immigrants in general. In addition, the consequences of these forms of exclusion are subtle because, through these actions, Moroccan immigrant children are excluded from symbolic membership in the social group, but not from more immediate and visible participation in everyday activities. Indeed, the indirectness and implicitness of these processes may be a crucial reason that it is usually difficult for the teachers to identify and address them for what they are: linguistically-mediated forms of racialized exclusion. Because of this, teachers often ended up reinforcing these processes, usually unintentionally, rather than intervening to disrupt them.

In light of the data analyzed primarily in Chapter 5, the indirect indexicality (Ochs 1990, 1992) may be effected by two facts. One is that these linguistically-mediated forms of racialized exclusion tend to occur in interactional sequences and modalities that are easily afforded by, and not extraneous to, the particular social situation or practice (e.g., tattling in children's cultures). The second is that these interactions are ethnically sanitized and produced instead in reference to fields of naturalized social norms and behaviors (e.g., eating chewing-gum in class or leaving homework at home). The ethnic-sanitation and implicitness of the exclusion can be analyzed as recipient-designed. An important aspect of this being that it successfully satisfies the demands of the social situation in a school that enacts policies to promote tolerance and respect. Indirect exclusion affords Spanish child-perpetrators protection from the disciplinary sanctions teachers were certain to impose in cases of overt discrimination, as well as affording protection to their social face by not appearing overly prejudiced in front of teachers and peers. In fact, as Moroccan immigrant children very candidly narrated in some of our interviews, other encounters of a racializing nature that occurred out of teachers' gaze or in environments with very limited numbers of *overhearers* (e.g., the school bathrooms or a lonely street corner in town), were much more direct and less ethnically sanitized. Manal put this more directly when she implied that her Spanish peers displayed shallow civility towards them only in front of the teacher that then turned into discriminatory behavior when the teachers were not present: "Se portan con nosotros bien cuándo estamos con el maestro [. . .] cuándo se va el maestro [. . .] hablan de nosotros mal. Dicen que somos sucios y todo y yo me ducho siempre por la noche" **(They behave well with us when we are with the teacher [. . .] when the teacher leaves [. . .] they talk about us badly. They say we're dirty and everything, and I always take a shower at night)** (see Chapter 4).

The interactional modalities of everyday racialized exclusion examined in this study include blaming, accusations, and fueling-the-fire sequences. Social markedness and exclusion boundaries are instantiated through aggravated directives and other linguistic structures that encode unmitigated, negative types of agency and responsibility. Participation frameworks

(Goffman 1981b), wherein Moroccan immigrant children are not ratified as speakers either or addressees but only as *overhearers*, are also analyzed as integral to the interactional organization of everyday racialization and negative social marking. The negative identities engendered by the acts and stances of Spanish peers in these linguistically and corporeally mediated forms of racialized exclusion have important consequences for Moroccan immigrant children's emerging sense of belonging and processes of identification as relational and indexical processes (Ochs 1993, 2002). The ways in which Moroccan immigrant children are differentially positioned in face-to-face encounters is fueled to a large extent by the politics of "difference" and "negative recognition" (Taylor 1994) at the core of their social relations and interactions with Spanish peers. In this light, forms of everyday "micro-aggressions of race" (Solórzano 1998), including interactionally-mediated forms of racialized exclusion, warrant attention, along with structural inequalities, in the current, much-touted debates about inclusion and integration. These everyday forms of racialized exclusion are also relevant in discussions about pervasive alienation among Muslim and North African immigrant youth in Europe, more generally.

Not without substance, a prominent theme that emerged in the person-centered interviews (Hollan 2001) conducted with some of the focal children was an acute awareness of being socially marked negatively and a widespread feeling of not being wanted or genuinely accepted by many of their peers. The interview fragments interspersed throughout the book, but particularly those in Chapters 4 and 5, speak powerfully of Moroccan immigrant children's insight into the politics of their own misrecognition. The stories they shared are a testament to their realization that it is precisely those racialized politics that fuel the behavior of their Spanish peers. This realization extends to situations in which Spanish children engage in more indirect forms of exclusion in the classroom (see, for example, Manal's reenactments of Spanish children's peer directives at school, along with Worda and Wafiya's commentaries on these reenactments, Chapter 5). Naturally, this realization also encompasses more directly racializing situations, such as when their Spanish peers refuse to sit with them on school trips (from Wafiya); when they do not want to eat the bread baked in Moroccan households (from Worda); when they do not want to play with them (from Manal); when they tell them to shower (from Sarah) and when they call them *moros* and other racial slurs (from Wafiya and Kamal). In reflecting upon the stories they tell, these group of children make clear their grasp of these racialized politics of misrecognition as something that affects their whole immigrant community. In the interviews, this is most evident when Wafiya remarks on the mechanisms of overgeneralization underlying racialization and stereotyping. After telling a story of how Karim showed up to class one day looking disheveled, she remarked on how this led some of the Spanish kids to imply, paraphrasing Wafiya, that "all the Moroccans" were dirty (Chapter 4).

In addition to their interview comments, children also exhibit awareness of the sociopolitical and economic consequences of this problematization in their everyday lives and interactions. This is perhaps most visible in the double-consciousness (Du Bois 1903/1994) Moroccan children display when they act as language brokers in the town's clinic, discussed in Chapter 7, and during the games of pretend-play with dolls described in Chapter 8. In Chapter 7, I considered how, when acting as interpreters between Spanish doctors and Moroccan families, immigrant children, such as Fatima or Asmaa, may be acting with an orientation to the importance of not conveying information to the doctor that could lead the pediatrician to misrepresent or misunderstand Moroccan immigrants' practices. Through their translational filters, these children engage in active facework to achieve a certain social presentation of self on behalf of Moroccan immigrant families. Children's *selective modifications-in-translation* illuminate their sophisticated understandings of how their families and communities are racialized and ascribed negative characteristics. From this perspective, it could be said that, in trying to shield their families from the kind of institutional scrutiny that could lead to reinforcement of negative stereotypes, these children are protecting their whole community from the routine misrecognition to which it is subjected.

Children's awareness of processes of racialized exclusion also underlies the peer games analyzed in Chapter 8. Through imaginary characters ascribed to their dolls, Moroccan immigrant girls position themselves as insiders with the power to destabilize these racialized positionings, as well as other structural class-based and gendered expectations. The girls' double-consciousness, as refracted through their imaginary characters in play, leaves a traceable echo in their ambivalent and clandestine orientation towards the activities enacted in play. An unmistakable index of children's double-consciousness is the polyphonic, reflexive, and dialogic nature (Bakhtin 1981, 1986) of the communicative practices that characterized medical interpreting encounters and neighborhood peer games. Children are aware of racialized models of personhood imposed upon Moroccans. Their double orientation to their own perspective of themselves and to the negative perspective others have of them is observable when in their *modifications-in-translation* they blend their own words with the words of others (Voloshinov-Bakhtin 1973/1986), resulting in *double-voiced* renditions of the original utterances (Bakhtin 1981). In peer play, children imagine possible future selves in which they contest others' racialized, gendered, and classed forms of misrecognition. The heteroglossic polyphony of voices in girls' bilingual play and in their ambivalent commentaries about their own play also constitutes a powerful example of their double-consciousness.

Since there is ample evidence to suggest that Moroccan immigrant children have a complex grasp of everyday and institutional processes of misrecognition, it is important to ponder whether this lack of positive recognition can acquire structural dimensions when teachers become unwitting collaborators of their peers' practices of exclusion, and in spite of official slogans and curricular goals built around the notion of inclusion. When teachers repeatedly treated as legitimate, even if unwittingly, Spanish classmates' reactions to Moroccan immigrant children's violations of classroom norms of conduct, the latter's categorization as outsiders is implicitly reinforced. The analyses demonstrate how teachers ratify, perhaps without awareness, Spanish children's accusations against Moroccan classmates. Moreover, the analyses also show how Spanish children manage to escalate a casual criticism by a teacher directed to a Moroccan student into a full-fledged censoring of that child. Indeed, when I asked focal children about whether they had ever approached teachers or administrators to tell them about the behavior of their Spanish peers, the children responded negatively, maintaining that they thought teachers would dismiss them or not believe them. Although throughout the interviews children spoke highly of a handful of teachers and administrators as fair and helpful, in general, they did not consider school staff as source of support for more subtle, everyday exclusion. Spanish peers' rejections coupled with Moroccan immigrant children's perceived lack of institutional support may affect these children's emerging sense of (non-)belonging, as well as contribute to a cycle of educational alienation.

Given the widespread research consensus concerning the importance of positive relations with teachers and peers in the successful educational trajectories of marginalized, minority and immigrant children,[3] understanding the everyday dynamics of exclusion in immigrant children's social worlds is essential to enhancing these trajectories. Until recently, discussions about immigrant children's lack of educational success have been dominated by arguments about immigrant children's linguistic problems, home-school discontinuities, and segmented assimilation.[4] Complementing these research findings, this study underscores the importance of the cumulative effect of everyday racializing, exclusionary social encounters on the documented *downward trajectory* (Suárez-Orozco, Suárez-Orozco, and Todorova 2008) that characterizes the educational path of many immigrant children. The importance of teachers and administrators' actions in perpetuating or changing the dynamics of these exclusionary social encounters cannot be underestimated. As I showed in Chapter 5, the more intense the scrutiny and the complicity, albeit unwitting, between Spanish peers and teachers, the more likely Moroccan children were to retreat into silence weighted down by unequal alignment structures in these participation frameworks. Yet, and at the same time, even the weakest teachers' disalignment with tattling actions performed by Spanish children was sufficient for Moroccan immigrant children not to feel so socially vulnerable and without sources of support.

9.2   Negotiating Membership and Belonging as the Outsiders' Inside

One of most noteworthy findings of this study is how Moroccan immigrant children negotiate the boundaries of simultaneous inclusion and exclusion in their daily lives. At the national political level, this inherent contradiction stems from a particularly restrictive set of citizenship laws, according to which children of immigrant parents are not considered Spanish nationals, even if they are born in Spain or brought to the country when they are toddlers (see García-Sánchez 2013). This is the case for all the focal children in this study. The scope of this contradiction widens, particularly at the level of jurisprudence and social policy, when, in spite of being considered Moroccan nationals, they have the same rights and access to social services as their Spanish peers, although only until their late teens. The mismatch of being treated institutionally like insiders, but being legally and ideologically considered outsiders, is also relevant to the *informal aspects of the politics of belonging* (Brubaker 2010), which has been the main focus of this study. In this sense, Moroccan immigrant children in Spain find themselves negotiating membership across social domains in which they are simultaneously "outside and inside, between exception and rule" (Agamben 1998, p.170).

Moroccan immigrant children encounter these boundaries of simultaneous inclusion and exclusion when they have to come to terms with the juxtaposition of official practices of inclusion in school settings (such as bilingual signs on walls and doors and the institutionalization of a multicultural curriculum specifically designed to "teach" children tolerance) and the quotidian technologies of surveillance and racialized exclusion (such as tattles and peer directives) that Moroccan immigrant children face in school. Curricular and pedagogical practices emphasize respect, interculturality, and friendship. Yet, Moroccan immigrant children face *microaggressions* and *negative* (or *lack of*) *recognition* in their everyday social activities at school (Chapter 5). This treatment goes beyond the walls of the school as evidenced by the lack of ethnically-mixed peer groups in the neighborhoods and parks of Vallenuevo (Chapters 4). This lack of Spanish friends was acutely felt by the children, as can be seen in Manal's quote that introduces Chapter 8.

Teachers, administrators, and sports coaches are aware of the value of not marking others as overtly different and take steps to prevent explicit exclusion and discrimination. Yet, Moroccan immigrant children's behavior is abnormalized and constructed as deviant by their Spanish peers (Chapter 5). Central to how Moroccan children are constituted as "outsiders" is their routine engagement in exclusionary interactional practices with their Spanish peers, as well as the linguistically-mediated regimes of surveillance to which they are habitually subjected. One characteristic of these practices of social exclusion is the active monitoring of Moroccan immigrant children's behavior that, in many ways, echoes the intense surveillance to which the Moroccan immigrant community as a whole is subjected at the national and local levels (Chapter 5). Knowledge and acceptance of Moroccan cultural practices was promoted in school activities. Yet, sociocultural and historical logics, chronotopic representations of *los moros*, and models of personhood position Moroccan diasporic communities as *unassimilable* and as a threat (Chapter 2).

The echoes of children's paradoxical positionalities as both insiders and outsiders can also be traced in their interactions with Moroccan adults. Although the children are legally considered Moroccan nationals, adults in the Moroccan community often fret about what it means to be a Moroccan in the diaspora context. They worry about whether their children may turn out to be "too Spanish," as well as the consequences this could have for their cultural and religious identifications (Chapter 6). There were diverse *ideoscapes* (Appadurai 2002) found among the Moroccan immigrant community regarding tradition versus modernity in achieving ethno-religious authenticity. Yet, there was also a significant common thread to all Moroccan adults' efforts to socialize children into religious practices and into varieties of Arabic, namely a fear that, without these, Moroccan immigrant children would grow up without a sense of who they are as Moroccans and as Muslims. Adult concerns usually revolved around two intertwined axes of fear. First, there was a fear of cultural absorption into dominant Spanish values at the expense of their Moroccan heritage; and, second, there was a fear that the loss of cultural and affective ties to their communities of origin would render their children more vulnerable to marginalization and self-destructive behaviors. For this reason, many Moroccan parents in Vallenuevo wanted their children to attend the after-school classes offered at the makeshift community oratory-mosque. Even in households where the children were not encouraged to attend these after-school classes, or at least not to attend them assiduously, Moroccan parents would often complement Arabic lessons at the public school with additional exposure to cartoons and children's books in Standard Arabic and French (as in Abdelkarim's house) or with exposure to daily prayers (as in Worda's house).

Moroccan adults' concerns about their children's linguistic and ethno-religious identity, however, clashed with the expectations of many Spanish people that Moroccan immigrant children should integrate as smoothly as possible into the community. These included expectations that the Moroccan children would learn Spanish, attend public school during the day, and in the afternoons, participate either in sports and or in the extra-curricular activities program in the school, like the other Spanish children (Chapter 4). Their expectations definitely did not include, however, Moroccan children attending Qur'anic lessons run by a local Islamic association at the town's oratory-mosque. Most Spanish people, in general, reluctantly tolerated the teaching of Arabic within the public school curriculum. They, however, viewed any other such language instruction, particularly as it was related to Qur'anic literacy, with feelings that ranged from guarded reservation to outright mistrust. For example, many people would imply that the Qur'anic lessons, prayers, and other activities occurring in the make-shift mosque at the edge of town were somehow shady or potentially illicit. Yet, many of these same people also opposed the construction of a permanent mosque in a more central location (see Chapter 2). Given the current geopolitical climate of suspicion surrounding Muslims and North African immigrants, it would be naïve not to identify the roots of Spanish fears with the contemporary anxieties discussed in Chapters 1 and 2. In this light, Moroccan adults' fears of cultural absorption and identity loss and Spanish fears of terrorism, insofar as they are conflated with Islamic symbols and piety among immigrant youth, feed off each other. These mirror-image fears create a social fabric in which Moroccan immigrant children and youth have to negotiate difference and belonging across community boundaries and across mutually reinforcing fears. On the one hand, children negotiate commonality of belonging in relation to a heritage community that attempts to socialize them into – sometimes similar, but sometimes conflicting – *authentic* ethno-religious identities (thereby allaying fears that the children may be becoming "too Spanish"). On the other hand, children also must negotiate their membership in relation to a dominant society that attempts to assimilate them in the midst of fears that they may be becoming "too Islamic." Acknowledging these mutually reinforcing fears, as well as the internal vitality and frictions of Muslim diasporic communities, is crucial to understanding the fraught experience of growing up Muslim in contemporary Spain and Europe, more generally.

Moroccan immigrant children also navigate paradoxical positionalities in translating for their families and for Spanish medical staff at the health center (Chapter 7). As language brokers, children come to embody a double role as agents of the institution, but also as advocates protecting their families from the ways in which institutions problematize the Moroccan community in Spain. In their dual role as agents of the institution and as representatives of their families and neighbors, these children can be viewed as *insiders* of the medical institution when they convey institutional views and values to Moroccan families, but they can also be viewed as *outsiders* when they take interactional steps in their translations to protect Moroccan immigrant adults from institutional surveillance. Chapter 7 analyzed children's selective modifications of translations for both Spanish doctors and adult Moroccan immigrants as distinct from linguistic mistakes and mistranslations. These selective modifications indicate that immigrant children perceive and manage the different ethical and social expectations implicated in their multiple roles as interpreters, as family representatives, and as children of racialized immigrants. When Moroccan immigrant children modify their translations for Spanish doctors, they often display greater awareness than adults of the racialization, negative stereotypes, and routine problematization to which they, their families, and their immigrant communities are routinely subjected. The children modify their translations around areas of sociocultural contention that could be particularly susceptible to misunderstanding and misrepresentation.

Similarly, in their selective modifications of translation for Moroccan adults, the children nuance the translations in fine attunement to Moroccan diasporic community values and practices that preserve intergenerational relations. In modifying translations for their families, the children may also be protecting themselves from familial disapproval of engaging in behaviors that could be considered inappropriate, or just simply attempting to avoid a personal sense of embarrassment. Given that children's modifications went both ways – to prevent racialized misrepresentations by doctors and to preserve intergenerational relations with their families – it could even be argued that these young children had at least a basic awareness of their multiple communities crisscrossing mirror-image fears discussed above. Thus, selective modifications can be viewed as practices that crystallize how Moroccan immigrant children navigate paradoxical positionalities in their daily lives. Furthermore, Moroccan immigrant children's contextual management of translation work evidences these children's sociocultural competence and ability to bridge successfully different situational expectations in an institutional setting that, unlike the school, allows them to exercise greater interactional agency.

Children's awareness of these crisscrossing fears, and their complex negotiation of simultaneous inclusion and exclusion, prevail in neighborhood play when Moroccan immigrant girls play together and attempt to hide themselves from adult surveillance. Peer-group activities take place outside the gaze of adults, providing relatively autonomous arenas of action for children's construction of their own sociocultural and linguistic worlds (Goodwin 1997). Moroccan immigrant children rehearse alternative processes of identification and ways of being in the world, as well as contribute to their processes of socialization and sociocultural learning. In neighborhood games with peers, Moroccan immigrant children construct identities for their play characters that position them as full-fledged insiders of Spanish society. Yet, throughout these games, the children also display their understanding of some of the constraints in achieving this sense of membership (Chapter 8). In these contexts, Moroccan immigrant girls engage in clandestine interactions and employ culturally subversive *tactics* (De Certeau 1984) through imaginative doll-play. In their fantasy games, they challenge and transform the restrictions and discrimination they may experience in their everyday lives from their classmates, teachers, and families. They also contest the subaltern socioeconomic positions of Moroccan immigrant families within Spanish society more generally. Heteroglossic linguistic practices, such as codeswitching between Moroccan Arabic and Spanish, allow a type of creative ambiguity in which young Moroccan immigrant girls act out their own idealized notions of Spanish femininity, while playfully exploring imagined transgressional possible identities and moral worlds.

The analyses in Chapter 8 show how *in-character dialogue* and *stage-setting* play function as powerful counter-narratives to the constraints Moroccan immigrant girls encounter. The play narratives establish them as *pretend insiders* in worlds that they are otherwise *excluded* from. The girls take interactional steps to protect themselves from their families's surveillance. They set up look-outs and codeswitch into Spanish as *tactics* in these clandestine activities. In this sense, Moroccan immigrant girls' pretend-play and hybrid language use therein constitute *serious games* (Ortner 1996, 1999, 2006) – or practices through which social actors (re)produce and/or transform the larger forces that impinge upon their lives –. These games have potentially important future implications for processes of continuity and change in both the Moroccan immigrant community and in the structures of Spanish society.

The gendered, sociopolitical, cultural, and moral valences with which Spanish and Moroccan Arabic are inflected in Moroccan girls' codeswitching also underscore the ambivalences with which Moroccan immigrant children's processes of identification are fraught. The gendered identifications that these girls construct for their dolls point to both their desire to realize idealizations of Spanish femininity, but also their moral ambivalence about such realizations. Through the juxtaposition of these girls' own voices and the voices of their dolls, they create in the play frame a safe zone for the exploration of ambivalences and contradictions. In this play frame, they position idealized identifications and future life paths for females *inside* the mainstream Spanish society but *outside* the low expectations that people often have for children of economic migrants.

A central aspect of the sociopolitical, cultural, and moral tensions embodied in the use of Moroccan Arabic and Spanish, is precisely the girls' awareness of the political economy of languages in their community of Vallenuevo. Thus, when they use Spanish to ventriloquate, in Bakhtin's sense (1981), their play characters and coveted lifestyle, they position Spanish as the dominant code of power and relegate Moroccan Arabic to the sidelines. This is revealing particularly in this community, where Moroccan immigrant children attend Arabic language classes in both the public school and in after-school lessons at small oratory-mosque, that are intended to promote linguistic pride and positive identifications with their sense of *Morocan-ness* (Chapter 6). Undoubtedly, some adults of the Moroccan diaspora community could interpret girls' play enactments as confirming some of their fears about children's loss of community ties and about children's cultural absorption by the larger Spanish polity. Certainly, the relegation of Moroccan Arabic in this pretend-play sequence bears the mark of the forces of acculturation and racialization at play in the children's lives.It is also interesting to ponder, however, whether language ideologies that downgrade colloquial Moroccan Arabic in the Arabic heritage language classrooms may indirectly collude with the assimilationist forces I allude to above.

9.3   A Final Note on Moroccan Immigrant Children's Worlds and Agency

Moroccan immigrant children in Vallenuevo are growing up in a small, but contested, multilingual and multicultural community, in which they are, no doubt, affected by crisscrossing fears and cross-cutting racializing practices. Yet, the Moroccan immigrant children whom I had the honor to know were not defeated by these larger forces. On the contrary, across the different contexts of their daily lives, they exhibited great resilience in the face of discrimination and also a tremendous sense of responsibility in navigating paradoxical positionalities of simultaneous inclusion and exclusion. Furthermore, the Moroccan immigrant children that I observed took an active part in negotiating membership and difference across communities and social situations, by asserting their attachment to multiple symbolic realms of belonging. They also took advantage of whatever interactional affordances available to them to challenge their differential positioning.

The interview quote by Kamal that opens this chapter – "Yo me siento las dos cosas porque si hablo marroquí y español, soy las dos cosas," **(I feel that I am both because if I speak Moroccan [Arabic] and Spanish, I am both)** – is an example of the firmness, yet flexibility, with which Moroccan immigrant children formulate their sense of belonging to multiple national and linguistic communities. In addition to its declarative content emphasizing the important link between language and group-affiliative forms of identification, the quote speaks of immigrant children's most agentive side with regard to their aspirations for membership. In the context of the interview, the quote was a vigorous, almost defiant, claim of Kamal's to belong to both Moroccan and Spanish communities, produced as a coda to a several narratives of discriminatory encounters. This series of stories was prompted by the initial reporting of an incident that had just happened to him at the local annual fair in which he felt he was misrepresented by some of his peers and one of his teachers. Beyond the immediate context of the interview, in the context of Vallenuevo more generally, the quote demonstrates Kamal's will not to be defeated by routine misrecognition and exclusion. It is on this hopeful note, by discussing the agency-within-constraints that immigrant children clearly exercise, that I would like to conclude this exploration of Moroccan immigrant childhoods.

Crucial to my attempt to take seriously the complex ways in which young immigrant children exercise agency is my effort to incorporate, on the one hand, Moroccan immigrant children's perspectives on their own life experiences, and to consider, on the other hand, the *multiple* contexts and activities that comprise their daily lives. This holistic approach to immigrant childhoods is important because children's agentive ability to define their identity or to contest negative identities ascribed to them in everyday exchanges varies in different social contexts. Another central aspect to my study of children's agency is my use of the analytic possibilities provided by the ethnopragmatically-informed (Duranti 2007) language socialization (Ochs and Schieffelin 2012) approach, with its powerful combination of ethnography and micro-analysis of language use in interaction. While undoubtedly, interactional modalities and participation frameworks are differentially configured through the structural constraints and affordances of different social fields, the ethnomethodological analysis of routine practices is particularly helpful for capturing the emergent and often unpredictable quality of much human social interaction. These include the small ways in which social actors, even young children, manage to exercise their agency and engage in everyday *tactics* (De Certeau 1984), even in the midst of formidable constraints. From this perspective, a linguistic anthropological approach has much to offer to the study of immigrant childhoods.

In reviewing how children encountered or creatively produced interactional affordances to become more active participants in negotiating their own sense of belonging, we first see the children in contexts where power and hierarchical disparities between them and their interlocutors are greatest. In these settings, Moroccan immigrant children are less able to manage these processes of belonging/exclusion, being instead defined by others as non-accepted members of Spanish society (Chapter 5) and as more or less *authentically* Moroccan (Chapter 6). This is particularly the case in the Spanish and Moroccan educational settings described in Chapters 5 and 6. In these social arenas, the children are under more direct adult supervision and bound by institutional expectations and norms of behavior, and thus, it is more difficult for them to counter these identifications.

However, even in these social contexts where Moroccan immigrant children have fewer opportunities to stand up for themselves, they often take up any interactional opportunities available to them to actively negotiate their social positioning and identity. Important in this regard are some of the examples discussed in Chapter 5. Even the most insignificant action of a teacher against a Spanish tattler is enough for Moroccan immigrant children to defend themselves, often confrontationally, against their peers' negative characterizations (Examples 5.8 through 5.10) and to reassign these negative social identities on the original perpetrators (Example 5.9). Such agency can also be found, though perhaps less visibly, in the context of Arabic language and Qur'anic lessons. Immigrant children actively negotiate their understandings of what being a Moroccan in a Spanish context means to them, including their incipient rejection of some of the notions espoused by Moroccan adults around them. Such incipient rejection is evident, for example, when some of the children, who were particularly vested in the Qur'anic lessons at the mosque, such as Mimon and Yimad, insisted on calling the Arabic teacher at the public school *fqih*, despite his displeasure at that. Another example is how some children, who excelled at the Arabic language classes at the public school (i.e., Sarah, Worda, and Abdelkarim) found reasons not to attend regularly the after-school Qur'anic lessons, sometimes with more acquiescence from their parents but sometimes with less.

Relative to the limited forms of agency available to Moroccan immigrant children in educational institutions, whether Spanish or Moroccan, children's role as language brokers in clinics allowed them greater autonomy for action. At the health center, children are still constrained by the norms and expectations of a Spanish institutional context, and under the supervision of adult authority figures. In spite of this, the hierarchical differential is not as great as in the two previous contexts, since children bring into this setting their bilingual expertise. While necessary to guarantee the success of medical interactions, it is an expertise that very few of the adults in Vallenuevo possessed. Because of these more horizontal participation frameworks, children have more opportunities to negotiate actively their roles and positions. Children use their position as mediators to engage in active facework to (re)present Moroccan families to Spanish doctors and to (re)present themselves to their families. In so doing, they display impressive common sense and insight in using translation filters as buffers to navigate the differences and tensions that can arise in these complex interpreting situations.

Moroccan immigrant girls' pretend-play is another arena in which children hold a great deal of decision-making authority. Ludic activities and peer-group communicative practices create critical affordances for negotiating racialization and structural constraints through play-acting as if the improbable were possible, all the while wary of scrutiny from potential adult overhearers. These affordances are essential particularly given the continuity that has been described between games and non-game domains of experience (Goodwin 1985; Rogoff 1998). In light of broader forces of racialized exclusion and negative social markedness, these affordances may not be enough to achieve commonality of belonging in their multiple communities. Nonetheless, ludic and translation practices (Chapters 7 and 8) raise the hopeful possibility that Moroccan immigrant children will be able to achieve this commonality of belonging while preserving their sense and practice of difference. At the very least, these practices demonstrate Moroccan immigrant children's agentive competence to bridge different expectations successfully and to negotiate their situated identities. I want to emphasize, then, that children are never just the products or victims of their social worlds, not matter how discriminatory, but also the creative interpreters, shapers, and creators of those worlds.

Notes

1 See e.g., Checa (ed.) 1998; Checa et al. (2001); Martín Muñoz, García Castaño, López Sala, and Crespo 2003.

2 Heidegger (1927/1962) discussed "ready-at-hand" (*zuhanden*) tools as technologies through which people are able to act in the world and accomplish social projects. Yet, these tools are invisible in that they remain in the background and their properties and functioning are themselves objects of overt attention. Heidegger establishes a contrast between "ready-at-hand" and "present-at-hand," (*vorhanden*) in which the tools become in themselves conspicuous objects of attention because they are defective or, otherwise, obtrusive.

3 See, e.g., Gil Conchas (2006); Goodwin (2006); Suárez-Orozco, Suárez-Orozco, and Todorova (2008); Ochs et al. (2001).

4 See, e.g., Carrasco Pons (2003); Carbonell, Simó, and Tort (2002); Erickson (1987); Franzé (1995); Gibson (1987); Heath (1983, 1986); Mijares (2004a); Ogbu (1987); Pease-Álvarez and Vásquez (1994); Pàmies-Rovira (2006); Philips 1983; Portes and Rumbaut (2001); Vásquez, Pease-Álvarez, and Shannon (1994).

Appendix 1
Working with Video-Recorded Discourse Data

In this appendix, I provide a description of how I worked with the video-recorded discourse data that I collected.

After logging and digitizing the mini-DV tapes using Final Cut Pro, I reviewed the Quicktime files, taking detailed notes of the activities taking place on film. I then used these notes to produce rough transcripts and to identify particular segments that I wanted to discuss with my native-speaker transcription assistants. The digitized files were stored on large-capacity external hard drives that I had brought with me to the field.

The video-recorded corpus yielded by this data collection was transcribed according to the conversation-analytic system developed by Sacks, Schegloff, and Jefferson (1974), as adapted by Goodwin (1990a). These are the transcription conventions that I used throughout this book:

:	Lengthening
°	Low volume
.	Falling contour
?	Rising contour
[	Overlap
=	Latching (no interval between turns)
<	Rapid speech
–	Sudden cut-off
(.)	Brief pause
( )	Material in parentheses indicates a hearing the transcriber was unsure about
(( ))	Comment by the transcriber. Not part of the talk being transcribed
<u>Bold underlined</u>	Speaker's emphasis or increased volume

Language and Muslim Immigrant Childhoods: The Politics of Belonging, First Edition. Inmaculada Mª García-Sánchez.
© 2014 John Wiley & Sons, Inc. Published 2014 by John Wiley & Sons, Inc.

This method of transcription aims at capturing as much as possible the structural and sequential details of participants' talk and actions, such as supra-segmental intonation features, phonetic dialectal variation, pauses and hesitations in speech, laughter, sudden cut-offs, and overlap in talk by multiple speakers. Because the act of transcription, as Ochs (1979) has argued, is already in itself a form of analysis and is largely driven by the analytical concerns of the researcher, I integrated into the transcripts information from my field notes, as well as video framegrabs or photographs next to the transcript when appropriate. These images were important to convey relevant information about gesture, eye gaze, body orientations, and the material arrangement of the physical context. The production of such detailed transcripts enables the researcher to conduct close analyses of participants' practices, taking into account how multiple features of the context affect the interaction, and vice versa, as activities unfold (Goodwin and Duranti 1989).

Additionally, in order to create ethnographically informed transcripts (Garrett 2008; Schieffelin 1979, 1990), all tapes involving the use of Moroccan and/or Classical/Standard Arabic were viewed by me and by two Moroccan and Standard Arabic native-speaker assistants. These assistants transcribed and checked the transcripts for accurate hearing and language coding. I translated all data in consultation with these native-speaker assistants. They also assisted in the ethnographic annotation of the transcripts, providing nuanced metalinguistic commentary on social practices, language use, and insights into cultural ideologies and attitudes toward that use. Also, questions concerning the actions and speech of the children, as well as the situations in which these occurred, were addressed to the children and to the children's caregivers (e.g., teachers and parents) during several interviews and consultation periods over the course of the study. The transcripts were also annotated with the information gained in these consultations.

Nevertheless, representing interactions involving varieties of Arabic in transcript form was challenging, particularly when the interactions involved multiple participants with varying degrees of linguistic competence. Varieties of Arabic were transcribed phonemically using a combination of the systems developed by Harrell, Abu-Talib, and Carroll (2003) and Brustad, Al-Batal, and Al-Tonsi (2004), which felt comfortable and slightly familiar to my research assistants. A list of Arabic transliteration symbols can be found in Appendix 2. Although distinguishing between varieties of Arabic was fairly straightforward most of the time, sometimes the task proved challenging, particularly when dealing with dialectal varieties of Moroccan Arabic or with a middle variety, which has been called alternately Educated Spoken Arabic or Modern Moroccan Arabic (Ennaji 2005). This variety is a form of dialectal Moroccan Arabic heavily permeated by Classical/Standard Arabic vocabulary and expressions used by educated, urban elites (such as the Arabic heritage-language teacher) in their everyday interactions in public space. My native-speaker research assistants helped mark words and utterances as Moroccan Arabic, Standard Arabic, or a combination, using different font colors. Annotations to the transcripts included these comments or ambiguities that arose during the process of transcription.

As I logged and described the contents of each tape as soon as possible following the recording session, I made rough transcriptions of the data, highlighting ambiguous segments that needed further clarification, or that were particularly interesting in a first viewing of the video-recordings. If interactions involved varieties of Arabic, I discussed these segments in more depth with my assistants, annotating and refining the transcripts in the manner described above. After completing rough transcriptions of most of the tapes, I began to focus on similar types/patterns of interactions and language practices. Grounding my analytic observations in the videos, field-notes, and transcripts at several stages of refinement, I coded the data according to social practice (such as tattling, recitation, prayer, scolding, lesson) or linguistic behavior (such as different types of codeswitching, directives, literal translations versus modified translation). Whenever I found material that was analytically interesting but did not seem to fit neatly in any of these categories, I marked the tape and the time code with the label "other" and a brief description of the events transpiring in those segments. I coded rough transcripts of interview data according to narrative content (such as background information, relations with teachers, relations with peers, family problems, relations with siblings, discrimination, favorite activities). Organizing data in this fashion allowed me to investigate a variety of significant issues across data types, in addition to facilitating the holistic integration of the ethnographic record in my analyses. After finishing the coding stage, I proceeded to transcribe in detail representative examples of interactions and language practices that are examined in the chapters of this book.

Appendix 2
Arabic Transliteration Symbols

ā = ا

b = ب

t = ت

z = ث

ž = ج

H = ح

kh = خ

d = د

Ḏ = ذ

r/rr = ر

ẓ = ز

s = س

š = ش

S = ص

ḍ = ض

T = ط

ṭ = ظ

ʿ = ع

ġ = غ

f = ف

g/q = ق

k = ك

l = ل

m = م

n = ن

h = ه

ī/y = ي

ʾ = ء

a/e = ´

u/o = ʼ

i = ̗

Language and Muslim Immigrant Childhoods: The Politics of Belonging, First Edition.
Inmaculada Mª García-Sánchez.
© 2014 John Wiley & Sons, Inc. Published 2014 by John Wiley & Sons, Inc.

References

Abu-Haidar, F. (1994). Language Loyalty: The Case of Algerian Immigrants' Children in France. In Y. Suleiman (ed.), *Arabic Sociolinguistics: Issues and Perspectives* (pp. 42–55). Surrey: Curzon Press Ltd.

Abu-Lughod, L. (1985). Honor and Sentiments of Loss in a Bedouin Society. *American Ethnologist*, 12(2), 245–261.

Acoach, C. L. and Webb, L. (2004). The Influence of Language Brokering on Hispanic Teenagers' Acculturation, Academic Performance, and Nonverbal Decoding Skills: A Preliminary Study. *The Howard Journal of Communication*, 15, 1–19.

Adida, C., Laitin, D. and Valfort, M. A. (2010). Identifying Barriers to Muslim Integration in France. *Proceedings of the National Academy of Sciences of the United States of America*, 107(52), 384–390.

Agamben, G. (1998). *Homo Sacer: Sovereign Power and Bare Life*. Stanford, CA: Stanford University Press.

Agamben, G. (2005). *State of Exception*. Chicago and London: The University of Chicago Press.

Agha, A. (2005). Voice, Footing, Enregisterment. *Journal of Linguistic Anthropology*, 15(1), 38–59.

Agha, A. (2007a). *Language and Social Relations*. Cambridge: Cambridge University Press.

Agha, A. (2007b). Recombinant Selves in Mass Mediated Spacetime. *Language and Communication*, 27, 320–335.

Agoumy, T. (2004). El Rif Central y Oriental: Uno de los Focos Más Importantes de la Emigración Internacional. In B. López García and M. Berriane (eds.), *Atlas de la Inmigración Marroquí en España*. Taller de Estudios Internacionales Mediterráneos (pp. 152–153). Madrid: UA Ediciones.

Augoustinos, M. and Every, D. (2007). The Language of "Race" and Prejudice: A Discourse of Denial, Reason, and Liberal-Practical Politics. *Journal of Language and Social Psychology*, 23, 123–141.

Language and Muslim Immigrant Childhoods: The Politics of Belonging, First Edition.
Inmaculada Mª García-Sánchez.
© 2014 John Wiley & Sons, Inc. Published 2014 by John Wiley & Sons, Inc.

Alegret, J. L. and Palaudaries, J. M. (1995). La Escolarización de los Niños y Niñas de Origen Magrebí en Gerona. In B. López García and M. Berriane (eds.), *Atlas de la Inmigración Magrebí en España.* Taller de Estudios Internacionales Mediterráneos (p. 220). Madrid: UA Ediciones.

Alexander, C. (2007). Violence, Gender and Identity: Re-imagining the "Asian Gang." In Y. Samad and S. Kasturi (eds.), *Islam in the European Union: Transnationalism, Youth and The War on Terror* (pp. 144-159). Oxford: Oxford University Press.

Algan, Y., Mayer, T., and Thoenig, M. (2013). The Economic Incentives of Cultural Transmission: Spatial Evidence from Naming Patterns Across France. Discussion Paper No. 9416. Center for Economic Policy Research. Retrieved January 8, 2014 from www.cepr.org/pubs/dps/DP9416.asp.

Alim, H. S. (2005). Hearing What's Not Said, and Missing What Is: Black Language in White Public Space. In S. F. Kiesling and C. Bratt Paulston (eds.), *Intercultural Discourse and Communication: The Essential Readings* (pp. 180–196). Oxford: Blackwell.

Alford, R. (1988). *Naming and Identity: A Cross-Cultural Study of Personal Naming Practices.* New Haven, CT: HRAF Press.

Allport, G. (1954). *The Nature of Prejudice.* Cambridge, MA., Addison-Wesley.

Alonso, I. and Baigorri, J. (2008). Enseñar la Interpretación en los Servicios Públicos: Una Experiencia Docente. *REDIT. Revista Electrónica de Didáctica de la Traducción y de la Interpretación*, 1, 1–25.

Amir-Moazani, S. and Salvatore, A. (2003). Gender, Generation, and the Reform of Tradition from Muslim Majority Societies to Western Europe. In S. Allievi and J. S. Nielsen (eds.), *Muslim Networks and Transnational Communities In and Across* (pp. 52–77). Leiden: Brill.

Anderson, B. (1983). *Imagined Communities: Reflections on the Origin and Spread of Nationalism.* London: Verso.

Angelelli, C. (2004). *Medical Interpreting and Cross-cultural Communication.* Cambridge: Cambridge University Press.

Antonini, R. (2011). The Invisible Mediators: Child Language Brokering in Italy. In G. Cortese, *Marginalized Identities in the Discourse of Justice: Reflections on Children's Rights* (pp. 229–250). Monza: Casa Editrice Polimetrica.

Appadurai, A. (1996). *Modernity At Large: Cultural Dimensions of Globalization.* Minneapolis, MN: University of Minnesota Press.

Appadurai, A. (2002). Disjuncture and Difference in the Global Cultural Economy. In J. Inda and R. Rosaldo (eds.), *The Anthropology of Globalization.* Oxford: Blackwell.

Appiah, K. A. (2006). The Politics of Identity. *Daedalus. Journal of the American Academy of Arts and Sciences*, 135(4), 15–22.

Aramburu, M. (2004). Imágenes Populares sobre la Inmigración Magrebí. In B. López García and M. Berriane (eds.), *Atlas de la Inmigración Marroquí en España.* Taller de Estudios Internacionales Mediterráneos (pp. 442–443). Madrid: UA Ediciones.

Arango Vila-Belda, J. (2002). La Inmigración en España a Comienzos del Siglo XXI: Un Intento de Caracterización. In *La Inmigración en España: Contextos y Alternativas*, Actas del 3° Congreso de Inmigración: Resúmenes y Ponencias. Volumen II (pp. 57–69). Laboratorio de Estudios Interculturales: Universidad de Granada.

Aronsson, K. and Thorell, M. (1999). Family Politics in Children's Play Directives. *Journal of Pragmatics*, 31, 25–47.

Arrojo, R. (1998). The Revision of the Traditional Gap between Theory and Practice and the Empowerment of Translation in Postmodern Times. *The Translator*, 4(1), 25–48.

Arrojo, R. (2013). Translators' Code of Ethics. In C. A. Chapelle (ed.), *The Encyclopedia of Applied Linguistics* (pp. 5945–5948). Oxford: Wiley-Blackwell.

Asad, T. (2000). Muslims and European Identity: Can Europe Represent Islam? In E. Hallam and B. Street (eds.), *Cultural Encounters. Representing Otherness* (pp. 11-27). New York: Routledge.

Asad, T. (2003). *Formations of the Secular: Christianity, Islam, Modernity*. Palo Alto, CA: Stanford University Press.

Auer, P. (ed.) (1998). *Code-switching in Conversation: Language, Interaction, and Identity*. London: Routledge.

Austin, J. L. (1962). *How to Do Things with Words*. Oxford: Oxford University Press.

Bakhtin, M. M. (1973). *Problems of Dostoevsky's Poetics*. Ann Arbor, MI: Ardis.

Bakhtin, M. M. (1981). *The Dialogic Imagination: Four Essays* (ed. M. Holquist, trans., C. Emerson and M. Holquist). Austin, TX: University of Texas Press.

Bakhtin, M. M. (1986). *Speech Genres and Other Late Essays*. Austin, TX: University of Texas Press.

Balibar, E. (1991). Is There a "Neo-Racism"? In E. Balibar and I. Wallerstein (eds.), *Race, Nation, Class: Ambiguous Identities* (pp. 17–28). New York: Verso.

Ballestín, B. (2011). Los Niños de la Inmigración en la Escuela Primaria: Identidades y Dinámicas de Des/vinculación escolar – Entre el Color-blindness y los Esencialismos Culturalistas. In M. I. Jociles, A. Franzé, and D. Poveda (eds.), *Etnografías de la Infancia y la Adolescencia* (pp. 133–159). Madrid: La Catarata.

Baquedano-López, P. (1998). *Language Socialization of Mexican Children in a Los Angeles Catholic Parish*. Unpublished Ph.D. Dissertation. University of California, Los Angeles.

Baquedano-López, P. (2000). Narrating community in *doctrina* classes. *Narrating Community*, 10(2), 1–24.

Baquedano-López, P. (2004a). Literacy Practices across Contexts. In A. Duranti (ed.), *Companion to Linguistic Anthropology* (pp. 245–268). Oxford: Blackwell.

Baquedano-López, P. (2004b). Traversing the Center: The Language Politics of Language Use in a Catholic Religious Education Program for Immigrant Mexican Children. *Anthropology and Education Quarterly*, 35(2), 212–232.

Baquedano-López, P. and Mangual Figueroa, A. (2012). Language Socialization and Immigration. In A. Duranti, E. Ochs, B. Schieffelin (eds.), *The Handbook of Language Socialization* (pp. 564–586). Oxford: Wiley-Blackwell.

Barbolla Camarero, D. (2001). *Inmigración Marroquí en la Zona de Talayuela (Cáceres) 1992–1996*. Mérida: Editora Regional de Extremadura.

Barbudo, T. (2004). Marroquíes en España: Un Negocio de Medio Millón de Personas. In B. López García and M. Berriane (eds.), *Atlas de la Inmigración Marroquí en España*. Taller de Estudios Internacionales Mediterráneos (pp. 27–28). Madrid: UA Ediciones.

Barker, M. (1981). *The New Racism: Conservatives and the Ideology of the Tribe*. London: Junction Books.

Barrett, S. (2007). The Role of Violence in the far right in Canada. In M. Prum, B. Deschamps, et al., (eds.). *Racial, Ethnic and Homophobic Violence: Killing in the Name of Otherness*. New York: Routledge-Cavendish.

Bateson, G. (1972). *Steps to An Ecology of Mind: Collected Essays in Anthropology, Psychiatry, Evolution, and Epistemology*. Chicago: University of Chicago Press.

Bauman, R. and Briggs, C. L. (1990). Poetics and Performance as Critical Perspectives on Language and Social Life. *Annual Review of Anthropology*, 19, 59–88.

Belarbi, A. (1995). The Child as an Economic Investment: Preliminary Reflections. In E. Warnock Fernea (ed.), *Children in the Muslim Middle East* (pp. 230–234). Austin, TX: University of Texas Press.

Benwell, B. and Stokoe, E. (2006). *Discourse and Identity*. Edinburgh: Edinburgh University Press.

Berleant-Schiller, R. (1977). Production and Division of Labor in a West Indian Peasant Community. *American Ethnologist*, 4(2), 253–272.

Berk-Seligson, S. (1990). *The Bilingual Courtroom: Court Interpreters in the Judicial Process*. Chicago: University of Chicago Press.

Bernard, H. R. (2002). Participant Observation. In H. R. Bernard (ed.), *Research Methods in Anthropology: Qualitative and Quantitative Methods* (pp. 322–364). Walnut Creek, CA: Altamira Press.

Berriane, M. (2004a). La Larga Historia de la Diáspora Marroquí. In B. López García and M. Berriane (eds.), *Atlas de la Inmigración Marroquí en España*. Taller de Estudios Internacionales Mediterráneos (pp. 24–26). Madrid: UA Ediciones.

Berriane, M. (2004b). El Rif y la Oriental Segundo Foco de la Emigración Marroquí hacia España. In B. López García and M. Berriane (eds.), *Atlas de la Inmigración Marroquí en España*. Taller de Estudios Internacionales Mediterráneos (pp. 154–158). Madrid: UA Ediciones.

Besnier, N. (1993). Literacy and Feelings: The Encoding of Affect in Nukulaelae Letters. In Brian V. Street (ed.), *Cross-cultural Approaches to Literacy* (pp. 62–86). Cambridge Studies in Oral and Literate Culture, 23. Cambridge: Cambridge University Press.

Besnier, N. (2009). *Gossip and the Everyday Production of Politics*. Honolulu, HI: University of Hawai'i Press.

Bilgrami, A. (2006). Notes Towards the Definition of Identity. *Daedalus. Journal of the American Academy of Arts and Sciences*, 135(4), 5–14.

Billig, M. (1988). Social Representation, Objectification and Anchoring: A Rhetorical Analysis, *Social Behaviour*, 3(1), 1–16.

Billig, M., Condor, S., Edwards, D., Gane, M., Middleton, D., and Radley A. (1998). *Ideological Dilemmas: A Social Psychology of Everyday Thinking*. London: Sage.

Blommaert, J. and Verschueren, J. (1998). *Debating Diversity: Analyzing the Discourse of Tolerance*. London: Routledge.

Blos, P. (1962). *On Adolescence: A Psychoanalytical Interpretation*. New York: The Free Press.

Blum, S. (1997). Naming Practices and the Power of Words in China. *Language in Society*, 26(3), 357–379.

Blum-Kulka, S. and Snow, C. (2004). Introduction: The Potential for Peer Talk. *Discourse Studies*, 6(3), 291–306.

Bonilla-Silva, E. (2002). The Linguistics of Color-blind Racism: How to Talk Nasty about Blacks without Sounding "Facist." *Critical Sociology*, 28(1/2), 41.

Bonilla-Silva, E. (2003). *Racism Without Racists: Color-Blind Racism and the Persistence of Racial Inequality in the United States*. Lanham, MD: Rowman & Littlefield.

Bourdieu, P. (1977). *Outline of a Theory of Practice*. Cambridge: Cambridge University Press.

Bourdieu, P. (1991). *Language and Symbolic Power*. Cambridge, MA: Harvard University Press.

Bourdieu, P. (1993). *The Field of Cultural Production: Essays on Art and Literature*. New York: Columbia University Press.

Bourdieu, P. and Passeron, J. C. (1977). *Reproduction in Education, Society and Culture*. Cambridge, MA: Harvard University Press.

Bowen, J. R. (2004a). Does French Islam Have Borders? Dilemmas of Domestication in a Global Religious Field. *American Anthropologist*, 106(1), 43–55.

Bowen, J. R. (2004b). Beyond Migration: Islam as a Transnational Public Space. *Journal of Ethnic and Migration Studies*, 30(5), 879–894.

Bowen, J. R. (2007). *Why the French Don't Like Headscarves: Islam, the State, and Public Space*. Princeton, NJ: Princeton University Press.

Bowen, J. R. (2009). *Can Islam Be French? Pluralism and Pragmatism in a Secularist State*. Princeton, NJ: Princeton University Press.

Bowen, J. R. (2010). Muslims in the West: Europe. In Robert W. Hefner (ed.), *The New Cambridge History of Islam, Vol. 6, Muslims and Modernity, Culture and Society since 1800* (pp. 218–237). Cambridge: Cambridge University Press.

Bowen, J. R. (2011). Islamic Adaptations to Western Europe and North America: The Importance of Contrastive Analyses. *American Behavioral Scientist*, 55, 1601–1615.

Bravo López, F. (2004). El Musulmán como Alter-ego Irreductible: La Expansión del Discurso Culturalista. In B. López García and M. Berriane (eds.), *Atlas de la Inmigración Marroquí en España* (pp. 433–437). Taller de Estudios Internacionales Mediterráneos. Madrid: UA Ediciones.

Brison, K. (1998). Giving Sorrow New Words: Shifting Politics of Bereavement in a Papua New Guinean Village. *Ethos*, 26, 363–386.

Brown, P. (2002). Everyone has to lie in Tzeltal. In S. Blum-Kulka and C. Snow (eds.), *Talking to Adults* (pp. 214–275). Mahwah, NJ: Erlbaum.

Brown, P. and Levinson, S. (1979). Social Structure, Groups, and Interaction. In K. Scherer and H. Giles (eds.), *Social Markers in Speech* (pp. 291–341). Cambridge: Cambridge University Press.

Brown, P. and Levinson, S. (1978). Universals in Language Use: Politeness Phenomena. In E. N. Goody (ed.), *Questions and Politeness Strategies in Social Interaction* (pp. 56–311). Cambridge: Cambridge University Press.

Brown, R. and Hanlon, C. (2004). Derivational Complexity and Order of Acquisition in Child Speech. In B. C. Lust and C. Foley (eds.), *First Language Acquisition: The Essential Readings* (pp. 155–175). Oxford: Blackwell.

Brubaker, R. (ed.) (1989). *Immigration and the Politics of Citizenship in Europe and North America*. Lanham, MD: The German Marshall Fund of the United States and University Press of America.

Brubaker, R. (1992). *Citizenship and Nationhood in France and Germany*. Cambridge, MA: Harvard University Press.

Brubaker, R. (1998). Migrations of Ethnic Unmixing in the New Europe. *International Migration Review*, 32(4), 1047–1065.

Brubaker, R. (2001). The Return of Assimilation? Changing Perspectives in Immigration and its Sequels in France, Germany, and the United States. *Ethnic and Racial Studies*, 24(4), 531–548.

Brubaker, R. (2004a). Ethnicity, Migration, and Statehood in Post-Cold War Europe. In Michel Seymour (ed.), *The Fate of the Nation-State* (pp. 357–374). Montreal: McGill-Queen's University Press.

Brubaker, R. (2004b). *Ethnicity Without Groups*. Cambridge, MA: Harvard University Press.

Brubaker, R. (2010). Migration, Membership, and the Modern Nation-State: Internal and External Dimensions of the Politics of Belonging Migration and Membership. *Journal of Interdisciplinary History*, 41, 61–78.

Brubaker, R. and Cooper, F. (2000). Beyond "Identity." *Theory and Society*, 29, 1–47.

Brustad, K., Al-Batal, M., and Al-Tonsi, A. (2004). *Alif Baa: Introduction to Arabic Letters and Sounds*. Washington, DC: Georgetown University Press.

Bucholtz, M. (1999). "You Da Man": Narrating the Racial Other in the Production of White Masculinity. *Journal of Sociolinguistics*, 3(4), 443–460.

Bucholtz, M. (2001). The Whiteness of Nerds: Superstandard English and Racial Markedness. *Journal of Linguistic Anthropology*, 11(1), 84–100.

Bucholtz, M. (2011). *White Kids: Language, Race, and Styles of Youth Identity*. Cambridge: Cambridge University Press.

Bucholtz, M. and Hall, K. (2004). Language and Identity. In A. Duranti (ed.), *Companion to Linguistic Anthropology* (pp. 369–394). Oxford: Blackwell.

Bucholtz, M. and Skapoulli, E. (2009). Youth Language at the Intersection: From Migration to Globalization. *Pragmatics*, 19(1), 1–16.

Buriel, R., Love, J. A., and, De Ment, T. L. (2006). The Relation of Language Brokering to Depression and Parent-child Bonding among Latino Adolescents. In M. H. Borstein and L. R. Cote (eds.), *Acculturation and Parent-Child Relationships: Measurement and Development* (pp. 240–270). Mahwah, NJ: Erlbaum.

Buriel, R., Perez, W., De Ment, T. L., Chavez, D. V., Moran, V. R. (1998). The Relationship of Language Brokering to Academic Performance, Biculturalism, and Self-efficacy among Latino Adolescents. *Hispanic Journal of Behavioral Sciences*, 20(3), 283–297.

Campesino Fernández, A. J. and Campos Romero, M. L. (2004). La Inmigración Marroquí en Extremadura. In B. López García and M. Berriane (eds.), *Atlas de la Inmigración Marroquí en España* (pp. 325–327). Taller de Estudios Internacionales Mediterráneos. Madrid: UA Ediciones.

Carbonell, J., Simó, N., and Tort, A. (2002). *Magribins a les aules*. Vic: Eumo.

Carrasco Pons, S. (2003). La Escolarización de Hijos e Hijas Inmigrantes y de Minorías Etnico-culturales en España. *Revista de Educación*, 330(MEC).

Castaño Madroñal, A. (1997). Las Familias Marroquíes Asentadas en el Poniente Almeriense: La Influencia del Ámbito Doméstico en la Integración de los Niños. In E. Zamora Acosta and P. Maya Álvarez (eds.) *Relaciones Interétnicas y Multiculturalidad en el Mediterráneo Occidental* (pp. 153–164). Melilla: V Centenario de Melilla, S.A.

Castién, I. (1995). Cambio Cultural e Integración: Marroquíes en Madrid. In In B. López García and M. Berriane (eds.), *Atlas de la Inmigración Magrebí en España* (pp. 230–232). Taller de Estudios Internacionales Mediterráneos. Madrid: UA Ediciones.

Cekaite, A. and Aronsson, K. (2004). Repetition and Joking in Children's Second Language Conversations: Playful Recyclings in an Immersion Classroom. *Discourse Studies*, 6(3), 373–392.

Cekaite, A. and Aronsson, K. (2005). Language Play, a Collaborative Resource in Children's L2 Learning. *Applied Linguistics*, 26(2), 169–191.

Celce-Murcia, M. and Larsen-Freeman, D. (1999a). Imperatives (Chapter 12). In *The Grammar Book: An ESL/EFL Teachers Course* (2nd ed.). Boston, MA: Heinle & Heinle.

Celce-Murcia, M. and Larsen-Freeman, D. (1999b). Reported Speech and Writing (Chapter 33). In *The Grammar Book: An ESL/EFL Teachers Course* (2nd ed.). Boston, MA: Heinle & Heinle.

Cesari, J. (2004). Islam in the West: Modernity and Globalization Revisited. In B. Schaebler and L. Stenberg (eds.) *Globalization and the Muslim World: Culture, Religion, and Modernity* (pp. 80–92). Syracuse, NY: Syracuse University Press.

Cesari, J. (2006). *When Islam and Democracy Meet: Muslims in Europe and in the United States*. New York: Palgrave Macmillan.

Cesari, J. (2007). The Hybrid and Globalized Islam of Western Europe. In Y. Samad and S. Kasturi (eds.), *Islam in the European Union: Transnationalism, Youth and The War on Terror*. Oxford: Oxford University Press.

Cesari, J. and McLoughlin, S. (eds.) (2005). *European Muslims and the Secular State*. The Network for Comparative Research on Islam and Muslims in Europe. Farnham, UK: Ashgate.

Chacón Rodríguez, L. (2003). La Inmigración en España: Los Desafíos de la Construcción de una Nueva Sociedad. *Migraciones*, 14, 219–304.

Chao, R. K. (2006). The Prevalence and Consequences of Adolescents' Language Brokering for their Immigrant Parents. In M. H. Bornstein and L. R. Cote (eds.), *Acculturation and Parent-Child Relationships: Measurement and Development* (pp. 271–296). Mahwah, NJ: Erlbaum.

Chaudron, C. (1988). *Second Language Classroom: Research on Teaching and Learning*. Cambridge: Cambridge University Press.

Checa, F. (1997). Los "Yu-Yus" de la Emigración: Boda Marroquí en España. Análisis de un Cambio Cultural. In E. Zamora Acosta and P. Maya Álvarez (eds.), *Relaciones Interétnicas y Multiculturalidad en el Mediterráneo Occidental* (pp. 225–246). Melilla: V Centenario de Melilla, S.A.

Checa, F. (ed.) (1998). *Africanos en la Otra Orilla: Trabajo, Cultura e Integración en la España mediterránea*. Barcelona: Icaria-Antrazyt.

Checa, F. et al. (2001). *El Ejido: La Ciudad Cortijo. Claves Económicas del Conflicto Étnico*. Barcelona: Icaria-Antrazyt.

Christensen, P. and James, A. (2000). Introduction. Researching Children and Childhood: Cultures of Communication. In P. Christensen and A. James (eds.), *Researching with Children: Perspectives and Practices* (pp. 1–8). London and New York: Falmer Press.

Chu, C. M. (1999). Immigrant Children Mediators (ICM): Bridging the Literacy Gap in Immigrant Communities. *The New Review of Children's Literature and Librarianship*, 85–94.

Chun E. W. (2001). The Construction of White, Black, and Korean American Identities through African American Vernacular English. *Journal of Linguistic Anthropology*, 11(1), 52–64.

Chun, E. W. (2009). Ideologies of Legitimate Mockery: Margaret Cho's Revoicing of Mock Asian. In A. Reyes and A. Lo (eds.), *Beyond Yellow English: Toward a Linguistic Anthropology of Asia Pacific America* (pp. 261–287). New York: Oxford University Press.

Chun, E. W. (2012). The Meaning of Ching Chong: Trajectories of Racist Words in New Media. Paper presented at the Center for Race, Ethnicity, and Language. Stanford University, May 3rd.

Cirillo, L., Torresi, I., and Valentini, C. (2010). Institutional Perceptions of Child Language Brokering in Emilia Romagna. *MediAzioni*, 10, 269–296. Retrieved January 8, 2014 from http://mediazioni.sitlec.unibo.it.

Clemente, I., Lee, S. H., and Heritage, J. (2008). Children in Chronic Pain: Promoting Pediatric Patients' Symptoms Accounts in Tertiary Care. *Social Science and Medicine*, 66, 1418–1428.

Clark, H. H. and Gerrig, R. J. (1990). Quotations as Demonstrations. *Language*, 66(4), 764–805.

Clifford, J. (1994). Diasporas. *Cultural Anthropology*, 9(3), 302–338.

Código Civil Español (1889). Boletín Oficial del Estado (BOE), núm. 206 de 25 de julio de 1889 (pp. 249–259). Retrieved January 8, 2014 from https://www.boe.es/buscar/doc.php?id=BOE-A-1889-4763.

Codó Olsino, E. (2008). *Immigration and Bureaucratic Control: Language Practices in Public Administration*. Berlin: Mouton.

Cohen, R. (2001). Children's Contribution to Household Labor in Three Socio-cultural Contexts: A Southern Indian Village, a Norwegian Town and Canadian City. *International Journal of Comparative Sociology*, XLII(4), 353–367.

Colectivo Ioé (2004). Distribución por Sexos del Alumnado Marroquí en España. In B. López García and M. Berriane (eds.), *Atlas de la Inmigración Marroquí en España*. Taller de Estudios Internacionales Mediterráneos (pp. 418–419). Madrid: UA Ediciones.

Collados Aís, A. and Fernández Sánchez, M. M. (eds.) (2001). *Manual de Interpretación Bilateral*. Granada, Spain: Editorial Comares.

Collier, J. F. (1997). Children, From Heirs to Parental Projects. In J. F. Collier, *From Duty to Desire: Remaking Families in a Spanish Village* (pp. 153–176). Princeton, NJ: Princeton University Press.

Collins, J. T. (1995). Literacies. *Annual Review of Anthropology*. Palo Alto, CA: Annual Review.

Collins, J. T. (2009). Social Reproduction in Classrooms and School. *Annual Review of Anthropology*, 38, 33–48.

Corsaro, W. (1988a). Routines in the Peer Cultures of American and Italian Nursery School Children. *Sociology of Education*, 61(1), 1–14.

Corsaro, W. (1988b). Peer Culture in the Preschool. *Theory into Practice*, 27(1), 19–24.

Corsaro, W. (1994). Discussion, Debate, and Friendship Processes: Peer Discourse in U.S. and Italian Nursery Schools. *Sociology of Education*, 67(1), 1–26.

Corsaro, W. (1997). *The Sociology of Childhood*. Thousand Oaks, CA: Pine Forge Press.

Corsaro, W. (2000). Early Childhood Education, Children's Peer Cultures, and the Futureof Childhood. *European Early Chilhood Education Research Journal*, 8(2), 89–102.

Covello, L. (1957). *The Heart is the Teacher*. New York: McGraw Hill.

Crawford, D. (2002). The Intellectual Economy of an Anthropology of Change. *Anthropology in Action*, 1(9), 3–12.

Cromdal, J. (2004). Building Bilingual Oppositions: Notes on Code-Switching in Children's Disputes. *Language in Society*, 33, 33–58.

Cromdal, J. and Aronsson, K. (2000). Footing in Bilingual Play. *Journal of Sociolinguistics*, 4, 435–457.

Cullen, R. (2002). Supportive Teacher Talk: The Importance of the F-move. *ELT Journal*, 56, 117–126.

De Certeau, M. (1984). *The Practice of Everyday Life*. Berkeley and Los Angeles, CA: University of California Press.

De Genova, N. (2005). *Working the Boundaries: Race, Space, and "Illegality" in Mexican Chicago*. Durham, NC: Duke University Press.

De León, L. (2005). *La Llegada del Alma: Lenguaje, Infancia y Socialización entre los Mayas de Zinacantán*. México: Publicaciones de la Casa Chata.

Deleuze, G. (1981/1988). *Spinoza: Practical Philosophy*. San Francisco, CA: City Lights Books.

Deleuze, G. and Guattari, F. (1980/1987). *A Thousand Plateaus: Capitalism and Schizophrenia*. Minneapolis, MN: University of Minnesota Press.

Delpit, L. (2006). *Other People's Children: Cultural Conflict in the Classroom*. New York: The New Press.

DeMent, T., Buriel, R., and Villanueva, C. (2005). Children as Language Brokers: A Narrative of the Recollection of College Students. In R. Hoosain and F. Salili (eds.), *Language in Multicultural Education* (pp. 255–272). Greenwich, CT: Information Age.

De Miguel, A. (2000). *Dos Generaciones de Jóvenes (1960–1998)*. Madrid: Ministerio de Trabajo y Asuntos Sociales, Instituto de la Juventud.

Devine, D. and Kelly, M. (2006). "I Just don't Want to Get Picked on by Anybody": Dynamics of Inclusion and Exclusion in a Newly Multi-ethnic Irish Primary school. *Children and Society*, 20(2), 128–139.

Dick, H. P. (2011). "Making Mexicans Illegal in Small Town USA." *Journal of Linguistic Anthropology*, 21(S1), 34–54.

Dietz, G. (2002). Mujeres Musulmanas en Granada: Discursos de Formación de Comunidad, Exclusión de Género y Discriminación. In F. J. García Castaño and C. Muriel López (eds.), *La Inmigración en España: Contextos y Alternativas*, Actas del 3° Congreso de Inmigración: Resúmenes y Ponecias. Volumen II (pp. 381–394). Laboratorio de Estudios Interculturales: Universidad de Granada.

Dietz, G. (2004). Frontier Hybridization or Culture Clash? Transnational Migrant Communities and Subnational Identity Politics in Andalusia, Spain. *Journal of Ethnic and Migration Studies*, 30, 1087–1112.

Dietz, G. (2005). *Muslim Women in Southern Spain: Stepdaughters of Al-Andalus*. La Jolla: Center for Comparative Immigration Studies.

Dominguez, V. R. (1994). A Taste for "The Other": Intellectual Complicity in Racializing Practices. *Current Anthropology*, 35(4), 333–348.

Dorner, L., Orellana, M. F., and Li-Grining, C. (2007). "I Helped my Mom and It Helped Me": Translating the Skills of Language Brokers into Improved Standardized Test Scores. *American Journal of Education*, 113(3).

Du Bois, W. E. B. (1903/1994). *The Soul of Black Folk*. New York: Dover.

Duff, P. (2000). Repetition in Foreign Classroom Interaction. In J. K. Hall and L. S. Verplaetse (eds.), *The Development of Second and Foreign Language Learning through Classroom Interaction* (pp. 109–138). Mahwah, NJ: Erlbaum.

Duranti, A. (1994). *From Grammar to Politics. Linguistic Anthropology in a Western Samoan Village*. Berkeley and Los Angeles: University of California Press.

Duranti, A. (1997a). Ethnographic Methods. In A. Duranti, *Linguistic Anthropology* (pp. 84–121). Cambridge: Cambridge University Press.

Duranti, A. (1997b). *Linguistic Anthropology*. Cambridge: Cambridge University Press.

Duranti, A. (2004). Agency in Language. In A. Duranti (ed.), *Companion to Linguistic Anthropology* (pp. 451–473). Oxford: Blackwell.

Duranti, A. (2005). *Lingua, Cultura e Intercultural: L'Italiano e le Altre Lingue*. Copenhagen Studies in Language, 31. Copenhagen: Samfundslitteratur Press.

Duranti, A. (2007). *Etnopragmatica. La Forza nel Parlare*. Roma: Carocci Editore.

Duranti, A. and Goodwin, C. (eds.) (1992). *Rethinking Context: Language as an Interactive Phenomenon*. Cambridge: Cambridge University Press.

Duranti, A. and Ochs, E. (1986). Literacy Instruction in a Samoan Village. In B. B. Schieffelin and P. Gilmore (eds.), *The Acquisition of Literacy: Ethnographic Perspectives* (pp. 213–232). Norwood, NY: Ablex.

Eckert, P. (2000). *Language Variation as Social Practice: The Construction of Identity in Belten High*. Oxford: Blackwell.

Eckert, P. and McConnell-Ginet, S. (1995). Constructing Meaning, Constructing Selves: Snapshots of Language, Gender and Class from Belten High. In K. Hall and M. Bucholtz (eds.), *Gender Articulated* (pp. 469–507). New York: Routledge.

Edwards, D. (2003). Analyzing Racial Discourse: The Discursive Psychology of Mind World Relationships. In H. van den Berg, H. Houtcoup-Steenstra, and M. Wetherell (eds.), *Analyzing Race Talk: Multidisciplinary Approaches to the Interview* (pp. 31–48). Cambridge: Cambridge University Press.

Eid, M. (1995). What's in a Name? Women in Egyptian Obituaries. In Y. Suleiman (ed.), *Arabic Sociolinguistics: Issues and Perspectives* (pp. 81–100). London: Routledge.

Eisele, J. (2003). Myth, Values, and Practices in the Representation of Arabic. *International Journal of the Sociology of Language*, 163, 43–59.

Ek, L. D. (2005). Staying on God's Path: Socializing Latino Immigrant Youth to a Christian Pentecostal Identity in Southern California. In A. C. Zentella (ed.), *Building on Strength: Language and Literacy in Latino Families and Communities* (pp. 77–92). New York: Teachers College Press and California Association for Bilingual Education.

El Siglo. (2004). La Lección de Aznar en Georgetown. No. 618, 4 de octubre de 2004. Retrieved January 8, 2014 from www.elsiglodeuropa.es/siglo/historico/politica/politica2004/618Aznar.htm.

Engbersen, G. (2007). Transnationalism and Identities. In Y. Samad and S. Kasturi (eds.), *Islam in the European Union: Transnationalism, Youth and The War on Terror*. Oxford: Oxford University Press.

Ennaji, M. (2005). *Multilingualism, Cultural Identity, and Education in Morocco*. New York: Springer.

Erickson, B. (2011). Utopian Virtues: Muslim Neighbors, Ritual Sociality, and the Politics of Convivencia. *American Ethnologist*, 38(1), 114–131.

Erickson, F. (1987). Transformation and School Success: The Politics and Culture of Educational Achievement. *Anthropology and Education Quarterly*, 18(4), 335–356.

Ervin-Tripp, S. and Reyes, I. (2005). Child Codeswitching and Adult Content Contrasts. *International Journal of Bilingualism*, 9(1), 85–102.

Evaldsson, A-C. (2005). Staging Insults and Mobilizing Categorizations in a Multiethnic Peer Group. *Discourse and Society*, 16(6), 763–786.

Ewing, K. (2008). *Stolen Honor: Stigmatizing Muslim Men in Berlin*. Palo Alto, CA: Stanford University Press.

Ezzaki, A., Spratt, J., Wagner, D. (1999). Childhood Literacy Acquisition in Rural Morocco: Effects of Language Differences and Quranic Preschool. In D.

Wagner (ed.), *The Future of Literacy in a Changing World* (pp. 183–198). Cresskill, NJ: Hampton Press, Inc.

Fader, A. (2001). Literacy, Bilingualism, and Gender in a Hasidic Community. *Linguistics and Education*, 12(3), 261–283.

Fader, A. (2009). *Mitzvah Girls: Bringing up the Next Generation of Hasidic Jews in Brooklyn.* Princeton, NJ: Princeton University Press.

Fasulo, A., Lloyd H., et al. (2007). Children's Socialization into Cleaning Practices: A Cross-Cultural Perspective. *Discourse and Society*, 18(1), 11–33.

Feitelson, D. (1980). Relating Instructional Strategies to Language Idiosyncrasies in Hebrew. In J. F. Kavanaugh and R. L. Venezky (eds.), *Orthography, Reading, and Dyslexia.* Baltimore, MD: University Park Press.

Fernea, E. W. (1995). Childhood in the Muslim Middle East. In E. W. Fernea (ed.), *Children in the Muslim Middle East* (pp. 3–17). Austin, TX: University of Texas Press.

Flesler, D. (2008). *The Return of the Moor: Spanish Responses to Contemporary Moroccan Immigration.* West Lafayette, IN: Purdue University Press.

Flesler, D. and Pérez Malagosa, A. (2003). Battles of Identity, Or Playing "Guest" and "Host": The Festivals of Moors and Christians in the Context of Moroccan Immigration in Spain. *Journal of Spanish Cultural Studies*, 4(2), 151–169.

Flores, V. (1999). "Language Skills Translate to Major Duties for Kids." *Chicago Sun-Times*, April 4:4.

Foucault, M. (1982). Technologies of the Self. In L. H. Martin, H. G. and P. H. Hutton (eds.), *Technologies of the Self: A Seminar with Michel Foucault* (pp. 16–49). Amherst: University of Massachusetts Press.

Franzé, A. (1995). La Población Infantil Marroquí en la Escuela Española. In B. López García and M. Berriane (eds.). In *Atlas de la Inmigración Magrebí en España.* Taller de Estudios Internacionales Mediterráneos (pp. 218–220). Madrid: UA Ediciones.

Friedman, D. (2006). *(Re)Imagining the Nation. Language Socialization in Ukranian Classrooms.* Unpublished Ph.D. Dissertation. University of California, Los Angeles.

Fung, H. (1999). Becoming a Moral Child: The Socialization of Shame among Young Chinese Children. *Ethos*, 27(2), 180–209.

Gal, S. (1987). Codeswitching and Consciousness in the European Periphery. *American Ethnologist*, 14(4), 637–653.

Gandy, O. H. Jr. (2006). Quixotics Unite! Engaging the Pragmatists on Rational Discrimination. In D. Lyon (ed.), *Theorizing Surveillance: The Panopticon and Beyond* (pp. 318–336). Portland, OR: Willan Publishing.

García Castaño, F. and Carrasco Pons, S. (eds.) (2011). Población Inmigrante y Escuela: Conocimientos y Saberes de Investigación. Madrid, Ministerio de Educación, Secretaría General Técnica.

García Coll, C. and Kerivan Marks, A. (eds.) (2009). *Immigrant Stories: Ethnicity and Academics in Middle Childhood (Child Development in Cultural Context).* Oxford: Oxford University Press.

García Coll, C. and Szalacha, L. A. (2004). The Multiple Contexts of Middle Childhood. *The Future of Children*, 14.

García Ortiz, P. and Díaz Hernández, R. (2004). Niños Marroquíes en España: Nacimientos y Segunda Generación. In B. López García and M. Berriane (eds.), *Atlas de la Inmigración Marroquí en España*. Taller de Estudios Internacionales Mediterráneos (pp. 228–234). Madrid: UA Ediciones.

García-Sánchez, I. M. (2005). More than Just Games: Language Socialization in an Immigrant Children's Peer Group. *Texas Linguistic Forum: Proceedings of the Thirteen Annual Symposium About Language and Society*, 49, 61–71.

García-Sánchez, I. M. (2009). *Moroccan Immigrant Children in a Time of Surveillance: Navigating Sameness and Difference in Contemporary Spain*. Unpublished Ph.D. Dissertation. University of California. Los Angeles.

García-Sánchez, I. M. (2010a). (Re)shaping Practices in Translation: How Moroccan Immigrant Children and Families Navigate Continuity and Change. *MediAzioni, Journal of Interdisciplinary Studies on Languages and Cultures*, 10, 182–214.

García-Sánchez, I. M. (2010b). Achieving Shared Understandings in Play: Multimodality and Participation in Immigrant Girls' Peer Groups. Paper Presented at the 2nd International Conference on Conversation Analysis. University of Mannheim, Germany. July 4–8.

García-Sánchez, I. M. (2012a). Visible Disruptions: When Exclusion Can No Longer Be Ignored. Paper presented at the 111th American Anthropological Association Annual Meeting. San Francisco. November, 14–18.

García-Sánchez, I. M. (2012b). Language Socialization and Exclusion. In A. Duranti, E. Ochs, B. Schieffelin (eds.), *The Handbook of Language Socialization* (pp. 391–420). Oxford: Wiley-Blackwell.

García-Sánchez, I. M. (2013). The Everyday Politics of "Cultural Citizenship" Among North African Immigrant Children in Spain. *Language and Communication*, 33, 481–499.

García-Sánchez, I. M. (Forthcoming). Multiculturalism and its Discontents: Essentializing Ethnic Moroccan and Roma Identities in Classroom Discourse in Spain. In H. S. Alim, A. Ball, and J. Rickford (eds.), *Racing Language and Languaging Race*. Palo Alto, CA: Stanford University Press.

García-Sánchez, I. M. and Orellana, M. F. (2006). The Construction of Moral and Social Identity in Immigrant Children's Narratives-in-Translation. *Linguistics and Education*, 17(3), 209–239.

García-Sánchez, I. M., Orellana, M. F., and Hopkins, M. (2011). Facilitating Intercultural Communication in Parent-Teacher Conferences: Lessons from Child Translators. *Multicultural Perspectives*, 13(3), 148–154.

Garrett, P. B. (2005). What a Language is Good For: Language Socialization, Language Shift, and the Persistence of Code-Specific Genres in St. Lucia. *Language in Society*, 34(3), 327–361.

Garrett, P. B. (2006). Language Socialization. *Elsevier Encyclopedia of Language and Linguistics* (2nd ed.), Vol. 6, pp. 604–613.

Garrett, P. B. (2007). Language Socialization and the Reproduction of Bilingual Subjectivities. In M. Heller (ed.), *Bilingualism: A Social Approach*. New York: Palgrave Macmillan.

Garrett, P. B. (2008). Language Socialization. In P. Duff and N. H. Hornberger (eds.), *Elsevier Encyclopedia of Language and Education* (2nd ed., vol. 8). New York: Springer Science + Business Media LLC.

Garrett, P. B. and Baquedano-López, P. (2002). Language Socialization: Reproduction and Continuity, Transformation and Change. *Annual Review of Anthropology*, 31, 339–361.

Gentile, A., Ozolins, U., and Vasilakakos, M. (1996). *Liaison Interpreting: A Handbook*. Melbourne: Melbourne University Press.

Gibson, M. A. and Carrasco Pons, S. (2009). The Education of Immigrant Youth: Some Lessons from the US and Spain, *Theory Into Practice*, 28(4), 249–257.

Gibson, M. A., Carrasco Pons, S., Pàmies, J., Ponferrada, M., and Ríos-Rojas, A. (2012). Different Systems, Similar Results: Immigrant Youth at School in California and Catalonia. In R. Alba and J. Holdaway (eds.), *The Children of Immigrants at School: A Comparative Look at Integration in the United States and Western Europe*. New York: New York University Press.

Gibson, M. A., Gándara, P., and Koyama, J. P. (2004). The Role of Peers in the Schooling of U.S. Mexican Youth. In M. A. Gibson, P. Gándara, J. P. Koyama (eds.), *School Connections: U.S. Mexican Youth, Peers, and School Achievement* (pp. 1–17). New York: Teachers College Press.

Gibson, M. G. (1987). The School Performance of Immigrant Minorities: A Comparative View. *Anthropology and Education Quarterly*, 18(4), 262–275.

Gil Conchas, G. (2006). *The Color of Success: Race and High-achieving Urban Youth*. New York: Teachers College Press.

Gill, G. K. (1998). The Strategic Involvement of Children in Housework: An Australian Case of Two Income Families. *International Journal of Comparative Sociology*, 39(3), 301–314.

Gill, H. (1999). Language Choice, Language Policy and the Tradition-Modernity Debate in Culturally Mixed Postcolonial Communities: France and the Francophone Maghreb as a Case Study. In Y, Suleiman (ed.), *Language and Society in the Middle East and North Africa* (pp. 125–136). London: Curzon.

Gilson, E. C. (2007). Zones of Indiscernibility: The Life of a Concept from Deleuze to Agamben. *Philosophy Today*, September, Supplement, 98–106.

Gingrich, A. (1998). Frontier Myths of Orientalism: The Muslim World in Public and Popular Cultures of Central Europe. In B. Baskar and B. Brumen (eds.), *Mediterranean Ethnological Summer School, Piran/Pirano Slovenia 1996. MESS vol. II* (pp. 99–127). Ljubljana: Institut za Multikulturne Raziskave.

Gingrich, A. (2010). Blame It on the Turks: Language Regimes and the Culture of Frontier Orientalism in Eastern Austria. In R. Cillia, H. Gruber, M. Krzyzanowski, and F. Menz (eds.), *Discourse, Politics, Identity: Festschrift for Ruth Wodak* (pp. 71–81). Tübingen: Stauffenburg Verlag.

Goffman, E. (1963). *Stigma: Notes on the Management of Spoiled Identity*. New York: Simon and Schuster.

Goffman, E. (1974). *Frame Analysis*. New York: Harper and Row.

Goffman, E. (1981a). Footing. In *Forms of Talk* (pp. 124–159). Philadelphia: University of Pennsylvania.

Goffman, E. (1981b). *Forms of Talk*. Philadelphia: University of Pennsylvania Press.

Goodwin, C. (1993). Recording Human Interaction in Natural Settings. *Pragmatics*, 3(2), 181–209.

Goodwin, C. (2007). Interactive Footing. In E. Holt and R. Clift (eds.), *Reporting Talk: Reported Speech in Interaction* (pp.16–46). Cambridge: Cambridge University Press.

Goodwin, C. and Duranti, A. (1992). Rethinking Context: An Introduction. In A. Duranti and C. Goodwin (eds.), *Rethinking Context: Language as an Interactive Phenomenon*. Cambridge: Cambridge University Press.

Goodwin, C. and Goodwin, M. H. (1992). Assessments and the Construction of Context. In A. Duranti and C. Goodwin (eds.), *Rethinking Context: Language as an Interactive Phenomenon* (pp. 147–189). Cambridge: Cambridge University Press.

Goodwin, C. and Goodwin, M. H. (2000). Emotion within Situated Activity. In N. Budwig, I. C. Uzgiris and J. V. Wertsch (eds.), *Communication: An Arena of Development* (pp. 33–54). Mahwah, NJ. Erlbaum (reprinted in A. Duranti (ed.) (2001) *Linguistic Anthropology: A Reader* (pp. 239–257). Oxford: Blackwell).

Goodwin, M. H. (1984). Aggravated Correction and Disagreement in Children's Conversations. *Journal of Pragmatics*, 7, 657–77.

Goodwin, M. H. (1985). The Serious Side of Jump Rope: Conversational Practices and Social Organization in the Frame of Play. *Journal of American Folklore*, 98, 315–330.

Goodwin, M. H. (1990a). *He-Said-She-Said: Talk as Social Organization Among Black Children*. Bloomington, IN: Indiana University Press.

Goodwin, M. H. (1990b). Tactical Uses of Stories: Participation Frameworks within Girls' and Boys' Disputes. *Discourse Processes*, 13, 33–71.

Goodwin, M. H. (1995). Co-Construction of Girls' Hopscotch. *Research on Language and Social Interaction*, 28, 261–282.

Goodwin, M. H. (1997). Children's Linguistic and Social Worlds. *Anthropology Newsletter*, 38(4), 1, 4–5.

Goodwin, M. H. (1998). Games of Stance: Conflict and Footing in Hopscotch. In S. Hoyle and C. Temple Adger (eds.), *Kids' Talk:Strategic Language Use in Later Childhood* (pp. 23–46). New York: Oxford University Press.

Goodwin, M. H. (1999a).Constructing Opposition within Girls' Games. In M. Bucholtz, A. C. Liang, and L. A. Sutton (eds.), *Reinventing Identities: The Gendered Self in Discourse* (pp. 388–409). New York: Oxford University Press.

Goodwin, M. H. (1999b). Participation. *Journal of Linguistic Anthropology*, 9(1–2), 173–76 (reprinted in A. Duranti (ed.) (2001) *Key Terms in Language and Culture* (pp. 172–175). Oxford: Blackwell.

Goodwin, M. H. (2000). Morality and Accountability in Girls' Play. *Texas Linguistic Forum: Proceedings of the Seventh Annual Symposium about Language and Society*, 43, 77–86.

Goodwin, M. H. (2002). Building Power Asymmetries in Girls' Interaction. *Discourse and Society*, 13(6), 715–730.

Goodwin, M. H. (2003). Gender, Ethnicity, and Class in Children's Peer Interactions. In J. Holmes and M. Meyerhoff (eds.), *Handbook of Language and Gender* (pp. 229–251). Oxford: Blackwell.

Goodwin, M. H. (2006). *The Hidden Life of Girls: Games of Stance, Status, and Exclusion*. Oxford: Blackwell.

Goodwin, M. H. and Alim, H. S. (2010). "Whatever (Neck Roll, Eye Roll, Teeth Suck)": the Situated Coproduction of Social Categories and Identities through Stancetaking and Transmodal Stylization. *Journal of Linguistic Anthropology*, 20(1), 179–194.

Goodwin, M. H., Cekaite, A., and Goodwin, C. (2012). Emotion as a Stance. In M-L. Sorjonen and A. Perakyla (eds.), *Emotion in Interaction* (pp. 16–41). Oxford: Oxford University Press.

Goodwin, M. H. and Goodwin, C. (1986). Gesture and Coparticipation in the Activity of Searching for a Word. *Semiotica*, 62(1/2), 51–75.

Goodwin, M. H., Goodwin, C., and Yaeger-Dror, M. (2002). Multi-modality in Girls' Game Disputes. *Journal of Pragmatics*, 34, 1621–1649.

Goodwin, M. H. and Kyratzis, A. (2007). Introduction. Children Socializing Children: Practices for Negotiating the Social Order among Peers. *Research on Language and Social Interaction*, 40(4), 279–289.

Goodwin, M. H. and Kyratzis, A. (2012). Peer Language Socialization. In A. Duranti, E. Ochs, and B. Schieffelin (eds.) *The Handbook of Language Socialization* (pp. 365–390). Oxford: Wiley-Blackwell.

Goytisolo, J. and Naïr, S. (2000). *El Peaje de la Vida: Integración o Rechazo de la Emigración en España*. Madrid: Aguilar.

Granados, A. (2004). El Tratamiento de la Inmigración Marroquí en la Prensa Española. In B. López García and M. Berriane (eds.), *Atlas de la Inmigración Marroquí en España*. Taller de Estudios Internacionales Mediterráneos (pp. 438–439). Madrid: UA Ediciones.

Graves, T. (1967). Psychological Acculturation in a Tri-ethnic Community. *South-Western Journal of Anthropology*, 23, 337–350.

Gregorio Gil, C. (1995). Familia y Entorno Social Migratorio: Dos Instancias Socializadoras en Conflicto. In B. López García and M. Berriane (eds.), *Atlas de la Inmigración Magrebí en España* (pp. 226–228). Taller de Estudios Internacionales Mediterráneos. Madrid: UA Ediciones.

Gudal, T. (1997). *Three Children, Two Languages: The Role of Code-selection in Organizing Conversation*. Unpublished Doctoral Dissertation. Norwegian University of Science and Technology at Trondheim.

Gumperz, J. J. (ed.) (1982). *Language and Social Identity*. Cambridge: Cambridge University Press.

Gutiérrez, K. (2008). Developing a Socio-critical Literacy in the Third Space. *Research Reading Quarterly*, 43(2), 148–164.

Hall, K. (1995). There's a Time to Act English and There's a Time to act Indian: The Politics of Identity among British Sikh Teenagers. In S. Stephen (ed.),

Children and the Politics of Culture (pp. 243–264). Princeton, NJ: Princeton University Press.

Hall, K. (2002). *Lives in Translation: Sikh Youth as British Citizens*. Philadelphia: University of Pennsylvania Press.

Hall, K. (2004). The Ethnography of Imagined Communities: The Cultural Production of Sikh and British Ethnicity. *Annals of the American Academy, AAPSS* 595, 108–121.

Hall, N. (2004). The Child in the Middle: Agency and Diplomacy in Language Brokering Events. In G. Hansen, K. Malmkjaer, and D. Gile (eds.), *Claims, Changes, and Challenges In Translation Studies: Selected Contributions from the EST Congress, Copenhagen 2001* (pp. 285–296). Benjamin Translation Library, 50.

Hallam E. and Street, B. (eds.) (2000). *Cultural Encounters. Representing Otherness.* New York: Routledge.

Halmari, H. and Smith, W. (1994). Code-switching and Register Shift: Evidence from Finnish-English Child Bilingual Conversation. *Journal of Pragmatics*, 21, 427–445.

Hanks, W. (2005). Explorations in the Deictic Field. *Current Anthropology*, 46(2), 191–220.

Harrell, R. S., Abu-Talib, M., and Carroll, W. S. (2003). *A Basic Course in Moroccan Arabic.* Washington, DC: Georgetown University Press.

Harris, B. (1977). The Importance of Natural Translation. *Working Papers in Bilingualism*, 12, 96–114.

Harris, B. and Sherwood, B. (1978). Translating as an Innate Skill. In D. Gerver and H. W. Sinaiko (eds.), *Language Interpretation and Communication* (pp. 155–170). New York: Plenum Press.

Hatim, B. (2006). Discourse Analysis and Translation. In M. Baker (ed.), *Routledge Encyclopedia of Translation Studies* (pp. 67–71) (6th ed.). London and New York: Routledge.

Hatim, B. and Mason, I. (1997). *The Translator as Communicator*. London: Routledge.

He, A. W. (2000). The Grammatical and Interactional Organization of Teachers' Directives: Implication for Socialization for Chinese-American Children. *Linguistics and Education*, 11(2), 119–140.

He, A. W. (2002). Speaking Variedly: Socialization in Speech Roles in Chinese Heritage Language Classes. In R. Baley and S. Schecter (eds.), *Language Socialization and Bilingualism*. Clevedon, UK: Multilingual Matters.

He, A. W. (2004). Identity Construction in Chinese Heritage Language Classes. *Pragmatics*, 14 (2/3), 199–216.

He, A. W. (2006). Toward an Identity-based Model for the Development of Chinese as a Heritage Language. *The Modern Language Journal*, 4. Retrieved January 8, 2014 from http://www.heritagelanguages.org.

Heath, S. B. (1983). *Ways With Words: Language, Life, and Work in Communities and Classrooms*. Cambridge: Cambridge University Press.

Heath, S. B. (1986). What no Bedstory Means: Narrative Skills at Home and School. In B. B. Schieffelin and E. Ochs (eds.), *Language Socialization Across Cultures* (pp. 97–124). Cambridge: Cambridge University Press.

Hefner, R. W. (2007). Introduction: The Culture, Politics, and Future of Muslim Education. In R. W. Hefner and M. Z. Zaman (eds.), *Schooling Islam: The Culture and Politics of Modern Muslim Education* (pp. 1–39). Princeton, NJ: Princeton University Press.

Heiddeger, M. (1927/1962). *Being and Time* (trans. J. Macquarrie and E. Robinson). San Francisco: Harper.

Hill, J. H. (1985). The Grammar of Consciousness and the Consciousness of Grammar. *American Ethnologist*, 12(4), 725–737.

Hill, J. H. (1998). Language, Race and White Public Space. *American Anthropologist*, 100(3), 680–689.

Hill, J. H. (2001). Mock Spanish, Covert Racism, and the (Leaky) Boundary between Public and Private Spheres. In S. Gal and K. A. Woolard (eds.), *Languages and Publics: The Making of Authority*. Manchester: St. Jerome.

Hill, J. H. (2008). *The Everyday Language of White Racism*. Oxford: Wiley-Blackwell.

Hill, J. H. (2009). White Virtue and a Public Racializing Practice: Decoding "code words." Paper presented at the Center for Language, Interaction, and Culture Symposium, University of California at Los Angeles.

Hoffman, K. (2002a). Generational Change in Berber Women's Song of the Anti-Atlas Mountains, Morocco. *Ethnomusicology*, 46(3), 510–540.

Hoffman, K. (2002b). Moving and Dwelling: Building the Moroccan Ashelhi Homeland. *American Ethnologist*, 29(4), 928–962.

Hoffman, K. and Crawford, D. (2000). Essentially Amazigh: Urban Berbers and the Global Village. In K. Lacey (ed.), *The Arab-Islamic World: Multidisciplinary Approaches* (pp. 117–133). New York: Peter Lang.

Hollan, D. W. (2001). Developments in Person-centered Ethnography. In C. C. Moore and H. F. Matthews (eds.), *The Psychology of Cultural Experience* (pp. 48–67). Cambridge: Cambridge University Press.

Hollan, D. W. and Wellenkamp, J. C. (1996). *The Thread of Life: Toraja Reflections on the Life Cycle*. Honolulu, HI: University of Hawai'i Press.

Holt, M. (1994). Algeria: Language, Nation and State. In Y. Suleiman (ed.), *Arabic Sociolinguistics: Issues and Perspectives* (pp. 25–41). Surrey: Curzon Press Ltd.

Howard, K. (2007). Kinship Usage and Hierarchy in Thai Children's Peer Groups. *Journal of Linguistic Anthropology*, 17(2), 204–230.

Huntington, S. (1996). *The Clash of Civilizations and the Remaking of World Order*. New York: Simon and Schuster.

Irvine, J. (1989). When Talk Isn't Cheap: Language and Political Economy. *American Ethnologist*, 16, 248–267.

Irvine, J. and Gal, S. (2000). Language Ideology and Linguistic Differentiation. In P. Kroskrity (ed.), *Regimes of Language: Ideologies, Polities, and Identities* (pp. 35–84). Santa Fe, NM: School of American Research.

Izquierdo Escribano, A. (2004). Los Preferidos Frente a los Inmigrantes Permanentes: La Inmigración Marroquí en los Inicios del Siglo XXI. In B. López García and M. Berriane (eds.), *Atlas de la Inmigración Marroquí en España* (pp. 112–114). Taller de Estudios Internacionales Mediterráneos. Madrid: UA Ediciones.

Jaffe, A. (1993). Obligation, Error and Authenticity: Competing Cultural Principles in the Teaching of Corsican. *Journal of Linguistic Anthropology*, 3(1), 99–114.

Jørgenssen, J. N. (1998). Children's Acquisition of Code-Switching for Power Wielding. *Code-switching in Conversation: Language, Interaction and Identity*. P. Auer. New York, Routledge.

Jørgensen, J. N. (2010). Languaging. Nine Years of Poly-lingual Development of Young Turkish-Danish Grade School Students, vols. I–II. Copenhagen Studies in Bilingualism, the Køge Series, vos. K15–K16. University of Copenhagen.

Juvonen, J. and Galván, A. (2008). Peer Influence in Involuntary Social Groups: Lessons from Research on Bullying. In M. J. Prinstein and K. A. Dodge (eds.), *Peer Influence Processes Among Youth* (pp. 225–244). New York: Guilford Press.

Katz, V. S. (2014). *Kids in the Middle: How Children of Immigrants Negotiate Community Interactions for their Families*. New Brunswick, NJ: Rutgers University Press.

Keane, W. (2010). Minds, Surfaces, and Reasons in the Anthropology of Ethics. In M. Lambek (ed.), *Ordinary Ethics* (pp. 64–83). New York: Fordham University Press.

Kerzazi, M. (2004). La Región Oriental. In B. López García and M. Berriane (eds.), *Atlas de la Inmigración Marroquí en España* (pp. 150–151). Taller de Estudios Internacionales Mediterráneos. Madrid: UA Ediciones.

Klein, W. L. (2007). *Punjabi Sikh Families in Los Angeles: Discourses of Identification and Youth Socialization Practices*. Unpublished Doctoral Dissertation. University of California, Los Angeles.

Klein, W. L. (2009). Turban Narratives: Discourses of Identification and Differences among Punjabi Sikh Families in Los Angeles. In A. Lo and A. Reyes (eds.), *Towards a Linguistic Anthropology of Asian-Pacific America*. Oxford: Oxford University Press.

Klein, W. L., Izquierdo, C., et al. (2008). Children's Participation in Household Work: Ideologies and Practices in 30 Los Angeles Families. *CELF Working Papers*.

Kroger, J. (2004). *Identity in Adolescence: The Balance between Self and Other*. New York: Routledge.

Kroskrity, P. (ed.) (2000). *Regimes of Language: Ideologies, Polities, and Identities*. Santa Fe, NM: School of American Research Press.

Kulick, D. (1992). *Language Shift and Cultural Reproduction: Socialization, Self, and Syncretism in a Papuan New Guinean Village*. Cambridge: Cambridge University Press.

Kulick, D. and Schieffelin, B.B. (2004). Language Socialization. In A. Duranti (ed.), *A Companion to Linguistic Anthropology* (pp. 349–368). Oxford: Blackwell.

Kuroshima, S. (2010). Another Look at the Service Encounter: Progressivity, Intersubjectivity, and Trust in a Japanese Sushi Restaurant. *Journal of Pragmatics*, 42(3), 856–869.

Kwan-Terry, A. (1992). Code-switching and Code-mixing: The Case of a Child Learning English and Chinese Simultaneously. *Journal of Multilingual and Multicultural Development*, 13, 243–259.

Kyratzis, A. (2000). Tactical Use of Narrative in Nursery School Same-Sex Groups. *Discourse Processes*, 29(3), 269–299.

Kyratzis, A. (2004). Talk and Interaction Among Children and the Co-construction of Peer Groups and Peer Cultures. *Annual Review of Anthropology*, 33, 625–649.

Kyratzis, A. (2010). Latina Girls' Peer Play Interactions in a Bilingual Spanish-English U.S. Preschool: Heteroglossia, Frame-shifting, and Language Ideology. *Pragmatics*, 20(4), 557–586.

Kyratzis, A. and Ervin-Tripp, S. (1999). The Development of Discourse Markers in Peer Interaction. *Journal of Pragmatics*, 31, 1321–1338.

Kyratzis, A. and Guo, J. (2001). Preschool Girls' and Boys' Verbal Conflict Strategies in the United States and China. *Research on Language and Social Interaction*, 34, 45–74.

LaBennet, O. (2011). *She's Mad Real: Popular Culture and West Indian Girls in Brooklyn*. New York: New York University Press.

Labov, W. (1964). Hypercorrection by the Lower Middle Class as a Factor in Linguistic Change. In W. Bright (ed.), *Sociolinguistics. Proceedings of the UCLA Sociolinguistics Conference, 1964*. Los Angeles: UCLA.

Labov, W. (1966). The Effect of Social Mobility on Linguistic Behavior. *Sociological Inquiry*, 36(2), 186–203.

Lahiou, M. (2004). Las Migraciones Clandestinas entre Marruecos y España: Por Qué, Cuántos, Qué Hacer. In B. López García and M. Berriane (eds.), *Atlas de la Inmigración Marroquí en España* (pp. 86–89). Taller de Estudios Internacionales Mediterráneos. Madrid: UA Ediciones.

Lambek, M. (2010). Toward An Ethics of the Act. In M. Lambek (ed.), *Ordinary Ethics: Anthropology, Language and Action*. New York: Fordham University Press.

Lapesa Melgar, R. (1996). *El Español Moderno y Contemporáneo: Estudios Lingüísticos*. Barcelona: Grijalbo-Mondadori.

Lapesa Melgar, R. (2000). *Estudios de Morfosintaxis Histórica del Español*. Madrid: Gredos.

Laouina, A. (2004). Rif Central y Oriental y Marruecos Oriental. In B. López García and M. Berriane (eds.), *Atlas de la Inmigración Marroquí en España* (pp. 147–151). Taller de Estudios Internacionales Mediterráneos. Madrid: UA Ediciones.

Lee, R. D. (1997). *Overcoming Tradition and Modernity: The Search for Islamic Authenticity*. Boulder, CO: Westview Press.

Lee, S. (2005). *Up Against Whiteness: Race, School, and Immigrant Youth*. New York: Teachers College Press.

Lerner, R. M. (1993). *Early Adolescence: Perspectives on Research, Policy and Intervention*. Mahwah, NJ: Erlbaum.

Lerner, G. H. (1995). Turn Design and the Organization of Participation in Instructional Activities. *Discourse Processes*, 19(1), 111–131.

Lerner, G. H. (2013). On the Place of Hesitating in Delicate Formulations: A Turn-Constructional Infrastructure for Collaborative Indiscretion. In J. Sidnell, M.

Hayashi, and G. Raymond (eds.), *Conversational Repair and Human Understanding*. Cambridge: Cambridge University Press.

Levidow, L. (2007). Terrorizing Communities: The So-called "War on Terror" in the UK. In Y. Samad and S. Kasturi (eds.), *Islam in the European Union: Transnationalism, Youth, and The War on Terror*. Oxford: Oxford University Press.

Levin, J. and Rabrenovic, G. (2007). The Impact of Interdependence on Racial Hostility: The American Experience. In M. Prum (ed.), *Killing In The Name Of Otherness: Racial, Ethnic, And Homophobic Violence* (pp. 149–160). New York: Routledge Cavendish.

Levinas, E. (1998). *Entre Nous: Thinking-of-the-Other*. New York: Columbia University Press.

Levinson, S. C. (1983). *Pragmatics*. Cambridge: Cambridge University Press.

Levy, R. I. and Hollan, D. W. (1998). Person-Centered Interviewing and Observation. In H. R. Bernard (ed.), *Handbook of Methods in Anthropology* (pp. 331–362). Walnut Creek, CA: Altamira Press.

Lo, A. (2009). Lessons about Respect and Affect in a Korean Heritage Language School. *Linguistics and Education*, 20(3), 2, 217–234.

Lo, A. and Fung, H. (2012). Language Socialization and Shaming. In A. Duranti, E. Ochs, and B. Schieffelin (eds.), *The Handbook of Language Socialization* (pp. 391–420). Oxford: Wiley-Blackwell.

Lo, A. and Howard, K. (2009). Mobilizing Respect and Politeness in Classrooms. *Linguistics and Education*, 20(3), 211–216.

López, N. (2003). *Hopeful Girls, Troubled Boys: Race and Gender Disparity in Urban Education*. New York: Routledge.

López García, B. (1993). Sindicalismo Magrebí y Emigración Norteafricana en Europa: Una Perspectiva Española. In J. Montabes-Pereira, B. López García, and D. del Pino (eds.), *Explosión Demográfica, Empleo, y Trabajadores Emigrantes del Mediterráneo Occidental* (pp. 553–564). Granada: Servicio de Publicaciones de la Universidad de Granada.

López García, B. (2002). Marroquíes en España 1991–2001: Confirmación de los Perfiles de Origen. In F. J. García Castaño and C. Muriel López (eds.), *La Inmigración en España: Contextos y Alternativas*. Actas del 3° Congreso de Inmigración. Volumen II (pp. 251–264). Laboratorio de Estudios Interculturales: Universidad de Granada.

López García, B. (2003). Los Olvidados: La Diáspora Marroquí. *Política Exterior*, 17(94), 95–104.

López García, B. (2004). La Evolución de la Inmigración Marroquí en España (1991–2003). In B. López García and M. Berriane (eds.), *Atlas de la Inmigración Marroquí en España*. Taller de Estudios Internacionales Mediterráneos (pp. 213–221). Madrid: UA Ediciones.

López García, B. (2006). La Inmigración de Magrebíes y Africanos. Asumir la Vecindad. In A. Alted y A. Asenjo (eds.), *De la España que Emigra a la España que Acoge* (pp. 480–489). Madrid: Caja Duero-Fundación Largo Caballero.

López García, B. and Berriane, M. (eds.) (2004). *Atlas de la Inmigración Marroquí en España*. Taller de Estudios Internacionales Mediterráneos. Madrid: UA Ediciones.

López García, B., et al. (1993). *Inmigración Magrebí en España: El Retorno de los Moriscos*. Madrid: Mapfre.

Losada-Campo, T. (1993). La Inmigración Marroquí en los Últimos 20 Años. In J. Montabes-Pereira, B. López García, and D. del Pino (eds.), *Explosión Demográfica, Empleo, y Trabajadores Emigrantes del Mediterráneo Occidental* (pp. 547–551). Granada: Servicio de Publicaciones de la Universidad de Granada.

Loyd, H. (2012). The Logic of Conflict: Practices of Social Control Among Inner City Neapolitan Girls. In S. Danby and M. Theobald (eds.), *Disputes in Everyday Life: Social and Moral Orders of Children and Young People* (pp. 325–353). Sociological Studies of Children and Youth, Volume 15, Emerald Group Publishing Limited.

Lucko, J. D. (2007). *God, Gangs, and Grades: Constructing Identity and Difference Among Ecuatorian Students in Madrid, Spain*. Unpublished Doctoral Dissertation. Berkeley, CA: University of California, Berkeley.

Lytra, V. (2007). *Play Frames and Social Identities: Contact Encounters in a Greek Primary School*. Amsterdam: John Benjamins.

Maira, S. M. (2002). *Desis in the House: Indian American Youth Culture in New York City*. Philadelphia: Temple University Press.

Malakoff, M. and Hakuta, K. (1991). Translation Skill and Metalinguistic Awareness in Bilinguals. In E. Bialystok (ed.), *Language Processing in Bilingual Children*. Cambridge: Cambridge University Press.

Mandel, R. (2008). *Cosmopolitan Anxieties: Turkish Challenges to Citizenship and Belonging in Germany*. Durham, NC: Duke University Press.

Mandeville, P. (2001). Reimagining Islam in Diaspora: The Politics of Mediated Community. *International Communication Gazette*, 63(1–2), 169–186.

Mandeville, P. (2007). Islamic Education in Britain: Approaches to Religious Knowledge in a Pluralistic Society. In R. W. Hefner and M. Qasimzaman (eds.), *Schooling Islam: The Culture and Politics of Modern Muslim Education* (pp. 224–241). Princeton, NJ: Princeton University Press.

Mangual Figueroa, A. (2011). Citizenship and Education in the Homework Completion Routine. *Anthropology and Education Quarterly*, 4(3), 263–280.

Markstrom, C. A. and Iborra, A. (2003). Adolescent Identity Formation and Rites of Passage: The Navajo Kinaaldá Ceremony for Girls. *Journal of Research on Adolescence*, 13(4), 399–425.

Martín Díaz, E. (2001). *Mercados de Trabajo e Inmigración Extracomunitaria en la Agricultura Mediterránea*. Sevilla: Consejería Asuntos Sociales.

Martínez, R. A., Orellana, M. F., Pacheco, M. and Carbone, P. (2008). Found in Translation: Connecting Translating Experiences to Academic Writing. *Language Arts*, 85(6), 421–431.

Martín Muñoz, G., García Castaño, F. J., López Sala, A., and Crespo, R. (2003). *Marroquíes en España. Un Estudio sobre su Integración*. Madrid: Fundación Repsol YPF.

Martín Rojo, L. (2000). Spain, Outerwalls of the European Fortress: Analysis of the Parliamentary Debates on the Immigration Policy in Spain. In R. Wodak and

T. van Dijk (eds.), *Racism at the Top. Parliamentary Discourses on Ethnic Issues in Six European States* (pp. 169–220). Klagenfurt: Drava Verlag.

Martín Rojo, L. (ed.) (2003). ¿Asimilar or Integrar? *Dilemas ante el Multilingüísmo en las Aulas*. Madrid: CIDE.

Martín Rojo, L. (2010). *Constructing Inequality in Multilingual Classrooms*. Berlin: Mouton.

Mason, I. (2001). Introduction. In I. Mason (ed.), *Triadic Exchanges. Studies in Dialogue Interpreting* (pp. i–vi). Manchester: St. Jerome.

Mason, I. (2006). Communicative/Functional Approaches. In M. Baker (ed.), *Routledge Encyclopedia of Translation Studies* (pp. 29–33) (6th ed.). London and New York: Routledge.

Mateo Dieste, J. L. (2012). *Health and Ritual in Morocco: Conceptions of the Body and Healing Practices*. Leiden: Brill.

Mayall, B. (2000). Conversations with Children: Working with Generational Issues. In P. Christensen and A. James (eds.), *Researching with Children: Perspectives and Practices* (pp. 120–135). London and New York: Falmer Press.

Meek, B. (2011). *We Are Our Language: An Ethnography of Language Revitalization in a Northern Athabaskan Community*. Albuquerque, AZ: University of Arizona Press.

Mehan, H. (1997). The Discourse of the Illegal Immigration Debate: A Case Study in the Politics of Representation. *Discourse and Society*, 8, 249–270.

Mendoza-Denton, N. (1999). Turn-Initial No: Collaborative Opposition among Latina Adolescents. In M. Bucholtz, A. C. Liang, L. A. Sutton (eds.), *Reinventing Identities: The Gendered Self in Discourse* (pp. 273–292). New York: Oxford University Press.

Mendoza-Denton, N. (2002). Language and Identity. In P. Trudgill, J. Chambers, and N. Schilling-Estes (eds.), *Handbook of Variation Theory* (pp. 475–499). Oxford: Blackwell.

Mendoza-Denton, N. (2008). *Homegirls: Language and Cultural Practice among Latina Youth Gangs*. Oxford: Wiley-Blackwell.

Mercado, S. (2008). *Linguistic Citizenship: Language Policy, Social Cohesion, and Immigration in Barcelona, Spain*. Unpublished Doctoral Dissertation. Department of Anthropology. University of California, Berkeley.

Merlini, R. and Favaron, R. (2007). Examining the "Voice of Interpreting" in Speech Pathology. In F. Pöchhacker and M. Shlesinger (eds.), *Healthcare Interpreting: Discourse and Interaction* (pp. 101–137). Amsterdam: John Benjamins.

Meyer, B. (2001). How Untrained Interpreters Handle Medical Terms. In I. Mason (ed.), *Triadic Exchanges: Studies in Dialogue Interpreting* (pp. 86–106). Manchester, and Northampton, MA: St. Jerome Publishing.

Mijares, L. (2004a). *Aprendiendo a Ser Marroquíes. Inmigración y Escuela en España*. Unpublished Ph.D. Dissertation. Madrid, Universidad Autónoma de Madrid.

Mijares, L. (2004b). Los Niños Marroquíes en la Escuela Española. In B. López García and M. Berriane (eds.), *Atlas de la Inmigración Marroquí en España*. Taller de Estudios Internacionales Mediterráneos (pp. 415–418). Madrid: UA Ediciones.

Mijares, L. and López García, B. (2004). Educación y Sociedad en Marruecos. In B. López García and M. Berriane (eds.), *Atlas de la Inmigración Marroquí en España*. Taller de Estudios Internacionales Mediterráneos (pp. 50–52). Madrid: UA Ediciones.

Mijares, L. and Relaño Pastor, A. M. (2011). Language Programs at Villababel High: Rethinking Ideologies of Social Inclusion. *International Journal of Bilingual Education and Bilingualism*, 14(4), 427–442.

Minks, A. (2010). Socializing Heteroglossia among Miskitu Children on the Caribbean Coast of Nicaragua. *Pragmatics*, 20(4), 495–522.

Minks, A. (2013). *Voices of Play: Miskitu Children's Speech and Song on the Atlantic Coast of Nicaragua*. Albuquerque, AZ: University of Arizona Press.

Mohammad-Arif, A. (2007). The Paradox of Religion: The Reconstruction of Hindu and Muslim Identities in the United States. *South Asia Multidisciplinary Academic Journal*, 1. Retrieved January 8, 2014 from http://samaj.revues.org/55.

Moore, L. (2006). Learning by Heart in Koranic and Public Schools in Northern Cameroon. *Social Analysis: The Interactional Journal of Culture and Social Practice*, 50. Thematic issue on the Cultural Politics of Education and Religiosity: Contesting the Boundaries of the Secular State, A. Stambach (ed.).

Mora Aliseda, J. (dir.) (2003). *La Inmigración en Extremadura*. Badajoz: Consejo Económico y Social de Extremadura.

Moreras, J. (2004). La Religiosidad en Contexto Migratorio: Pertenencias y Observancias. In B. López García and M. Berriane (eds.), *Atlas de la Inmigración Marroquí en España*. Taller de Estudios Internacionales Mediterráneos (pp. 412–415). Madrid: UA Ediciones.

Morrell. E. (2008). *Critical Literacy and Urban Youth: Pedagogies of Access, Dissent, and Liberation*. London: Routledge.

Mouhssine, O. (1995). Ambivalence du Discours sur l'Arabisation. *International Journal of the Sociology of Language*, 112, 45–62.

Munárriz, D. (1995). Breve Descripción Geográfica de Marruecos. In B. López García and M. Berriane (eds.), *Atlas de la Inmigración Magrebí en España*. Taller de Estudios Internacionales Mediterráneos (pp. 42–43). Madrid: UA Ediciones.

Myers, K. (2005). *Racetalk: Racism Hiding in Plain Sight*. Lanham, MD: Rowman and Littlefield.

Nida, E. A. (1964). *Toward a Science of Translating*. Leiden: Brill.

Nieto, S. (2000). *Affirming Diversity: The Socio-political Context of Multicultural Education*. New York: Longman.

Nishina, A. and Juvonen, J. (2005). Daily Reports of Witnessing and Experiencing Peer Harassment in Middle School. *Child Development*, 76(2), 435–450.

Observatorio Permanente de Inmigración. (2013). Extranjeros con Certificado de Registro o Tarjeta de Residencia en Vigor. Ministerio de Empleo y Seguridad Social. Gobierno de España. Retrieved January 8, 2014 from http://extranjeros.empleo.gob.es/es/Estadisticas/operaciones/con-certificado/index.html.

Ochs, E. (1979). Transcription as Theory. In E. Ochs and B. B. Schieffelin (eds.), *Developmental Pragmatics* (pp. 43–72). New York: Academic Press.

Ochs, E. (1988). *Culture and Language Development: Language Acquisition and Language Socialization in a Samoan Village.* Cambridge: Cambridge University Press.

Ochs, E. (1990). Indexicality and Socialization. In J. W. Stigler, R. Shweder, and G. Herdt (eds.), *Cultural Psychology: Essays on Comparative Human Development* (pp. 287–308). Cambridge: Cambridge University Press.

Ochs, E. (1992). Indexing Gender. In A. Duranti and C. Goodwin (eds.), *Rethinking Context* (pp. 335–358). New York: Cambridge University Press.

Ochs, E. (1993). Constructing Social Identity: A Language Socialization Perspective. *Research on Language and Social Interaction*, 26(3), 287–306.

Ochs, E. (2002). Becoming a Speaker of Culture. In C. Kramsch (ed.) *Language Socialization and Language Acquisition: Ecological Perspectives* (pp. 99–120). New York: Continuum.

Ochs, E. (2012). Experiencing Language. *Anthropological Theory*, 12, 142–160.

Ochs, E. and Izquierdo, C. (2010). Responsibility in Childhood: Three Developmental Stories. *Ethos*, 37(4), 391–413.

Ochs, E. and Schieffelin, B. B. (1984). Language Acquisition and Socialization: Three Developmental Stories. In R. Shweder and R. LeVine (eds.), *Culture Theory: Mind, Self, and Emotion* (pp. 276–320). Cambridge: Cambridge University Press.

Ochs, E. and Schieffelin, B. B. (1989). Language Has a Heart. *Text*, 9(1), 7–25.

Ochs, E. and Schieffelin, B. B. (2012). The Theory of Language Socialization. In A. Duranti, E. Ochs, and B. Schieffelin (eds.), *The Handbook of Language Socialization* (pp. 1–21). Oxford: Wiley-Blackwell.

Ochs, E., Kremer-Sadlik, T., Solomon, O., and Sirota, K. G. (2001). Inclusion as a Social Practice: Views of Children with Autism. *Discourse Studies*, 10(3), 399–419.

Ogbu, J. U. (1987). Variability in Minority School Performance: A Problem in Search of an Explanation. *Anthropology and Education Quarterly*, 18(4), 312–334.

Ong, A. (1996). Cultural Citizenship as Subject-Making: Immigrants Negotiate Racial and Cultural Boundaries in the United States. *Current Anthropology*, 37(5), 737–762.

Ong, A. (1999). *Flexible Citizenship: The Cultural Logics of Transnationality.* Durham, NC: Duke University Press.

Ong, A. (2003). *Buddha is Hiding: Refugees, Citizenship, the New America.* Berkeley and Los Angeles: University of California Press.

Ong, A. (2006). *Neoliberalism as Exception: Mutations in Citizenship and Sovereignty.* Durham, NC: Duke University Press.

Orellana, M. F. (2001). The Work that Kids Do: Mexican and Central American Immigrant Children's Contributions to Households and Schools in California. *Harvard Educational Review*, 71(3), 366–389.

Orellana, M. F. (2003). Responsabilities of Children in Latino Immigrant Homes. *New Directions for Youth Development*, 100(Winter), 25–39.

Orellana, M. F. (2009). *Translating Childhoods: Immigrant Youth, Language, and Culture.* New Brunswick, NJ: Rutgers University Press.

Orellana, M. F., Dorner, L., and Pulido. L. (2003a). Accessing Assets: Immigrant Youth's Work as Family Translators or "Para-phrasers." *Social Problems*, 50(4), 505–524.

Orellana, M. F., Reynolds, J., Dorner, L. M. and Meza, M. (2003b). In Other Words: Translating or "Para-phrasing" as a Family Literacy Practice in Immigrant Households. *Reading Research Quarterly*, 38(1), 12–34.

Orellana, M. F. and Reynolds, J. (2008). Cultural Modeling: Leveraging Bilingual Skills for School Paraphrasing Tasks. *Reading Research Quarterly*, 43(1), 48–65.

Ortega y Gasset, J. (1921/1921). *La España Invertebrada.* Barcelona: Espasa Libros, S.L.U.

Ortner, S. (1996). Making Gender: Toward a Feminist, Minority, Postcolonial, Subaltern . . . etc. Theory of Practice. In S. Ortner (ed.), *Making Gender: The Politics and Erotics of Culture* (pp. 1–20). Boston: Beacon Press.

Ortner, S. (1999). *Life and Death on Mt. Everest: Sherpas and Himalayan Mountaineering.* Princeton, NJ: Princeton University Press.

Ortner, S. (2006). Power and Projects: Reflections on Agency. In S. Ortner (ed.), *Anthropology and Social Theory: Culture, Power, and the Acting Subject* (pp. 129–153). Durham, NC: Duke University Press.

Pagliai, V. (2009). Conversational Agreement and Racial Formation Processes. *Language in Society*, 38, 1–31.

Pàmies-Rovira, J. (2006). *Dinámicas Escolares y Comuntarias de los Hijos e Hijas de Familias Inmigradas de la Yebala en la Periferia de Barcelona.* Unpublished Ph.D. Dissertation. Department d'Antropologia Social i Cultural. Barcelona, Universidad Autónoma de Barcelona.

Panizo Rodríguez, J. (2000). Camino de Compostela. *Revista de Folklore*, 230, 68–72.

Parke, R. D. and Buriel, D. (1995). Socialization in the Family: Ethnic and Ecological Perspectives. In N. Eisenberg (ed.), *Handbook of Child Psychology: Social, Emotional, and Personality Development*, Vol. 3, New York: John Wiley & Sons, Inc.

Paugh, A. L. (2005). Multilingual Play: Children's Code-switching, Role Play, and Agency in Dominica, West Indies. *Language in Society*, 34, 63–86.

Paugh, A. L. (2012). *Playing with Languages: Children and Change in a Caribbean Village.* New York and Oxford: Berghahn Books.

Pease-Álvarez, C. and Vásquez, O. (1994). Language Socialization in Ethnic Minority Communities. In F. Genesse (ed.), *Educating Second Language Children: The Whole Child, The Whole Curriculum, The Whole Community* (pp. 82–102). Cambridge: Cambridge University Press.

Pêdziwiatr, K. (2007). Muslims in Europe: Demography and Organization. In Y. Samad and S. Kasturi (eds.), *Islam in the European Union: Transnationalism, Youth and the War on Terror.* Oxford: Oxford University Press.

Petit Caro, A. (2001). Los Códigos de Conducta y el Tratamiento a las Minorías en los Medios. In F. Mariño Menéndez and C. R. Fernández Liesa (eds.),

Minorías y Medios de Comunicación. Universidad Carlos III. Instituto de Estudios Internacionales y Europeos "Francisco de Vitoria." Madrid: Imprenta Nacional del Boletín Oficial del Estado.

Philips, S. U. (1983). *The Invisible Culture: Communication in Classroom and Community on the Warm Springs Indian Reservation*. New York: Longman.

Philips, S. U. (2004). Language and Social Inequality. In A. Duranti (ed.), *A Companion to Linguistic Anthropology* (pp. 474–495). Oxford: Blackwell.

Pillet-Shore, D. M. (2001). *"Doing Pretty Well": How Teachers Manage the Interactional Environment of Unfavorable Student Evaluation in Parent-teacher Conferences*. Unpublished Master's Thesis. Department of Sociology. University of California, Los Angeles.

Pöllabauer, S. (2013). Community Interpreting. In C. A. Chapelle, *The Encyclopedia of Applied Linguistics* (pp. 746–753). Oxford: Wiley-Blackwell.

Pollock, M. (2004). *Colormute: Race Talk Dilemmas in an American School*. Princeton, NJ: Princeton University Press.

Pomerantz, A. M. (1975). *Second Assessments: A Study of Some Features of Agreements/Disagreements*. Unpublished Ph.D. Dissertation. School of Social Science. University of California, Irvine.

Pomerantz, A. M. (1978). Attributions of Responsibility: Blamings. *Sociology*, 12, 132–2, 115–121.

Pomerantz, A. M. (1984). Agreeing and Disagreeing with Assessments: Some Features of Preferred/Dispreferred Turn Shapes. In M. Atkinson and J. Heritage (eds.), *Structures of Social Action: Studies in Conversation Analysis* (pp. 57–101). Cambridge: Cambridge University Press.

Pomerantz, A. M. (1986). Extreme Case Formulations: A Way of Legitimizing Claims. *Human Studies*, 9(2–3), 219–229.

Portes, A. and Rumbaut, R. G. (2001). *Legacies: The Story of the Immigrant Second Generation*. Berkeley, CA: University of California Press and Russell Sage Foundation.

Portes, A. and Rumbaut, R. G. (2006). *Immigrant America: A Portrait* (3rd ed.). Berkeley, CA: University of California Press.

Portes, A. and Zhou, M. (1993). The New Second Generation: Segmented Assimilation and Its Variants. *The Annals of the American Academy of Political and Social Sciences*, 530, 74–96.

Poveda, D. and Marcos, T. (2005). The Social Organization of a "Stone Fight": Gitano Children's Interpretive Reproduction of Ethnic Conflict. *Childhood*, 12(3), 327–349.

Programa MUS-E. Fundación Yehudi Menuhin España. Retrieved January 8, 2014 from http://www.fundacionmenuhin.org/programas/muse1.html.

Prum, M., Deschamps, B., et al. (eds.) (2007). *Racial, Ethnic and Homophobic Violence: Killing in the Name of Otherness*. New York: Routledge-Cavendish.

Pumares, P. (1995). La Inmagración Marroquí en la Comunidad de Madrid. In B. López García and M. Berriane (eds.), *Atlas dela Inmigración Magrebí en España*. Taller de Estudios Internacionales Mediterráneos (pp. 165–174). Madrid: UA Ediciones.

Quiroz, B., Greenfield, P. M., and Altchech, M. (1998). Bridging Cultures between Home and School: The Parent-teacher Conference. *Connections*, 1, 8–11.

Quiroz, B., Greenfield, P. M., and Altchech, M. (1999). Bridging Cultures with a Parent-teacher Conference. *Educational Leadership*, 56(7), 68–70.

Ramadan, T. (1999). *To Be a European Muslim*. Leicester: Islamic Foundation.

Ramadan, T. (2004). *Western Muslims and the Future of Islam*. Oxford: Oxford University Press.

Ramírez, A. (1995). La Progresiva Feminización del Colectivo Marroquí. In B. López García and M. Berriane (eds.), *Atlas de la Inmigración Magrebí en España*. Taller de Estudios Internacionales Mediterráneos (p. 76). Madrid: UA Ediciones.

Ramírez, A. (2004). Las Mujeres Marroquíes en España a lo Largo de los Noventa. In B. López García and M. Berriane (eds.), *Atlas de la Inmigración Marroquí en España*. Taller de Estudios Internacionales Mediterráneos (pp. 223–224). Madrid: UA Ediciones.

Rampton, B. (1995). *Crossing: Language and Ethnicity among Adolescents*. London: Longman.

Rampton, B. (1998). Crossing: Language and Ethnicity among Adolescents. In P. Auer (ed.), *Language, Interaction and Identity* (pp. 290–317). New York: Routledge.

Rampton, B. (1999). Styling the Other: Introduction. *Journal of Sociolinguistics*, 3(4), 421–427.

Rampton, B. (2009). Interaction Ritual and Not Just Artful Performance in Crossing and Stylization. *Language in Society*, 38, 149–176.

Reddy, M. (1979). The Conduit Metaphor: A Case of Frame Conflict in Our Language about Language. In A. Ortony (ed.), *Metaphor and Thought* (pp. 284–324). Cambridge: Cambridge University Press.

Redfield, R., Linton, R., and Herskovits, M. H. (1936). Memorandum on the Study of Acculturation. *American Anthropologist*, 38, 149–152.

Relaño-Pastor, A. M. (2009). Policy and Practice in Madrid Multilingual Schools. *Theory into Practice*, 48(4), 258–266.

Reyes, A. (2007). *Language, Identity, and Stereotype among Southeast Asian American Youth: The Other Asian*. Mahwah, NJ: Erlbaum.

Reyes, A. (2011). Racist!: Metapragmatic Regimentation of Racist Discourse by Asian American Youth. *Discourse and Society*, 22(4), 458–473.

Reynolds, J. F. (2008). Socializing *Puros Pericos*: The Negotiation of Respect and Responsibility in Antonero Mayan Sibling and Peer Networks. *Journal of Linguistic Anthropology*, 18(1), 82–107.

Reynolds, J. F. (2010). Enregistering the Voices of Discursive Figures of Authority in Antonero Children's Socio-dramatic Play. *Pragmatics*, 20(4), 467–494.

Reynolds, J. F. and Orellana, M. F. (2009). New Immigrant Youth Interpreting in White Public Space. *American Anthropologist*, 111(2), 211–223.

Riley, K. C. (2007). To Tangle or Not To Tangle: Shifting Ideologies and the Socialization of *Charabia* in the Marquesas, French Polynesia. In M. Makihara and B. B. Schieffelin (eds.), *Consequences of Contact: Language Ideologies and Sociocul-*

tural Transformations in Pacific Societies (pp. 70–95). New York: Oxford University Press.

Rogoff, B. (1998). Cognition as a Collaborative Process. In W. Damon, D. Kuhn, and R. S. Siegler (eds.), *Handbook of Child Psychology. Vol. 2: Cognition, Perception, and Language* (pp. 679–744). New York: John Wiley & Sons, Inc.

Rogoff, B. (2003). *The Cultural Nature of Human Development*. New York: Oxford University Press.

Rogoff, B., Paradise, R., Mejía Arauz, R., Correa-Chávez, M., Angelillo, C. (2003). First Hand Learning through Intent Participation. *Annual Review of Psychology*, 54, 175–203.

Rogozen-Soltar, M. (2007). Al-Andalus in Andalusia: Negotiating Moorish History and Regional Identity in Southern Spain. *Anthropological Quarterly*, 80, 863–886.

Rogozen-Soltar, M. (2012a). Ambivalent Inclusion: Anti-racist and Racist Gatekeeping in Andalusia's Immigrant NGOs. *Journal of the Royal Anthropological Institute*, 18, 633–651.

Rogozen-Soltar, M. (2012b). Managing Muslim Visibility: Conversion, Immigration, and Spanish Imageries of Islam. *American Anthropologist*, 114(4), 612–624.

Ronkin, M. and Karn, H. E. (1999). Mock Ebonics: Linguistic Racism in Parodies of Ebonics on the Internet. *Journal of Sociolinguistics*, 3(3), 360–380.

Romero, V. (2001). Tratamiento de las Minorías en los Informativos de T.V. In F. Mariño Menéndez and C. R. Fernández Liesa (eds.), *Minorías y Medios de Comunicación*. Universidad Carlos III. Instituto de Estudios Internacionales y Europeos "Francisco de Vitoria." Madrid: Imprenta Nacional del Boletín Oficial del Estado.

Rosaldo, R. (1994). Cultural Citizenship and Educational Democracy. *Cultural Anthropology*, 9(3), 402–441.

Rosaldo, R. (1999). Cultural Citizenship, Inequality, and Multiculturalism. In R. D. Torres, L. F. Mirón, and J. X. Inda (eds.), *Race, Identity, and Citizenship: A Reader* (pp. 253–261). Oxford: Blackwell.

Rosello, M. (2001). *Post-colonial Hospitality: The Immigrant as Guest*. Stanford, CA: Stanford University Press.

Ruth-Gordon, J. (2007). Racing and Erasing the Playboy: Slang, Transnational Youth Subculture, and Racial Discourse in Brazil. *Journal of Linguistic Anthropology*, 17(2), 246–265.

Rumbaut, R. G. and Portes, A. (eds.) (2001). *Ethnicities: Children of Immigrants in America*. Berkeley, CA: University of California Press.

Rumsey, A. (2010). Ethics, Language, and Human Sociality. In M. Lambek (ed.), *Ordinary Ethics: Anthropology, Language, and Action* (pp. 105–122). New York: Fordham University Press.

Russo, M. (2013). Liaison Interpreting. In C. A. Chapelle (ed.), *The Encyclopedia of Applied Linguistics* (pp. 3394–3400). Oxford: Wiley-Blackwell.

Rymes, B. (1996). Naming as a Social Practice: The Case of Little Creeper from Diamond Street. *Language in Society*, 25(2), 237–260.

Rymes, B. (2001). *Conversational Borderlands: Language and Identity in an Alternative Urban High School*. New York: Teachers College Press.

Sacks, H. (1992). *Lectures on Conversation* (ed. G. Jefferson, 2 vols). Oxford: Blackwell.

Sacks, H., Schegloff, E. A., and Jefferson, G. (1974). A Simplest Systematics for the Organization of Turn-taking for Conversation. *Language*, 50, 696–735.

Sadiqi, F. (2003). *Women, Gender, and Language in Morocco*. Leiden: Brill.

Said, E. (1978). *Orientalism*. London: Routledge.

Sakkouni, A. (1998). Immigration et Langue; Quel Rapport a la Langue Arabe chez les Enfants d'Origine Marocaine? *Migrations Société*, 10, 5–22.

Samad, Y. (2007). Ethnicization of Religion. In Y. Samad and S. Kasturi (eds.), *Islam in the European Union: Transnationalism, Youth and The War on Terror*. Oxford: Oxford University Press.

Samad, Y. and Kasturi, S. (eds.) (2007). *Islam in the European Union: Transnationalism, Youth, and The War on Terror*. Oxford: Oxford University Press.

Santa Ana, O. (1999). "Like an Animal I was Treated": Anti-immigrant Metaphor in U.S. Public Discourse. *Discourse and Society*, 10, 191–224.

Santa Ana, O. (2002). *Brown Tide Rising: Metaphors of Latinos in Contemporary American Discourses*. Austin, TX: University of Texas Press.

Sapir, E. (1949). Cultural Anthropology and Psychiatry. In D. G. Mandelbaum (ed.), *Selected Writings of Edward Sapir in Language, Culture, and Personality* (pp. 509–521). Berkeley and Los Angeles: University of California Press.

Sargent, C. and Larchanché, S. (2011). Transnational Migration and Global Health: The Production and Management of Risk, Illness, and Access to Healthcare. *Annual Review of Anthropology*, 40, 345–361.

Sarroub, L. (2005). *All American Yemeni Girls: Being Muslim in a Public School*. Philadelphia: University of Pennsylvania Press.

Schaefer Davis, S. and Davis, D. A. (1995). Love Conquers All? Changing Images of Gender and Relationship in Morocco. In E. W. Fernea (ed.), *Children in the Muslim Middle East* (pp. 93–108). Austin, TX: University of Texas Press.

Schegloff, E. A. (1991). Reflections on Talk and Social Structure. In D. Boden and D. H. Zimmerman (eds.), *Talk and Social Structure: Studies in Ethnomethodology and Conversation Analysis* (pp. 44–70). Oxford: Polity Press.

Schegloff, E. A. (1992). In Another Context. In A. Duranti and C. Goodwin (eds.), *Rethinking Context: Language as an Interactive Phenomenon* (pp. 193–227). Cambridge: Cambridge University Press.

Schegloff, E., Jefferson, G., and Sacks, H. (1977). The Preference for Self-Correction in the Organization of Repair in Conversation. *Language*, 53(2), 361–382.

Schieffelin, B. B. (1979). Getting It Together: An Ethnographic Approach to the Study of the Development of Communicative Competence. In E. Ochs and B. B. Schieffelin (eds.), *Developmental Pragmatics* (pp. 73–110). New York: Academic Press.

Schieffelin, B. B. (1990). *The Give and Take of Everyday Life: Language Socialization of Kaluli Children*. Cambridge: Cambridge University Press.

Schieffelin, B. B. (1999). Introduction. In D. Wagner (ed.), *The Future of Literacy in a Changing World* (pp. 175–181). Cresskill, NJ: Hampton Press.

Schieffelin, B. B. (2000). Introducing Kaluli Literacy: A Chronology of Influences. In P. Kroskrity (ed.), *Regimes of Language: Ideologies, Politics, and Identities* (pp. 293–327). Santa Fe, NM: School of American Research Press.

Schieffelin, B. B. (2003). Language and Place in Children's Worlds. *Proceedings of the Tenth Annual Symposium About Language and Society. Texas Linguistic Forum*, 45, 152–166.

Schieffelin, B. B. and Gilmore, P. (eds.) (1986). *The Acquisition of Literacy: Ethnographic Perspectives*. Norwood, NY: Ablex.

Schieffelin, B. B. and Ochs, E. (eds.) (1986a). *Language Socialization Across Cultures*. Cambridge: Cambridge University Press.

Schieffelin, B. B. and Ochs, E. (1986b). Language Socialization. *Annual Review of Anthropology*, 15, 163–191.

Schwartzman, H. (2006). Materializing Children: Challenges for the Archaeology of Childhood. *Archaeological Papers of the American Anthropological Association*, 15, 123–131.

Scribner, S. and Cole, M. (1978). Literacy Without Schooling: Testing for Intellectual Effects. *Harvard Educational Review*, 48, 4.

Scribner, S. and Cole, M. (1981). *The Psychology of Literacy*. Cambridge, MA: Harvard University Press.

Shankar, S. (2008). *Desi Land: Teen Culture, Class, and Success in Silicon Valley*. Durham, NC: Duke University Press.

Shankar, S. (2009). Reel to Real: Desi Teen Linguistic Engagement with Bollywood. In A. Reyes and A. Lo (eds.), *Beyond Yellow English: Toward a Linguistic Anthropology of Asia Pacific America* (pp. 309–324). New York: Oxford University Press.

Sheldon, A. (1990). Pickle Fights: Gendered Talk in Pre-School Disputes. *Discourse Processes*, 13(1), 5–31.

Sidnell, J. (2010). The Ordinary Ethics of Everyday Talk. In M. Lambek (ed.), *The Anthropology of Ordinary Ethics: Anthropology, Language, and Action*. New York: Fordham University Press.

Silverman, D., Baker, C., and Keogh, J. (1998). The Case of the Silent Child: Advice-giving and Advice-reception in Parent-teacher Interviews. In I. Hutchby and J. Moran-Ellis (eds.), *Children and Social Competence: Arenas of Action* (pp. 222–240). London: Falmer.

Silverstein, M. (1976). Shifters, Linguistic Categories, and Cultural Description. In K. H. Basso and H. A. Selby (eds.), *Meaning in Anthropology* (pp. 11–56). Albuquerque, NM: University of New Mexico Press.

Silverstein, M. (1992). The Indeterminacy of Contextualization. In A. DiLuzio and P. Auer (eds.), *The Contextualization of Language* (pp. 55–75). Amsterdam: John Benjamins.

Silverstein, M. (2001). The Limits of Awareness. In A. Duranti (ed.), *Linguistic Anthropology: A Reader* (pp. 382–401). Oxford: Blackwell.

Silverstein, M. (2003). Indexical Order and the Dialectics of Sociolinguistic Life. *Language and Communication*, 23(3–4), 193–229.

Silverstein, M. and Urban, G. (eds.) (1996). *Natural Histories of Discourse*. Chicago: University of Chicago Press.

Silverstein, P. A. (2004). *Algeria in France: Transpolitics, Race, and Nation*. Bloomington, IN: Indiana University Press.

Silverstein, P. A. (2005). Immigrant Racialization and the New Savage Slot: Race, Migration, and Immigration in the New Europe. *Annual Review of Anthropology*, 34, 363–384.

Solórzano, D. G. (1998). Critical Race Theory, Racial and Gender Microaggressions, and the Experience of Chicana and Chicano Scholars. *International Journals of Qualitative Studies in Education*, 11, 121–136.

Solórzano, D. G., Allen, W. R., and Carroll, G. (2002). Keeping Race in Place: Racial Microaggressions and Campus Racial Climate at the University of California, Berkeley. *Chicano-Latino Law Review*, 23(15), 15–112.

Solórzano, D. G., Ceja, M., and Yosso, T. (2000). Critical Race Theory, Racial Microaggressions, and Campus Racial Climate: The Experiences of African American College Students. *Journal of Negro Education*, 69(1/2), 60–73.

Solórzano, D. G., and Yosso, T. J. (2001). From Racial Stereotyping and Deficit Discourse Toward a Critical Race Theory in Teacher Education. *Multicultural Education*, Fall, 2–7.

Song, M. (1997). "You're Becoming More and More English:" Investigating Chinese Siblings' Cultural Identity. *New Community*, 23(3), 343–362.

Spratt, J. E. and Wagner, D. A. (1986/2011). The Making of a Fqih: The Transformation of Traditional Islamic Teachers in Modern Cultural Adaptation. In M. I. White, and S. Pollak (eds.), *The Cultural Transition: Human Experience and Social Transformation in the Third World and Japan* (pp. 59–73). London: Routledge.

Sterponi, L. (2004). *Reading as Involvement with Text*. Unpublished Ph.D. Dissertation. Department of Applied Linguistics. University of California, Los Angeles.

Sterponi, L. and Santagata, R. (2000). Mistakes in the Classroom and at the Dinner Table: A Comparison between Socialization Practices in Italy and the United States. *Crossroads of Language, Interaction, and Culture*, 3, 57–72.

Stivers, T. (2001). Negotiating Who Presents the Problem: Next Speaker Selection in Pediatrics Encounters. *Journal of Communication*, 51(2), 252–282.

Street, B. (1993). Introduction: The New Literacy Studies. In. B. Street (ed.), *Cross-cultural Approaches to Literacy* (pp. 1–22). Cambridge: Cambridge University Press.

Suárez-Navaz, L. (2004). *Rebordering the Mediterranean: Boundaries and Citizenship in Southern Europe*. New York: Berghahn.

Suárez-Orozco, C. (2000). Identities under Siege: Immigration Stress Among the Children of Immigrants. In M. M. Suárez-Orozco (ed.), *Cultures Under Siege: Collective Violence and Trauma* (pp. 194–226). Cambridge, MA: Harvard University Press.

Suárez-Orozco, C. (2004). Formulating Identities in a Globalized World. In M. M. Suárez-Orozco and D. Qin-Hilliard (eds.), *Globalization: Culture and Education in the New Millennium* (pp. 173–202). Berkeley and Los Angeles: University of California Press.

Suárez-Orozco, C., Suárez-Orozco, M. M. and Todorova, I. (2008). *Learning a New Land: Immigrant Students in American Society*. Cambridge, MA: Harvard University Press.

Suleiman, Y. (1994). Nationalism and the Arabic Language: A Historical Overview. In Y. Suleiman (ed.), *Arabic Sociolinguistics: Issues and Perspectives* (pp. 3–24). London: Curzon Press Ltd.

Suleiman, Y. (2003). *The Arabic Language and National Identity*. Washington, DC: Georgetown University Press.

Tates, K. and Meeuwesen, L. (2001). Doctor-parent-child Communication. A Review of the Literature. *Social Science and Medicine*, 52(6), 839–851.

Taylor, C., Appiah, K. A., Habermas, J., Rockefeller, S., Walzer, M., and Wolf, S. (1994). *Multiculturalism: Examining the Politics of Recognition* (ed. Amy Gutman). Princeton, NJ: Princeton University Press.

Terren, E. (2004). Opinión Pública y Visibilidad: Las Encuestas Sobre Racismo y Xenofobia. In B. López García and M. Berriane (eds.), *Atlas de la Inmigración Marroquí en España* (pp. 439–441). Taller de Estudios Internacionales Mediterráneos. Madrid: UA Ediciones.

Tetreault, C. (2008). La Racaille: Figuring Gender, Generation, and Stigmatized Space in a French Cité. *Gender and Language*, 2(2), 141–170.

Tetreault, C. (2009). Cité Teens Entextualizing French TV Host Register: Crossing, Voicing, and Participation Frameworks. *Language in Society*, 38(2), 201–231.

Tetreault, C. (2010). Collaborative Conflicts: Teens Performing Aggression and Intimacy in a French Cité. *Journal of Linguistic Anthropology*, 20(1), 72–86.

Thompson, M. J. (ed.) (2003). *Islam and the West: Critical Perspectives on Modernity*. Lanham, MD: Rowman and Littlefield.

Thorne, B. (1993/1995). *Gender Play: Girls and Boys in School*. New Brunswick, NJ: Rutgers University Press.

Thorne, B. (2008). The Chinese Girls and the "Pokémon Kids": Children Constructing Difference in Urban California. In J. Cole and D. Durham (eds.), *Figuring the Future: Children, Youth, and Globalization* (pp. 73–97). Santa Fe, NM: School for American Research.

Tibi, B. (2002). Muslim Migrants in Europe: Between Euro-Islam and Ghettoization. In N. AlSayyad, N. and M. Castells (eds.), *Muslim Europe or Euro-Islam* (pp. 31–53), Lanham, MD: Lexington Books.

Tilmatine, M. (2002). Hijos de Inmigrantes Norteafricanos: Elementos de Aproximación a Una Política de Integración desde el Aspecto Lingüístico. In *II Semanario sobre la Investigación Extranjera en Andalucía* (pp. 187–194). Dirección General de Políticas Migratorias. Consejería de Gobernación. Junta de Andalucía.

Trouillot, M. R. (1991). Anthropology and the Savage Slot: The Poetics and Politics of Otherness. In R. G. Fox (ed.), *Recapturing Anthropology: Working in the Present* (pp. 17–44). Santa Fe, NM: School of American Research Press.

Trumbull, E., Rothstein-Fisch, C., Greenfield, P. M., and Quiroz, B. (1998). *Improving Cross-cultural Relationships between Home and School: A Handbook with a Focus on Immigrant Latino Families*. San Francisco: WestEd.

Trumbull, E., Rothstein-Fisch, C., Greenfield, P. M., and Quiroz, B. (2001). *Bridging Cultures between Home and School: A Guide for Teachers*. Mahwah, NJ: Erlbaum.

Tse, L. (1995). Language Brokering Among Latino Adolescents: Prevalence, Attitudes, and School Performance. *Hispanic Journal of Behavioral Sciences*, 17, 2, 180–193.

Tse, L. (1996a). Language Brokering in Linguistic Minority Communities: The Case of Chinese- and Vietnamese-American Students. *The Bilingual Research Journal*, 20(3–4), 485–498.

Tse, L. (1996b). Who Decides? The Effect of Language Brokering on Home-School Communication. *The Journal of Educational Issues of Language Minority Students*, 16, 225–233.

Turner, B. (2007). Orientalism and Otherness. In Y. Samad and S. Kasturi (eds.), *Islam in the European Union: Transnationalism, Youth, and The War on Terror*. Oxford, Oxford University Press.

Unamuno, V. and Codó Olsino, E. (2007). Categorizar a Través del Habla: La Construcción Interactiva de la Extranjeridad. *Discurso and Sociedad*, 1(1), 116–147.

Urban, G. (1996). Entextualization, Replication, and Power. In M. Silverstein and G. Urban (eds.), *Natural Histories of Discourse* (pp. 21–44). Chicago: University of Chicago Press.

Urciouli, B. (1996). *Exposing Prejudice: Puerto Rican Experiences of Language, Race, and Class*. Boulder, CO: Westview Press.

Urciouli, B. (2009). Talking/Not Talking about Race: The Enregisterments of *Culture* in Higher Education Discourses. *Journal of Linguistic Anthropology*, 19(1): 21–39.

Urciouli, B. (2011). Discussion Essay: Semiotic Properties of Racializing Discourses. *Journal of Linguistic Anthropology*, 21(S1), E113–E122.

Urla, J. and Swedlund, A. C. (1995). The Anthropology of Barbie: Unsettling Ideals of the Femenine Popular Culture. In J. Terry and J. Urla (eds.), *Deviant Bodies: Critical Perspectives on Difference*. Bloomington, IN: Indiana University Press.

Valdés, G. (ed.) (2003). *Expanding Definitions of Giftedness: The Case of Young Interpreters from Immigrant Countries*. Mahwah, NJ: Erlbaum.

Valdés, G., Chávez, C., and Angelleli, C. (2000). Bilingualism from Another Perspective: The Case of Young Interpreters from Immigrant Communities. In A. Roca (ed.), *Research on Spanish in the United States: Linguistic Issues and Challenges* (pp. 42–81). Somerville, MA: Cascadilla Press.

Valdés, G., Chávez, C., and Angelelli, C. (2003). A Performance Team: Young Interpreters and Their Parents. In G. Valdés (ed.), *Expanding Definitions of Giftedness: The Case of Young Interpreters from Immigrant Countries* (pp. 25–62). Mahwah, NJ: Erlbaum.

Valenzuela, A. (1999). *Subtractive Schooling: U.S. Mexican Youth and the Politics of Caring*. Albany: State University of New York Press.

Valero Garcés, C. (2001). Estudio para Determinar el Tipo y Calidad de la Comunicación Lingüística con la Población Extranjera en los Centros de Salud. *Ofrim Suplementos*, 9. *El Impacto de la Inmigración en la Población Autóctona*. Madrid: Comunidad de Madrid, Consejería de Servicios Sociales.

Valero Garcés, C. (2008). *Formas de Mediación Intercultural, Traducción e Interpretación en los Servicios Públicos*. Granada: Comares Interlingua.

Valero Garcés, C., Lázaro Gutiérrez, R., and Peña Díaz, C. (eds.) (2008). *Investigación y Práctica en Traducción e Interpretación en los Servicios Públicos: Desafíos y Alianzas / Research and Practice in Public Service Interpreting and Translation: Challenges and Alliances* (CD-Rom). Universidad de Alcalá: Servicio de Publicaciones.

Vásquez, O. A., Pease-Álvarez, L., and Shannon, S. (1994). *Pushing Boundaries: Language and Culture in a Mexicano Community*. New York: Cambridge University Press.

van Ausdale, D. and Feagin, J. R. (2001). *The First R: How Children Learn Race and Racism*. Lanham, MD: Rowman and Littlefield.

van de Wetering, S. (1992). The Arabic Language and Culture Teaching Program to Moroccan Children. In W. A. R. Shadıd and P. S. van Koningsveld (eds.), *Islam in Dutch Society: Current Developments and Future Prospects* (pp. 90–106). Kampen: Kok Pharos Publishing House.

van Dijk, T. (1984). *Prejudice in Discourse*. Philadelphia: John Benjamins.

van Dijk, T. (1987). *Communicating Racism: Ethnic Prejudice in Thought and Talk*. Newbury Park, CA: Sage.

van Dijk, T. A. (1991). *Racism and the Press. Critical Studies in Racism and Migration*. London: Routledge.

van Dijk, T. A. (1993). *Elite Discourse and Racism*. Newbury Park, CA: Sage.

van Dijk, T. A. (2000). Ideologies, Racism, and Discourse: Debates on Immigration and Ethnic Issues. In J. ter Wal and M. Verkuyten (eds.), *Comparative Perspectives on Racism* (pp. 91–116). Farnham: Ashgate.

van Dijk, T. A. (2005). *Racism and Discourse in Spain and Latin America*. Philadelphia: John Benjamins.

van Dulmen, A. M. (1998). Children's Contributions to Pediatric Outpatient Encounters. *Pediatrics*, 102, 563–568.

Van Leeuwen, T. A. and Wodak, R. (1999). Legitimizing Immigration Control: A Discourse-Historical Analysis. *Discourse Studies*, 1, 83–118.

Van Lier, L. (1988). *The Classroom and the Language Learner*. New York: Longman.

Van Valin, R. D. and Wilkins, D. P. (1996). The Case for "Effector": Case Roles, Agents, and Agency Revisited. In M. Shibatani and S. A. Thompson (eds.), *Grammatical Constructions. Their Form and Meaning*. Oxford: Oxford University Press.

Venutti, L. (1998). *The Scandals of Translation – Towards an Ethics of Difference*. Oxford: Oxford University Press.

Verkuyten, M. (1998). Personhood and Accounting for Racism in Conversation. *Journal for the Theory of Social Behavior*, 28(2), 147–167.

Verkuyten, M. (2001). "Abnormalization" of Ethnic Minorities in Conversation. *The British Psychological Society*, 40, 257–278.

Verkuyten, M. and Thijs, J. (2001). Peer Victimization and Self-esteem of Ethnic Minority Group Children. *Journal of Community and Applied Social Psychology*, 11, 227–234.

Verkuyten, M. and Thijs, J. (2006). Ethnic Discrimination and Global Self-worth in Early Adolescents: The Mediating Role of Ethnic Self-esteem. *International Journal of Behavioral Development*, 30(2), 107–116

Voloshinov, V. N. and Bakhtin, M. M. (1973/1986). *Marxism and the Philosophy of Language*. Cambridge, MA: Harvard University Press.

Vygotsky, L. S. (1966/1967). Play and Its Role in the Mental Development of the Child. *Soviet Psychology*, 5(3), 6–18.

Wagner D., Messick B., and Spratt J. (1986). Studying Literacy in Morocco. In B. B. Schieffelin and P. Gilmore (eds.), *The Acquisition of Literacy: Ethnographic Perspectives* (pp. 233–260). Norwood, NY: Ablex.

Wagner, D. (1993). *Literacy, Culture, and Development: Becoming Literate in Morocco*. Cambridge: Cambridge University Press.

Waldinger, R. (ed.) (2001). *Strangers at the Gates: New Immigrants in Urban America*. Berkeley, CA: University of California Press.

Waldinger, R. (2008). Between "here" and "there": Immigrant Cross-border Activities and Loyalties, *International Migration Review*, 42(1), 3–29.

Waldinger, R. (2010). Rethinking Transnationalism. *Empiria: Revista de Metología en Ciencias Sociales*, 19, 21–38.

Wandensjö, C. (1993/2002). The Double Role of Dialogue Interpreters. In F. Pöchhacker and M. Shlesinger (eds.), *The Interpreting Studies Reader* (pp. 354–370). London: Routledge.

Wandesjö, C. (1998). *Interpreting as Interaction*. London and New York: Addison Wesley Longman.

Wandesjö, C. (2001). Interpreting in Crisis: The Interpreter's Position in Therapeutic Encounters. In I. Mason (ed.), *Triadic Exchanges: Studies in Dialogue Interpreting* (pp. 71–85). Manchester and Northampton, MA: St. Jerome Publishing.

Wandesjö, C. (2006). Community Interpreting. In M. Baker (ed.), *Routledge Encyclopedia of Translation Studies* (pp. 33–37) (6th ed.). London and New York: Routledge.

Warnock Fernea, E. (1995). Childhood in the Muslim Middle East. In E. Warnock Fernea (ed.), *Children in the Muslim Middle East* (pp. 3–17). Austin, TX: University of Texas Press.

Weisskirch, R. S. and Alva, S. A. (2002). Language Brokering and the Acculturation of Latino Children. *Hispanic Journal of Behavioral Sciences*, 24, 369–378.

Werbner, P. (2002). *Imagined Diasporas among Manchester Muslims: The Public Performance of Transnational Pakistani Identity Politics*. Santa Fe, NM: School American Research Press.

Werbner, P. (2005). Islamophobia. *Anthropology Today*, 21(1), 5–9.

Wertsch. J. (2002). *Voices of Collective Remembering*. New York: Cambridge University Press.

Wikan, U. (1989). Managing the Heart to Brighten Face and Soul: Emotions in Balinese Morality and Health Care. *American Ethnologist*, 16, 294–312.

Wilce, J. (1995). "I Can't Tell You All My Troubles": Conflict, Resistance, and Metacommunication in Bangladeshi Illness Interactions. *American Ethnologist*, 22(4), 927–952.

Wiley, T. G. (2001). On Defining Heritage Languages and Their Speakers. In J. K. Peyton, D. A. Ranard, and S. McGinnis (eds.), *Heritage Languages in America: Preserving a National Resource* (pp. 29–36). Washington, DC: Center for Applied Linguistics.

Wiley, T. G. (2005). The Reemergence of Language and Community Language Policy in the US National Spotlight. *The Modern Language Journal*, 89(4), 594–601.

Wiley, T. G. and Lukes, M. (1996). English Only and Standard Language Ideologies in the US. *TESOL Quarterly*, 30(3), 511–535.

Wingo, E. (2004). *Moroccan and Ecuadorian Migration to Spain: The Role of Cultural Bias in Immigration and Immigrant Policy and in the Differential Treatment of Immigrant Groups*. Unpublished Honors Essay. Curriculum in International and Area Studies, University of North Carolina at Chapel Hill.

Wirtz, K. (2011). Cuban Performances of Blackness as the Timeless Past Still Among Us. *Journal of Linguistic Anthropology*, 21(S1), E11–E34.

Wodak, R. and Reisigl, M. (1999). Discourse and Racism: European Perspectives. *Annual Review of Anthropology*, 28:175–99.

Wodak, R. and van Dijk, T. (eds.) (2000). *Racism at the Top. Parliamentary Discourses on Ethnic Issues in Six European States*. Klagenfurt: Drava Verlag.

Woolard, K. A. (1989). Sentences in the Language Prison: The Rhetorical Structuring of an American Language Policy Debate. *American Ethnologist*, 16(1), 268–278.

Woolard, K. A. (1990). Voting Rights, Liberal Voters and the English-Only Movement: An Analysis of Campaign Rhetoric in San Francisco's Proposition O. In K. Adams and D. Brink (eds.), *Perspectives on Official English: The Campaign for English as the Official Language of the USA* (pp. 125–137). Berlin and New York: Mouton.

Woolard, K. A. (2004). Codeswitching. In A. Duranti (ed.), *A Companion to Linguistic Anthropology* (pp. 73–94). Oxford: Blackwell.

Woolard, K. A. and Schieffelin, B. B. (1994). Language Ideology. In W. Durham et al. (eds.), *Annual Review of Anthropology*, 23. Palo Alto, CA: Annual Review Inc.

Wortham, S., Allard, E., Lee, K., and Mortimer, K. (2011). Racialization in Pay-Day Mugging Narratives. *Journal of Linguistic Anthropology*, 21(S1), E56–E75.

Wortham, S., Mortimer, K., and Allard, E. (2009). Mexicans as Model Minorities in the New Latino Diaspora. *Anthropology and Education Quarterly*, 40, 388–404.

Wright, W. E. (2005). The Political Spectacle of Arizona's Proposition 203. *Education Policy*, 19(5), 662–700.

Zelizer, V. A. (1985). *Pricing the Priceless Child: The Changing Social Value of Children*, Princeton, NJ: Princeton University Press.

Zelizer, V. A. (2005). The Priceless Child Revisited. In J. Qvortrup (ed.), *Studies in Modern Childhood: Society, Agency, and Culture*, London: Palgrave Macmillan.

Zentella, A. C. (1996). The Chiquitification of U.S. Latinos and Their Languages: Or Why We Need An Anthropological Linguistics. *Proceedings of the Third*

Annual Symposium about Language and Society – Texas Linguistic Forum, 36, 1–18.

Zentella, A. C. (1997). *Growing Up Bilingual: Puerto Rican Children in New York.* Oxford: Blackwell.

Zentella, A. C. (1998). Multiple Codes, Multiple Identities: Puerto Rican Children in New York. In S. Hoyle and C. T. Adger (eds.), *Language Practices of Older Children* (pp. 95–112). New York: Oxford University Press.

Zentella, A. C. (2005a). Premises, Promises, and Pitfalls of Language Socialization Research in Latino Families and Communities. In *Building on Strength: Language and Literacy in Latino Families and Communities* (pp. 13–30). New York: Teachers College Press.

Zentella, A. C. (ed.) (2005b). *Building on Strength: Language and Literacy in Latino Families and Communities.* New York: Teachers College Press.

Index

Figures, tables and notes are indexed as, for example, 136f, 146t, 24n.

Language and Muslim Immigrant Childhoods: The Politics of Belonging, First Edition.
Inmaculada Mª García-Sánchez.
© 2014 John Wiley & Sons, Inc. Published 2014 by John Wiley & Sons, Inc.